Study Guide

to accompany

Macroeconomics

Sixteenth Edition

Paul Samuelson
Professor Emeritus,
Massachusetts Institute of Technology

William Nordhaus
Yale University

Prepared by
Laurence Miners
Department of Economics
Fairfield University

Kathryn Nantz
Department of Economics
Fairfield University

 Irwin
McGraw-Hill

Boston   Burr Ridge, IL   Dubuque, IA   Madison, WI   New York   San Francisco   St. Louis
Bangkok   Bogotá   Caracas   Lisbon   London   Madrid
Mexico City   Milan   New Delhi   Seoul   Singapore   Sydney   Taipei   Toronto

Irwin/McGraw-Hill

A Division of The McGraw·Hill Companies

Study Guide to accompany
MACROECONOMICS

1 2 3 4 5 6 7 8 9 0 BBC/BBC 9 0 9 8

ISBN 0-07-059251-0

http://www.mhhe.com

TABLE OF CONTENTS

CHAPTER 1
The Fundamentals of Economics

I. CHAPTER OVERVIEW

In this beginning chapter basic economic concepts are discussed. The first part of this chapter has been designed to provide a rough outline of what the discipline of economics is all about. The primary objective here is to give you the "lay of the land," as well as a feel for why people would ever want to concern themselves with the study of economics in the first place. We need to consider how, in broad and general terms, such a study should be conducted.

In the second part of the chapter the three main problems of economic organization are presented and discussed. In the last section there is a discussion of the production-possibility frontier that every society faces. Together, these sections help to describe the constraints placed on all economies as they deal with the problem of scarcity.

Finally, there is an appendix to this chapter, focusing on the use of graphs in economic analysis. Basic equations related to the use and interpretation of graphs are presented. Following the format of your text, there is an appendix to this chapter in the *Study Guide* that you can use to review this material.

II. LEARNING OBJECTIVES

After you have read Chapter 1 in your text and completed the exercises in this *Study Guide* chapter, you should be able to:

1. Recognize that while there are numerous specific examples of economic problems and decisions, they are all illustrations of the b*asic definition of economics: Economics is the study of how societies use scarce resources to produce valuable commodities and distribute those commodities among various people.*
2. Understand the *what*, the *how*, and the *for whom* of economic decision making.
3. Define the three primary inputs in the production of outputs: land, labor, and capital.
4. Distinguish between microeconomics and macroeconomics.
5. Understand and avoid the common fallacies in economic reasoning.

6. Distinguish between positive and normative economics.
7. Understand the concept of *productive efficiency* and how it relates to both the use of **inputs** and the basic definition of economics.
8. Use the **production-possibility frontier** to illustrate the choices that societies face.
9. Understand the concept of **opportunity cost** and explain its relationship to the production possibilities frontier.

III. REVIEW OF KEY CONCEPTS

Match the following terms from column A with their definitions in column B.

A	B
___ Scarcity	1. The branch of economics concerned with the overall performance of the economy.
___ Efficiency	2. Commodities or services, such as land, labor or capital, that are used by firms in their production processes.
___ Free goods	3. Measurement of cost based on the value of the next-best forgone alternative.
___ Economic goods	4. Using the economy's resources as effectively as possible to satisfy people's needs and desires.
___ Macroeconomics	5. Describes the facts and behavior of an economy.
___ Microeconomics	6. Assuming that what is true for part of a system is also true for the whole system.
___ Normative economics	7. Commodities and resources that we value are limited in supply.
___ Positive economics	8. Goods and services that result from the production process.

___ Laissez-faire

___ Inputs

___ Outputs

___ *Post hoc* fallacy

___ Fallacy of composition

___ Opportunity cost

9.   A market economy in which the government has almost no role.

10.   Assuming that one event causes another simply because it happens first.

11.   Goods that we value that are limited in supply.

12.   Involves value judgments and ethical precepts about an economy.

13.   Commodities and resources that are available without limit.

14.   Branch of economics concerned with the behavior of individual entities such as markets, firms, and households.

IV. SUMMARY AND CHAPTER OUTLINE

This section summarizes the key concepts from the chapter.

A. Introduction

1.   Economics exists as a discipline of study because the "things" that we value in our world are not available in a limitless supply. These "things" include, but certainly are not limited to, raw materials and resources, clean air and water, and all types of manufactured goods and services. If everyone in the world had all they could possibly hope for, there would be no need for economics.

2.   Economics is the study of how societies use scarce resources to produce valuable commodities and distribute them among different people.

3.   In an attempt to meet the (unfulfilled) needs of people, economies strive to produce goods and services efficiently. When an economy is producing efficiently, it cannot produce more of one good without producing less of another.

4.   Within the study of economics, a significant distinction is made between the behavior of individual components of an economy (individuals, households, firms, industries, etc.), on the one hand, and the functioning of the economy taken as a whole, on the other. The former, called **microeconomics**, looks at the small building blocks of a larger system. How are vegetable prices set? How do people negotiate their employment contracts? These are the types of questions that are asked in the study of microeconomics.

5.   By way of contrast, **macroeconomics** focuses on broader sorts of questions. What is the relationship (if any) between the rate of unemployment and the rate of inflation? What should we expect to see as a consequence of enormous federal government budget deficits? These are typical macroeconomic issues.

6.   The textbook distinction between microeconomics and macroeconomics is somewhat less clear in reality.

Unemployment, for example, is not just a national problem, but a household problem as well. When is an industry so large that an analysis of its response to a certain tax treatment is a question of macroeconomics rather than microeconomics? Recognizing this blurring is not, however, nearly as important as recognizing that macroeconomic and microeconomic views of how the world behaves must be consistent with each other.

7.   Even though economics is a social science, economists often use a scientific approach when tackling economic problems. They identify economic problems, formulate theories, collect and analyze data, and use **econometrics**, a specialized branch of statistics, in an attempt to accept or refute economic theories. As in any scientific investigation, efforts are made to control for other factors related to the problem under consideration. For example, if we are interested in explaining the relationship between the price of CDs and the quantity purchased by a consumer, we would want to hold the consumer's income constant. Normally, we would expect that when the price of a product goes up, the quantity demanded will fall. However, it is possible that a consumer may coincidentally get a better paying job or a raise in pay just as the firm is increasing the price of CDs. So unless we hold income constant we may conclude that when price increases the consumer will demand more CDs.

8.   "*Post hoc*" is Latin for "after this." Just because one event precedes another, it does not mean that it caused the events that follow. This is the *post hoc* fallacy. Finally, the **fallacy of composition** says that what is true for the part is not necessarily true for the whole. For example, one firm may cut prices to steal customers away from competitors and make more profit. On the other hand, if all firms cut prices, they may wind up stealing customers from no one and wind up losing money due to lower revenues.

B. The Three Problems of Economic Organization

1.   Since we are faced with both scarcity and the wants of the people, each society must decide "what" goods and services to produce. No country has enough resources to meet *all* the wants of *all* its citizens. Scarcity means that choices have to be made.

2.   "How" deals primarily with the production process. Typically, there may be several different ways of producing a particular product. For example, a painter could use a compressor and spray gun to paint a building. Alternatively, the painter could hire several workers with paintbrushes to help with the work. Depending upon the availability (and cost) of these alternative **inputs**, either method could prove to be the best way to do the job. **Technology**, or the knowledge used to combine inputs, is also an important factor in determining *how* to produce outputs.

3.   Finally, society must determine who will get the outputs that are produced. This is the "for whom" part of the

economic problem. This is a very difficult decision, and often issues of fairness and equity come into play when deciding how to distribute a nation's output.

4. There are two fundamentally different ways that societies use to address these three problems. In a **market economy** individuals and private firms make the major decisions about *what, how,* and *for whom.* In a **command economy** these decisions are made by the government. No contemporary society falls completely into either of these polar categories. Rather, all societies are **mixed economies,** with elements of both market and command decision making.

C. Society's Technological Possibilities

1. Firms use **inputs** to produce goods and services, which are called **outputs.** The three main categories of inputs are **land, labor,** and **capital.**

2. The *land* includes the earth itself and all the precious (and scarce) **natural resources** that we get out of it. In our congested world we need to broaden our definition of "land" beyond natural resources and include **environmental resources** such as air, water, and climate. These, too, are becoming scarce and are often adversely affected by our production decisions.

3. *Labor* consists of all human time spent in production. There are skilled workers and unskilled workers. There are managers and assembly line workers. There are doctors, lawyers, engineers, and even economists. Labor is both the most familiar and the most crucial input for an advanced industrial economy. Resources and capital may be imported—every country has its own labor force.

4. *Capital* resources are durable goods, the output of some previous production process, which are then used to produce other goods and services. Examples of capital goods include factories, trucks, computers, washing machines, compressors, and spray guns for paint.

5. Economists often use diagrams to explain economic concepts. The *production possibility frontier (PPF)* is used to illustrate the concept of scarcity and the production choices that society faces.

6. **Opportunity costs** measure the cost of doing something in terms of the next-best alternative that is given up. The opportunity cost of going to college is four (or more) years of work, plus the next-best way of using the money spent on tuition and fees. In a two-good *PPF* world, the opportunity cost of producing more of one commodity is the amount of the other good that must be given up. Because economic resources are scarce, society is forced to make choices. The cost of these choices can be measured in terms of opportunity cost.

must make choices. Look back at the eight definitions/examples of economics at the beginning of the textbook chapter. Make sure you see how they relate to the concept of scarcity.

2. All decisions therefore relate in some sense to economics. On a personal level, your time (like your income) is a scarce resource and you continually decide how best to use it. The decision to stay in bed an extra hour, or go to class, or study, or eat breakfast is ultimately tied back to the concepts of scarcity and choice. The sooner you buy into and grasp this most basic notion of economics, the happier you (and your instructor) will be!

3. Inputs are often referred to as **factors of production.** The two expressions can be used interchangeably.

4. Capital is one of those terms (there will be others) that have special meaning for economists. To the noneconomist, "capital" is often used synonymously with money. It is not uncommon for business associates to talk of the capital they have invested in a project. For students of economics, however, capital is a factor of production. It is itself an output from some previous production process. Remember, capital is something physical, like a piece of equipment, that firms use as an input to produce goods and services. Money is not capital.

5. The terms *outputs* and *goods and services* can be used interchangeably.

6. Economists frequently use diagrams, like the production-possibility frontier (*PPF*), to simplify and explain concepts. The *PPF* illustrates the tradeoff that society faces when it produces one good instead of another. Of course, in reality, an economy produces thousands of goods. In a three-dimensional *PPF* diagram, a third axis could be added to show the tradeoff among three goods. While no one can draw a four-dimensional diagram, conceptually the interpretation is the same as for our two-dimensional diagram.

7. Economics is an inexact science, and unlike the natural sciences, experiments are usually not performed in a controlled environment. Always take care to know what is and what is not being held constant. Make sure that you understand the *post hoc* fallacy and the fallacy of composition too.

8. **Opportunity cost** is a very important term in economic analysis. Economists are always measuring costs and benefits, and weighing the pros and cons of economic decisions. Opportunity costs provide a useful way to measure the cost of a particular economic decision. Remember, opportunity costs are measured in terms of the next-best foregone alternative, not in terms of money. This concept is used over and over again in economics.

V. HELPFUL HINTS

1. All economic issues and problems ultimately relate back to the idea of scarcity. Since we are faced with scarcity, we

VI. MULTIPLE CHOICE QUESTIONS

These questions are organized by topic from the chapter outline. Choose the best answer from the options available.

A. Introduction

1. Economics is concerned primarily with:
   a. money.
   b. determining corporate profits and losses.
   c. the allocation of scarce resources.
   d. balancing your checkbook.
   e. all of the above.

2. When Samuelson and Nordhaus write that "goods are limited while wants seem limitless," they mean that:
   a. people are basically greedy and not willing to share.
   b. the government needs to redistribute output.
   c. current methods of production are inefficient.
   d. there is no simple solution to the basic economic problems of scarcity and unlimited human wants.
   e. none of the above.

B. The Three Problems of Economic Organization

3. Which of the following are economic goods?
   a. Atlantic Ocean sea water.
   b. Iowa farm land.
   c. California coast line.
   d. All of the above.
   e. All of the above, except **a**.

4. The *post hoc* fallacy occurs when:
   a. one problem follows another.
   b. you think something that is true for one unit is true for all.
   c. many variables may change at the same time and you fail to adjust for the changes.
   d. you assume one event was caused by another simple because the other event occurred first.
   e. economists from different schools of thought approach the same economic problem.

5. The fallacy of composition occurs when:
   a. one problem follows another.
   b. you think something that is true for one unit is true for all.
   c. many variables may change at the same time and you fail to adjust for the changes.
   d. you assume one event was caused by another simply because the other event occurred first.
   e. economists from different schools of thought approach the same economic problem.

6. The problem of failing to hold other things constant occurs when:
   a. one problem follows another.
   b. you think something that is true for one unit is true for all.
   c. many variables may change at the same time and you fail to adjust for the changes.
   d. you assume one event was caused by another simple because the other event occurred first.

   e. economists from different schools of thought approach the same economic problem.

7. The three fundamental questions of economic organization are:
   a. closely related to the concept of scarcity.
   b. not nearly as important today as they were at the dawn of civilization.
   c. *what, how,* and *why.*
   d. *land, labor,* and *capital.*
   e. all of the above.

8. The economic problem of *what* goods to produce:
   a. may be a problem for any individual firm seeking to make a profit but is not in any sense a problem for society as a whole.
   b. can be illustrated as the problem of choosing a point on the production-possibility curve.
   c. arises only when the stock of productive resources is very small.
   d. arises only when all productive inputs are so specialized that each can be used only in the production of one good and no other.
   e. none of the above.

9. The economic problem of *how to* produce goods would not exist:
   a. if the required proportions of inputs were fixed for all commodities, so substitution of one input for another input in production would be impossible.
   b. if production had not been carried to the point where there was full employment of all the economy's resources.
   c. if the economy's stock of capital were small relative to its labor force.
   d. in a technically advanced society, since proper technology would have established the best possible method of producing each good.
   e. in any circumstance, because the problem of how to produce goods is an engineering problem throughout and not an economic problem.

10. Which of the following statements applies to a mixed economy?
    a. There is confusion and a lack of organization.
    b. The allocation of resources changes from production period to production period.
    c. There are no real examples of truly mixed economies.
    d. Mixed economies include aspects of both market and command economies.
    e. None of the above statements apply.

C. Society's Technological Possibilities

11. Capital is:
    a. the same as money.
    b. the headquarters of economic planning.
    c. both an input and an output.

d.   all of the above.

e.   none of the above.

12. Land, labor, and capital are:.

a.   available only in finite amounts.

b.   used to produce outputs.

c.   the primary factors of production.

d.   combined with technology in the production process.

e.   all of the above.

13. Which of the statements below does *not* apply to the production-possibility frontier, or *PPF*?

a.   The *PPF* is closely related to the concept of scarcity.

b.   Quantities of inputs are measured along the axes of the *PPF*.

c.   The *PPF* may shift over time.

d.   Movements along the *PPF* may occur as the allocation of resources changes.

e.   Technology may change the shape of the *PPF*.

14. Which of the statements below is a reason why an economy might produce a level of output that is beneath its production-possibility frontier?

a.   The available resources are not equally suited to the production of both outputs.

b.   The available body of technological knowledge is not being fully utilized.

c.   Society prefers one product over the other.

d.   In reality, economies produce thousands of goods not just two.

e.   There are no frontiers left anymore.

15. Which of the following statements is false? When an economy is on its *PPF*:

a   more of one product cannot be produced without sacrificing some of the other.

b.   resources are fully employed.

c.   the economy is producing with *productive efficiency*.

d.   consumers will have all that they need.

e.   a strike by workers will move the economy beneath the *PPF*.

16. Which of the following statements could be used to explain an outward shift in the production-possibility frontier?

a.   There is an increase in technology.

b.   The population of the country increases.

c.   The country decides to postpone current consumption in favor of capital investment.

d.   New natural resources are discovered under the ocean.

e.   All of the above apply.

17. Which of the following are measured along the axes of a *PPF* graph?

a.   quantities of productive inputs or resources.

b.   quantities of finished commodities.

c.   values of finished commodities.

d.   all of the above.

e.   none of the above.

18. Each and every point in a production-possibility diagram (whether on the curve or off it) stands for some combination of the two goods produced. With a given input stock, some of these points are attainable, while others are not. Specifically, with respect to production, the economy *could* operate:

a.   anywhere on the curve and only on the curve.

b.   anywhere on the curve or anywhere inside it (below and to the left).

c.   anywhere on the curve, inside it, or outside it.

d.   all of the above.

e.   none of the above.

19. In order to shift the *PPF* out (above and to the right), an economy would have to:

a.   somehow increase its stock of inputs.

b.   remove some incompetent bureaucrats from their jobs.

c.   eliminate the sources of significant abuse of monopoly power.

d.   all of the above.

e.   none of the above.

20. If an economy did somehow add to its input stock, or if it did discover new production techniques, then the production-possibility curve would:

a.   remain unchanged.

b.   move appropriately inward and to the left.

c.   move appropriately outward and to the right.

d.   all of the above.

e.   none of the above.

Please use Figure 1-1 to answer questions 21 through 24.

Figure 1-1

21. On the dark production frontier labeled *ABCD*, which point corresponds to the economy's valuing food most heavily?

a.   A.

b.   B

c.   C.

d.   D.

e.   E.

22. A shift in the dark *PPF* curve to the position indicated by the line marked "1" would be appropriate to illustrate:
    a. a change in the tastes of the population whereby its members want more food produced and less clothing.
    b. the appearance of some new resources useful only in the clothing industry.
    c. an improvement in technology applicable to both industries.
    d. a change in the production mix involving an increase in clothing output and a decrease in food output.
    e. the development of a better technology in the food industry alone.

23. Which alternative in question 22 would have applied if the dark *PPF* had shifted to position 2?
    a.
    b.
    c.
    d.
    e.

24. Which alternative in question 22 would have applied if the dark *PPF* had shifted to position 3?
    a.
    b.
    c.
    d.
    e.

Please use Figure 1-2 to answer questions 25 through 27.

Figure 1-2

25. As the economy moves from point *A* to point *B*:
    a. it gives up 8 units of housing and gains 40 units of food.
    b. it gives up 8 units of food and gains 40 units of housing.
    c. idle resources become fully employed.
    d. the economy becomes more efficient.
    e. there is a breakthrough in technology.

26. As the economy moves from point *B* to point *C*:
    a. it gives up 20 units of food and gains about 17 units of housing.
    b. it gives up 20 units of housing and gains about 17 units of food.
    c. idle resources become fully employed.
    d. the economy becomes more efficient.
    e. there is a breakthrough in technology.

27. Assume that an advance in technology is responsible for the shift from *PPF I* to *PPF II*. It appears that technology
    a. affected both industries equally.
    b. had a relatively greater influence on the food industry.
    c. had a relatively greater influence on the housing industry.
    d. was actually destroyed.
    e. none of the above.

28. The concept of opportunity cost is:
    a. useful only when discussing the production possibility frontier.
    b. used to measure costs in terms of the next-best alternative.
    c. measured in dollars and cents.
    d. used only by professional economists.
    e. none of the above.

29. The opportunity cost of repairing the roads in town could be:
    a. putting an addition on the school.
    b. purchasing new snow removal equipment.
    c. changing from a volunteer to a full-time fire department.
    d. any of the above, depending upon which is the next-best alternative.
    e. none of the above.

VII. PROBLEM SOLVING

The following problems are designed to help you apply the concepts that you learned in the chapter.

A. Introduction

1. To exercise your understanding of the distinction between *micro*economics and *macro*economics, consider the following list of publications. Each appears in a footnote somewhere later in the textbook. On the basis of the content suggested by the titles, indicate whether you expect the research to be primarily related to *micro* or *macro* economics. Use the letters **MI** for *micro,* and **MA** for *macro.*
    a. Arthur Okun, *The Political Economy of Prosperity* ___

    b. Orley Ashenfelter, "Union Relative Wage Effects," in Stone and Petersen (eds.), *Econometric Contributions to Public Policy* ___

c.   Edward Denison, "Is U.S. Growth Understated because of the Underground Economy? Employment Ratios Suggest Not," *Review of Income and Wealth* ___

d.   R. J. Gordon, "Inflation, Flexible Exchange Rates and the Natural Rate of Unemployment," in M. N. Baily (ed.), *Workers, Jobs and Inflation* ___

e.   A. A. Berle, Jr., and Gardner Means, T*he Modern Corporation and Private Property* ___

B. The Three Problems of Economic Organization

2.   This question focuses on the difference between *normative* and *positive* economic statements. Indicate which of the following are statements of *normative* (**N**) or *positive* (**P**) character.

a.   Taxes should be progressive. ___

b.   Taxes discourage work effort. ___

c.   Inflation tends to be high when unemployment is low. ___

d.   Inflation is less harmful than unemployment. ___

e.   Pollution restraints cost jobs. ___

f.   Pollution restraints are worth the cost. ___

C. Society's Technological Possibilities

Capital is essential to any modern economy, and a heavy reliance on capital is a characteristic of successful advanced economies in the world today.

3.   Circle *all* the following *that qualify* as capital:

a.   An oil refinery.

b.   An issue of General Motors stock.

c.   Cash in a business owner's safe.

d.   A screwdriver used by a carpenter.

e.   Money borrowed by a business firm from a bank to expand its operations.

f.   A steel-ingot inventory held by a steel company.

g.   Unsold automobiles held by an auto manufacturer.

h.   An inventory of groceries held by a supermarket.

4.   Any developed nation possesses a large stock of capital, and much of each day's productive effort goes into maintenance and expansion of that stock. Consequently, today's productive effort to maintain and expand capital is signifi-

cantly devoted to satisfying (**yesterday's / today's / tomorrow's**) needs, while the consumer goods actually enjoyed today result from (**yesterday's / today's / tomorrow's**) effort.

5.   Circle as many of the following as are correct:

a.   The larger the available stock of capital, the larger the output of consumer goods that is possible.

b.   In terms of a production-possibility frontier, additions to the stock of capital can push the frontier upward and outward.

c.   A decision to produce or to not produce more capital goods is not part of the decision of *what* goods to produce.

d.   In a fully employed economy, a decision to produce more capital goods is a decision to produce fewer consumer goods in the immediate future.

Consider the production-possibility curves drawn in Figure 1-3. Use the different *PPFs* to answer questions 6 through 10. In each panel the *lighter* schedule represents an *original* curve, while the *darker* schedule represents what happens to the frontier after something has *changed* the economy.

6.   Suppose that scientific invention increased the productivity of resources used only in the production of X Which panel most accurately reflects this development? ___

7.   Many scientists believe that we are exhausting our natural resources. Assume that natural resources used to produce X are being depleted, but that the production of Y, at least for the time being, is not affected. ___

8.   Assume that the labor force grows and the new workers receive specialized training to produce commodity Y. ___

9.   Technological knowledge increases and both industries benefit, more or less equally, from the new technology. ___

10. A war depletes some of the resources used to produce X. ___

VIII. DISCUSSION QUESTIONS

Answer the following questions, making sure that you can explain the work you did to arrive at the answers.

Table 1-1 shows the production possibilities for the country of Economainia for two commodities: apartments

(1)

(2)

(3)

(4)

(5)

Figure 1-3

and bread. At each production point listed in Table 1-1, all of Economainia's resources are fully employed and all the available technological knowledge is being utilized.

TABLE 1-1 Economainia's Production Possibilities

Apartments (thousands of units)		Bread (millions of loaves)
0	A	30
6	B	29
2	C	26
18	D	22
24	E	16
30	F	0

1. Use Figure 1-4 to plot the points and draw Economainia's *PPF*. Use the letters from the table (A

Figure 1-4

through F) to label the points on your *PPF*. Before you start, note how the axes on the diagram are labeled.

2. Is point *C* a point of productive efficiency? Please explain. What about points *A, B, D, E*, and *F*?

3. Find the point where Economainia is producing 16,000 apartments and 10,000,000 loaves of bread. Label this point *G*. Assuming that your *PPF* remains where it is (at least for now), list two reasons why Economaninia could be producing at point *G*.

4. Is point *G* a point of productive efficiency? Please explain.

5. Suppose Economaninia's *PPF* shifts so that it now goes through point *G*, and not points *A* through *F*. Draw this new *PPF* on your diagram. What could have caused this shift in the *PPF*?

6. Find the point where Economaninia is producing 50,000 apartments and 50,000,000 loaves of bread. Label this point *H*. Given your current *PPF* can Economaninia actually produce this combination of goods? Please explain why, or why not.

Suppose some changes occur in the Economaninia economy such that a new set of production possibilities becomes possible. Table 1-2 lists the new production options.

TABLE 1-2 Economaninia's New Production Possibilities

Apartments (thousands of units)	Bread (millions of loaves)
0	50
6	48
12	46
18	40
24	40
30	34
36	16
42	0

7. Add these points to your diagram and draw Economaninia's new *PPF*. Give two reasons for the shift in the *PPF*.

Figure 1-5

8. Given your new *PPF*, can Economaninia now product at point *H*? Please explain.

The next two questions refer to Figure 1-5, which is also Figure 1-5 in your textbook.

9. Explain the difference between points A_1, A_2, and A_3 in panel (*a*).

10. What is the relationship between the three points in Figure 1-5 (*a*) and the three *PPFs* in Figure 1-5 (*b*)?

11. When an economy decides to produce more capital goods, must it usually (at least for the time being) produce fewer consumer goods? Why, or why not?

12. List the opportunity costs associated with going to college for four years. Explain why the amount spent for room and board should or should not be included in your list.

IX. ANSWERS TO STUDY GUIDE QUESTIONS

III. Review of Key Concepts

7	Scarcity
4	Efficiency
13	Free goods
11	Economic goods
1	Macroeconomics
14	Microeconomics
12	Normative economics
5	Positive economics
9	Laissez-faire economy
2	Inputs
8	Outputs
10	*Post hoc* fallacy
6	Fallacy of composition
3	Opportunity cost

VI. Multiple Choice Questions

1. C 2. D 3. E 4. D 5. B 6. C
7. A 8. B 9. A 10. D 11. C 12. E
13. B 14. B 15. D 16. E 17. B 18. B
19. A 20. C 21. D 22. B 23. E 24. C
25. B 26. A 27. B 28. B 29. D

VII. Problem Solving

1. a. MA
   b. MI
   c. MA
   d. MA
   e. MI
2. a. N
   b. P
   c. P
   d. N
   e. P
   f. N
3. a, d, f.

4. tomorrow's, yesterday's
5. a, b, d.
6. (3)
7. (4)
8. (5)
9. (1)
10. (4)

VIII. Discussion Questions

1.

Figure 1-4

2. Point *C*, as well as points *A, B, D, E*, and *F*, all represent points of productive efficiency. Society is on its frontier. There is full employment of all resources and the only way to produce more of one good is by producing less of the other.

3. Economainia could be at *G* due to unemployment (of any resource) or some other inefficiency, such as strikes or political turmoil.

4. Since point *G* is beneath society's frontier, it represents a point of *in*efficiency—society could do better.

5. A leftward shift in the *PPF* can occur when society depletes or loses resources.

6. Point *H* is currently unattainable. Economainia has neither the resources nor the technological know-how to produce at point *H*.

7. The *PPF* may shift to the right due to advances in technology or the discovery or acquisition of more resources.

8. Point *H* is still unattainable. Society can produce either 42,000 apartments and no bread, or 50,000,000 loaves of bread and no apartments.

9.   As the economy moves from A_1 to A_3, it is giving up or trading current consumption goods for capital goods. The increase in capital goods will enable this economy to produce more goods and services in the future. All the points in Figure 1-5 (*a*) represent points of full employment and efficient use of the available technology.

10. As the economy allocates more resources to capital investment in Figure 1-5 (*a*), it is providing for more economic growth in the future. The points A_1, A_2, and A_3 represent three different choices, made by three different countries with equal resource endowments. Country 1 decides to allocate all its resources to current consumption. It does not grow, and the *PPF* in Figure 1-5 (*b*) is similar to the one in Figure 1-5 (*a*). Countries 2 and 3 allocate more resources to capital investment. The more resources that are allocated to capital the more the economy grows, and the further out to the right the *PPF* shifts in the future.

11. Yes. Resources are scarce, and tradeoffs occur. While allocating more resources to capital goods will help an economy grow and produce more of both consumer and capital goods in the future, it must sacrifice some current consumption. This is not a huge problem. Since the production of capital goods is typically financed (at least in part) by saving, households send a signal to producers that they do not need consumer goods in the present. They are postponing consumption until some point in the future, when the capital investment will enable the economy to produce more.

12. The opportunity costs of going to college include the next-best use of your time, probably the money lost from not working at a market job, and the next-best use of the money spent on tuition, books, and fees, perhaps some financial investment. The amount spent for room and board is not part of opportunity cost. Regardless, of how the four years are spent, living expenses must be paid. Of course, if there is a substantial difference between college and non-college living costs, the alternative use of any extra costs should be included.

CHAPTER 1: APPENDIX
How to
Read Graphics

I. CHAPTER OVERVIEW

Economics makes extensive use of graphs and charts. They appear in nearly every chapter of the text, and the appendix to Chapter 1 in the text is included to provide the reader with a basic review of their foundation. This associated appendix extends that review.

Graphs and charts are tools with which the fundamental notions of economic reasoning can be illustrated, exercised, and stretched. Graphs provide an easy context within which to explore many economic phenomena that would otherwise require pages of prose. To proceed without a minimal understanding of graphs would be to proceed at a great disadvantage; it would be like playing defense in basketball with both hands tied behind your back.

This appendix is designed to present both a brief review of the basics of graphical analysis and some small insight into its usefulness. If you are already comfortable with graphs, you may still want to scan this appendix for a glimpse of things to come. Graphs are used in economics, most fundamentally, to illustrate how sets of numbers are related to each other.

II. LEARNING OBJECTIVES

After you have read the appendix to Chapter 1 in your text and completed the exercises in this *Study Guide* chapter, you should be able to:

1. Interpret economic relationships that are presented in diagrams and graphs.
2. Plot your own diagrams using (economic) data.
3. Evaluate the slopes of curves.
4. Understand the relationship that exists between variables that are plotted in a graph.
5. Use an equation to describe a linear relationship between two variables.

III. REVIEW OF KEY CONCEPTS

Match the following terms from column A with their definitions in column B.

A

__ Slope

__ Intercept

__ Origin

__ Positive slope

__ Negative slope

__ X axis

__ Y axis

__ Grid lines

__ Tangent

__ Scatter diagram

B

1. A straight line that just touches, but does not cross, a curved line at a particular point. Used to measure the slope of the curve at that point.
2. Indicates a direct relationship between two variables such that they both move (increase or decrease) in the same direction.
3. A diagram illustrating how a variable has changed with the passage of time. Time is measured on the horizontal axis in this diagram.
4. The point of intersection between a line on a diagram and the vertical axis.
5. Horizontal and vertical lines on a diagram that aid in plotting points.
6. Vertical axis on a diagram. Measurement along this axis is from bottom to top.
7. The change in the variable on the vertical axis per unit of change in the variable on the horizontal axis.
8. A plot of pairs of points, used to visualize the relationship between two variables.
9. Indicates an inverse or indirect relationship between two variables such that they move in opposite directions. (When one increases, the other decreases and vice versa.)
10. Horizontal axis on a diagram. Measurement along this axis is from left to right.

___ Time-series
    diagram

11. The bottom, left-hand corner, or beginning point of reference in a graph.

Note to Students *Since the emphasis in this appendix is to give you practice working with graphs, we are changing our usual format at this point to give you more practice working through examples of graphs.*

IV. EXAMPLES

Example One: Study Hours and Leisure Hours

Suppose that you decide to plan your working day. A considerable part of each 24 hours must be given over to sleep, meals, and class attendance. Suppose that these matters take up 14 hours per day. This leaves the remaining 10 hours to divide between study, on the one hand, and leisure and recreation, on the other.

That 10 hours could be divided in an infinite number of ways. At one extreme would be 10 hours for leisure and 0 hours for study. This particular time allocation must be considered unsatisfactory in the sense that its pursuit tends to lead to unpleasant interviews with the dean of students. It is, nonetheless, a possible allocation of time. At the other extreme would be 10 hours for study and 0 for leisure and recreation, i.e., the typical week before examinations allocation. Between the two extremes is a wide selection of alternatives. Among these choices are the allocations indicated in Table 1A-1.

TABLE 1A-1

	A	B	C	D	E	F	G
Leisure hours	10	8	7	6	4-1/2	2-1/2	0
Study hours	0	2	3	4	5-1/2	7-1/2	10

Table 1A-1 shows two sets of numbers. One set gives the number of possible study hours; the other gives the corresponding number of leisure hours (given a total of 10 hours to allocate between leisure and study). The numbers are, in other words, inexorably tied to one another; each study-hour number is paired with a leisure-hour figure. It is always this type of pairing process that a graph illustrates. The leisure-study tradeoff provides a perfect example. All the pairs in Table 1A-1 are characterized by one relationship: the sum of the hours spent studying and the hours spent relaxing must always equal 10.

All these points are captured somewhere along the line *AG* in Figure 1A-1 (assuming that negative numbers of hours are not allowed). To see how, notice that the vertical line at the left of Figure 1A-1 and the horizontal line at the bottom are the axes against which the pairwise linkage is to be charted. Each is divided off with a number scale, and the meaning of the numbers is indicated by the labels: Hours of Study Time" (horizontally) and "Hours of Leisure Time" (vertically).

The slanting line carrying points labeled *A* through *G* has already been identified as the actual graph of the leisure-study relationship. Each point identified along that line corresponds to a pair in Table 1A-1. Take point *B*. for example. Point *B* in Table 1A-1 pairs 2 hours of study with 8 hours of leisure time. The dashed lines in Figure 1A-1 do the same thing. Passing down from point *B* to the study-time horizontal axis, note that 2 hours is associated with point *B*; moving left to the leisure-time vertical axis, similarly note that 8 hours is associated with point *B*. Table 1A-1 and Figure 1A-1 illustrate the same thing, for point *B* and every other point along the line.

Figure 1A-1

1. In Figure 1A-1, point *B* stands for the combination of 2 hours of (**study / leisure**) and 8 hours of (**study / leisure**).
2. In Figure 1A-l, leisure hours are measured (**vertically / horizontally**) and study hours are measured (**vertically / horizontally**).
3. Point *D* stands for __ hours of leisure and __ hours of study; 9 study hours and 1 leisure hour would be a pair indicated by a point between points (**A and B / D and E / F and G**).
4. The rate at which study hours can be turned into leisure time is __ hour(s) for every 1 hour of study time sacrificed.
5. The slope of the line in the diagram is __.
6. Take any point inside the triangle formed by the three lines (*AG* and the two axis lines). The pair of measurements for any such point:
   a. must together total more than 10.
   b. must together total less than 10.
   c. must together total 10.

d.   may total more than 10 or less than 10.

7.   Which alternative in question 6 correctly describes the pair of measurements belonging to any point outside line *AG* (above and to the right)? (**a / b / c / d**)

8.   If we redid this example by assuming that there were a total of 11 hours to allocate, rather than 10, what would happen to line *AG* (as the line indicating all possible combinations) ?

   a.   It would move outward (i.e., upward and to the right), remaining parallel to the present line.

   b.   It would move inward (i.e., downward and to the left), remaining parallel to the present line.

   c.   Its position would not change.

   d.   It would pivot or rotate outward on point *A*.

Example Two: Money, Apples, and Oranges

Suppose that someone particularly interested in either apples or oranges decides that he will allocate $40 to the purchase of one or the other, or both. Let apples cost $2 per bushel, and let oranges cost $1 per dozen. Table 1A-2 records a few possible combinations of apples and oranges that this person might consider. Notice, for example, that devoting the entire $40 to apples would allow him to bring 20 bushels of apples home (point *A* in Table 1A-2). Devoting the entire $40 to oranges would allow him to bring 40 dozen oranges home (point *G* in Table 1A-2). Other intermediate combinations, designated elsewhere in Table 1A-2, would also be possible and should not be ignored. It is likely, in fact, that these intermediate points would be preferred to "specializing" exclusively in the consumption of one fruit or the other.

Figure 1A-2

TABLE 1A-2

	A	B	C	D	E	F	G
Apples (bushels)	20	18	15	10	5	2	0
Oranges (dozens)	0	4	10	20	30	36	40

Figure 1A-2 is blank save for a series of vertical and horizontal "grid lines," used to help locate the point that matches up with any given pair of numbers. On Figure 1A-2, draw a graph that illustrates the points in Table 1A-2. First label your axis lines. Then pick a scale for each of the axes, i.e., choose how much distance you are going to use to represent 1 bushel of apples and 1 dozen oranges. With these scales in mind, plot the seven points of Table 1A-2 and label each with its letter identification. They should all lie along a straight line much like the one drawn in Figure 1A-1. After you have satisfied yourself that they do, draw the entire line by connecting the points. This "smoothing" allows the graph to reflect all the points that you could have marked off if you had the time and patience—all combinations of oranges and apples (including fractions) that could be purchased with $40. The concept introduced in the last line above bears repeating. Looking back at Figure 1A-1, note that you cannot possibly find any combination of two positive numbers which add up to 10 that does not appear somewhere on line *AG*. Line *AG* includes every possible pair that satisfies this linking rule. Moreover, line *AG* can be trusted in another respect: it contains no point that does not meet the linking rule. In other words, line *AG* is an exact graphical representation of the "sum-to-10 rule" in the sense that (1) it includes *all* points that satisfy this rule, and (2) it includes *only* points that satisfy this rule. Similarly, the line that *you* drew in Figure 1A-2 includes *all* the combinations of apples and oranges which cost $40 and *only* those combinations which, indeed, cost $40.

9.   In this example, our fruit lover would have loved to have purchased 20 dozen oranges and 20 bushels of apples. He (**could / could not**) do that, however, because he had (**more than enough money / insufficient funds**).

10. That combination, i.e., 20 of each fruit, would cost ___.

11. In the study-leisure example, the rate of exchange between study time and relaxation time was ___ hour devoted to studying for every 1 hour of forgone relaxation. In the apples-oranges example, the tradeoff is ___ dozen oranges for every bushel of forgone apples.

Example Three: The Guns-or-Butter Diagram

The first graphical diagram that you encountered in the text was the guns-or-butter chart of Chapter 1. As shown in Table 1A-3 (reproduced from Table 1-1 in the text), it involves pairs of figures once again.

TABLE 1A-3

	A	B	C	D	E	F
Butter (millions of pounds)	0	1	2	3	4	5
Guns (thousands)	15	14	12	9	5	0

The background of the guns-or-butter case is fundamentally one of scarcity. The economy has only a limited and fixed stock of machinery, labor, and all the other things needed to produce such items as guns or butter. Some of these resources can be used in the production of either commodity. Labor, for instance, can be transferred from the production of guns to the production of butter, or vice versa (with due allowance for the training time that might be required to make labor proficient in its new location). If labor were switched from, say, work on guns to work on butter, the result would be an increase in the output of butter and a corresponding reduction in the output of guns. If resources were fully employed, the inevitable cost of getting more of one commodity must, by extension of this example, always be a reduction in the supply of another.

The "guns-or-butter" metaphor first arose in Nazi Germany. By the end of the 1930s, Hitler's government had turned so much of German industry toward rearmament that there were shortages of some civilian goods, butter among them. The late and generally unlamented Hermann Goering made a famous speech in which he sought to appease the public's complaints by declaring, "We must choose between guns and butter!" Some choice.

As a further exercise in graph drawing, draw the guns-or-butter diagram for yourself in Figure 1A-3 using the figures in Table 1A-3. As before, first label your two axes. Measure quantity of guns in the vertical dimension (as the text does) and quantity of butter horizontally. Ordinarily, you want to make use of all the space available on a graph. In Figure 1A-3, the maximum butter quantity to be recorded is 5 (million pounds); so put 5 at the bottom right-hand corner. There are 15 little squares sitting on the horizontal axis line; if 5 goes below the end of the fifteenth square, then 1 must go below the end of the third one, 2 below the end of the sixth, and so on. As to guns, your maximum is 15 (thousand); so put 15 at the top left, with the smaller numbers below. Notice that (in the matter of graph distances) your

two number scales can be different. Here, the same distance in inches which measures 5 million pounds of butter (horizontally) records 15,000 guns (vertically).

Having put labels and numbers on your axes, indicate on the graph the six points in the table. (This is known as plotting the points.) Identify them by letter and join them with a smooth curve. You have now completed a graph of the guns-butter production-possibility frontier (*PPF*). What can you learn from this graph? Why was it worth the trouble? Four different observations spring to mind:

1. The area of the graph above and to the right of the frontier (the curved line *ABCDEF*) represents more desirable but unattainable territory. Points in that region represent larger guns-butter combinations than those represented by the frontier line, but they are unattainable unless or until the economy acquires more productive agents or develops better techniques for using what it has. The process of economic growth can be represented as a gradual outward shifting of the frontier.
2. The graph area below and to the left of the frontier is fully attainable. If the economy's actual guns-butter production were to be represented by a point in this area, it would signify (a) that the economy was not fully using all its available resources, or (b) that although it was employing them fully, it was somehow failing to use them to the best advantage. We assume that the economy can reach any point on the frontier without disrupting its social order and without undue strain on its productive agents and that its people will want production to reach this line. Both of the two commodities are scarce relative to the desire for them.
3. If both the unattainable area above the curve and the undesirable area below the curve were removed from consideration, then only the frontier would remain. The decision which people in this economy (or their leaders) must somehow make about what to produce can thus be represented as the problem of deciding which point along the frontier *ABCDEF* to choose. To describe this as a "guns-or-butter" decision can be a bit misleading; it suggests (all) guns or (all) butter. If both guns and butter were desirable, though, it is most likely that points *A* and *F* would both be rejected in lieu of some intermediate point such as *C* or *D*.
4. In actual life, decisions about what to produce have been being made for a long time, and they are still being made. A decision of this nature is not something that can be made only once and then forgotten, for tastes change and so do productive conditions. It is a little more realistic, then, to think of an economy which is currently operating at some point such as *D*, and which might, for example, be disposed to spend its "peace dividend" and move toward having a little more butter. This would mean a movement away from point *D* and toward point *E*.

Figure 1A-3

12. The figures in the guns-or-butter table represent (**maximum / minimum**) combinations of these two commodities that some imaginary community could produce per unit of time. The figures stand for (**money values / physical quantities**) of guns and butter.

13. If all available resources or inputs were devoted to butter production, butter output would be ___ million pounds and gun output would be ___ thousand guns. If the economy wished to have 9000 guns per period, butter output could not exceed ___ million pounds.

14. Suppose that the community is producing a total of 1 million pounds of butter. If it wants to increase this by another 1 million pounds, then the required decrease in gun production would be ___ thousand. If the community were producing 4 million pounds of butter and wanted to increase this by 1 million (to a total of 5 million), then the required decrease in gun production would be ___ thousand.

15. Suppose that the community is producing 15,000 guns and is considering a reduction to 14,000. The change would make possible a butter increase of ___ million pounds. Alternatively, if the community currently produces 9000 guns and decides on a reduction to 5000, then a butter increase of ___ million pounds would be possible. If gun production were to be increased from 9000 to 10,000, this increase of 1000 would call for a reduction in butter output of approximately ___ million pounds.

Notice that your two answers in question 14 were different, indicating that the cost of butter in terms of guns changed as more butter was produced. This notion will be important later.

One essential distinction that pervades economic thought is the difference between movement along a curve and shifts of a curve. It has already been noted in the context of the guns-or-butter example of Table 1A-3 that a society disposed toward having a little more butter could move from a point like D toward a point like E. Notice, however, that such a move clearly indicates that more butter means fewer guns. Point D represents 3 million pounds of butter and 9000 guns; point E represents 4 million pounds of butter but only 5000 guns. Without any increase in resources or advances in technology, this sort of movement along the PPF is society's only option.

When the things which are normally held constant in the construction of a curve are allowed to change, however, the entire curve can actually shift. Suppose, for example, that the economy whose guns-or-butter tradeoff was represented in Table 1A-3 was to discover a better way to make butter—a way that would use fewer resources that are applicable to the production of guns. Table 1A-4 reflects such a change.

Compare Tables 1A-3 and 1A4. The technological improvement reflected in Table 1A-4 shows that butter production doubles for any given level of gun production except the maximum.

Table 1A-4

	A'	B'	C'	D'	E'	F'
Butter (millions of pounds)	0	2	4	6	8	10
Guns (thousands)	15	14	12	9	5	0

Hint In general, if a variable that is important to the analysis of some issue changes *and* it is *not measured on one of the axes* of your diagram, then this will cause the curve to shift. In the example at hand, there was a change in technology. (Note, technology is not measured on the axes of the PPF; just guns and butter are.) Since technology is very relevant to this analysis, the PPF will shift when technology changes. Alternatively, a change in guns or in butter will not cause the PPF to shift; rather, as we trade guns for butter, we move along the PPF.

Figure 1A-4

Graph the production-possibility frontier defined in Table 1A-4 on Figure 1A-4. (You will need a different scale on the butter axis.) Label the points and smooth the curve. Now replicate your graph of the production-possibility frontier from Table 1A-3 on Figure 1A-4. The frontier should have shifted out in moving from Table 1A-3 to Table 1A-4 for every level of gun production but one—the one in which no butter at all is produced so that 15,000 guns can be manufactured. That makes sense, though, because the technological advances in the production of butter increase the opportunities of the economy except in the case where it ignores the new butter technology and specializes entirely in the production of guns. Movement from D to E is no longer necessary. Shifting from D to D' increases butter production to 4 million pounds even though gun production holds at 9000.

Example Four: Slope—Straight Lines

One way to describe a straight-line relationship between some variable X and another variable Y is to assert that X and Y are linked so that any given change in X always generates exactly the same change in Y. Starting with X and Y occupying some initial positions, we often ask, 'What would happen to Y if X were to change its position (i.e., its value)?' In a more useful way, perhaps, we might ask, "What change in Y would be forthcoming if X were to increase or decrease by 1 unit?"

To get a picture of what is going on, think of starting somewhere on a straight-line graph and making little movements to the right in two stages. Think, in particular, first about making a strictly horizontal movement of sufficient length to indicate a 1-unit increase in the X value. Since the move was horizontal, the Y value will not have changed. Then think about a vertical movement up or down to signify a change in Y of a very special dimension: a vertical distance precisely equal to the amount of movement required to return to the straight line. For example, in either of the two little diagrams composing Figure 1A-5, the true path traced out is $ABDE$, but the movement from B to D can be considered in two parts. First, there is a probing movement from B to C (the 1-unit change in X which takes the point momentarily off its true path along the line). Then there is a second, correcting movement from C to D (the matching change in Y required to get back on the line). If BC's length indicates a 1-unit increase in X, then CD's length must indicate the rate at which Y must change in response to X to stay on the straight line. On the graph, this vertical measure of the change is called the slope of the line $ABDE$.

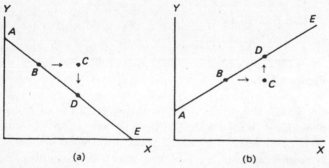

Figure 1A-5

Several points about the slope of a line should now be clear:

1. *Slope* is always a number that measures a *rate of change*. It is the amount by which some variable Y must change in response to a 1-unit change in X if we are to stay on the same straight line.

2. If the graph line is straight, one single number measures its slope at any and all points. This is just another way of saying that a straight line is one whose direction does not change.

3. The slope always assumes a negative value if the X-Y relation is an inverse one—one in which a positive increase in X requires a reduction in Y. Both the study-leisure (Figure 1A-1) and the apples-oranges (Figure 1A-2) examples qualify, and both straight lines drawn in those two diagrams have negative slopes. In terms of what we draw, therefore, the slope is negative if the graph falls down to the right. Conversely, the slope is positive and the line climbs up toward the right if the X-Y relation is a direct one.

Now consider a little more fully the technique for measuring or illustrating graphically the slope of a straight line. We have said that the slope of either graph line $ABDE$ in Figure 1A-5 is measured by the length of CD. This assumes that BC is of a length equal to 1 unit of X. We could equally well have said that slope is measured by the fraction CD/BC, with the lengths of CD and BC representing the numbers for which they stand. Since BC corresponds to the number 1, CD/BC reduces to CD anyway. The only objection to defining slope to be CD/BC is that at first it seems needlessly clumsy; but measuring slope as the more general fraction CD/BC is a reminder that the Y movement (CD) can be considered only relative to the amount of movement envisioned in the variable X (BC).

Some people find it helpful to think of slope as "the rise over the run." The "rise" is the vertical distance involved; in Figure 1A-5's terms, the rise is CD. The "run" is the horizontal distance; it is BC in Figure 1A-5's terms. So the "rise over run" rule would, in this instance, cause us to place CD over BC.

It is tempting to associate the measure of slope with the steepness with which the graph line rises or falls, so a steeply tilted line is often assumed to be one with a high slope value, positive or negative. Sometimes this conclusion is valid, but don't overlook the fact that the steepness with which a graph line rises or falls depends in part on the scale chosen for the graph. Diagrams (*a*) and (*b*) in Figure 1A-6 both portray exactly the same relationship, and either is a perfectly respectable illustration. Notice, however, that the horizontal scale has been stretched in (*b*) in comparison with that used in (*a*). This stretching makes the line look flatter in (*b*) than in (*a*) even though the slope in both cases is +1/2.

The trick is that relative steepness accurately reflects relative slope only when the scales are the same. When you have two lines on the same graph, therefore, you can certainly say that the steeper line has the larger slope, in absolute value—more negative if the two lines are negatively sloped and downward-sloping or more positive if the two lines are positively sloped and upward-sloping. In Figure 1A-6(*c*), for example, line I has a slope of 4, line II has a slope of 2, and I is clearly steeper than II. In Figure 1A-6(*d*), line I has a slope of -4, line II has a slope of -2; the number 4 is still greater than 2 -and -4 is more negative than -2, so line I is again steeper than line II.

Figure 1A-6

Figure 1A-7 contains six different graphs. In each, the variable X signifies the magnitude being measured horizontally, and Y signifies the magnitude being measured vertically. Use the letters beneath the diagrams to answer questions 16 through 25. Some questions may have more than one correct answer.

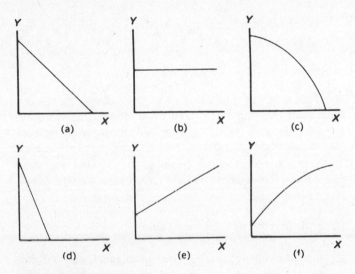

Figure 1A-7

16. Diagrams (**a / b / c / d / e / f**) illustrate an inverse relation between X and Y.

17. In diagram (**a / b / c / d / e / f**), Y's response to a change in X is zero.

18. The X-Y relation is positive rather than inverse in diagram(s) (**a / b / c / d / e / f**).

19. Among the diagrams illustrating an inverse relation, the slope is constant in diagram(s) (**a / b / c / d / e / f**).

20. The diagram best suited to illustrate the relation between an adult's daily food intake in calories, measured along the X axis, and his or her weight, measured along the Y axis, would be (pick two which could be correct) (**a / b / c / d / e / f**).

21. The relationship between a child's age (X) and height (Y) would probably be illustrated best by (**a / b / c / d / e / f**).

22. The most probable relation between the number of study hours you put in before a given examination (X) and the examination grade you can expect to earn (Y) is illustrated best by (or is supposed to be illustrated best by) diagram(s) (**a / b / c / d / e / f**).

23. Assume, in diagram (*d*), that the graph line meets the Y axis at 10 units and that it meets the X axis at 5 units. (You may want to write these figures on the diagram.) A 1-unit increase in X must therefore be accompanied by a (**0 / .5 / 1 / 2 / 4 / 10**) unit (**increase / decrease**) in Y.

24. In diagram (*b*), let the graph line meet the Y axis at 4 units. When the value of X is 0, then the value of Y must be (**0 / 1 / 2 / 4 / can't tell**). Similarly, when the value of X is 10, then the value of Y must be (**0 / 1 / 2 / 4 / can't tell**).

25. In diagram (*e*), let one point on the graph line represent the point where $X = 0$ and $Y = 4$. This point on the diagram is called the (**intercept / origin / slope**). Let another point on the graph line represent the point where $X = 3$ and $Y = 5$. These two points indicate an underlying relation which holds that every single unit increase in the value of X must be accompanied by (**an increase / a decrease**) in the value of Y equal to (**.25 / .33 / 1 / 3 / 4**).

Note **If you find yourself stuck on any of these questions, or if you have answered incorrectly, do not be too concerned: the unfamiliar is seldom easy. Go back and review earlier material if necessary, until you are reasonably sure you understand why each answer is correct.**

26. Slope is a measure of the rate at which the value of Y changes for each change of (**0 units / 1 unit / the same number of units**) in the value of X.

27. When a graphed line has the same slope value throughout, we can be certain that the line is (**curved / rising / straight / falling**).

28. We can graphically illustrate or measure slope of a line by using a right-angled triangle below the graph line. Slope is the fraction or ratio obtained by putting the length of the (**vertical / horizontal**) side of the triangle over the length of the (**vertical / horizontal**) side.

29. When an X-Y relation is inverse, then its graphical illustration will look like the path of a point which (**falls / rises**) as it moves to the right. The slope value of such a relation is (**positive / zero / negative**).

30. In diagram (*b*) of Figure 1A-7, the slope of the line illustrated is (**positive / negative / zero / impossible to tell**).

31. Two positions of *X* on a straight graph line are 5 and 7. What is the value of slope if the corresponding values for *Y* are:
   a. 5 and 7? (**-3 / -2 / -1/ 0 / 1 / 2 / 3 /infinity**)
   b. 4 and 2? (**-3/ -2/ -1/ 0 / 1 / 2 / 3 / infinity**)
   c. 2 and -2? (**-3 / -2 / -1 / O / 1 / 2 / 3 / infinity**)
   d. 4 and 4? (**-3 / -2/ -1 / 0 / 1 / 2 / 3 / infinite**)
   e. -2 and -8? (**-3 / -2 / -1 / 0 / 1 / 2 / 3 / infinity**)
   f. -8 and -2? (**-3 / -2 / -1 / 0 / 1 / 2 / 3 / infinity**)

Example Five: Equations for Straight Lines

While a picture is often worth a thousand words, a single equation can completely describe a linear relationship between two variables. Assume there are two variables, *X* and *Y*, and they are linearly related. The following equation can be used to describe their relationship:

$$Y = a + bX$$

where a is the intercept of the line and *b* is its slope. (You may recall that the intercept is the point where a line crosses the *Y*, or vertical axis.) Look, for example, back at Figure 1A-1 in this appendix which illustrates the relationship between leisure time and study time. The *Y* axis intercept of that line is 10 and the slope is -1. Therefore, the equation for that line is:

$$Y = 10 - 1X$$

32. Look at Figure 1A-2 which illustrates the relationship between apples and oranges. Write an equation which completely describes this relationship. (Unlike in the leisure and study-time example, the slope in this diagram is not -1. So there are two possible answers, depending upon which fruit you plotted on the vertical axis.)

33. Look at Figure 1A-7, panel (*e*). Suppose that the *Y* intercept is 3 and the slope of the line is 2. Write the equation for this line.

34. Look at Figure 1A-7, panel (*b*). Suppose that the *Y* intercept is 4. Write the equation for this line. (*Hint*: What is the slope of a horizontal line?)

In addition to writing equations from lines drawn on graphs, you can also formulate equations from tables of data. Once you derive the equation, it is very easy to precisely plot the line! Suppose you are presented with the following data for *Y* and *X*:

TABLE 1A-5

Y	X
22	20
25	25
28	30

At this point, we know neither the slope nor the intercept of this linear relationship. The relationship is a positive one, however (*Y* and *X* increase together).

The first thing we need to do is find the slope. As we move down the table, *Y* always increases by 3 units and *X* always increases by 5 units. So the slope, measured by the *change* in *Y* over the *change* in *X* is +3/5, or +0. 6. At this point we can write the equation for the line as:

$$Y = a + 0.6X$$

To solve for the intercept, *a*, we can pick *any pair of Y* and *X* numbers from Table 1A-5 above. For example, pick the 28 and the 30. Substitute these numbers into our equation and solve for *a*.

$$28 = a + 0.6(30)$$
$$28 = a + 18$$
$$28 - 18 = a$$
$$10 = a$$

The data in Table 1A-5 can now be represented with the following equation:

$$Y = 10 + 0.6X$$

This is a very powerful statement! Even though the table includes only three pairs of numbers, you can now solve for any value of *Y* as long as you are told what the corresponding value of *X* is.

35. When *X* is 85, *Y* will be equal to ___. Unless you have either a very large table or a very large piece of graph paper, it is difficult to determine the answer without the equation.

Example Six: Slope—Curved Lines

A curved line is one whose slope continually changes; i.e., the amount of change in *Y* required to accommodate a 1-unit change in *X* varies according to the position from which this change begins. Consider the curved line *ABCDEF* in Figure 1A-8. Suppose we are at point *B*. If we know the exact *X* and *Y* values associated with every point on this line, then we should have no difficulty in learning what the changes in both *X* and *Y* would be as a result of moving from point *B* to point *E*. Moreover, we could put the usual right-angled triangle underneath the line segment between *B* and *E*, with corners at points *B* and *E*, and from it develop a value for the slope—a value called the *arc slope* from *B* to *E*.

The arc slope would not, however, be the slope of the curved line itself; it would really measure the slope of the straight line running between points *B* and *E*. We would get a different and somewhat higher slope figure if we dealt similarly with a change from point *B* to point *D*, and a still different value for a change between points B and C.

For some purposes, it is quite sufficient to know the arc slope from point *B* to *E*, or to *D*, or to *C*. For other problems, however, it can be essential to know the value of

Figure 1A-8

the slope of the curved line exactly at some point like point *B*.

Does it make sense to speak of the slope of a line precisely at a single point? Certainly point *B*, considered in isolation, has no slope and no direction. When point *B* is considered as part of the line *ABCDEF*, however, its slope is another matter. The slope of the line is a measure of the direction in which it runs, computed in terms of the scales on the two axes. Think for the moment of *ABCDEF* as the path traced by a moving automobile traveling around a curve. The direction of the automobile changes continually, since it follows the curve, but we can say that the automobile is headed in a specific direction at any specific moment, like the exact moment when it passes over point *B*. We can certainly do so in the sense that a compass mounted on the car's dashboard at that exact moment would give an exact reading.

But how is this direction at *B* to be indicated on a piece of graph paper? The accepted answer is quite simple: by a *tangent* drawn to the curved line at point *B*. The tangent to a curved line is itself, by definition, a straight line; it does not cross the curved line, and it touches it at only one point. By inspection of Figure 1A-9(a), for example, it is easy to see how the slope of the tangent line *FJ* is to be considered as a measure of the slope of the curved line at point *B*; and line *GH* does the same for point *D*. We can then, of course, apply the usual right-angle technique for computing the slope of each straight line.

What does this slope mean? Figure 1A-9(b) redraws the guns-or-butter production-possibility frontier from Table 1A-4. At point *B*, a tangent line is drawn, and its slope, — (*JN/MN*), represents the slope of the guns-or-butter schedule at point *B*. It is, intuitively, a reflection of how many guns need to be sacrificed to increase the production of butter not by 1 million pounds but by 1 pound—a much smaller number. In reality, the slope of the line at point *B* is the sacrifice in guns required to finance a minuscule increase in butter

(a)

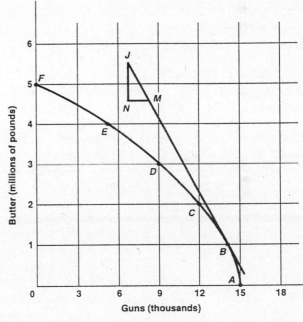

(b)

Figure 1A-9

production; and after all, 1 pound is a small quantity when it is compared with 1 million pounds.

36. Figure 1A-10 consists of eight separate diagrams, each illustrating a small segment of a graph line. In each, the numbers indicate the length of the adjacent straightline segment. Use the numbers in parentheses below to indicate the slope of line *AB* in each of the panels, (*a*) through (*h*). Where line *AB* is curved, it is the slope at point *C* that is desired. Circle the correct answer for each panel.

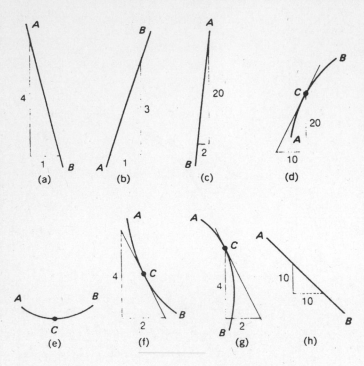

Figure 1A-10

a. (-4 / -3 / -2 / -1 / 0 / 1 / 2 / 3 / 4 / 10 / infinity)
b. (-4 / -3 / -2 / -1 /0 / 1 / 2 / 3 / 4 / 10 / infinity)
c. (-4 / -3 / -2 / -1 / 0 / 1 / 2 / 3 / 4 /10 / infinity)
d. (-4 / -3 / -2 / -1 / 0 / 1/ 2 / 3 / 4 / 10 / infinity)
e. (-4 / -3 / -2 / -1 / 0 / 1 / 2 / 3/ 4 / 10 / infinity)
f. (-4 / -3/ -2 / -1 / 0 / 1 / 2 / 3 / 4 / 10 / infinity)
g. (-4 / -3 / -2 / -1 / 0 / 1 / 2 / 3 / 4 / 10 / infinity)
h. (-4 -3 / -2 / -1 / 0 / 1 / 2 / 3 / 4 / 10 / infinity)

Example Seven: Two or More Lines on a Graph
So far our discussion has run in terms of the interpretation of a single line on a graph. But most text diagrams will include two or more lines, usually intersecting at one or more points on the graph. The supply-and-demand diagrams of Chapter 3 in your textbook are good examples. The demand line, or demand curve, is drawn as usual—from two sets of figures paired together. Table 1A-6 provides one example of a demand curve.

Table 1A-6 shows a relationship between the quantities of wheat that buyers in some market would demand (i.e., be prepared to buy) if the price were to stand at any one of five possible levels.

TABLE 1A-6

	Price of Wheat (per bu)	Quantity Demanded (million bu per month)
A	$5	9
B	4	10
C	3	12
D	2	15
E	1	20

It does not matter whether this is a real market or an imaginary one. The precise figures in the table are not especially important, either. This schedule is intended simply to illustrate the reasonable (and important) notion that as the price of wheat falls, buyers probably will want to buy a larger total amount than they did before. In other words, quantity of wheat bought should be expected to be inversely related to the price of wheat.

It is also possible to prepare another schedule, indicating what sellers of wheat (the producers of wheat, the suppliers of wheat) are prepared to do. In this case, it seems reasonable to assume that if the price were to go up, then suppliers would try to supply a larger quantity because the higher price would generate a higher return on their efforts. Alternatively, if the price were to fall, then they would choose to supply less. Table 1A-7 represents this different relation, showing quite clearly that the quantity of wheat supplied is directly related to the price of wheat.

TABLE 1A-7

	Price of Wheat (per bu)	Quantity Supplied (million bu per month)
A	$5	18
B	4	16
C	3	12
D	2	7
E	1	0

At this stage, it is not particularly essential that you fully understand the ideas conveyed by the demand and supply schedules. What matters for the moment is that you recognize something familiar in the construction: the demand curve consists of two sets of inversely related figures, neatly paired one with the other; the supply curve consists of two sets of positively related figures, equally neatly paired with each other. This means that each can be depicted as a line on a graph—and both can even be depicted together on the same graph.

Why? Despite their differences, there is a fundamental similarity between the two schedules. Although they represent the attitudes or the intentions of two entirely different groups of people, *the two schedules match one another in that one column refers to price and the other to quantity.*

It is only because they match in this respect that both can be depicted on the same graph. If we are to make any sense out of two or more lines on the same graph, these lines must refer to the same kinds of things, measured in the same kinds of units.

In Figure 1A-11, draw the lines corresponding to these two schedules. (Plot the five points for each schedule and join them with a smooth curve.) Label your demand curve *DD* and your supply curve *SS*.

Your two lines should cross at one point and one point only: the point signifying a price of $3 per bushel and a quantity of 12 million bushels. Its significance is that at this level of price, and no other, the intentions of buyers and the intentions of sellers match. In these circumstances, the price of $3 will be called an "equilibrium price," and the quantity of 12 million bushels an "equilibrium quantity." At a price of $3, buyers want to purchase exactly the 12 million bushels that suppliers are willing to deliver.

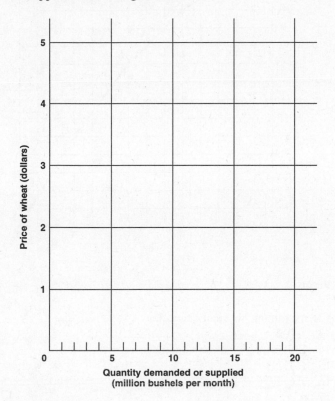

Figure 1A-11

V. REVIEW

37. One point on a graph indicates a value for *X* of 4 and a value for *Y* of 10. Another point indicates that *X* = 5 and *Y* = 8. If these two points are joined by a straight line, then the slope of that line is ___.

38. The slope of a straight line is -3. Movement from one point to another along that line results in an increase in *Y* from 10 to 16. What was the associated change in *X*? It must have (**risen / fallen**) by (**6 / 3 / 2 / 1 / 0.5**).

39. A line on a graph appears as the upper half of a circle: it starts out at the origin of the graph, rises, and then falls, until finally it drops to the horizontal axis from which it started. Which of the following correctly describes the slope of this line as it moves from the origin to the right?

    a. It will have a changing but positive slope value throughout.

    b. It will first have a negative slope (toward the left-hand side), and its value will grow larger as the line

proceeds to the right. Eventually, though, the slope will turn positive.

    c. It will first have a positive slope, and its value will grow larger as the line proceeds to the right. Eventually, though, the slope will turn negative.

    d. It will first have a positive slope, but its value will diminish as the line proceeds to the right. The slope will eventually reach a value of zero at the top of the semi-circle, and then it will turn negative.

40. In Figure 1A-11, the *DD* curve has a (**negative / positive**) slope. Its value is (**constant / changing**) throughout the line. The *SS* curve in this figure has a (**negative / positive**) slope. Its value is (**constant / changing**) throughout the line.

VI. CONCLUSION

Graphs were made to help people grasp ideas with as little expenditure of time and effort as possible; but if you want to take advantage of this device, you must learn the rules and you must ask the right questions:

1. What does the graph measure on each axis? What are the labels on the axes? Each line on a graph indicates some kind of relation or linking rule between the two sets of numbers.

2. Which way does the line run? Does it fall to the right or rise to the right? If it falls, then the relation between the two sets of numbers is an inverse one—as one rises, the other falls. If it rises to the right, then the two sets of numbers move in the same direction and represent a direct relationship.

3. Is the line straight or curved? If it is straight, the ratio of the change in the value of *Y* to the change in the value of *X* is constant. If the line curves, this ratio varies.

4. If there are two or more lines on a graph, then there are two or more schedules in the background. What kind of relationship is involved in each schedule, and why is it important to bring the schedules together on the same graph? Usually the two lines cross one another at some point, and usually this intersection is important because at this point the two schedules match one another.

5. If the variables under consideration change, should you move along the curve or will the curve shift? Generally, if the variable that is changing is measured along one of the axes in the diagram, then you move along the curve. If some other relevant variable changes, say technology in the *PPF* analysis, then the curve will shift to illustrate the change. The importance of understanding this concept—the difference between movements along and shifts in curves—cannot be stated too strongly.

VII. ANSWERS TO STUDY GUIDE QUESTIONS

III. Review of Key Concepts

7   Slope
4   Intercept
11 Origin
2   Positive slope
9   Negative slope
10 *X* axis
6   *Y* axis
5   Grid lines
1   Tangent
8   Scatter diagram
3   Time-series diagram

IV. Examples

1. study, leisure
2. vertically, horizontally
3. 6, 4, *F* and *G*
4. 1
5. -1
6. b
7. a
8. a
9. could not, insufficient funds
10. $60
11. 1, 2

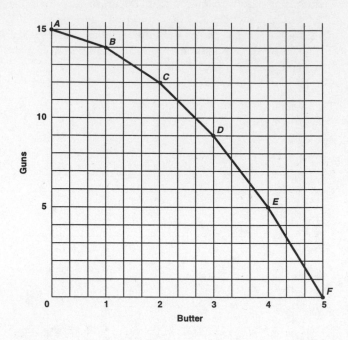

Figure 1A-3

12. maximum, physical quantities
13. 5, 0, 3
14. 2, 5
15. 1, 1, .33
16. a, c, d
17. b
18. e, f
19. a, d
20. e, f

Figure 1A-2

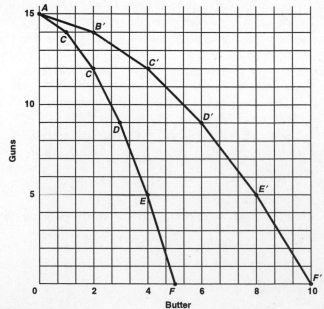

Figure 1A-4

21. f
22. e
23. 2, decrease
24. 4, 4
25. intercept, an increase, .33
26. 1 unit
27. straight
28. vertical, horizontal
29. falls, negative
30. zero
31. a. 1
    b. -1
    c. -2
    d. 0
    e. -3
    f. 3
32. If apples (AP) are on the vertical axis: AP = 20 -0.5 ×
OR.
    If oranges (OR) are on the vertical axis: OR = 40 -2.0 ×
AP.
33. $Y = 3 + 2X$
34. $Y = 4$
35. 61
36. a. -4
    b. 3
    c. 10
    d. 2
    e. 0
    f. -2
    g. -2

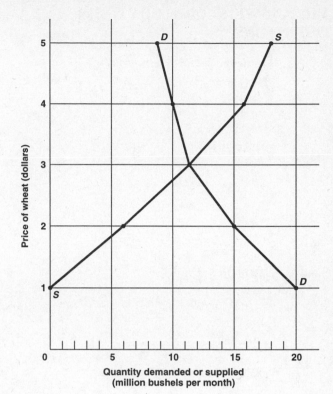

h. -1
Figure 1A-11

37. 2
38. fallen, 2
39. d

CHAPTER 2
The Shifting Boundary
Between Markets and Government

I. CHAPTER OVERVIEW

This chapter introduces a series of fundamental ideas and concepts which define the essence of the economic problem and the source of economic opportunity for an advanced economy. They are important because they form the foundation for the analysis of a market economy. The tools and methods that you learn here will be carried throughout the text and developed in greater detail as you make your way through the course. It is essential, therefore, that you grasp each of them before you proceed.

II. LEARNING OBJECTIVES

After you have read Chapter 2 in your text and completed the exercises in this *Study Guide* chapter, you should be able to:

1   Describe what is meant by the term **market** and describe the process of achieving **equilibrium** in a market economy.

2.   Use your definition of market equilibrium to address three basic economic problems that confront all societies.

3.   Explain how the price system works as an **invisible hand**, allocating goods and services in a market economy.

4.   Understand the importance of (a) specialization, (b) the division of labor, (c) money, (d) factors of production, and (e) capital and property rights in the functioning of a modern economy.

5.   Use a **circular-flow diagram** to illustrate the relationships between agents and markets in a modern economy.

6.   Make a case for government intervention in a mixed market economy in order to promote **efficiency, equity,** and **macroeconomic growth** and **stability**.

III. REVIEW OF KEY CONCEPTS

Match the following terms from column A with their definitions in column B.

A	B
__ The market mechanism	1 A market structure in which a commodity is supplied by a single firm.
__ Market equilibrium	2. Involves issues of "fairness" in the distribution of income.
__ Perfect competition	3. Productive inputs that include all durable produced goods that are in turn used in production.
__ The invisible hand	4. Arrangements whereby buyers and sellers interact to determine the prices and quantities exchanged of a commodity.
__ Specialization and division of labor	5. The use of economic resources that produces the maximum level of satisfaction possible with the given inputs and technology.
__ Capital	6. Thc balancing of supply and demand in a market.
__ Efficiency	7. A government's program with respect to its own spending and taxation.
__ Equity	8. Situations in which production or consumption yields positive or negative effects on outside parties.
__ Monopoly	9. A method of organizing production whereby each group of people concentrates its efforts on a particular set of tasks.
__ Externalities	10. With each participant pursuing his or her own private interest, a market system works to the benefit of all.
__ Fiscal policy	11. Markets in which no firm or consumer is large enough to affect market price.

IV. SUMMARY AND CHAPTER OUTLINE

This section summarizes the key concepts from the chapter.

A. What Is a Market?

1. A market economy has at its heart the actions of buyers and sellers who exchange goods and services with one another. There is no higher authority that directs the behavior of these economic agents; rather, it is the *invisible hand* of the marketplace that allocates final goods and services, as well as factors of production.

2. Buyers and sellers receive signals from one another in the form of prices. If buyers want to buy more of a good, prices rise and sellers respond by supplying more to the marketplace. If buyers want to buy less of a good, prices fall and sellers respond by supplying less to the marketplace. This is what is meant by the term *invisible hand*. Prices rise and fall naturally as people change their behavior; there is no need for a higher authority. Price signals tell sellers what to do with their production levels.

3. Market equilibrium occurs when the price is such that the quantity that buyers are interested in purchasing is equal to the quantity that sellers are interested in supplying to the market.

4. The market mechanism allows an economy to simultaneously solve the three economic problems of *what, how,* and *for whom*. Consumers indicate their preferences over *what* is produced through their willingness to pay for a good or service. Firms respond to this by considering the mix of final products that will maximize their own profits, that is, the difference between their revenues from sales and their production costs. This must involve the question *how,* since firm production costs are determined by the prices of inputs and technology used in the production process. Once these questions have been addressed, *for whom* is found to be those consumers who have the money to pay for the goods and services produced.

B. Trade, Money, and Capital

1. Advanced economies use complex systems of trade in order to accumulate the bundle of goods and services that the people in that economy want to consume. People produce the goods and services that they can produce most efficiently, and then they trade their excess for other items that they need.

2. Money is *not* an input or factor of production. Consumers and firms use money in order to more efficiently carry out market transactions; it is a kind of lubricating oil that allows the machinery of an economy to operate with a minimum of friction.

3. In this course, the term *capital* does *not* refer to money. Instead, the term refers to productive inputs that have, themselves, been manufactured. The notion of capital includes durable items like blast furnaces, factory buildings, machine tools, electric drills, tack hammers, and so on. It also includes stocks of semifinished goods. These are goods which are on the way to becoming consumer goods but which are still manufactured inputs to be used in later stages of the production process.

4. Capital accumulation is an important determinant of economic growth. An economic system that builds a strong capital base is investing in a factor of production that will make all other factors more productive, or useful. Capital is typically privately owned in a market economy, so that private individuals can make decisions about its use. Because these individuals will directly benefit from the use of their capital, they have some incentive to make sure that it is employed efficiently.

C. The Economic Role of Government

1. In the real world, markets do not always operate as smoothly as we might like. Market imperfections lead to a wide range of problems, and governments step in to address them.

2. Governments intervene in a market economy in order to promote *efficiency*.

   a. Market allocations are only efficient when conditions of *perfect competition* hold; this means that no firm or consumer is large enough to affect input or output market prices. When there are many small firms in a market, competition forces all firms to operate with lowest possible costs and prices.

   b. Market allocations become inefficient when *externalities* occur. Externalities are the positive or negative effects on outside parties that production or consumption in an industry yields. For example, when people receive education, schools and students benefit, but so do others in the community who now have neighbors who are better educated.

   c. Market allocations often do not work well, if at all, in the case of public goods. A *public good* is something that is nonrival (my consumption of the good does not exclude your consumption of it) and that can be collectively consumed (we can both enjoy it at the same time). Because it is difficult, or at least expensive, to exclude consumers once the good is available, these types of goods are often provided by the government. One example is snow removal. Once the street has been plowed, everyone on the block can use it; however, it is very impractical to charge residents every time they use the plowed street.

3. Governments intervene in a market economy in order to promote *equity,* or fairness, in the distribution of resources and income. This is a difficult concept because there is no universal definition of fairness. Markets distribute goods and services to those who have the money to purchase them, not necessarily to those who need or deserve them the most.

4. Governments intervene in a market economy in order to promote *macroeconomic growth and stability*. Fiscal policies of government (the power to tax and spend) and monetary policies (the power to adjust the money supply and interest rates) help to move an economy along a stable path, avoiding periods of excessive inflation and unemployment.

V. HELPFUL HINTS

1. Over the past few years, monumental changes have taken place around the world that have led to the development of market economies. The Soviet Union collapsed of exhaustion and Russia and the newly-independent states are in the process of initializing market reforms. China now allows many small farmers to exchange their products in markets. These large economies, formerly dominated by central economic planning, found that the old (command) system did a poor job of alleviating the problems of scarcity.

2. Markets do not provide the only solutions to economic problems. In fact, some economies use goodwill and/or command to motivate resources that are commonly owned by the group. For example, the *kibbutz* system in Israel encourages collective consumption as well as joint ownership of the means of production. These small, intentional communities have provided very efficiently and equitably (according to group standards) for the needs of their citizens.

3. It is easy to assume that when a market economy is operating efficiently it is also providing an equitable distribution of income and opportunity. However, this is not always the case. In the United States, some people inherit wealth and property from their relatives, while others inherit nothing. Likewise, while some people have the opportunity to attend Harvard University, others are not even able to complete high school before they must enter the work force. These factors are not always determined by the market and at times may lead to distributions that seem very unfair to some people.

VI. MULTIPLE CHOICE QUESTIONS

These questions are organized by topic from the chapter outline. Choose the best answer from the options available.

A. What Is a Market?

1. Markets can occur:
   a. whenever buyers and sellers of the same product can communicate with one another.
   b. only if buyers and sellers have some form of currency to use for exchange.
   c. only if the government steps in and regulates the behavior of buyers and sellers.
   d. all of the above.
   e. none of the above.

2. If a commodity such as peanuts becomes overstocked, sellers will:
   a. raise their prices in order to make up for the fact that sales are lower.
   b. raise their prices in order to increase the demand for peanuts.
   c. lower their prices hoping to lure additional buyers into the marketplace.
   d. lower their prices in order to encourage competition from rival firms.
   e. grow more peanuts next year to make up for losses this year.

3. A market equilibrium is defined as occurring when:
   a. government has balanced out the forces of demand and supple
   b. the price is such that the quantity that buyers want to buy is equal to the quantity that sellers want to sell.
   c. price and quantity are equal.
   d. prices are rising.
   e. prices are falling.

4. The three economic problems of *what, how,* and *for whom* goods shall be produced apply:
   a. mainly to totalitarian or centrally planned societies, in which the problem of planning arises directly.
   b. only (or principally) to free enterprise or capitalist societies, in which the problem of choice is most acute.
   c. only (or principally) to less developed societies, since development alone is largely a question of dealing with these three problems.
   d. to all societies, regardless of stage of development or form of political organization.
   e. to none of the above necessarily, since they are problems for the individual business firm or family not for society.

5. There cannot be a problem of *what* goods to produce if:
   a. the supply of a productive resource is very small, so it must be devoted to the production of goods selected from a set of essential necessities.
   b. production has not yet reached the stage at which the law of diminishing returns begins to operate.
   c. the supply of productive resources is sufficiently large to make possible the production of some luxury goods.
   d. each productive input is so specialized that it can be used only in the production of one good and no other.
   e. production can be carried on under conditions of decreasing or constant cost, rather than increasing cost.

6. The "invisible hand" refers to:
   a. the role of government in the marketplace.
   b. a system of taxation that redistributes wealth from the rich to the poor.
   c. the fact that individuals, pursuing their own self-interest, achieve the best good for all when operating in a market economy.

d. a production system whereby each individual performs the task to which he or she is best suited.

e. a production system whereby each country produces the products that best suit each particular resource base.

B. Trade, Money, and Capital

7. An example of specialization in production can be seen when:

a. wheat is produced in the United States and exchanged for autos produced in Japan.

b. most of the potatoes produced in the United States are grown in Idaho and Maine, where the soil and climate are optimal for their production.

c. faculty in a university teach courses in their areas of expertise.

d. all of the above.

e. none of the above.

8. Specialization (or division of labor) is rampant in a modern economy because it increases the output obtainable from a given resource supply. The consequences of specialization include (circle as many as are correct):

a. the exchange of goods.

b. the use of money.

c. social interdependence.

d. an intensified law of scarcity.

e. possibly a sense of alienation on the part of members of the society involved.

9. Capital, in an economic sense, includes all the following *except*:

a. inventory on a grocer's shelf.

b. a $100 bill.

c. ten new computers that are being used by your university's accounting department.

d. a new hammer that is purchased by a carpenter.

e a new boiler that is used to heat your student center cafeteria.

10. Money is *not* counted as part of capital because it:

a. is essential to production.

b. has no part to play in production.

c. is not actually useful in production, although it is essential to have money in order to buy the real inputs that are needed for production.

d. is counted as part of labor.

e. none of the above.

11. When reference is made to "a capitalist economy," the speaker is probably contemplating an economy:

a. in which most capital goods are privately owned.

b. in which the stock of capital is large relative to the population of that economy.

c. that is under communist or socialist direction, so property rights to the capital flow to the government.

d. suffering from high and increasing rates of inflation.

e. that has limited economic resources with which to work.

12. Due in part to the heavy use of automobiles in the United States this century, Congress passed the Clean Air Act in 1991. Basically, this act is an attempt to:

a. encourage specialization in production.

b. better define property rights over use of the air.

c. prohibit division of labor in the production of power in the United States.

d. eliminate property rights over the use of the air.

e. none of the above.

C. The Economic Role of Government

13. The philosophy of laissez-faire means that:

a. government controls the economy through a central planning board.

b firms are allowed to monopolize industries in the economy to make greater profits.

c. barter is used instead of money to make all transactions.

d. the government uses taxing and spending policies to redistribute income and wealth.

e. government interferes as little as possible in economic affairs.

14. Government's role in a modern economy is to:

a. ensure efficiency.

b. correct an unfair distribution of income.

c. promote economic growth and stability.

d. all of the above.

e. none of the above.

15. Perfect competition means that:

a. all goods and services have prices and are traded in markets.

b. no firm or consumer is large enough to affect the market price.

c. each industry is controlled by a single, monopolistic firm.

d. **a** and **b**.

e. all of the above.

16. Many governments subsidize primary research because it often benefits all citizens, even those who are not actively involved in research. This makes primary research a(n):

a. negative externality.

b. private good.

c. public good.

d. efficient good.

e. equity good.

17. A government policy that aims to provide a more equitable distribution of resources might involve:

a. decreasing transfer payments.

b. abolishing progressive taxation.

c. providing national health insurance.

d. subsidizing housing for low-income families.

e. any of the above, depending on the definition of equity used by the economy.

VII. PROBLEM SOLVING

The following problems are designed to help you to apply the concepts that you learned in this chapter.

A. What Is a Market?

1. Determine whether the following events would lead to store shelves that are **understocked** or **overstocked,** and explain the effect of this on prices in a market economy.

a. Flooding in the midwest destroys a large portion of the corn crop. Will store shelves tend to be **understocked** or **overstocked** with corn? Prices will go **(up / down).**

b. Your college wins the NCAA basketball championship. Will bookstore shelves tend to be **understocked** or **overstocked** with sweatshirts? Prices will go **(up / down).**

c. Scientists find that much of the popcorn sold at movie theaters is bad for our health. Will theaters tend to be **understocked** or **overstocked** with popcorn? Prices will go **(up / down).**

2. Draw a circular-flow diagram in the space below, showing the interaction between households and firms in goods markets and in input markets. Use your diagram to show how this market economy would answer the *what, how,* and *for whom* questions that face all societies.

B. Trade, Money, and Capital

3. Many people have speculated that the Soviet Union's demise was a result of its investing too many resources in military equipment and too few resources in consumer products.

a. Draw a hypothetical production-possibility frontier (from Chapter 1) in Figure 2-1. (Assume that as you try to specialize in the production of either good, it becomes increasingly harder to produce additional units of it.) Explain why you would expect the frontier to have the shape it does.

Figure 2-1

b. As this economy produces increasingly more military goods, what happens to the *PPF*? Carefully explain. Given this information, why might you have predicted the eventual demise of the Soviet Union? Explain.

C. The Economic Role of Government

4. Consider the following events. Do they indicate a movement **toward** or **away from** the notion of laissez-faire?

a. President Ronald Reagan fires the nation's striking air traffic controllers. **(Toward / Away from)**

b. President Bill Clinton supports the notion of nationalized health insurance. **(Toward / Away from)**

c. British Prime Minister Margaret Thatcher "privatizes" national industries, like British Airways, by selling them to private investors. **(Toward / Away from)**

d. The Federal Reserve takes actions to decrease the money supply, thereby increasing interest rates. **(Toward / Away from)**

e. The government requires all auto manufacturers to install safety belts in newly produced automobiles. **(Toward / Away from)**

VIII. DISCUSSION QUESTIONS

Answer the following questions, making sure that you can explain the work you did to arrive at the answers.

1. For the past several decades, governments have been taking steps to preserve the environment. Recently, a new policy initiative has emerged that uses basic economic concepts to provide incentives for polluters. Markets have emerged in which pollution "rights" are traded between "owners" of these rights. Government authorities establish maximum amounts of pollutants that firms can emit into the air on a region-by-region basis. They then dole these rights out to firms in the area, who are allowed to emit pollutants only as long as they own the rights to emit them.
   a. Using this information, explain how markets for pollution rights emerge. How are property rights established, and why is it important to establish these property rights?
   b. Why might this policy fail to provide incentives for firms to limit pollution to the greatest extent possible? Explain.
2. If money is not categorized as capital by economists, why do we use money in an economic system at all? What purpose does it serve? Explain.
3. Discuss the pros and cons of promoting laissez-faire in an economic system. Would you be in favor of such a policy? Why or why not?
4. Define what is meant by the term *equity*. Why is it difficult for economists to come up with a definitive definition of an equitable distribution of resources? Explain.
5. Define what is meant by the term *progressive taxation*. How might this help to provide a more equitable distribution of income?

IX. ANSWERS TO STUDY GUIDE QUESTIONS

III. Review of Key Concepts
4 The market mechanism
6 Market equilibrium
11 Perfect competition
10 The invisible hand
9 Specialization and division of labor
3 Capital
5 Efficiency
2 Equity
1 Monopoly
8 Externalities
7 Fiscal policy

VI. Multiple Choice Questions
1. A 2. C 3. B 4. D 5. D 6. C
7. D 8. A, B, C, E 9. B 10. C 11. A
12. B 13. E 14. D 15. B 16. C 17. E

VII. Problem Solving
1. a. understocked, up
   b. understocked, up
   c. overstocked, down
2.

3. a. Resources are not equally suited to the production of both commodities. Starting at point A in Figure 2-1, a relatively large amount of consumer products are produced as society gives up military equipment. However, as more and more consumer products are produced, the resources that are left are less and less suited to the production of them. Consequently, more and more military equipment must be given up.

Figure 2-1

b. As the Soviet economy produced more and more military goods, fewer and fewer consumer products were available for its citizens. Furthermore, some of the resources that were being used to produce military goods were much better suited to the production of other commodities. It became increasingly more difficult to efficiently and equitably distribute the few consumer products that were available. Finally, the economy collapsed.
4. a. away from
   b. away from
   c. toward
   d. away from
   e. away from

VIII. Discussion Questions

1. a. Each firm in an industry is given the right to pollute a certain (limited) amount of air. If a firm pollutes more than its limit, it can be fined by the government. In essence, each firm "owns" a certain amount of air. If a firm pollutes more than what it "owns," it can expect to be penalized. However, if a firm does not pollute all the air it is allowed to, it can sell its remaining allotment to another firm. In this way the firm that reduces pollution is rewarded, and firms that pollute excessively are penalized. By establishing property rights for air, firms are given an incentive to take care of what they "own."

   b. As long as firms are given property rights to a certain amount of air, they may have little incentive to reduce pollution beneath their allotment. Firms are essentially told that a certain amount of pollution is free.

2. Money is very useful as a medium of exchange. When sellers accept it as a means of payment, it eliminates the need to provide the seller with some desirable (from the seller's perspective) commodity that the buyer may not have. Sellers can use the money they receive to purchase the commodities they desire.

3. *Pros*: Freedom of choice in occupations and production; low taxes mean that the successful retain most of their rewards; society, not the government, decides how to allocate resources.

   Cons: No program of economic stabilization; no provision for the production of public goods; less consumer protection; no oversight of externalities.

4. *Equity* deals with fairness. Economists have difficulty with this concept because we all have different tastes and preferences as well as different needs and abilities. Should individuals be rewarded according to their efforts or according to their needs? The answer to this question entails subjective evaluation.

5. *Progressive taxation* occurs when the *percent* of income that is paid in taxes increases with increases in income. The very wealthy would pay the highest percentage of their income in taxes. These tax revenues could be redistributed by the government to the poorest families. This would make the distribution of income more equitable.

CHAPTER 3
Basic Elements of Supply and Demand

I. CHAPTER OVERVIEW

This chapter lays the foundation for the rest of your course by describing the interaction between buyers and sellers in a market economy. Properly framed, almost any economic question can be approached from a supply-and-demand perspective; because resources are limited but wants are unlimited, the magic of the market is to direct signals between people who are looking to consume and people who are looking to produce. Our implicit assumption is that *prices* carry this information between buyers and sellers, and hence prices are discussed as the most important factor determining behavior on both sides of the market.

II. LEARNING OBJECTIVES

After you have read Chapter 3 in your text and completed the exercises in this *Study Guide* chapter, you should be able to:

1. Define **demand** in a market using words, tables, and diagrams.
2. Illustrate the shifts in demand caused by changes in factors other than price that influence a consumer's willingness to purchase.
3. Explain the difference between changes in demand and changes in quantity demanded.
4. Define **supply** in a market using words, tables, and diagrams.
5. Illustrate the shifts in supply caused by changes in factors other than price that influence a firm's willingness to produce and sell.
6. Explain the difference between changes in supply and changes in quantity supplied.
7. Use the concepts of **shortages** and **surpluses** to illustrate the natural tendency of a market to move toward equilibrium.
8. Show the effects of shifts in supply or demand using diagrams.

III. REVIEW OF KEY CONCEPTS

Match the following terms from column A with their definitions in column B.

A	B
__ Effective demand	1. One explanation for an increase in labor supply.
__ Increase in supply	2. A factor other than price that changes supply.
__ Consumer income	3. A factor other than price that changes demand.
__ Technology	4. One reason why we have an upward-sloping supply curve.
__ Prices of substitutes	5. The quantities of a good demanded per unit of time at alternative prices, all else being fixed.
__ Immigration	6. An increase in this factor will shift demand to the right.
__ The laws of diminishing returns	7. The price and quantity at which there is no surplus or shortage.
__ Equilibrium level of output	8. Occurs when the price of a product falls.
__ Surplus	9. Occurs when the quantity supplied is greater than the quantity demanded.
__ Decrease in quantity supplied	10. The recent explosion of computer echnology has caused this.

IV. SUMMARY AND CHAPTER OUTLINE

This section summarizes the key concepts from the chapter.

Many forces can operate to push the observed price of any given commodity higher or lower: changes in people's tastes, changes in their incomes, changes in the costs of production, changes in the prices of substitute products, changes in government policy, etc. For example, the price of tickets to see a Grateful Dead concert might fall if their music becomes less popular, if the incomes of music lovers fall, if the price of guitars doubles, if the price of Rolling Stones concerts falls, or if the government decides to place taxes on concert tickets.

In order to assess the impact of any of these single events, we need to divide these forces into too groups: those that have their initial impact on the demand side of the market and those that have their initial impact on the supply side of the market.

A. The Demand Schedule

1.   When economists refer to the *law of downward-sloping demand,* they are speaking of a particular kind of behavior among buyers that is observed with so few exceptions that it can be designated as a "law" of behavior.

2.   It is essential to keep in mind that a demand curve is a conditional schedule; it answers an "if this, then that" type of question. It shows, in particular, that if the price of some good were to stand at some specified level, then consumers would be willing to purchase the indicated quantity.

3.   The quantity of a good or service that is read from a demand curve does not depend at all upon whether or not that quantity is feasible to supply at the given price. It reflects only the desires of consumers who worry only about their own preferences and what they can afford.

4.   Remember that price is not the only factor that influences consumers' decisions to buy. Average income, number of buyers, price and availability of related goods, and tastes and preferences all define the behavior of buyers. Any changes in these factors will cause the demand curve to shift.

B. The Supply Curve

1.   The quantity of a good or service that is read from a supply curve does not depend upon whether or not people want to buy that much. It reflects only the ambitions of suppliers who worry only about their costs and their anticipated profits (given the quoted price).

2.   The *supply schedule* (and *supply curve*) for a commodity shows the relationship between its market price and the amount of that commodity that producers are willing to produce and sell, other things being held equal.

3.   Technology, input prices, prices of related goods, and government policy all define the behavior of sellers. Thus, changes in any of these factors will cause the supply curve to shift.

C. Equilibrium of Supply and Demand

1.   The division between buyers and sellers is nearly absolute. In all but a very few exceptional cases, economic forces *directly* influence either the demand side of a market or the supply side of a market, *but not both.*

2.   Market-clearing equilibrium prices are achieved when the quantity supplied matches the quantity demanded.

3.   When the quantity demanded exceeds the quantity supplied, the resulting shortage pushes the price up toward equilibrium. On the other hand, when the quantity demanded is less than the quantity supplied, the resulting surplus pushes the price down.

4.   When we draw demand and supply schedules, we are defining a relationship between quantities demanded or supplied and the relative price of the product. When relative prices change, consumers or producers change their behavior *along* the demand and supply curves. Demand and supply curves shift only when a factor *other than* the own-price of the product has changed.

V. HELPFUL HINTS

Understanding demand-and-supply diagrams is crucial to understanding how a market economy operates. Simply memorizing all the movements and shifts in curves that can be applied to different market situations does not work well. For your part as a student, it takes thoughtfulness and practice. Nevertheless, there are several guidelines that can help you in your study of markets.

1.   Whenever you are confronted with a supply and demand problem (even in a multiple choice or true/false problem), *draw* the appropriate diagram and use it to illustrate the changes that you anticipate in the market. The discipline of envisioning the graph will help you keep track of what is changing and what is staying the same, first on the demand side and second on the supply side. You will find it easier to avoid errors caused by confusing changes in quantities demanded and supplied (movement along curves) with changes in demand and supply (shifts of curves).

2.   In *any* diagram, if a variable that is measured on one of the axes changes, the curve will not shift. You simply move along the curve to measure the response to the change in the variable. For example, in demand-and-supply diagrams, price is measured along the vertical axis. According to this rule, if there is a change in price, the curves will not shift. After all, in order to draw the demand and supply curves in the first place, we had to know how much would be demanded or supplied at each price. If *any other* variable changes and it has bearing on the market, then the curve(s) will shift.

3.   When demand and supply curves shift, think of these shifts in terms of *left* and *right,* rather than up or down. Up usually implies there is more of something rather than less. However, when supply curves shift up, less is being supplied at every price. To avoid this pitfall, think of shifts in terms of *left* and *right.*

4.   When equilibrium is reached in a market, this means that the market clears; that is, all consumers who are willing to pay the market price are able to find the product. Producers sell all they are willing to bring to market at that price. Market equilibrium does not necessarily mean, however, that all consumers or producers are completely satisfied with the equilibrium position. Some consumers may want to purchase the commodity but may not be able to afford the market-clearing price. I may *want* to purchase an Infinity automobile, but I am currently "priced out" of that marketplace. Automobile manufacturers, on the other hand, may *want* to produce more luxury automobiles but refrain from doing so because they think the established market price is too low.

5. *Excess demand* means the same thing as *shortage*.
6. *Excess supply* means the same thing as *surplus*.

VI. MULTIPLE CHOICE QUESTIONS

These questions are organized by topic from the chapter outline. Choose the best answer from the options available.

A. The Demand Schedule

1. A demand curve for widgets shows:
   a. how people's spending patterns change as their income changes.
   b. that people spend more money on widgets as the price of widgets increases.
   c. the quantity of widgets that would be purchased per unit of time at each alternative price, holding other factors influencing demand fixed.
   d. that firms are willing to supply more output, per unit of time, as prices increase.

2. As the price of airline tickets increases, the:
   a. demand for airline tickets increases.
   b. supply of airline tickets decreases.
   c. quantity of tickets demanded decreases.
   d. quantity of tickets supplied decreases.

3. The law of downward-sloping demand holds that:
   a. a surplus of goods will cause price to fall.
   b. people normally buy more of a good as their incomes rise.
   c. the quantity of a good that consumers willingly purchase increases as the price of the good falls.
   d. the quantity of a good purchased will decrease as it goes out of style or is replaced by something of better quality.

Use Figure 3-1 to answer questions 4 through 7.

Figure 3-1

4. A patient must purchase some exact quantity of a particular drug (no less, no more) and will pay any price in order to obtain it. Which of the diagrams best illustrates this situation?
   a. (*a*)
   b. (*b*)
   c. (*c*)
   d. (*d*)

5. The government declares that it is prepared to purchase any and all gold supplied to it by domestic gold mines at a price of $410 an ounce. Which of the diagrams best illustrates this situation?
   a. (*a*)
   b. (*b*)
   c. (*c*)
   d. (*d*)

6. An increase in consumers' money incomes prompts them to demand a greater quantity of good *X* at any price. Which of the diagrams best illustrates this situation?
   a. (*a*)
   b. (*b*)
   c. (*c*)
   d. (*d*)

7. I can buy *any amount* of sugar in my local supermarket at a fixed price of 40 cents per pound. No matter how much I buy, I always pay the same price per pound. Which of the diagrams best illustrates this situation?
   a. (*a*)
   b. (*b*)
   c. (*c*)
   d. (*d*)

8. Any of the following could cause an increase in the demand for Wheaties *except*:
   a. a decrease in the price of wheat used to produce cereal.
   b. a new report from the Surgeon General suggesting that wheat helps to cure sunburns.
   c. a picture of a popular sports figure, such as Michael Jordan, on the Wheaties box.
   d. an increase in the price of a competing cereal, such as Cheerios.

9. Suppose that the demand curve for commodity *X* shifts to the left. One reasonable explanation for this shift would be:
   a. the supply of *X* has decreased for some reason.
   b. the price of *X* has increased, so people have decided to buy less of it than they did before.
   c. consumer tastes have shifted in favor of this commodity, and they want to buy more of it than they did before at any given price.
   d. the price of *X* has fallen, so people have decided to buy more of it than they did before.
   e. none of these events.

10. Four of the five events described below might reasonably explain why the demand for beef has shifted to a new position. Which one is not a suitable explanation?
   a. The price of some good which consumers regard as a substitute for beef has risen.
   b. The price of beef has fallen.
   c. Money incomes of beef consumers have increased.

d.   A widespread advertising campaign is undertaken by the producers of beef.

e.   There is a change in people's tastes with respect to beef.

11. When applied to the demand for commodity X the phrase "other things equal," or "other things constant," means that:

a.   the price of X is held constant.

b.   both buyer incomes and the price of X are held constant.

c.   buyer incomes, tastes, and the price of X are held constant.

d.   all factors that might influence the demand for X including the price of X are held constant.

e.   none of the above.

12. If IBM and Compaq computers are substitutes, a decrease in the price of IBM PCs will cause:

a.   a decrease in the demand for Compaq computers.

b.   an increase in the demand for IBM computers.

c.   an increase in the supply of IBM computers.

d.   an increase in the supply of Compaq computers.

B. The Supply Curve

13. The supply curve describes:

a.   an inverse relationship between price and quantity supplied.

b.   a direct relationship between income and quantity supplied.

c.   a cyclical relationship between consumption and savings.

d.   a direct relationship between price and quantity supplied.

14. An increase in the cost of materials needed to produce snow skis causes the following change in the snow ski market:

a.   the demand curve shifts to the right.

b.   the supply curve shifts to the left.

c.   both the demand and supply curves shift to the left.

d.   neither curve shifts.

15. Consider the producer who makes leather shoes and leather purses. An increase in the price of leather shoes would cause:

a.   a decrease in the supply of leather purses.

b.   movement along the supply curve for purses.

c.   a shift in the demand curve for leather shoes.

d.   the supply curve for leather shoes and the supply curve for purses to shift to the left.

16. The demand for snowboards has increased recently as more people have taken up the sport. This will cause the supply curve for snowboards to:

a.   shift to the left.

b.   shift to the right.

c.   remain the same.

d.   decrease next year.

17. Supply curves are typically "positively sloped." The meaning conveyed by any such curve is that:

a.   any increase in costs of production will result in a movement up along the supply curve.

b.   the lower the price, the larger the supply that consumers are prepared to buy.

c.   the higher the price, the larger the quantity suppliers will wish to sell.

d.   the larger the quantity suppliers have to sell, the lower the price they will have to quote in order to dispose of it.

e.   none of the above.

18. Which of the following will *not* help to determine the position of the supply curve?

a.   Technology

b.   Resource costs.

c.   Consumer income.

d.   Government taxes.

C. Equilibrium of Supply and Demand

19. Equilibrium in a market indicates:

a.   the price at which quantity supplied equals quantity demanded.

b.   that every buyer who wants to buy can buy at the equilibrium price, and every seller who wants to sell can sell at the equilibrium price.

c.   there is no tendency for price to change.

d.   all of the above.

e.   none of the above.

20. In prosperous times, *both* the equilibrium price *and* the quantity of some commodity X may go up simultaneously. Such a situation:

a.   is one of the few recognized exceptions to the law of downward-sloping demand.

b.   is precisely what the law of downward-sloping demand says is to be expected.

c.   is the consequence of a demand curve running from southwest to northeast.

d.   cannot be explained by means of ordinary supply-curve and demand-curve analysis.

e.   is caused by a rightward-shifting demand curve and a stable supply curve.

21. Beef supplies are sharply reduced because of drought in the beef-raising states, and consumers turn to pork as a substitute for beef because they believe there are health benefits. *In the beef market,* these two phenomena would be described in terms of supply and demand as:

a.   a leftward shift in the demand curve.

b.   a leftward shift in the supply curve.

c.   a rightward shift in the demand curve.

d.   a rightward shift in the supply curve.

e.   both the supply curve and the demand curve will shift to the left.

22. Which alternative in question 21 would be correct with respect to the events described had that question asked about *the pork market*?
    a.
    b.
    c.
    d.
    e.

23. Let the initial price of a good be $5. If buyers wish to purchase 4000 units per week at that price while sellers wish to sell 5000 units per week, then:
    a. price will tend to increase in the future.
    b. firm output will tend to increase in the future.
    c. price and output will tend to remain the same in the future.
    d. price will tend to decrease in the future.
    e. something is wrong—this could not happen.

Figure 3-2 shows conditions in the market for home heating oil last year. The initial equilibrium position in the market is shown by price P_1 and quantity Q_1. Please use the diagram to answer questions 24 and 25.

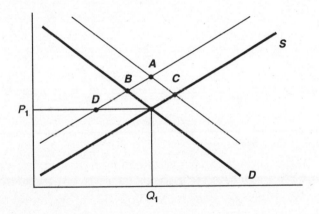

Figure 3-2

24. This winter has been unusually cold and snowy in the northeast, with a record number of snowstorms. The new equilibrium in the market for home heating oil is best represented by point:
    a. *A*.
    b. *B*.
    c. *C*.
    d. *D*.

25. At the old equilibrium price, there now exists a(n):
    a. shortage.
    b. surplus.
    c. equilibrium.
    d. excess supply.

Table 3-1 contains data pertaining to the market for mountain bikes. Please use the data to answer questions 26 and 27.

TABLE 3-1

Price	Quantity Supplied (weekly)	Quantity Demanded (weekly)
$100	1000	4000
200	2000	3500
300	3000	3000
400	4000	2500
500	5000	2000

26. The equilibrium price in this market is:
    a. $100.
    b. $200.
    c. $300.
    d. $400.

27. The equilibrium quantity exchanged in this market is:
    a. 2000 bikes.
    b. 3000 bikes.
    c. 4000 bikes.
    d. 5000 bikes.

28. A recent *Wall Street Journal* article (6/24/93) details the increased popularity of "Doc Martens" shoes and boots among college-aged students. This fad has had a big impact on the market for Reebok sneakers, a substitute for Doc Martens. We would expect the equilibrium:
    a. price of Reeboks to fall and the equilibrium quantity exchanged to increase.
    b. price and quantity of Reeboks exchanged to increase.
    c. price and quantity of Reeboks exchanged to decrease.
    d. price of Reeboks to increase and the equilibrium quantity exchanged to decrease.

VII. PROBLEM SOLVING

The following problems are designed to help you to apply the concepts that you learned in this chapter.

1. For each of the following statements, put a **T** if the statement is *true*, an **F** if the statement is *false*, and a **U** if you are *uncertain* about the validity of the statement.

A. The Demand Schedule

____ a. The substitution effect tells us that people will buy more as prices fall because their purchasing power is increasing.

____ b. The demand for cars has increased in the past 50 years because the price has fallen.

____ c. When demand decreases, the price falls, so supply shifts to the left.

B. The Supply Curve

____ d. Over the past few years, the price of compact disc players has fallen, and at the same time firms are supplying many more compact disc players. The law of supply is invalid in this case.

___ e.　An improvement in technology will cause the supply curve to shift to the right.

___ f.　If the price of Pepsi goes up, it is likely that the market supply curve for Coke will shift to the right.

___ g.　If the wages of autoworkers increase, the supply of automobiles will shift to the left.

C. Equilibrium of Supply and Demand

___ h.　Markets for goods are defined by the behavior of suppliers who determine prices and output levels.

___ i.　If the actual price in a market is above the equilibrium price, we would expect to see downward pressure on output and price.

___ j.　In a market economy, goods are allocated by the price system to those people who can afford them.

2.　Table 3-2 focuses on the factors that will shift either the demand curve or the supply curve. In each case, determine which curve will shift, and write in **demand** or **supply** as appropriate; then write in whether the shift will be to the **right** or the **left**. In addition, determine whether equilibrium price and output will be **higher** or **lower**. The first case has been completed as an example.

TABLE 3-2

Shift Factor	Demand or Supply	Shifts	Left or Right	Price Will Be	Output Will Be
a. Population increases.	demand	shifts	right	higher	higher
b. Input prices go up.	____	shifts	____	____	____
c. Tariffs are removed.	____	shifts	____	____	____
d. Average income falls.	____	shifts	____	____	____
e. Technology improves.	____	shifts	____	____	____
f. Product becomes more desirable/popular.	____	shifts	____	____	____

(a)

(b)

(c)

(d)

Figure 3-3

3.　This problem deals with shifts in demand and supply curves. Figure 3-3 illustrates four different shifts in demand or supply. Take a moment to consider each shift.

Table 3-3 considers changes that occur in seven different markets. Determine which diagram—(a), (b), (c), or (d)—is most appropriate for each market. Then identify the specific *shift factor* that caused the curve to shift. Finally, determine whether equilibrium price and output will be *higher* or *lower*. The first case has been completed as an example.

TABLE 3-3

Change in Market	Diagram	Shift Factor	Price Will Be	Output Will Be
a. Good X is clothing that has gone out of style	b	change in taste shifts DD left	lower	lower
b. Pollution tax on supplier	____	_____	____	____
c. Opening of market to foreign buyers	____	_____	____	____
d. Price of substitute good falls	____	_____	____	____
e. Market structure requires more advertising	____	_____	____	____
f. A 10% across-the-board income-tax cut	____	_____	____	____
g. Robot makes production more efficient	____	_____	____	____

4.　This problem deals with the market for fish and the effect of a papal decree issued by Pope Paul VI in 1966 which gave local Catholic bishops the authority to allow Roman Catholics to eat meat on Fridays. We will use hypothetical data to analyze the effect of the decree on the market for fish. (For a more accurate analysis see Frederick W. Bell, "The Pope and the Market for Fish," *American Economic Review* 58 [December 1968], pp. 1346-1350.)

Table 3-4 presents market data for the price per pound of codfish (measured in cents) and the quantity demanded and supplied at those prices (measured in thousands of pounds) . (*For the time being, ignore the column on the right labeled "New Quantity."*)

a.　Every time the price of codfish decreases by 60 cents per pound, the quantity demanded increases by

_____.

b.　Every time the price of codfish decreases by 60 cents per pound, the quantity supplied decreases by

_____.

TABLE 3-4

Price	Quantity Demanded	Quantity Supplied	New Quantity
300	0	15	0
240	2	12	0
180	4	9	2
120	6	6	4
60	8	3	6
0	10	0	8

c. On Figure 3-4, plot the market demand and supply curves.

d. What are the equilibrium price and quantity in this market? _____

e. Now suppose the papal decree is issued. Which curve will be affected by this change?

_____

f. Which *shift factor* will cause the curve to shift?

_____

Suppose the column labeled "New Quantity" in Table 3-4 represents the change in the market.

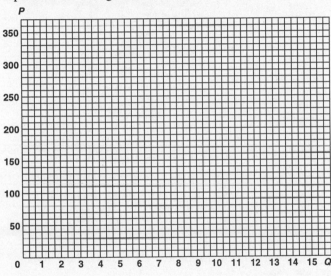

Figure 3-4

g. Plot the new curve on Figure 3-4. (Is there any doubt about which curve shifted?)

h. Approximately, what are the new equilibrium price and output? _____

i. What type of change would have resulted in a movement along the demand curve and *not* a shift in it?

_____

j. Will the supply curve shift as a result of the papal decree? Will the quantity of fish supplied change? Explain. _____

_____

5. What would happen to used-car prices in a recession as family incomes fall? The first three columns in Table 3-5

can be used to illustrate *price, quantity supplied,* and *quantity demanded* before the recession hits the economy.

TABLE 3-5

Price	Quantity Supplied	Quantity Demanded	New Quantity
$500	100	400	_____
600	150	300	_____
700	200	200	_____
800	250	100	_____
900	300	0	_____

a. Use the grid in Figure 3-5 to plot the supply and demand curves in this market.

b. Determine the equilibrium price and output.

_____

c. At what price would the quantity supplied fall to zero? _____

d. What is the price axis intercept of the supply curve?

_____

e. What are the slopes of the supply and demand curves? _____

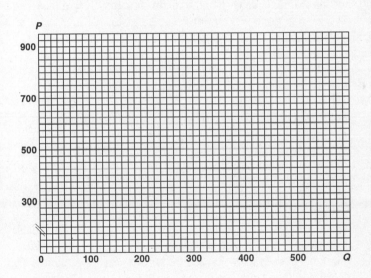

Figure 3-5

One special feature of this market is that households, or consumers, are both suppliers and demanders of used cars. When the recession comes a new relationship is established between *price* and *quantity*. Suppose a new relationship is established between price and quantity as shown in Table 3-6.

TABLE 3-6

P	Q
$500	55
700	155
900	255

f.   Use these numbers to fill in the last column in Table 3-5. Note that there are gaps in your data!

g.   Calculate and then fill in the missing numbers in the column.

h.   Add this new curve to your diagram in Figure 3-5.

i.   Approximately, what are the new equilibrium price and output? _____

j.   For what reason(s) did the curve shift?

_____
_____

k.   Can you think of any reasons why the curve might shift in the opposite direction instead?

_____
_____

l.   Finally, suppose, as a result of the recession, some households decide to purchase a used car rather than a new one. Suppose further that some households that were previously planning to buy a used car decide to postpone the purchase of a car altogether. Assume that this second change dominates, or is stronger than, the first one mentioned. Illustrate this change in your diagram in Figure 3-5 and explain the effect it will have on market price and output. _____

_____
_____

6.   The last market example that Samuelson and Nordhaus discuss in this chapter focuses on the supply of and demand for workers, or labor. *Labor, land,* and *capital* are considered the *primary factors of production* that firms use to produce goods and services. The exchange of the factors of production takes place in *factor* markets. Goods and services, on the other hand, are exchanged in *product* markets. To make sure that the functions of these markets are clear to you, we suggest that you review the circular-flow diagram of a market economy (Figure 2-1) in Chapter 2 of the text.

In the *factor* market for labor, the roles of individuals and firms are reversed from their positions in the *product* market. In the factor market, individuals are the suppliers of labor services, and firms are now the consumers or demanders of labor services. Workers will supply more of their labor services at higher prices or wage rates, and all other things held equal, firms will demand more labor services as wages fall.

Figure 3-6 illustrates demand and supply curves for labor in a competitive market. As indicated, the equilibrium market wage is $5 (per hour).

a.   If the wage rate were beneath the equilibrium wage, would you expect either the demand or supply curve to shift? Explain why or why not. _____

_____
_____

b.   If the wage rate were beneath the equilibrium wage, what forces would move the market toward equilibrium?

_____

c.   Suppose the government passed a law which said that all workers in this industry must be paid at least $6 per hour. Would you expect either the demand curve or the supply curve to shift? Explain why or why not.

_____
_____
_____

d.   Assuming that there are no other changes, describe the effect that this legislation would have on wages, employment, and unemployment in this market.

_____
_____
_____

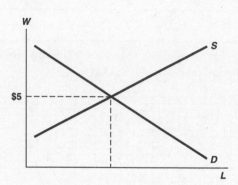

Figure 3-6

VIII. DISCUSSION QUESTIONS

Answer the following questions, making sure that you can explain the work you did to arrive at the answers.

1.   Explain why the market supply curve for any commodity has a positive slope.

2.   Explain why the market demand curve for any commodity has a negative slope.

3.   Explain the importance of the concept "all other things held equal" in supply-and-demand analysis.

4.   Suppose that we are studying the market for cornflakes. Suppose further that during the summer of 1999 the following events both occur: (1) The weather in the farm belt is extraordinarily hot, with very little rain; and (2) A new research study is published and widely disseminated which proves that eating cornflakes makes people healthier and adds years to their lives. Figure 3-7 illustrates the initial equilibrium position in the cornflake market.

a.   Show how the two events described above will change this market.

b.   Can you say what will happen to the equilibrium price in this market? Please explain your answer.

c.   Can you say what will happen to the equilibrium quantity in this market? Please explain your answer.

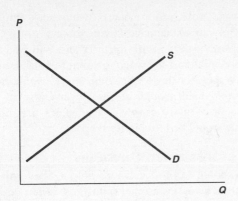

Figure 3-7

5. In the last section of the chapter, Samuelson and Nordhaus discuss "rationing by prices."
    a. What exactly does this mean?
    b. What other methods can societies use to ration goods and services?

IX. ANSWERS TO STUDY GUIDE QUESTIONS

III. Review of Key Concepts

5	Effective demand
10	Increase in supply
3	Consumer income
2	Technology
6	Prices of substitutes
1	Immigration
4	The law of diminishing returns
7	Equilibrium level of output
9	Surplus
8	Decrease in quantity demanded

VI. Multiple Choice Questions

1. C   2. C   3. C   4. B   5. A   6. C
7. A   8. A   9. E   10. B   11. E   12. A
13. D   14. B   15. A   16. C   17. C   18. C
19. D   20. E   21. E   22. C   23. D   24. C
25. A   26. C   27. B   28. C

VII. Problem Solving

1. a. F
    b. F
    c. F
    d. F
    e. T
    f. F
    g. T
    h. F
    k
2. b. supply, left, higher, lower

c. supply, right, lower, higher
d. demand, left, lower, lower
e. supply, right, lower, higher
f. demand, right, higher, higher

3. b. (*d*) Increase in costs shifts *SS* left. higher, lower
    c. (*a*) Increase in the number of buyers shifts *DD* right, higher, higher
    d. (*b*) Decrease in substitute's price shifts *DD* left. lower, lower
    e. (*d*) Increase in costs shifts *SS* left. higher, lower
    f. (*a*) Increase in income shifts *DD* right. higher, higher
    g. (*c*) Increase in technology shifts *SS* right. lower, higher

4. a. 2 (thousand)
    b. 3 (thousand)
    c.

Figure 3-4

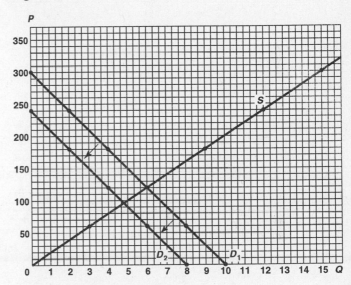

d. P_1 = 120 cents or $1.20 per pound.
    Q_1 = 6 thousand pounds.
e. Demand will shift to the left.
f. Consumers' tastes and preferences will be affected by the decree.
g. See Figure 3-4.
h. P_2 is approximated 96 cents or $0.96 per pound.
    Q_2 is approximately 4.8 thousand pounds.
i. If there is a change in the price of codfish, consumers will move along the demand curve.
j. The papal decree will cause the demand curve to shift, not the supply curve. Producers will move down the existing supply curve to the new demand curve. If as a result of the lower prices, less profits are made, this may encourage firms to exit the industry. If and when this occurs, the supply curve will shift to the left. But

the papal decree has no direct effect on the position or shape of the supply curve

5. a.

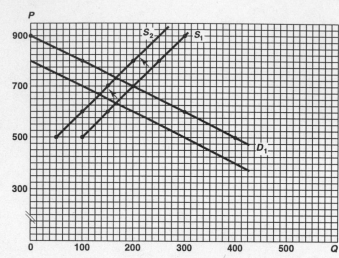

Figure 3-5

b. $P_1 = \$700$.
    $Q_1 = 200$.
c. $300.
d. $300.
e. Slope of supply = 2.
    Slope of demand = -1.

TABLE 3-5

	Price	Quantity Supplied	Quantity Demanded	New Quantity
f.				
g.	$500	100	400	55
	600	150	300	105
	700	200	200	155
	800	250	100	205
	900	300	0	255

h. See Figure 3-5.
i. P_2 is approximately $730.
    Q_2 is approximately 162.
j. Automobile owners are holding on to their cars longer during the recession. Perhaps their pay has been cut or they have lost their jobs.
k. If household income falls dramatically, people may be forced to sell their cars for money. (This would probably be a depression.)
l. See Figure 3-5. The demand curve will shift to the left. Market price and output will both fall.
6. a. Neither curve will shift. Since the wage rate is measured along the Y axis, you would move along the curves to the equilibrium wage.
    b. There would be an excess demand for labor. Firms would want to hire more workers than they could find.

As wages rose, more workers would seek employment, and firms would demand fewer workers.
c. Neither curve will shift. There will be an excess supply of labor if the wage is raised to $6 an hour.
d. Wages, for those who found work, would be higher. Unemployment would increase because firms would lay some previously employed workers off, and more people would be looking for work.

VIII. Discussion Questions

1. If firms are to produce more output, they will have to bid resources away from other industries. Their costs go up, so to produce more, they must be paid more.
2. As consumers purchase commodities, the additional satisfaction they receive from additional units begins to decrease. So their willingness to pay for the commodity declines as well.
3. It is very difficult to explain how the economy works if we cannot (at least in the classroom) hold other things equal. When more than one change occurs at a time, it becomes impossible to explain causal relationships.
4. a.

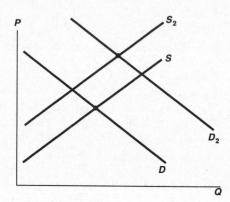

Figure 3-7

b. Since people recognize health benefits, and since supply has been reduced, the price will go up.
c. We cannot be certain about quantity. Consumers want more. Firms want to supply less. Whichever curve shifts more will dominate and determine the direction of the change in output.
5. a. In a market system, goods and services are rationed by the marketplace. Consumers "vote" with their dollars and determine what will be produced.
    b. An alternative rationing plan can be imposed by the government. This is a command economy. Remember, all societies are faced with scarcity and must devise some way to ration goods and services.

CHAPTER 4
Overview of
Macroeconomics

I. CHAPTER OVERVIEW

The study of macroeconomics is the study of the "big picture." It is the study of how entire economies make decisions about using resources. It ponders the sources of growth, inflation, unemployment, and business cycles. It ponders the ability of governments to help (or hinder) their economies by manipulating a wide variety of policy instruments. It asks why some policies work and why some fail.

Applied macroeconomists who study the impact of economic policy on the economy as a whole have found that certain policy objectives, and the instruments used to achieve them, may at times be incompatible. While a particular policy objective may be admirable when considered at face value, strenuous pursuit of that policy may be damaging to other objectives of arguably equal importance. For example, policies which produce low unemployment rates may also generate increased inflation.

Once you complete your work on this overview, you will not have many answers. You will, instead, have collected a multitude of questions whose answers will be addressed over the course of the next 16 chapters. Your work on this list of questions will not, however, be an exercise in futility. In noting the significance and the context of each question, you will build a strong foundation which can support your acquisition of greater macroeconomic knowledge.

II. LEARNING OBJECTIVES

After you have read Chapter 20 in your text and completed the exercises in this *Study Guide* chapter, you should be able to:

1. Explain the difference between microeconomics and macroeconomics.
2. Identify the major goals of macroeconomic policy.
3. Identify the major macroeconomic policy instruments used to achieve these goals.
4. Understand some of the major economic events and the related governmental policies that influenced the United States during this century.
5. Appreciate the contribution of John Maynard Keynes to the development of governmental macroeconomic policy.
6. Recognize the potential for tradeoffs between two or more policy objectives (e.g., price stability versus high employment, rapid growth versus high current consumption, etc.).
7. Understand how **policy instruments** and **exogenous variables** affect **induced** (or endogenous) **variables**.
8. Appreciate the importance of the international economy and a nation's connection to it.
9. Develop the fundamentals of aggregate supply, aggregate demand, and macroeconomic equilibrium.
10. Use aggregate supply and aggregate demand analysis to illustrate how *policy instruments* and *external variables* can influence either the demand or the supply side of the macroeconomy.

Note to Students *As you begin the macro section of the text there are many new terms and concepts to learn. A little extra time and effort on your part to learn them now will pay off later!*

III. REVIEW OF KEY CONCEPTS

Match the following terms from column A with their definitions in column B.

A	B
__ Employment Act of 1946	1. A sudden change in conditions of cost or productivity that shifts **aggregate supply** sharply.
__ Business cycle	2. Total quantity of goods and services that the nation's businesses are willing to produce and sell in a given period.
__ Fiscal policy	3. Short term decline in an economy's real output.
__ Monetary policy	4. Monitors the cost of a fixed basket of goods and services bought by the typical urban consumer.

__ Incomes policies

__ Gross domestic product (GDP)

__ Nominal

__ Real

__ Potential GDP

__ GDP gap

__ Unemployment rate

__ Consumer Price Index

__ Net exports

__ Trade policies

__ External variables

__ Induced variables

__ Aggregate supply

__ Aggregate demand

__ International financial management

__ Supply shock

__ Recession

__ Inflation

5.   Numerical value of the difference between the value of exports and imports.

6.   Percent of the labor force that is unemployed.

7.   Exogenous variables which influence economic activity but are unaffected by the economy.

8.   Pattern of expansion and contraction of economic activity.

9.   The central bank's management of the nation's money, credit, and banking system to affect macroeconomic activity.

10. Rate of growth or decline of the price level from one year to the next.

11. Governmental policies used to control wages and prices.

12. Total amount that different sectors of the economy willingly spend on goods and services in a given period.

13. Maximum level of output that is also compatible with stable prices.

14. Endogenous economic variables which are influenced both by policy instruments and external variables.

15. Measurements at current market prices.

16. Manner in which a country establishes the price of its own currency in terms of the currency of other nations.

17. With this, the federal government declared its responsibility to promote maximum employment, production, and purchasing power.

18. Use of government expenditure and taxes to affect macroeconomic variables.

19. The difference between potential and actual GDP.

20. Measurements at constant market prices.

21. Tariffs, quotas, and other regulations that restrict or encourage imports and exports.

22. Market value of all final goods and services produced in a country during a year.

IV. SUMMARY AND CHAPTER OUTLINE

This section summarizes the key concepts from the chapter.

A. Key Concepts of Macroeconomics

1. **Macroeconomics** is the study of the behavior of the economy *as a whole*. It examines the overall level of a nation's output, employment, and prices. **Microeconomics**, on the other hand, studies *individual* prices, quantities, and markets.

2. As a result of the Great Depression, many economists and policymakers alike recognized that the government had to be more involved in stabilizing the nation's economic health. *The General Theory of Employment Interest and Money*, written by John Maynard Keynes, revolutionized macroeconomics. Keynes pointed out that (a) market economies may not, by themselves, be able to achieve a position of full employment and economic prosperity, but could instead be stuck in a position of high unemployment and underutilized production capacity; and (b) the government could use **fiscal** and **monetary policies** to reduce unemployment and shorten economic downturns.

3. In broad terms, a healthy economy is characterized as one with a high and steady level of economic growth, a high level of employment and low *un*employment, and stable (or gently rising) prices. In an attempt to achieve these objectives, most governments use a combination of **fiscal** and **monetary policy**. **Incomes policies** are used less frequently to control wages and prices in an economy.

4. Economic growth is subject to erratic upturns and downturns referred to as **business cycles**. The government uses its **policy instruments** to lessen these swings in economic activity and strives to keep GDP at or close to its potential.

5. The labor force is divided into two groups: those individuals who are working and those who are seeking work. The **unemployment rate** measures the percent of the labor force that is seeking work. Individuals who are neither working nor seeking work are not in the labor force. These individuals include young children, full-time students, retirees, and full-time household caregivers. These individuals are *not* counted by economists as being unemployed, because they are not seeking employment. Individuals who would like to work full-time but are currently stuck in part-time jobs are counted as employed.

6. Stable prices are a critically important component of economic health. Rapid price changes distort the economic decisions of both companies and individuals. The most common measure of the overall price level is the **consumer price index (CPI)**.

7. Our economy is tied very closely with the rest of the world through trade and finance. Political leaders and central bankers around the globe increasingly attempt to coordinate their macroeconomic policies, for a nation's fiscal and monetary policies can spill over to affect its neighbors.

B. Aggregate Supply and Demand

1. A nation's **aggregate supply (AS)** depends on the price level that businesses can charge, as well as the economy's capacity or potential output. **Potential output** (or **GDP**) is itself determined by the availability of productive inputs and the managerial and technical efficiency with which those inputs are combined.

2. **Aggregate demand (AD)** refers to the total amount that different sectors in the economy willingly spend on goods and services in a given period. Aggregate demand is the sum of spending by consumers, businesses, and governments. *AD* is influenced by the level of prices, as well as monetary policy, fiscal policy, and other factors.

3. The interaction of the downward-sloping **aggregate demand schedule** and the upward-sloping **aggregate supply schedule** determines the total output of the economy. National output and the price level settle at that level where demanders willingly buy what businesses willingly sell. The resulting output and price level determine employment, unemployment, and net exports.

4. The *AS* and *AD* schedules can be used to analyze some of the major economic events that have influenced the U.S. economy this century: (a) the economic expansion during the Vietnam war, (b) the stagflation caused by the supply shocks of the 1970s, (c) the deep recession caused by the monetary contraction of the 1980s, and (d) the phenomenal record of economic growth for this century.

5. The major task of macroeconomic policy is to diagnose the condition of the economy and to prescribe the right medicine. For sure, there is not always agreement among economists or even among fiscal and monetary policymakers in the administration as to what should be done. Nevertheless, the influence of government policy on economic activity can be very large.

V. HELPFUL HINTS

1. When calculating the **unemployment rate** make sure that you include only those individuals who are *actively looking for work*. Remember, the **labor force** includes the unemployed and those who are working in the marketplace.

2. Economic growth is *always* measured in **real** or inflation-adjusted terms. If nominal GDP increases from one year to the next by 8 percent, and if inflation during that year also increases by 8 percent, then there has been *no* growth in the economy. Prices have simply increased by 8 percent, and that is why (nominal) GDP is 8 percent higher than it was the year before. There is no such thing as **nominal** economic **growth**!

3. In order to make comparisons in GDP over time, or across countries, *real* numbers should be used. (Economists love to measure data in real terms.)

4. Economic growth is often measured in percentage terms. Percentage changes are fairly easy to calculate. Any percentage change is simply the change in some variable, divided by some base or initial value, multiplied by 100. For example, if you have two apples and you give one to a friend, we could say that your holding of apples has been reduced by 50 percent. The change is 1, and the base value is 2; we multiplied by 100 to get 50 (percent). It is that simple. In footnote number 2 in this chapter of your text, Samuelson and Nordhaus use the following expression to calculate the rate of inflation in the CPI:

$$\text{Rate of inflation of consumer prices} = \frac{\text{CPI (this year)} - \text{CPI (last year)}}{\text{CPI (last year)}} \times 100$$

This expression is clearly recognizable as a *percentage change*.

5. The warning from the text on *AS* and *AD* curves is worth repeating. Do not confuse the macroeconomic *AD* or *AS* curves with the microeconomic demand and supply curves. In *micro*, the demand and supply curves show the quantities and prices of commodities in *individual markets*, with such things as national income and other goods' prices held constant. In *macro*, however, the *aggregate* supply and *aggregate* demand curves show the determination of *total* output and the *overall* price level, with such things as the money supply, fiscal policy, and the capital stock held constant. The two sets of curves have a family resemblance, but they explain very different phenomena.

6. When analyzing *AS* and *AD* diagrams, watch for movements *along* the curves as compared to *shifts* in the curves. If the price level changes, the curves will *not* shift. Remember, since the price level is measured along the vertical axis, changes in it can be explained by movements along the curves—this was how the two schedules were constructed in the first place. If any other relevant variable changes (e.g., fiscal policy, monetary policy, or even the weather), then (at least) one of the curves will shift. Review the appendix to Chapter 1 if you need to work on this concept.

7. Like the production-possibility frontier, the aggregate supply and aggregate demand diagram is a model of the economy. We make some simplifying assumptions and hold other variables constant in order to better understand and explain some economic issue.

8. As you continue your study of *macro*economics, relate these new concepts back to issues of scarcity and the production-possibility frontier presented in Chapter 1. Note, too, the relationship to such *micro*economic issues as businesses, markets, and individuals.

VI. MULTIPLE CHOICE QUESTIONS

These questions are organized by topic from the chapter outline. Choose the best answer from the options available.

A. Key Concepts of Macroeconomics

1. The study of macroeconomics includes, among other topics, which of the following?
   a. the sources of inflation, unemployment, and growth.
   b. the microeconomic foundations of aggregate behavior.
   c. the reasons why some economies succeed and some fail.
   d. policies that can be enacted to improve the likelihood of success in achieving macroeconomic objectives.
   e. all the above.

2. The practice of directing government policy to support the macroeconomic health of the United States was initiated formally in:
   a. the Humphrey-Hawkins Act of 1978.
   b. the Tax Reform Act of 1986.
   c. the Full Employment and Balanced Growth Act of 1946.
   d. Balanced Budget Act of 1985.
   e. none of the above.

3. The objective of stable prices can, in the view of at least some economists, be tackled by adjustments in:
   a. fiscal policy.
   b. monetary policy.
   c. incomes policies.
   d. all the above.
   e. none of the above.

4. The main difference between nominal and real GDP is that:
   a. real GDP is adjusted for price changes while nominal is not.
   b. nominal GDP is adjusted for price changes while real is not.
   c. nominal GDP is better for comparing output across several years.
   d. real GDP increases more during periods of inflation.
   e. Keynes argued that nominal GDP was calculated incorrectly during the Great Depression.

5. The main difference between a recession and a depression is that:
   a. depressions usually precede recessions.
   b. unemployment is higher and lasts longer during a depression.
   c. recessions tend to be caused by inappropriate fiscal policy, while depressions are usually caused by poor monetary policy.
   d. recessions are considered part of the business cycle, while depressions are not.
   e. economic forecasters do a better job of predicting depressions.

6. If *potential GDP* is greater than *actual GDP* then:
   a. exports must be greater than imports.
   b. inflation has increased from the year before.
   c. there is probably some unemployment in the economy.
   d. comparisons should be made in *nominal* terms.
   e. *both* **a** and **b**.

7. Policies directed at stimulating exports can influence:
   a. the domestic employment picture.
   b. price stability.
   c. the growth of actual GDP relative to potential GDP.
   d. the foreign trade balance.
   e. all of the above.

8. John Maynard Keynes is probably *best* remembered for his:
   a. marriage to a Russian ballerina.
   b. shrewd investments on behalf of King's College.
   c. advice to the British treasury.
   d. collection of modern art and rare books.
   e. new way of looking at macroeconomics and macroeconomic policy.

9. Which of the following pairs of objectives seems to be mutually contradictory?
   a. low inflation and low unemployment.
   b. low unemployment and high rates of growth in actual GDP.
   c. high rates of growth in actual GDP and balance in foreign trade.
   d. price stability and balance in foreign trade.
   e. price stability and rapid growth in potential GDP.

10. Unemployment, inflation, and the rate of growth of actual GDP are all examples of:
    a. policy variables.
    b. external variables.
    c. international variables.
    d. variables determined by the economy.
    e. none of the above.

11. Which of the following is a determinant of potential output in the long run?
    a. taxes.
    b. money.
    c. technology.
    d. capital investment.
    e. *both* **c** and **d**.

B. Aggregate Supply and Demand

12. The aggregate supply curve is positively sloped in the short run because of:
    a. increasing costs of production.
    b. decreasing returns to scale.
    c. output prices generally rising more quickly than input prices.
    d. the potential for high unemployment.
    e. none of the above.

13. In a macroeconomic model of the economy, which of the following is most likely to be considered as an exogenous variable?

a. Foreign exports to the United States.
b. Domestic exports.
c. Interest rates.
d. Taxes.
e. Monetary policy.

14. In a macroeconomic model of the economy, which of the following is most likely to be considered as an induced variable?
a. Supply shocks.
b. Foreign exports.
c. Population growth.
d. World War II.
e. National output.

15. The short-run effect of increased defense spending that is not accommodated by increased taxation could be:
a. higher prices and higher GDP.
b. higher prices and lower GDP.
c. lower prices and lower GDP.
d. lower prices and higher GDP.
e. lower prices and the same GDP.

16. If the *AD* schedule had shifted to the right in order to accommodate the OPEC oil shock, then:

a. both prices and GDP would have remained stable.
b. output would have remained the same, albeit with higher prices.
c. output would have increased and prices decreased.
d. domestic oil prices would have fallen.
e. none of the above.

17. The effect of the orchestrated increase in interest rates in the United States in the early 1980s can be best illustrated in an *AS-AD* graph by:
a. a shift left in the *AS* curve.
b. a shift right in the *AS* curve.
c. a shift left in the *AD* curve.
d. a shift right in the *AD* curve.
e. no shift in either the *AD* or the *AS* curve.

18. 1973 has been referred to as the "year of the seven plagues" because:
a. of the repeated cover-ups of the Watergate break-in.
b. of numerous antiwar protests around the country.
c. severe supply shocks and turmoil in markets that disrupted the world economy.
d. the return of the seven plagues to Egypt.
e. none of the above.

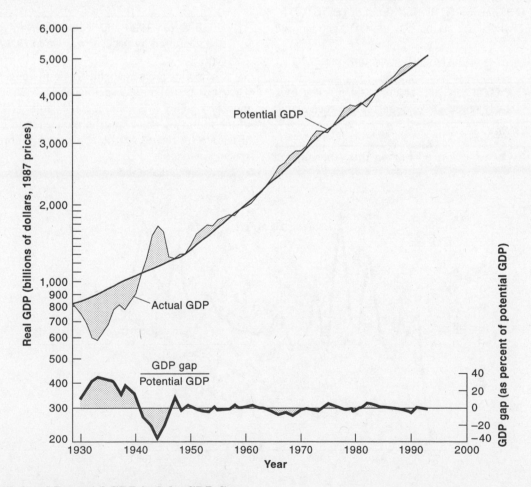

Figure 4-1 Actual and Potential GDP and the GDP Gap

VII. PROBLEM SOLVING

The following problems are designed to help you apply the concepts that you learned in the chapter.

A. Key Concepts of Macroeconomics

1. Output is usually measured in terms of gross domestic product, its most comprehensive yardstick. Figure 20-2 from the text is reproduced here as Figure 4-1 (see previous page). Use it to answer parts **e, f, g,** and **h** of this question.

a. GDP is the (**market / discounted / stable**) value of all goods and services produced during any given year.

b. When measured at current prices, this measure is termed (**nominal / real / potential**) GDP.

c. When measured after correcting for inflation, it is termed (**nominal / real / potential**) GDP.

d. When measured in terms of maximum sustainable output, it is termed (**nominal / real / potential**) GDP.

e. During the late 1970s, periods of high inflation caused real GDP to (**match potential GDP / exceed nominal GDP / fall short of nominal GDP**).

f. Periods of high unemployment during the early 1980s caused nominal GDP to (**exceed potential GDP / fall short of potential GDP / fall short of real GDP**) .

g. During what time period was the GDP gap largest? ___

Historically, what occurred during this time period?

____

h. When the GDP gap as a percent of GDP is negative, what can you say about the relationship between *actual* and *potential* GDP?

____

Historically, what occurred during this (these) time period (s)?

____

____

2. Price stability, as a goal of macroeconomic policy, does not mean absolute stability of all prices. Absolute stability would eliminate the natural role of changes in relative prices in allocating goods and services. Figure 20-4 from the text is reproduced here as Figure 4-2. Use it to answer parts **c, d, e,** and **f** of this question.

a. Price stability is, instead, an objective stated in terms of a price index like the CPI that (**ignores price movements across goods and services / averages price movements across goods and services / includes only price increases across goods and services**).

b. Inflation, then, is measured as (**the rate of change in the index / the absolute value of the price index / the absolute price levels of a representative number of goods**).

c. In what year was inflation the highest? ___.

d. In the last 25 years, inflation peaked in the (**mid-1970s and early 1980s / mid-1980s and early 1990s / mid-1970s and mid-1980s**).

e. How would you explain the dramatic fall in prices during the first years depicted in Figure 4-2?

____

f. Between 1929 and 1988, the average rate of inflation measured by the CPI was about (**8.7 / 1.2 / 3.4**) percent.

3. The policy tools available to the policymaker are varied. They fall under three general rubrics: fiscal policy (FP), monetary policy (MP), and incomes policy (IP). Match each of the following more specific policies with its general classification by recording the appropriate abbreviation in the space provided:

a. A change in federal income tax rates. ___

Figure 4-2 The Rising Trend of Consumer Price Inflation, 1929-1994

b.   An increase in the money supply. ___

c.   A tax penalty on high wage settlements. ___

d.   An increase in defense spending. ___

e.   The elimination of the interest rate deduction against taxable income. ___

f.   A change in the rate of interest that banks pay when *they* borrow money. ___

g.   A presidential order limiting the price increase that manufacturers can charge for newly produced goods. ___

4.   Which of the following are policy instruments (PI), and which are external variables (EV) that may shock the economy from beyond its boundaries? Identify each by recording the appropriate abbreviation in the space provided:

a.   Money supply ___

b.   Wars ___

c.   Expanding grain sales to the Soviet Union ___

d.   Government spending ___

e.   Sunspots ___

f.   Population growth ___

g.   Import tariffs ___

h.   Tax deductions ___

i.   Changes in the weather ___

j.   Public employment programs ___

k.   OPEC oil embargo ___

5.   Suppose the population of the country is 200 million people. Suppose further that there are 96 million people working at jobs in the marketplace and there are 4 million people looking for work.

a.   How large is the labor force? ___

b.   What is the unemployment rate? ___

c.   For each of the statements below determine what will happen to the *labor force* and the *unemployment rate*.

1.   A student graduates from college and starts to search for a job.

The labor force will (**increase / decrease / remain the same**), and the unemployment rate will (**go up / go down / remain unchanged**).

2.   A student graduates from college and is immediately hired by her mother's business.

The labor force will (**increase / decrease / remain the same**), and the unemployment rate will (**go up / go down / remain unchanged**).

3.   Jane Jones quits her job and starts looking for a better one.

The labor force will (**increase / decrease / remain the same**), and the unemployment rate will (**go up / go down / remain unchanged**).

4.   John Jones quits his job to spend more time with his kids.

The labor force will (**increase / decrease / remain the same**), and the unemployment rate will (**go up / go down / remain unchanged**).

5.   Sam Smith is unhappy at his current job. He starts looking for a new job but does not quit his current job.

The labor force will (**increase / decrease / remain the same**), and the unemployment rate will (**go up / go down / remain unchanged**).

6.   Question 8 at the end of the chapter ("Discussion Questions") mentions a price index known as the *GDP deflator*. This price index is similar to the *CPI* in that it is an overall measure of inflation or price increases in the country. One of the key differences between the two indexes is that the *CPI* includes a sample of typical *consumer goods and services* while the *GDP deflator* includes *all* goods and services produced in the economy. (There are some other differences, too, but we can postpone a discussion of those until we have a more detailed discussion about inflation in Chapter 30.)

One year is chosen as the base year for the price index. In the base year the price index has a value of 100. Since prices generally rise over time, the price index will usually be less than 100 in years prior to the base year and greater than 100 in years after the base year.

To calculate real GDP from nominal GDP we would divide by the price index, or GDP deflator, and then multiply by 100. Or we can write:

$$\text{Real GDP} = \frac{\text{nominal GDP}}{\text{GDP deflator}} \times 100$$

Similarly, nominal GDP could be calculated from real GDP with the following formula:

$$\text{Nominal GDP} = \frac{\text{real GDP} \times \text{GDP deflator}}{100}$$

Table 4-1 includes hypothetical numbers for GDP in five different years.

TABLE 4-1

Year	Nominal GDP	Real GDP	GDP Deflator	Percent Change In Real GDP
1	___	3690	84	------
2	3800	___	91	___
3	4000	___	100	___
4	4240	___	106	___
5	___	4800	110	___

a.   Calculate real GDP in years 2, 3, and 4.

b.   Calculate nominal GDP in years 1 and 5.

c.   Explain the relationship between nominal and real GDP in year 3.

d.   Calculate the percentage change in real GDP from year to year.

e.   According to your calculations, which year was the best? Explain.

f. Explain the growth rate in GDP from year 3 to year 4.

g. According to your calculations, which year was the worst? Explain.

h. Can you think of a historical example in the United States when the GDP deflator actually decreased from one year to the next? (*Hint*: Look back at Figure 4-2.)

B. Aggregate Supply and Demand

7. Figure 4-3 uses aggregate supply and demand to illustrate four possible reactions to changes in the macroeconomic environment. In each panel, *AD* and *AS* represent initial positions of aggregate demand and aggregate supply, respectively In panels (*a*) and (*b*), *AS'* represents a new position for the aggregate supply curve; in panels (*c*) and (*d*), *AD'* represents a new position for aggregate demand.

Figure 4-3

Table 4-2 lists six possible changes in the macroeconomic environment.

a. Use column 2 to identify which panel in Figure 4-3 best illustrates each change.

b. Use columns 3 and 4 to indicate the direction of the change in price and output. Use a "+" sign for increases and a "-" sign for decreases.

TABLE 4-2 Changes In the Macroeconomic Environment

(1) Condition	(2) Panel	(3) Price	(4) Output
1. Increase in defense spending	___	___	___
2. Weather-related crop failure	___	___	___
3. Large cut in personal taxes	___	___	___
4. Increase in interest rates	___	___	___
5. Reduction in government taxation of inputs	___	___	___
6. Reduction in money supply by the central bank	___	___	___

8. Suppose that Figure 4-4 illustrates the effect of a sudden negative energy shock.

Figure 4-4

a. *AD* would represent the preshock aggregate demand curve, (AS_1 / AS_2) would represent the preshock aggregate supply curve, and (AS_1 / AS_2) would represent the postshock aggregate supply curve.

b. (**An increase / A decrease / No change**) in aggregate demand would be required in the short run to accommodate the shock and keep output at its preshock level.

c. As a result of the change in **b**, (**prices / output**) would be even (**smaller / greater**) than after the initial energy shock.

VIII. DISCUSSION QUESTIONS

Answer the following questions, making sure that you can explain the work you did to arrive at the answers.

1. Briefly explain Keynes's main contribution to macroeconomics.

2. In what ways did the Employment Act of 1946 indicate a change in federal government policy?

3. Describe the primary policy instruments that the government uses to influence the economy. Indicate which part or branch of the government controls each instrument.

4. What is meant by a "tight money" policy? What effect did this policy have on the United States from 1979 to 1982?

5. How should the United States respond if a major oil price shock were to occur today? Describe how the policy instruments that are used may be incompatible.

IX. ANSWERS TO STUDY GUIDE QUESTIONS

III. Review of Key Concepts

17   Employment Act of 1946
8   Business cycle
18   Fiscal policy
9   Monetary policy
11   Incomes policies
22   Gross domestic product (GDP)
15   Nominal
20   Real
13   Potential GDP
19   GDP gap
6   Unemployment rate
4   Consumer Price Index
5   Net exports
21   Trade policies
7   External variables
14   Induced variables
2   Aggregate supply
12   Aggregate demand
16   Exchange-market management
1   Supply shock
3   Recession
10   Inflation

VI. Multiple Choice Questions

1. E   2. C   3. D   4. A   5. B   6. C
7. E   8. E   9. A   10. D   11. E   12. C
13. B   14. E   15. A   16. B   17. C   18. C

VII. Problem Solving

1. a. market
    b. nominal
    c. real
    d. potential
    e. fall short of nominal GDP
    f. fall short of potential GDP
    g. 1930s, the Great Depression
    h. actual GDP exceeds potential GDP, World War II and the Vietnam war
2. a. averages price movements across goods and services
    b. the rate of change in the index
    c. 1947
    d. mid-1970s and early 1980s
    e. The dramatic fall in prices accompanied the decline

in output and widespread unemployment during the Great Depression.
    f. 3.4
3. a. FP
    b. MP
    c. IP
    d. FP
    e. FP
    f. MP
    g. IP
4. a. PI
    b. EV
    c. PI
    d. PI
    e. EV
    f. EV
    g. PI
    h. PI
    i. EN
    j. PI
    k. EV
5. a. 100 million
    b. $(4/100) \times 100 = 4$ percent
    c. 1. increase, go up
        2. increase, go down
        3. remain the same, go up
        4. decrease, go up
        5. remain the same, remain unchanged
6. a. $(3800/91) \times 100 = 4175.82$, 4000, $(4240/106) \times 100 = 4000.00$
    b. $(3690 \times 91)/100 = 3099.60$, $(4800 \times 110)/100 = 5280.00$
    c. Year 3 is the base year since the GDP deflator equals 100. In that year nominal and real GDP will be the same.
    d. $[(4175.82 - 3690.00)/3690] \times 100 = 13.17$
        $[(4000.00 - 4175.82)/4175.82] \times 100 = -4.21$
        $[(4000.00 - 4000.00)/4000] \times 100 = 0$
        $[(4800.00 - 4000.00)/4000] \times 100 = 20$
    e. Year 5 was the best in terms of real GDP growth. From looking at the numbers for the GDP deflator, it also appears that year 5 had the smallest increase in inflation.
    f. From year 3 to year 4, real GDP was unchanged so there was no growth.
    g. Year 3 was the worst since real GDP fell. The economy was in a recession. To make matters worse, inflation increased by $(9/91) \times 100 = 9.89$ percent, more than any other year.
    h. If prices fall from one year to the next, the GDP deflator will fall. This happened during the Great Depression.

7.

TABLE 4-2 Changes in the Macroeconomic Environment

(1) Condition	(2) Panel	(3) Price	(4) Output
1. Increase in defense spending	c	+	+
2. Weather-related crop failure	b	+	-
3. Large cut in personal taxes	c	+	+
4. Increase in interest rates	d	-	-
5. Reduction in government taxation of inputs	a	-	+
6. Reduction in money supply by the central bank	d	-	-

8. a. AS_1, AS_2
    b.   An increase
    c.   prices, greater

VIII. Discussion Questions

1.   In 1936, Keynes challenged the current views on economic theory and policy. He argued for a much wider role of the government in fighting the Depression and establishing economic policy.

2.   For the first time the federal government affirmed its role in promoting economic growth, full employment, and price stability.

3.   The two main policy instruments of the government are monetary policy and fiscal policy. Monetary policy is controlled by the Federal Reserve System, and fiscal policy is determined by the executive and legislative branches of the government. Monetary policy relies primarily on changes in interest rates and the money supply, while fiscal policy refers to government spending and taxes.

4.   A "tight money" policy occurs when the Federal Reserve reduces the growth rate of the money supply. In 1979, the Fed was very concerned about the high rate of inflation in the United States. The tight money policy which it pursued slowed the economy down and reduced inflation, but it also contributed to the subsequent recession.

5.   As a result of the oil-price shock, prices will increase and output will fall. If the government tries to limit the price increases with tight monetary policy or restrictive fiscal policy, it will make the output and unemployment problem worse. If, instead, the government tries to maintain employment and output, prices will go even higher. Ideally, the government could enact some sort of supply-side change to shift the aggregate supply curve back to the right.

CHAPTER 5
Measuring Economic Activity

I. CHAPTER OVERVIEW

This important chapter must be approached carefully and patiently. You will, however, discover that there is really only one basic idea being presented here. It is surrounded by complication, to be sure, but the point of this chapter is singular: *The accounting procedure with which a nation measures its total output in any one year simply adds up the market value of all the goods and services that it produces.* Every nation uses its limited stock of labor, machines, and materials to produce commodities and services.

There are many difficulties associated with computing the output for an entire nation. Your job is not to do the counting. Your job, instead, is to understand the rules that govern the counting. Having completed your work in this chapter, you will have achieved the objectives listed below. Without this achievement, you will find it very difficult to understand what economists mean when they talk about growth, unemployment, and inflation.

II. LEARNING OBJECTIVES

After you have read Chapter 21 in your text and completed the exercises in this *Study Guide* chapter, you should be able to:

1. Describe what **gross domestic product (GDP)** is and why it is so important to have an accurate measurement of the nation's output.
2. Define the **flow-of-product** approach and the **earnings** or **cost** approach to computing GDP.
3. Understand **intermediate products** and the **value-added** approach to computing GDP.
4. Explain how focusing on either final product in the product approach or value added in the earnings approach helps statisticians avoid **double counting** in the computation of GDP.
5. Explain the difference between **nominal** and **real** GDP, paying close attention to the role of the GDP deflator.
6. Divide GDP into its major component parts in the flow-of-product approach: consumption (*C*), gross private domestic investment (*I*), government purchases of

goods and services (*G*), and net exports (*X*). That is, explain why:

$$GDP = C + I + G + X, \text{ or}$$
$$GDP = C + I_n + G,$$

where $I_n = I + X$ representing total gross national investment.

7. Understand the differences between **gross domestic** product, **net domestic** product, and **gross national** product.
8. Understand the process by which GDP is related to the **disposable income** of households.
9. Argue why, in general, total gross national investment (I_T) must equal the sum of all private saving (*PS*), and government surplus (*GS*).
10. Understand what GDP does and does not measure, and appreciate why economists have begun developing "augmented national accounts."
11. Distinguish between the three different price indexes, the CPI, the GDP deflator, and the PPI, and understand how they are used to adjust for inflation.

III. REVIEW OF KEY CONCEPTS

Match the following terms from column A with their definitions in column B.

A	B
__ Final product	1. Gross investment minus capital depreciation.
__ Real GDP	2. Exports minus imports of goods and services.
__ Nominal GDP	3. Household income minus personal taxes.
__ GDP deflator	4. The difference between a firm's sales and its purchases of materials and services from other firms.
__ Intermediate good	5. Adjusts for rapid shifts in relative prices by changing the base period for constructing prices and quantities more quickly.

__ Value added

__ Net exports

__ Net domestic product

__ Government transfer payments

__ Disposable income

__ Gross national investment

__ Net investment

__ National income

__ Chain weights

__ Consumer Price Index

__ Producer Price Index

6. Good or service that is produced and sold for consumption or investment.

7. GDP evaluated at the actual market prices of the current year.

8. Government payments to individuals that are not made in exchange for goods and services.

9. Gross domestic investment plus net foreign investment.

10. Good used to produce other goods.

11. Measures the cost of buying a standard basket of consumer goods and services at different time periods.

12. GDP minus capital depreciation.

13. Price index used to convert nominal GDP to real GDP.

14. GDP evaluated at a set of constant prices.

15. Based on approximately 3400 commodity prices and measures the level of prices at the wholesale or producer stage.

16. Total factor incomes received by labor, capital, and land.

IV. SUMMARY AND CHAPTER OUTLINE

This section summarizes the key concepts from the chapter.

1. The gross domestic product (or **GDP**) is the most comprehensive measure of a nation's total output of goods and services. It enables the President, the Congress, and the Federal Reserve to judge whether the economy is contracting or expanding, whether the economy needs a boost or should be reined in a bit, and whether a severe recession or inflation threatens. Without measures of economic aggregates like GDP, policymakers would be adrift in a sea of unorganized data. In addition, macroeconomic theory would be impossible to understand without GDP and other indicators of national output.

2. There are two different ways of measuring GDP: a **flow-of-product** approach and an **earnings or cost** approach. In a world of perfectly precise measurement, these two methods would arrive at the exact same number for GDP. In reality, the two approaches provide a useful check for one another.

3. In the **flow-of-product** approach, GDP is measured by how much is spent on products (or goods and services) in the economy. In the macroeconomy there are four main areas of spending:

a. purchases by households or consumers (C)
b. investment spending by businesses (I)
c. purchases of goods and services by the government (G)
d. *net* exports, which is the difference between the value of our exports to other countries and the value of the products that we import from abroad (X)

The inclusion of *net* exports in GDP may seem a little confusing. If foreigners purchase some of the goods and services that are produced in this country, we would want to include that spending in our calculation of GDP. However, if some of our spending is used to purchase products that were produced in other countries, we need to subtract that figure from GDP since it does not reflect production at home.

4. The **earnings or cost** approach is used to calculate GDP by summing up all the costs of doing business. These costs include the wages paid to labor, the rents paid to land, and the profits paid to capital. Since households ultimately provide the land and the money used to acquire capital, these business costs also represent the earnings that households receive. When we include the wearing out of capital equipment (**depreciation**) and the influence of the government (i.e., **taxes** and **transfer payments**), the analysis becomes somewhat more complicated, but the basic thrust of the analysis remains the same: *the total dollar value of all spending must equal the total value of all earnings*.

5. GDP is measured as the total production of *final* goods and services during a year. A *final product* is one that is sold for consumption purposes or is an investment good. The point here is that the product is not changed or modified and sold again to someone else. The product has reached its final stage and is now being used either as a consumption good or a piece of capital equipment. When a car manufacturer orders glass from a glass company to use in its automobiles, the glass is considered an *intermediate good* The value of this glass should *not* be measured as part of GDP, because when the car (i.e., the final product) is sold, the purchase price will include the value of the glass. If we counted the glass when the car manufacturer purchased it, we would have counted the glass twice. This is the *double-counting problem* that GDP statisticians try to avoid.

To adjust for this problem in the *earnings or cost* approach, statisticians measure only the *value added* by businesses at each stage of production. The value added is calculated as the difference between a firm's sales and its purchases of materials and services from other firms.

6. When we evaluate the nation's current output at current market prices, we measure *nominal GDP*. This is equivalent to multiplying output by price, for all units of every commodity that is produced, and then adding all these numbers up. So, nominal GDP is a huge sum of prices times quantities (PQ). Therefore, if nominal GDP changes from one year to the next it could be due to a change in P, or Q, or both. Since we are very interested in the growth of the economy

over time, we need to know which component(s) of GDP is (are) changing.

Suppose, for example, that prices increase from one year to the next, and output decreases such that the result of multiplying P times Q remains exactly the same. Nominal GDP will be unchanged, and looking only at GDP, it will appear as if the economy is in the same spot it was a year ago. In fact, this economy has a couple of new problems. Prices are higher, so there is an increase in inflation. Output is lower, so there is probably an increase in unemployment, too. When both inflation and unemployment increase together, economists refer to this situation as **stagflation**. (The economy slows down or *stagnates* at the same time that prices increase.)

In order to accurately assess the **real** growth of the economy over time, we need to measure output with a constant set of prices. One year is chosen as the base year and then every year's output is evaluated in terms of the prices in the base year. (The base year that the United States uses to calculate real GDP is 1987.) Finally, if we divide nominal GDP by real GDP (and multiply by 100), we get the overall price index which we call the **GDP deflator**.

$$\frac{\text{Nominal GDP}}{\text{Real GDP}} =$$

$$\frac{(\text{current } P \text{ times current } Q)}{(\text{base year } P \text{ times current } Q)} = \text{GDP deflator}$$

7.   Until a few years ago (1991), the United States relied primarily on gross *national* product, rather than GDP, as its primary measure of output. GNP focuses on the ownership of resources, while GDP is concerned with where the production takes place. For example, Fords produced in Britain with U.S.-owned capital would be included in U.S. GNP but excluded from U.S. GDP. For a nation like the United States, which owns a great number of production facilities abroad but also has a large number of foreign firms producing goods and services within its domestic economy, the two measures are nearly identical. There are two main reasons for making the switch. First, most other countries were already using GDP as their measure of aggregate output, so changing to GDP made it somewhat easier to make comparisons with other countries. Second, GDP probably gives us a more reliable picture of the health of the domestic economy, which is critically important in setting macroeconomic policy.

8.   The relationship between savings and investment in an economy is important. Consider first a simple economy with no government, no foreign sector, and no business savings. In the *earnings or cost approach*, GDP equals *total* household income. Households spend most of their income (C), but some household income is saved (S) as well. In the *flow-of-product* approach to GDP, total spending in the economy consists of household consumption spending (C) and investment spending by firms (I). Therefore, we can calculate GDP in either of the two following ways:

$$\textit{Earnings or cost GDP} = \text{total household incom} = C + S$$
$$\textit{Flow-of-product GDP} = C + I$$

The linkage between S and I should be apparent; and there is a logical explanation for the relationship between these two variables. When households save, they are sending a signal to the market economy. Households are saying to producers, "We are not interested in purchasing goods and services today. We are putting some of our income aside so that we will have more to spend in the future." On the other hand, when firms invest, they are using some of their (scarce) resources to acquire or build capital equipment. They produce fewer goods and services today so that they will have greater production capabilities in the future—just at the time consumers want them if all goes well. It should also be pointed out that firms usually finance their investment projects by borrowing the funds from the credit market. The primary source of funds flowing into the credit market is household *savings*.

In a sense, savings can be viewed as a *leakage* from the economy—it represents money which is not spent directly by the household. If we consider consumption spending as the primary source of spending in the economy, investment spending by firms can be considered as a supplement or *injection* which adds to total spending. In our circular-flow analysis, all leakages should match all injections.

In an expanded economy which includes foreign trade and the government, we should include net exports (X) as another injection of spending, and the government surplus (GS), if there is any, as a leakage. In the case where private savings (PS) includes both personal saving and business saving, an injection-leakage identity can be written as:

$$I + X = PS + GS$$

9.   The essence of *investment* in all its various forms is that it is production for future benefit. A newly finished machine tool yields no direct consumer satisfaction whatsoever. It is built to yield future benefit; it is expected to contribute to consumer-goods production in the future, throughout its coming 5-year or 10-year life. A *new* house counts within the investment category in a similar way; it is expected to contribute to consumer satisfaction over a long number of years.

A manufacturer's additional inventory at the end of the year must receive the same treatment. Suppose a shirt company made $1000 worth of shirts in 1994 which it did not sell in that year. The shirts it did sell count as part of consumption. The shirts it made but did not sell must also go into GDP (because they were made in 1994), but because they weren't sold they do not go into consumption. They are included in investment because they will be consumed in the future, presumably *next* year.

This inventory rule works both ways. Had the shirt company's beginning inventory been $4000 and its closing inventory $3000, then we would include a figure of *minus* $1000 within *investment*.

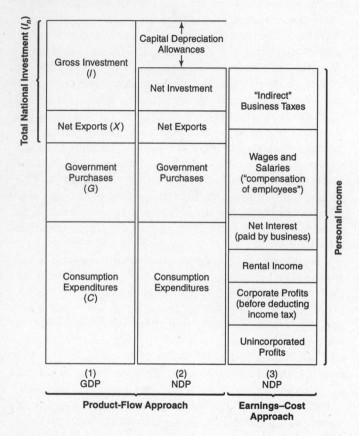

Figure 5-1

10. Figure 5-1 can be used to review the basics of national income accounting and illustrate the equivalence of the *flow-of-product* and *earnings or cost* approaches. The flow-of-product approach is illustrated in columns 1 and 2 as the sum of government purchases (*G*), consumption expenditures (*C*), net exports (*X*), and investment (*I*). The difference between GDP and NDP is clearly shown as depreciation. Total national investment (investment plus net exports) appears at the top of both—*gross* in column 1 and *net of depreciation* in column 2. The third column depicts the earnings or cost approach to the same accounting problem. Note that there are essentially five fundamental categories represented there:

    a.   Wages and salaries
    b.   Interest earned (by people lending money to firms)
    c.   Rentals and other property income (paid to people who supply property)
    d.   Corporate and unincorporated profits
    e.   Indirect business taxes (levied on businesses)

The profits noted in item **d** above are, by definition, the difference between the value of outputs and the cost of inputs. They are, in other words, the residual values that guarantee that the earnings or cost approach generates the same result as the flow-of-product approach.

11. GDP is at best an accurate measure of a nation's output. It is not, nor is it intended to be, a measure of overall well-being or satisfaction. Economists have begun developing "augmented national accounts" that include estimates of the *underground economy* and subtract the costs of pollution.

12. Inflation is measured as a rate of change in a price index from one period (e.g., 1 year) to the next. If P_1 represents the price index recorded in year 1 and P_2 represents the index recorded in year 2, then inflation between years 1 and 2 would be:

$$\frac{P_2 - P_1}{P_1} \times 100\%$$

When an economy experiences inflation it does not necessarily mean that *all* prices have increased. Rather, inflation indicates an increase in the *general* level of prices and costs.

13. Different price indexes are used to measure inflation in the economy. One commonly quoted price index, based on the prices of the things that a typical consumer buys, is the *Consumer Price Index* (CPI). It is based on the cost of a market basket of goods and services computed across 364 classes of commodities. The weights given to the categories in the CPI represent the share of income devoted to purchases in the indicated category observed in a survey conducted between 1982 and 1984.

A second widely used price index is the *Producer Price Index* (PPI). It is based on the wholesale prices of approximately 3400 products.

The GDP deflator, discussed above, can be viewed as a price index for all the components of GDP. Since the GDP deflator is based on current output, the weights, in essence, change every year. This makes the GDP deflator somewhat more difficult to calculate. The weights used in both the CPI and PPI are based on previous years, so the only current information needed to calculate these indexes are current prices. To calculate the GDP deflator data are needed on both current output and prices.

V. HELPFUL HINTS

1. In macroeconomics, the term *simple economy* is usually used to describe an economy with just a household and a business sector. Once the model is developed for this narrowly defined economy, it can then be expanded to include the government and international trade.

2. *Investment* is another one of those terms that has special meaning to economists (and to students of economics).

Investment spending is undertaken by firms to acquire or build new capital equipment and buildings which then add to the firms' productive capability in the future. Investment, to an economist, is *not* money. Investments represent additions to the (physical) stock of durable capital goods.

3.   Capital goods, like everything else, wear out or *depreciate* over time. Consequently, a portion of each year's investment is used to replace worn out plant and equipment. This replacement of "used up" capital does not really add to economic growth—it helps prevent the economy from slipping backward but does not push the economy forward. Ideally, *net domestic product (NDP)* which equals *GDP minus depreciation*, would give a better picture of the nation's economic health. However, depreciation is difficult to measure, so GDP is the universally accepted measure of output.

4.   The linkage between savings and investment is very important. The additional linkage between investment and economic growth is also very important. Look for this in the chapters that follow.

5.   Be careful to distinguish between government spending on goods and services and government *transfer payments*. The G in C + I + G + X includes the government's purchases of final goods and services (medicines for V.A. hospitals, books for schools, airplanes for the Air Force). It does not (and should not) include transfer payments like veterans' benefits and social security payments. These transfer payments are a very large part of the government's budget but should not be included in the *flow-of-product* calculation of GDP. Note that these transfer payments would be shown as a flow from government to households, *not* to firms. The government's budget includes *both* what it spends for goods and services and the transfer payments that it makes to its citizens.

6.   In the national income accounts the term *capital consumption allowance* is often used for *depreciation*. The two terms mean the same thing and thus are interchangeable.

7.   Taxes that are paid out of income include personal and corporate income taxes. These are *direct taxes*. Other taxes that firms collect, and then send to the government, like sales taxes and excise taxes, are considered as *indirect taxes*.

8.   Take another look at Figure 5-4, "From GDP to National Income to Disposable Income," in your text. It should be clear that the numbers in the first bar of the chart (GDP) are calculated from the *product approach* and that the second bar (NI) is found using the *earnings or cost approach*.

9.   Price indexes suffer from two main deficiencies. They do not, for one thing, take quality changes in account. Better products that cost more would cause any price index to rise. This should not be measured as inflation. Second, price indexes with fixed weights fail to reflect the consumer's substitution out of more expensive items and into cheaper products as prices rise. This pattern of behavior diminishes the impact of product-specific inflation.

10.   Remember, economic growth is *always* measured in real

terms. there is no way to make meaningful comparisons between years if price changes are not controlled for. Stay away from people who talk about nominal growth.

VI. MULTIPLE CHOICE QUESTIONS

These questions are organized by topic from the chapter outline. Choose the best answer from the options available.

1.   The *flow-of-product* and *earnings or cost* approaches to GDP:
a.   measure two different aspects of GDP and are therefore unrelated to each other.
b.   are two different ways of measuring the same thing.
c.   should both arrive at the same number if GDP is measured in real terms, but not if GDP is measured nominally.
d.   have nothing to do with the circular-flow diagram.
e.   none of the above.

2.   The double-counting problem refers to:
a.   the inclusion of both intermediate and final products in the calculation of GDP.
b.   the nominally higher value for GDP when prices double.
c.   the equivalence of the *flow-of-product* and *earnings or cost* approaches.
d.   the problems caused by using value-added measures in the lower loop.
e.   all the above.

3.   There would be double counting in the computation of GDP if statisticians were to sum the:
a.   net value added by the iron-mining industry and the net value added by the steel manufacturing industry.
b.   net increase in inventories of flour mills and the net increase in inventories of bakeries.
c.   total output of iron ore and the total output of iron.
d.   value added by bakers and the value of flour mills.
e.   total of consumer services purchased and the total of investment goods produced.

4.   To compute a firm's contribution to GDP on a value added basis, the value at market price of the goods that it has produced must be diminished by:
a.   all indirect business taxes paid.
b.   any undistributed profits.
c.   depreciation.
d.   all sales to other business firms.
e.   none of the above.

5.   Economic growth is always measured in real terms because:
a.   output changes from year to year.
b.   the *flow-of-product* approach does not always yield the same figure as the *earnings or cost* approach.
c.   the differences in nominal GDP from year to year

are too large.

  d. the price level changes from year to year.

  e. all the above.

6. In GDP statistics, investment includes:

  a. any product produced for the government during the year in question.

  b. any purchase of common stock issued during the year in question.

  c. any increase in the amount of year-end inventories over inventories held at the beginning of the year in question.

  d. any commodity bought by a consumer but not fully consumed by the end of the year in question.

  e. none of these items.

7. In GDP statistics, a negative gross investment figure:

  a. could never occur.

  b. could appear if the total of depreciation on buildings and equipment was sufficiently large.

  c. would automatically occur if there was no production of buildings or equipment during the year.

  d. could be caused by a sufficiently large reduction in inventories during the year.

  e. would mean that the economy had produced more than it had consumed.

8. In NDP statistics, a negative investment figure:

  a. could never occur.

  b. could appear if the total of depreciation on buildings and equipment was sufficiently large.

  c. would automatically occur if there was no production of buildings or equipment during the year.

  d. could be caused by a sufficiently large increase in inventories during the year.

  e. would mean that the economy had produced more than it had consumed.

9. In GDP statistics, the value of housing services, in which the houses are occupied by their owners, is:

  a. not counted, since property services are not considered production.

  b. not counted, since such property services are included in the value of the house itself.

  c. not counted in GDP, but it does appear in NDP using an arbitrary estimate of rental value.

  d. counted in GDP using an arbitrary estimate of rental value.

  e. counted in NDP, but not in GDP.

10. One of the five items listed below is *not* in the same class as the other four for purposes of national income accounting. Which one?

  a. corporation income (or profits).

  b. government transfer payments.

  c. net interest payments by business.

  d. rental income.

  e. wages and salaries.

11. If you want to compute disposable personal income

from NDP, then one thing you must *not* do is:

  a. deduct depreciation.

  b. add government transfer payments.

  c. deduct indirect business taxes.

  d. deduct social security levies.

  e. deduct undistributed corporation profits.

12. In computing the size of the government spending component of GDP, all government:

  a. expenditures on commodities and services are counted.

  b. expenditures on commodities are counted; those on services are not.

  c. expenditures on final commodities and services are counted as well as all government transfer payments.

  d. transfer payments are counted, but not expenditures on commodities or services.

  e. none of the above is correct.

13. The term *national income* (*NI*) as used in the national product and national income statistics means:

  a. NDP plus all taxes that are not considered taxes paid out of income—i.e., NDP plus indirect business taxes.

  b. NDP minus all taxes that are considered taxes paid out of income, such as the personal and corporation income taxes.

  c. NDP plus all taxes that are considered taxes paid out of income, such as the personal and corporation income taxes.

  d. NDP minus all taxes that are not considered taxes paid out of income—i.e., NDP minus indirect business taxes.

  e. none of the above.

14. If nominal GDP was $360 (billion) in 1992 and if the price level rose by 20 percent from 1990 to 1992, then the 1992 GDP, measured in 1990 prices, was (in billions):

  a. $300.

  b. $320.

  c. $340.

  d. $360.

  e. $432.

15. In computing the national income and national product accounts, it would be incorrect to add together which of the following two items?

  a. consumption expenditures and personal saving.

  b. net investment and consumption expenditures.

  c. corporate profits and net interest paid by business.

  d. government purchases and consumption expenditures.

  e. government purchases and wages and salaries.

16. Statisticians use chain weights:

  a. to connect the weights of products together.

  b. when constructing price indexes for the metal industries.

  c. when nominal GDP is increasing faster than real

GDP.

d. when real GDP is increasing faster than nominal GDP.

e. when related prices of products are shifting rapidly.

17. The consumer price index is in part based upon the share of income devoted to which of the following major categories?

a. shelter.

b. food.

c. medical expenses.

d. transportation expenses.

e. all of the above.

18. Inflation measured in terms of annual changes in the CPI using a single year's spending weights might overestimate the impact of inflation on individual purchasing power because it:

a. ignores the likely substitution out of relatively expensive categories.

b. ignores the depressing effect of world prices on American goods.

c. ignores the effects of unemployment on aggregate demand.

d. inaccurately includes the price effects of improved production technology.

e. does all of the above.

19. The 1983 price index for the medical care component of the CPI was 357. It must therefore be true that the 1983 value of the CPI:

a. must have been greater than 357.

b. must have been less than 357.

c. must have been exactly equal to 357.

d. could have been anything because medical expenses are really not included in the CPI.

e. was none of the above.

VII. PROBLEM SOLVING

The following problems are designed to help you apply the concepts that you learned in the chapter.

1. Suppose, in a simple economy, that national output consists of only two commodities: X, a consumer good, and Y, a capital good (some form of machine or tool needed in production). In 1994, just 500 units of X were produced and sold to consumers at a price of $2 each. Twenty units of Y were produced and sold to business firms, at a price of $10 each.

a. The total output for 1994 was ($500 / $800 / $1000 / $1200 / $1500 / $2000).

The figure computed above is the *gross* domestic product. To produce this total output, however, the nation's existing stock of capital goods must have been, to some extent, used up or worn out; that is to say, the capital stock must have depreciated. Suppose that the nation began the year

with a stock of 100 Y machines (assuming, for simplicity, that there is just one kind of capital good involved). By the year's end, a few of these machines, the oldest, will have become completely worn out, and all the others will have moved just a little closer to the scrap heap.

Suppose, now, that the best possible estimate of this depreciation for 1994 is $50. There is no cash expenditure in a depreciation figure; it is just an estimate of the extent of "wearing out" during the year. With the price of a new Y machine being $10, it is *as though* five Y machines, brand new at the year's beginning, had been completely worn out by the year's end in the production of the national product for 1994.

The gross domestic product figure of $1200 included the value of the 20 new Y machines produced. But in making these machines and also in making the 500 units of consumer good X, the *equivalent* of five new Y machines were totally used up.

b. The available capital stock had not, therefore, *grown* by 20 machines by year's end; it had, instead, increased by only (5 / 10 / 15) machines.

c. With "gross" meaning "no allowance for depreciation" and "net" meaning "after allowance for depreciation," this nation's gross domestic product (GDP) for 1994 was $1200, and its net domestic product (NDP) was ($1000 / $1050 / $1100 / $1150 / $1200).

There are certain distinctions that are made among the goods that comprise either GDP or NDP. The most basic of these distinctions is the division between (a) goods that were produced to be consumed during the year in question and (b) goods that were produced during the year not to be consumed but to be added to the existing stock of capital. This is precisely the difference noted above, with X representing a consumption good and Y representing an investment good.

The *consumption* goods total is the same figure in both GDP and NDP. The *investment* goods figure in GDP is gross investment: total production of new capital goods without depreciation allowance. The investment figure in NDP is net investment: value of new capital goods produced after a deduction for depreciation.

d. In the example above, the GDP of $1200 would divide between consumption of ($200 / $800 / $1000 / $1150 / $1200) and gross investment of ($0 / $100 / $150 / $200 / $250 / $300).

e. The NDP of $1150 would divide between consumption of ($200 / $800 / $1000 / $1200 / $1500) and net investment of ($0 / $100 / $150 / $200 / $250 / $300).

2. Government statisticians use *value-added* measurements when using the cost or earnings approach to GDP. Table 5-1 shows the (hypothetical) steps and costs involved in producing a ton of steel. In our simplified example, the miner purchases no intermediate products or goods. We can assume that the miner's family has owned the iron ore mine for years and that the manufacturer works the mine and trucks the ore

away. We are also assuming that all the relevant costs of production are included in the table below.

Table 5-1

Stage of Production	(1) Sales Receipts		(2) Cost of Intermediate Materials		(3) Value Added
1. Miner	$4	-	$0	=	$4
2. Iron manufacturer	9	-	___	=	___
3. Steel manufacturer	16	-	___	=	___
4. Steel retailer	20	-	___	=	___

a. Fill in columns (2) and (3) in the table.

b. Which firm adds the most value to the final product? ___

c. What is the total of all sales receipts? ___

d. What is the total of all the value addeds? ___

e. Which figure belongs in GDP? ___ Briefly explain why.

f. Compare the steel retailer's sales receipts with the sum of the value addeds. Explain the relationship between these two numbers.

3. The country of Easyliving produces just three goods: apples, T-shirts, and bicycles. The prices of each good and the outputs for three years are listed in Table 5-2.

Table 5-2

Product	Year 1		Year 2		Year 3	
	P_1	Q_1	P_2	Q_2	P_3	Q_3
Apples	$ 1	50	$ 3	60	$ 4	70
T-shirts	6	100	8	140	7	160
Bicycles	80	90	100	100	90	110

a. Calculate nominal GDP for each year.
  1. nominal GDP_1 =
  2. nominal GDP_2 =
  3. nominal GDP_3 =

b. Assume that the first year is used as the base year. Calculate real GDP for each year.
  1. real GDP_1 =
  2. real GDP_2 =
  3. real GDP_3 =

c. Calculate the value of the GDP deflator for each year.
  1. GDP deflator$_1$ =
  2. GDP deflator$_2$ =
  3. GDP deflator$_3$ =

d. Measure the increase in the rate of inflation from:
  1. year 1 to year 2.
  2. year 2 to year

(**Hint**: These are percentage changes in the GDP deflator.)

e. By how much did the economy of Easyliving grow from:

1. year 1 to year 2?
2. year 2 to year 3?

(**Remember**: Economic growth is always measured in real terms.)

f. Suppose year 2 is used as the base year instead of year 1. Recompute your figures for real GDP, the GDP deflator, and the change in inflation.

real GDP_1 = GDP deflator$_1$ =

real GDP_2 = GDP deflator$_2$ = % change =

real GDP_3 = GDP deflator$_3$ = % change =

(**Note**: The percentage changes in inflation should be comparable to part **d** above!)

4. A nation's GDP was $260 billion in 1980 and $325 billion in 1990. Both figures were computed as usual in terms of market prices for the year involved. The price index rose from 100 in 1980 to 130 in 1990.

a. Real output (**increased / decreased**) from 1980 through 1990.

b. In terms of 1990 prices, the 1980 GDP would be $___.

c. In terms of 1980 prices, the 1990 GDP would be $___.

d. The overall rate of inflation during the ten years is about ___.

5. A firm's income statement begins with the value of its sales for a given period. Say, for example, that a given firm's 1994 sales amount to $800. All costs incurred in making and selling these goods are then listed: depreciation, wages, interest paid, rents paid. Suppose depreciation was $25 and the other three items summed to $650. Profit could then be computed as the revenue that remains after deducting all such costs.

a. In this instance, profit would be (**$0 / $25 / $50 / $75 / $100 / $125 / $150**).

b. The initial sales figure of $800 would be this firm's contribution to the flow-of-product computation of GDP. Deduct depreciation, and its NDP contribution would be (**$700 / $725 / $750 / $775**).

c. Its earnings or cost figure would meanwhile equal the total of wages, interest paid, rent paid, and profit: (**$700 / $725 / $750 / $775**). This earnings or cost figure would therefore be (**less than / equal to / greater than**) the (net) flow-of-product figure.

d. Profit is the residual item which makes things come out even. Had our firm paid out wages, interest, and rents totaling $775, its profit (allowing for depreciation) would have been (**$0 / $25 / $50 / $70 / $100**). The earnings or cost figure would (**still / no longer**) be $775, so it would (**still / no longer**) match the (net) product flow estimate.

6. Suppose that a house built in the first half of 1994 is sold as a rental property for $90,000 in the same year. Let total rental income for the 6 months be $6000, and estimate

$600 of depreciation for this same period. In the 1994 statistics, the proper entries for this house would be:

a. gross investment of (**$0 / $600 / $6000 / $89,400 / $90,000**),

b. net investment of (**$0 / $600 / $6000 / $89,400 / $90,000**), and

c. consumption expenditures of (**$0 / $600 / $6000 / $89,400 / $90,000**).

The construction and use of this house would therefore appear in the 1994 GDP and NDP statistics as follows:

d. GDP (**$89,400 / $90,000 / $95,400 / $96,000**);

e. NDP (**$89,400 / $90,000 / $95,400 / $96,000**).

7. Table 5-3 includes data for the economy of Simple economy. These figures are complete—there are no government or foreign sectors.

a. The difference, in year 1, between 110 consumer goods produced and 90 consumer goods consumed is explained by (**an increase / a decrease**) in inventories on hand at the (**beginning / end**) of the year.

Table 5-3

	Year 1	Year 2
New buildings produced................	5	5
New equipment produced	10	10
Consumer goods produced..............	110	90
Consumer goods consumed	90	110
Estimated depreciation on existing buildings during year..........	10	10
Estimated depreciation on existing equipment during year	10	10
Inventories of consumer goods at beginning of year.................	30	50
Inventories of consumer goods at close of year	50	30

Table 5-4

	Year 1	Year 2
Gross domestic product...............	(1) ___	(7) ___
Breakup of GDP into:		
Consumption	(2) ___	(8) ___
Gross investment	(3) ___	(9) ___
Net domestic product	(4) ___	(10) ___
Breakup of NDP into:		
Consumption	(5) ___	(11) ___
Net investment....................	(6) ___	(12) ___

b. The difference, in year 2, between 90 consumer goods produced and 110 consumer goods consumed is explained by (**an increase / a decrease**) in inventories on hand at the (**beginning / end**) of the year.

c. Complete Table 5-4 for the years 1 and 2.

d. A negative *net* investment figure (**could / could not**) appear in the national product statistics if *total depreciation* exceeded the total value of new buildings and equipment produced. A negative *gross* investment figure (**could / could not**) appear if the value of

inventory reduction exceeded the total value of new buildings and equipment produced.

8. Columns (1) and (2) in Table 5-5 record hypothetical price indexes for the five major categories in the CPI for two successive years. Columns (3) and (4) indicate the proportions of income allocated to the five categories in the two years. The information in columns (3) and (4) are used to weight the relative importance of the various categories.

a. Based upon the CPI formula using year 1 weights, the price index for year 1 would be _____ .

b. Again based upon the CPI formula using year 1 weights, the price index for year 2 would be _____ .

c. On the basis of this calculation, the rate of inflation would be calculated as _____ %.

Now suppose that the year 2 price index is computed on the basis of year 2 weights.

d. The index would then equal _____ , with the resulting inflation rate (**rising / falling**) to _____ %.

e. If year 2 weights were used to compute the index for year 1, then the year 1 index would equal _____ , and the inflation rate would instead equal _____ %.

The point of this exercise is not that one index is correct and others are wrong. It is, instead, that the selection of weights can be critical in the computation of inflation.

f. However, on the basis of the substitution that occurred, it can be said that the computation that used year 1 weights for both years probably (**overestimated / underestimated / correctly estimated**) the effect of inflation on the real well-being of the population.

Table 5-5

	Underlying Price Indexes		Underlying Income Shares	
	(1)	(2)	(3)	(4)
Category	Year 1	Year 2	Year 1 (%)	Year 2 (%)
Food	100	110	20	20
Clothing	100	150	20	5
Fuel	100	100	20	35
Medical	100	110	20	15
Transport	100	105	20	25

VIII. DISCUSSION QUESTIONS

Answer the following questions, making sure that you can explain the work you did to arrive at the answers.

1. Explain, in your own words, why measuring GDP in real terms is important.

2. Explain the use of value-added measurements in the earnings or cost approach to GDP.

3. Explain the linkage between savings and investment in an economy.

4. Figures 21-2 and 21-3 from the text are reproduced here (also as Figures 21-2 and 21-3).

a. What has happened to the ratio of net investment to GDP since the late 1970s?

b.   What can you say about the growth in (real!) GDP since the late 1970s?

c.   What could possibly account for the change in the ratio of net investment to GDP?

d.   Does this have any implications for the economy's future growth?

5.   Briefly explain the difference between GDP and GNP. Why did the United States switch to the use of GDP as its main measurement value for the macroeconomy?

6.   Briefly explain why GDP may not be a good measure of overall well-being or happiness.

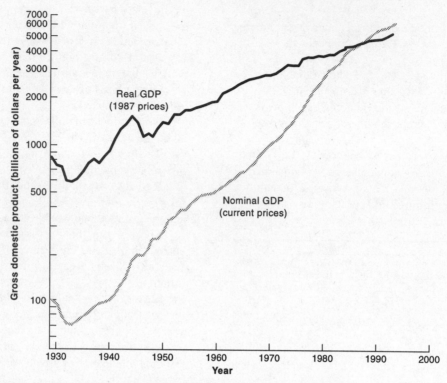

Figure 5-2 Nominal GDP Grows Faster Than Real GDP because of Price Inflation

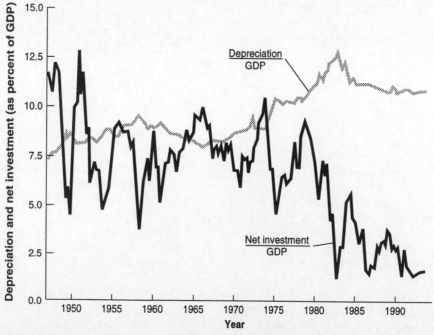

Figure 5-3 Fraction of National Output Devoted to Net Investment Has Plummeted

IX. ANSWERS TO STUDY GUIDE QUESTIONS

III. Review of Key Concepts

6 Final product
14 Real GDP
7 Nominal GDP
13 GDP deflator
10 Intermediate good
4 Value added
2 Net exports
12 Net domestic product
8 Government transfer payments
3 Disposable income
9 Gross national investment
1 Net investment
16 National income
5 Chain weights
11 Consumer Price Index
15 Producer Price Index

VI. Multiple Choice Questions

1. B 2. A 3. C 4. E 5. D 6. C
7. D 8. B 9. D 10. B 11. A 12. A
13. D 14. A 15. E 16. E 17. E 18. A
19. E

VII. Problem Solving

1. a. $1200
   b. 15
   c. $1150
   d. $1000, $200
   e. $1000, $150
2. a.

Table 5-1

Stage of Production	(1) Sales Receipts	(2) Cost of Intermediate Materials		(3) Value Added
1. Miner	$4	—	$0 =	$4
2. Iron manufacturer	9	—	4 =	5
3. Steel manufacturer	16	—	9 =	7
4. Steel retailer	20	—	16 =	4

b. The steel manufacturer
c. $49
d. $20
e. $20. If you add up all the sales receipts, all of the intermediate products would be counted twice.
f. The steel retailer sells the finished steel. It is that value that belongs in GDP. When value addeds can be measured accurately, they will always add up to the price of the finished product.

3. a. 1. $50 + $600 + $7200 = $7850
      2. $180 + $1120 + $10,000 = $11,300
      3. $280 + $1120 + $ 9900 = $11,300
   b. 1. $ 7850
      2. $(60 \times \$1) + (140 \times \$6) + (100 \times \$80) = \$8900$
      3. $(70 \times \$1) + (160 \times \$6) + (110 \times \$80) = \$9830$
   c. 1. 100.00
      2. 126.97
      3. 114.95
   d. 1. $[(126.97 - 100.00)/100.00] \times 100 = 26.97\%$
      2. $[(114.95 - 126.97)/126.97] \times 100 = -9.47\%$
   e. 1. $[(8900 - 7850)/7850] \times 100 = 13.38\%$
      2. $[(9830 - 8900)/8900] \times 100 = 10.45\%$
   f. real GDP$_1$ = $9950 GDP deflator$_1$ = 78.89
      real GDP$_2$ = $11,300 CDP deflator$_2$ = 100 change = +26.76
      real GDP$_3$ = $12,490 GDP deflator$_3$ = 90.47 to change = -9.53
4. a. decreased
   b. $260 \times 1.30 = $338 billion
   c. $325/1.30 = $250 billion
   d. 30 percent
5. a. $800 - $675 = $125
   b. $775
   c. $650 + $125 = $775, equal to
   d. $0, still, still
6. a. $90,000
   b. $89,400
   c. $6,000
   d. $96,000
   e. $95,400
7. a. an increase, end
   b. a decrease, end
   c. (1) 125, (2) 90, (3) 35, (4) 105, (5) 90, (6) 15, (7) 105, (8) 110, (9) -5, (10) 85, (11) 110, (12) -25
   d. could, could
8. a. 100
   b. 115
   c. 15 %
   d. 107.25 ([110 × .2] + [150 × .05] + [100 × .35] + [110 × .15] + [105 × .25]), falling to 7.25%
   e. 100, 7.25%
   f. overestimated

VIII. Discussion Questions

1. Measurement in real terms is important to get an accurate picture of changes in GDP from year to year. Unless you adjust for price changes, you may get the impression that the economy has experienced a growth in output, when in fact it may have suffered from inflation.
2. Most products pass through different stages of production. At each step in the production process, we should consider just what changes are made at that particular step. If we do not, the value of someone's work will be counted

again, and we will wind up overstating the value of the product. The value-added approach provides a useful check on the expenditures approach to GDP measurement.

3. There are (at least) two important signals that an increase in savings sends to the economy. First, when households save they spend less, so firms get a signal that consumers do not, at least in the present, want to purchase as many goods and services as firms perhaps thought they would. Second, the increase in savings increases the availability of loanable funds from the credit market. Interest rates are pushed lower, and firms are more likely to increase investment spending. Since consumption spending is lower, firms are encouraged to use their investment spending to add to their productive capability in the future, rather than increase current production of goods and services.

4. a. The ratio of net investment to GDP has fallen since the late 1970s.

b. Real GDP has grown since the late 1970s, but since the real GDP line is rather flat, the rate of growth has been low.

c. A number of factors could account for the decrease in the net investment to GDP ratio. The savings rate could have fallen, the economy could be in a prolonged recession, or government budget deficits could have increased which would drain more funds from the credit market.

d. Lower rates of investment in the present suggest that the economy's rate of growth in the future will be lower.

5. GDP is a geographic measure of output. It measures output that takes place within the borders of a country, regardless of who owns the resources. GNP measures output according to who owns the resources. When Nissan produces cars in Tennessee, that output is part of U.S. GDP because the production takes place within the United States. However, if we were measuring GNP, the value of those automobiles would be part of Japan's GNP since Nissan is a Japanese corporation. Many foreign corporations currently produce goods and services in the United States, but many U.S. corporations produce goods and services abroad. So for the United States, these two measures of aggregate output are nearly equal.

Most of the other nations in the world use GDP as their measure of output, so it is convenient that the United States does too. GDP also tends to give a more accurate assessment of the current economic health of the domestic economy. This is important when determining economic policy.

6. Economists recognize that GDP is a measure of output; it is not a measure of economic well-being, or satisfaction, or happiness. Many things we value currently go unmeasured. Examples include work done in the home, leisure time, and unreported economic transactions. Some items that most people do not like go unmeasured as well. These things include crime, pollution, and the fear and psychic costs of armed conflict. Currently, data are not available to measure these things accurately. We are left with a measure of output, not a measure of well-being.

CHAPTER 6
Consumption and Investment

I. CHAPTER OVERVIEW

In this chapter we begin to build a new model of the macroeconomy. Remember, economists use models to get a better understanding of some economic issue. We used the *production-possibility frontier* model to explain scarcity and the allocation of resources. We used the *circular-flow* model to better understand the flow of resources, products, and money in the economy. The circular-flow model also proved to be very useful in the last chapter in explaining the *flow-of-product* and *earnings or cost* approaches to GDP accounting.

The focus of this new model is on the main building blocks of the macroeconomy (**C, I, G,** and **X**) and the use of policy instruments to implement change in the economy. This work will take us several chapters. In this chapter we focus on the two main components of the private-market economy, consumption and investment spending. The tools described in these pages were outlined by Keynes more than 60 years ago in *The General Theory*. Even though their application in macroeconomics has been debated and changed over the intervening years, the impact of their development is still felt today. Therefore, it is useful to study the basic Keynesian construction of the major components of aggregate demand for at least two reasons.

First, a careful review of the Keynesian foundations builds an understanding of the antecedents of modern macroeconomic theory. Without such an understanding, contemporary macro theory can often appear isolated and impenetrable; students find it hard to understand why certain questions were ever raised, much less fathom their proposed answers.

Second, it is equally important to view the evolutionary process which brought us to our current state of economic awareness. To do this, particularly in macroeconomic analysis, we need a point of departure—a historical benchmark against which the reasons behind changes in viewpoint can be cast. The original Keynesian construction is an excellent starting point in this effort, and the integration of monetary policy into that model is an equally good example of the type of change that has occurred.

II. LEARNING OBJECTIVES

After you have read Chapter 22 in your text and completed the exercises in this *Study Guide,* you should be able to:

1. Understand the deterministic relationship between income and consumption (household spending on food, clothing, etc.). Understand, too, that saving, the mirror image of consumption, is also determined in large part by income.

2. Define (a) the consumption function, (b) the savings function, (c) the marginal propensity to consume, and (d) the marginal propensity to save.

3. Follow the aggregation of *individual* consumption functions into a *national* consumption function determined by disposable income, wealth, **permanent income**, and the life-cycle hypothesis.

4. Recognize that the U.S. savings rate has declined sharply over the last decade, and discuss some of the reasons behind the decline.

5. Recognize investment spending as a second major component of total spending. Understand that the level of investment spending in an economy depends upon anticipated revenues, costs, and expectations about the future.

6. Formalize the relationship between the interest rate and the level of investment in the investment demand schedule.

7. Visualize consumption and investment as two of the key components of *aggregate demand* in the economy.

III. REVIEW OF KEY CONCEPTS

Match the following terms from column A with their definitions in column B.

A	B
__ Disposable income	1. Assumes that people save in order to smooth their consumption spending over their lifetime.
__ Dissave	2. Shows the relationship between interest rates and investment spending.

___ Break-even point

___ Consumption function

___ Savings function

___ Marginal

___ Marginal Propensity to consume

___ Marginal propensity to save

___ Permanent income

___ Life-cycle hypothesis

___ Wealth effect

___ Accelerator principle

___ Investment demand curve

3.   Level of income that house-holds receive when all temporary influences are removed.

4.   Used throughout the study of economics to mean extra or additional.

5.   The rate of investment will be primarily determined by the rate of change of output in the economy.

6.   The level of household income, after taxes have been paid, that is left for consumption spending and saving.

7.   The fraction of an extra dollar of income that goes into saving.

8.   Where a household neither saves nor dissaves, but consumes all its income.

9.   The relationship between higher levels of wealth and higher levels of consumption spending.

10.   The extra amount that people consume when they receive an extra dollar of income.

11.   Shows the relationship between the level of consumption expenditures and disposable income.

12.   Shows the relationship between the level of savings and income.

13.   To draw down on wealth, or borrow.

IV. SUMMARY AND CHAPTER OUTLINE

This section summarizes the key concepts from the chapter.

A. Consumption and Saving

1.   Consumption (C) is determined primarily by disposable income (DI); a *consumption function* therefore relates consumption to disposable income. Saving (S) is the amount of disposable income not devoted to consumption. The *savings function* is the mirror image of the consumption function because saving plus consumption always exhausts disposable income.

2.   The marginal propensity to consume (MPC) is the ratio of a change in consumption to the underlying change in disposable income. The marginal propensity to save (MPS) is the corresponding ratio of a change in saving with respect to a change in disposable income. $MPC + MPS = 1$ because $C + S = DI$.

3.   *Individual* consumption functions can be aggregated to estimate a *national* consumption function. It, too, depends upon disposable income. Trends in national consumption spending are important for two reasons:

   a.   Consumption is the largest component of spending in our economy, and our task in this chapter, and those that follow, is to understand the determination of aggregate demand.

   b.   Whatever portion of income is not consumed (i.e., saved) is available to the nation for investment, and investment serves as a driving force behind long-term economic growth.

4.   The consumption function diagram is plotted with consumption expenditure on the vertical axis and disposable income on the horizontal axis. As is *always* the case, if some other relevant variable changes, like *wealth* or *permanent income*, the consumption function (and the corresponding saving function) will shift up or down.

5.   The decrease in the personal savings rate in the United States has been significant. The savings rate is critically linked to the long-term health of the economy. The level of national savings determines the rate of capital formation. The capital stock, in turn, determines the level of economic growth and potential output. When a nation's savings rate is low, its equipment and factories become obsolete and its infrastructure begins to rot away.

6.   The reasons behind the decline in the personal savings rate in the United States have been the subject of much debate. Some of the possible explanations include:

   a.   The social security system, which guarantees (at least a minimal level of) income for retirees and thereby encourages less personal saving.

   b.   The improvement of capital and credit markets, which has made it easier for households to borrow.

   c.   The slow growth in income and the slowdown in the economy's growth rate. Be careful here—this almost sounds like a "chicken and egg" type argument: Does economic growth influence the savings rate, or does the savings rate determine economic growth? Samuelson and Nordhaus point to an example (Japan after 1973) where a decrease in the GDP growth rate *preceded* a fall in the personal savings rate.

   d.   Changes in attitudes about debt, and demographic structure of the population.

B. The Determinants of Investment

1.   Investment—spending on new housing, plants and equipment, and additions to inventories is the second major component of aggregate demand. It is important not only for its role in determining aggregate demand but also for its relationship to the stock of capital, the long-term growth of the economy, and aggregate supply.

2.   An important determinant of investment is the overall level of output or GDP in the economy. Firms are more

likely to invest in new plant and equipment if managers believe there is a strong market for their products. Hence if the economy is growing and sales are rising, firms are more likely to invest. This relationship between the rate of change of output and the rate of investment is known as the **accelerator principle**.

3.   A second important determinant of investment is cost. Because capital equipment usually lasts a number of years and is expensive, firms typically finance investment projects by borrowing. Therefore, *interest rates* are an important cost associated with investment. An additional cost factor related to investment is the corporate *tax* levied on firms by the government. Taxes decrease profits, thereby decreasing the attractiveness of investment projects. Alternatively, investment tax credits, given by the government, may encourage firms to expand investment.

4.   Investment is the most *volatile* component of aggregate demand. One of the reasons behind the volatility of investment is the importance of *expectations* in determining the level of investment spending. Since investment projects, by their very nature, depend upon the future, corporate leaders spend a great deal of time and effort trying to establish accurate forecasts of the business climate and the economy.

5.   The investment demand curve relates the interest rate to the level of investments It is downward-sloping and can shift up or down as the level of output in the economy, tax rates, and expectations about the future change.

6.   Figures 22-7 and 22-9 from the text are reproduced here as Figures 6-1 and 6-2. Note how the pattern of consumption spending is fairly stable and predictable. As disposable income in the economy increases, so does consumption spending. It almost looks like a one to one relationship. In fact, if the savings rate in the economy is five percent, the slope would be 0.95. Investment spending, on the other hand, is indeed more volatile. As the rate of growth – of course, you remember that growth is always measured in *real* terms – in GDP increases, so does the rate of change in real investment. However, the relationship is not as stable as the one between consumption and disposable income. When the rate of growth in GDP varies between two and four percent, the rate of change in investment varies from slightly less than zero to over ten percent!

Figure 6-2

V. HELPFUL HINTS

1.   If you are unfamiliar with graphs, slopes, and plotted lines, head back immediately to the appendix to Chapter 1.

2.   There is a precise accounting relationship between *disposable income, consumption*, and *saving*. After taxes have been paid, households are left with disposable income. This money is either consumed or saved—there are no other choices. Any two of these three terms will always, by definition, determine the value of the third.

3.   Economists are very fond of marginal analysis and *margin means change* (especially small change). Change, you should recall, is also how we measure a line's slope (*change*

Consumption Relates to Income

Figure 6-1

in *Y* axis over *change* in *X* axis between two points) . So margin is the same thing as slope. This concept is very useful for economists. For example, from microeconomics: the *slope* of total cost is *marginal* cost, and the *slope* of total revenue is *marginal* revenue; and from macroeconomics: the *slope* of the consumption function is the *marginal* propensity to consume, and the *slope* of the savings function is the *marginal* propensity to save. The sooner you learn this, the easier your time as a student of economics will be!

4. The 45° line plays an important part in several economic diagrams. As long as the same scale of measurement applies to both axes, the 45° line will provide a direct and equivalent mapping from the numbers on one axis to the same numbers on the other axis. In our consumption function diagram, points along the 45° line illustrate observations where consumption equals disposable income, the break-even level of income. (Note that the slope of the 45° line is 1.)

5. As you work with the consumption function and the investment demand schedule remember how to distinguish between movements along the curve and shifts in the curve. If a variable measured along the axis changes, like disposable income in the consumption function, you move along the curve to determine the new point of observation. On the other hand, if a variable changes that is not measured on the graph, and it is relevant to the analysis, like expectations in the investment demand schedule, then the curve will shift to illustrate the change.

VI. MULTIPLE CHOICE QUESTIONS

These questions are organized by topic from the chapter outline. Choose the best answer from the options available.

A. Consumption and Saving

1. The marginal propensity to consume is:
   a. the ratio of total consumption to total income at any income level.
   b. the change in income caused by a change (increase or decrease) in consumption spending.
   c. a schedule showing the amount of consumption spending for each income level.
   d. the ratio of a change in consumption to a change in income level at any income level.
   e. none of these things.

2. At the **break-even** level of income:
   a. the *MPC* is equal to the *MPS*.
   b. the *MPS* is equal to 0.
   c. consumption is equal to saving.
   d. saving is equal to 0.
   e. households are borrowing more than they are saving.

3. The break-even point on a family's consumption function is the point at which:

a. its saving equals its income.
b. its income equals its consumption.
c. its saving equals its consumption.
d. its consumption equals its investment.
e. the marginal propensity to consume equals 1.

4. The relationship between the marginal propensities to consume and to save holds that:
   a. their sum must equal 1, since some fraction of marginal income must go to extra consumption spending and the remaining fraction to extra saving.
   b. the ratio between them must indicate the average propensity to consume.
   c. their total must indicate the current total of disposable income received, since *DI* must divide between consumption and saving.
   d. the point at which they are equal must be the break-even level of income.
   e. their total must equal 0.

5. *Personal saving*, as the term is used in this chapter in connection with national income and national product analysis, reflects:
   a. the total of all assets held by families.
   b. income received within the period in question but not spent on consumption.
   c. the total of all assets held by families minus the total of their liabilities.
   d. income received within the period in question and either used only to buy a security or deposited in a bank.
   e. income received within the period in question but not spent on consumption or used to buy a security or deposited in a bank.

6. If people do not consume all their incomes and if they put the unspent amount into a bank, they are, in national income and product terms:
   a. saving but not investing.
   b. investing but not saving.
   c. both saving and investing.
   d. neither saving nor investing.
   e. saving, but investing only to the extent that they buy securities.

Use Figure 6-3 to answer questions 7 through 10.

Figure 6-3

7. The solid line *CC* is the consumption function for some family or community. If the total amount of consumption expenditure were *EA*, then the amount of disposable income must be:
   a. *AB*.
   b. *FD*.
   c. *FA*.
   d. *DA*.
   e. none of the above.

8. Equivalently, given the same total amount of consumption expenditure *EA* in the diagram, then the amount of disposable income must also be:
   a. *EA*.
   b. *GB*.
   c. *ED*.
   d. *0A*.
   e. none of the preceding.

9. If the consumption function is given as line *C'C'*, and disposable income is equal to *GB*, then savings must be equal to:
   a. *GJ*.
   b. *HJ*.
   c. *FG*.
   d. *DJ*.
   e. *FE*.

10. A change in consumption expenditure from *HB* to *EA* could be the result of:
    a. a decision to spend more and save less at each level of income.
    b. a decrease in disposable income from *0B* to *0A*.
    c. a decision to spend less and save more at each level of income.
    d. an increase in disposable income from *0A* to *0B*.
    e. none of the preceding.

Use Figure 6-4 to answer questions 11 through 13.

Figure 6-4

11. A shift in the consumption function from the solid line *CC* upward to the broken line *C'C'* would illustrate:
    a. an increase in consumption expenditure resulting from a rise in disposable income.

    b. a decision on the part of the family or community involved to consume more and save less at any given level of disposable income.
    c. a decrease in consumption expenditure resulting from a fall in disposable income.
    d. a decision on the part of the family or community involved to consume less and save more at any given level of disposable income.
    e. none of these events.

12. If the consumption function were indicated by the solid line *CC* and the amount of disposable income were *0K* then the amount of saving out of disposable income *0K* must be:
    a. *PK*
    b. *MK*.
    c. *PM*.
    d. *NM*.
    e. none of the preceding.

13. If the amount of disposable income were to change from *0K* to *0L*—the solid *CC* line still indicating the consumption function—then the amount of saving out of income would become:
    a. *SM*.
    b. *QR*
    c. *PQ*.
    d. *RS*.
    e. *QS*.

14. With regard to *both* of the consumption function diagrams (Figures 22-3 and 22-4), the primary difference between them is that:
    a. the *MPC* (marginal propensity to consume) is constant in Figure 6-3, and the *MPC* decreases as income increases in Figure 6-4.
    b. the *MPC* decreases as income increases in Figure 6-3, and the *MPC* is constant in Figure 6-4.
    c. the *MPC* increases as income increases in Figure 6-3, and the *MPC* is constant in Figure 6-4.
    d. the *MPC* is constant in Figure 6-3, and the *MPC* increases as income increases in Figure 6-4.
    e. in both instances, the *MPC* falls as income increases, but it falls more rapidly in Figure 6-4.

15. The consumption function refers to:
    a. the level of income at which consumption spending just equals income.
    b. the inclination on the part of some consumers to "keep up with the Joneses" in their consumer spending.
    c. the fraction of extra income that will be spent on consumption.
    d. a schedule showing the amount a family (or community) will spend on consumption at different levels of income.
    e. the fact that, at low incomes, families spend more on consumption than the amount of their incomes.

16. According to the statistical evidence, which of the following characterizes the typical American family's behavior with respect to consumption?
    a.   An increasing proportion of income is spent on consumption as income increases.
    b.   The same proportion of income is spent on consumption at all except very low income levels.
    c.   The same proportion of income is spent on consumption at all income levels.
    d.   A decreasing proportion of income is spent on consumption as income increases.
    e.   The same proportion of income is spent on consumption at all except very high income levels.
17. A family spends $2000 on consumption when its income is 0, and $6000 on consumption when its income is $6000. Assume that its consumption function is a straight line. This family's marginal propensity to consume is:
    a.   2/3.
    b.   3/4.
    c.   4/5.
    d.   1.
    e.   greater than 1.
18. The family from question 17 has a marginal propensity to save equal to:
    a.   1/3.
    b.   2/3.
    c.   3/4.
    d.   1/4.
    e. $2000.
19. **Permanent income** can be best described as:
    a.   money which has been saved for years and not likely to be spent by the household.
    b.   income left for the household after all taxes have been paid.
    c.   the sum of consumption and saving over the long run.
    d.   the long-run trend in household income.
    e.   none of the above.
20. Which of the statements below about savings is *false*?
    a.   One of the possible reasons for the decline in the personal savings rate is social security.
    b.   The improvement of capital and credit markets may have contributed to the decline in the savings rate.
    c.   Saving can be viewed as a residual of what is left over after households spend their income.
    d.   The savings rate is higher in the United States than in Japan.
    e.   All of the statements above are *true*.

B.   The Determinants of Investment

21. Which of the following would be regarded as investment by an economist?

    a.   any purchase of a corporate bond.
    b.   any amount saved out of income and not hoarded.
    c.   any purchase of a *new* corporate bond.
    d.   any productive activity resulting in present consumption.
    e.   none of the preceding.
22. Investment spending does *not* include:
    a.   purchases of new housing.
    b.   purchases of new factories.
    c.   additions to a firm's inventory of finished goods.
    d.   the issuing of new stock.
    e.   *All* of the above are considered as part of investment.
23. Which of the following best describes the relationship between interest rates and the level of investment spending?
    a.   They are directly related to each other.
    b.   They are inversely related to each other.
    c.   They move together but in no discernible relationship.
    d.   They are unrelated.
    e.   None of the above.
24. The *accelerator principle* states that:
    a.   as the economy heats up, inflation increases.
    b.   as the pace of economic growth quickens, investment will increase.
    c.   as government spending increases, investment increases as well.
    d.   an increasing supply of money accelerates the growth of investment.
    e.   it is very difficult to slow down a rapidly growing economy.
25. We would move along the *demand-for-investment* schedule to a new level of investment spending if:
    a   corporate profits taxes increased.
    b.   Congress passed an investment tax credit.
    c.   business managers became more optimistic about the future.
    d.   interest rates changed.
    e.   all the above.
26. Which statement below best describes the terms *investment and consumption*?
    a.   Both activities are undertaken by the same group (i.e., households), although not always for the same reasons.
    b.   Both are demands calling for the current use, or employment, of the economy's stock of productive inputs.
    c.   Both are components of disposable income.
    d.   In both cases, the only factor of major consequence which governs them is the level of national product or disposable income.
    e.   None of the preceding.

VII. PROBLEM SOLVING

The following problems are designed to help you apply the concepts that you learned in the chapter.

A. Consumption and Saving

1. Suppose that a certain family's weekly expenditure on consumption (C) is governed by this rule: Spend $100 plus one-half of weekly *DI*. Its consumption and saving at various income levels could then be represented in tabular form.

a. Fill in the blanks in Table 6-1. (*Remember*: *S* must be the difference between *DI* and *C*; at low income levels, therefore, *S* will be a negative amount.)

Table 6-1

DI	C	S
$ 0	$___	$___
100	___	___
200	___	___
300	___	___
400	___	___
500	___	___

b. Use the grid in Figure 6-5 to plot the points relating consumption (C) to disposable income for the six *DI* values in your table. Join these points with a line.

Figure 6-5

c. Now draw a diagonal line from the bottom left corner to the top right corner of your diagram. (If possible, use a different color to distinguish this line from the consumption function.)

You have just drawn a 45° line running through all the points for which *C = DI*. The 45° line runs through

the point marking off $100 of *DI* and $100 of *C*, through the point marking $200 *DI* and $200 *C*, through $300 *DI* and $300 *C*, and so on. In fact, the 45° line can be represented algebraically by *C = DI* (consumption equals disposable income).

It should be clear, at this point, that the 45° line can be used to identify the particular *DI* level at which the family just "breaks even," spending on consumption an amount exactly covered by its disposable income. The *break even point* appears on the 45° line where that line intersects the consumption schedule.

d. For the family depicted in your diagram, this intersection occurs where *DI* equals (**$100 / $200 / $300 / $400**). To the left of this intersection, the consumption function lies (**above / below**) the 45° line, and the family spends on *C* (**more / less**) than its *DI*. To the right of the intersection, the consumption function lies (**above / below**) the 45° line, and the family spends (**more / less**) than its *DI*. Given an income in excess of $200, therefore, the family would save part of its *DI*.

e. When *DI* equals $400, the vertical distance up to the 45° line from the *X* axis is (**$500 / $400 / $300**). At this point, the vertical distance up to the consumption function from the horizontal axis is (**$500 / $400 / $300**); this is the amount of *C* spending. The difference of (**$0 / $100 / $200**), or the vertical distance between the two lines, is the amount of saving (*S*).

f. Your diagram also indicates that if the family's *DI* were $300, it would (**save / dissave**) (**$0 / $50 / $100 / $150**). If *DI* were $100, then it would (**save / dissave**) (**$0 / $50 / $100 / $150**).

The family will, in fact, dissave for any *DI* for which the consumption function lies above the 45° line. This means simply that the family would draw on past savings or borrow in order to supplement *DI* currently received for *C* spending should its income ever fall (temporarily) below the break-even *DI* level of $200.

g. The amount of saving can be plotted directly on a saving-*DI* graph. Use the *DI* and *S* data from Table 6-1 to plot the savings schedule on the grid in Figure 6-6.

Figure 6-6

2.   It follows from the construction of a consumption function that any change in *DI* is likely to produce some *changes*
in both consumption spending (*C*) and saving (*S*). When
economists talk about change, they are really talking about
marginal analysis—in this case, the marginal propensity to
consume (*MPC*) and the marginal propensity to save (*MPS*).
  a.   Use the data from the last question to fill in the
  blanks below:
    1.   *MPC* = ___.
    2.   Slope of consumption schedule = ___.
    3.   *MPS* = ___.
    4.   Slope of savings schedule = ___.
  Now consider another (individual) consumption function which is defined in Table 6-2.

Table 6-2

Yearly Dl	Yearly C	Increase in C
$12,000	$11,600	
		$640
13,000	12,240	
		590
14,000	12,830	

  b.   Use the data from Table 6-2 to fill in the blanks
  below:
    1.   For a change in yearly *DI* from $12,000 to
  $13,000, *MPC* = ___ and MPS = ___.
    2.   For a change in yearly *DI* from $13,000 to
  $14,000, *MPC* = ___ and *MPS* = ___.
3.   Assume that a family has a weekly disposable income
of $450. Like the household in the first question, its con-
sumption spending equals $100 plus one-half of weekly *DI*.
  a.   Consumption spending equals ___.
  b.   One family member now leaves home, so the consumption function changes. It now becomes one-half of
  DI, plus $75. If family *DI* were unaffected by the
  change, then its weekly *C* spending would now be (**$300
  / $325 / $350 / $375**).
  c.   On a consumption function graph this change
  would be represented as (pick one):
    1.   a movement downward along the existing
  curve.
    2.   a movement upward along the existing curve.
    3.   a shift of the entire consumption function
  upward to a new position.
    4.   a shift of the entire consumption function
  downward to a new position.
  d.   Has the value of the marginal propensity to consume changed? (**No. / Yes, it has risen. / Yes, it has
  fallen.**)
  Suppose, finally, that a new consumption function is
established such that consumption spending becomes two-
fifths of *DI*, plus $75.
  e.   The value of the *MPC* would then have (**fallen /
  remained unchanged / risen**).

f.   The value of the *MPS* would now equal
g.   Write an equation that describes this consumption
function.

---

4.   The solid line *CC* in the diagram in Figure 6-7 illustrates
a community's consumption function. One possible level of
total *DI* is indicated by the horizontal measure 0*A*; the corresponding level of consumption expenditure is measured by
the vertical distance 0*D*.

Figure 6-7

a.   Suppose we observe an increase in the community's
C expenditure from 0*D* to 0*E*. This increase could be
the consequence of:
    1.   only an increase in *DI* from level 0*A* to level
0*B*.
    2.   only some factor other than a *DI* increase—a
factor causing the consumption function to shift upward
to a new position indicated by the broken line *C'C'*.
    3.   either of the above—an increase in *DI* or a
decision to spend more prompted by some factor other
than an increase in *DI*.
b.   A respected economic authority predicts a coming
recession. His prediction is influential, and people
decide that they should spend less and save more as a
precaution against coming hard times (even though *DI*
has not fallen—not yet, at any rate) . If this decision
were to be illustrated in Figure 6-7, it would imply (pick
one):
    1.   a movement downward and to the left along a
given consumption function, say, the solid *CC* one, to
indicate the reduced *C* spending caused by reduced disposable income.

2.   an upward movement of the entire consumption function, say, from the position indicated by the solid *CC*: line upward to the broken *C'C'* line.

3.   a downward movement of the entire consumption function, say, from the position indicated by the broken *C'C'* line downward to the solid *CC* line.

5.   Which of the following would cause the consumption function to shift up (**U**), shift down (**D**), or not shift at all (**NS**) ?

a.   An anticipated down-turn in business conditions that leads people to worry that they might lose their jobs. (**U / D / NS**)

b.   A reduction in the interest rate paid by banks that makes saving less attractive to everyone. (**U / D / NS**)

c.   A reduction in taxes that enables people to retain more of their incomes after taxes. (**U / D / NS**)

d.   An actual contraction in the economy that causes a reduction in the availability of outside or overtime employment. (**U / D / NS**)

B. The Determinants of Investment

6.   *Investment*, as the term is used in economics, generates employment while the investment item in question is being built, and thereby generates income for those people employed in the item's construction. In this sense, do the following, by themselves, constitute investment?

a.   Having a contractor build a new house for you. (**yes / no**)

b.   Buying a house built a year ago. (**yes / no**)

c.   Buying duPont stock on the stock market. (**yes / no**)

d.   Buying stock in a newly formed corporation. (**yes / no**)

e.   Using money obtained from the bond or stock issue of item **d** to build a new factory building. (**yes / no**)

7.   Indicate whether each of the following is true (**T**) or false (**F**):

a.   A firm is considering building a new plant to add to its output capacity. To do this sensibly, it must try to evaluate the future market for its product to be sure there is likely to be sufficient demand to justify the resulting increase in production. This evaluation requires that the firm estimate, among other things, the likely degree of competition from rival firms and the coming "general business conditions"—i.e., the probable future course of GDP. (**T / F**)

b.   This means, then, that the flow of investment expenditure is governed by many considerations frequently having to do with forecasts about the future. (**T / F**)

c.   A large corporation which has been steadily adding new plant and equipment may stop doing so because it feels it has caught up with probable demand for its product for the time being. If it stops, the investment flow will be correspondingly reduced even though the stock of capital is maintained net of depreciation. (**T / F**)

d.   Such investment plans may be postponed or canceled because the firm is fearful of a recession, that is, a drop or pause in GDP. This would again mean a drop in the flow of investment spending. (**T / F**)

e.   If any such reduction in the investment-spending flow were to occur, then it would be reasonable to assume that there would be an immediate and matching reduction in the flow of personal saving. (**T / F**)

f.   Suppose that the economy goes through a period of high interest rates caused by a variety of internal and external factors. The result should be a reduction in both the investment financed through borrowing and the investment financed through retained earnings. (**T / F**)

8.   Table 6-3 highlights the characteristics of four separate investment projects. Suppose that the annual cost of investment is based on market interest rates. Four different possible values of interest rates are given in the table: 3, 6, 10, and 15 percent, respectively. Assuming that the interest rate is the only cost of each investment, we can compare the annual revenue of each $1000 invested (found in column 3) with the annual interest cost per $1000 borrowed. For example, at 3 percent the cost of borrowing $1000 is $30 per year.

a.   At 6 percent the cost of borrowing $1000 is $___ per year.

At 10 percent the cost of borrowing $1000 is $___ per year.

At 15 percent the cost of borrowing $1000 is $___ per year.

As long as the annual revenue per $1000 exceeds the annual cost, the investment project will add to the firm's profit and should be undertaken.

b.   Now you are ready to complete the annual profit columns in the table. The numbers for project A are already filled in. Fill in the blanks for projects B, C, and D.

c.   Given these rates of interest, will the firm ever *not*

Table 6-3

(1) Project	(2) Total Investment (millions)	(3) Annual Revenue per $;1000	Annual Profit per $1000 at:			
			3%	6%	10%	15%
A	$10	$1000	$970	940	900	850
B	6	250	—	—	—	—
C	14	100	—	—	—	—
D	5	50	—	—	—	—

invest in project A? ___ What about project B?

   d.   At what rate of interest will this firm stop investing in project C? In project D?

The firm's total demand for investment is the total of all the investment projects that the firm is willing to fund at various rates of interest. For example, at 3 percent all the investment projects are profitable and the firm would spend $35 million on investment (10 + 6 + 14 + 5).

   e.   Fill in the blanks in Table 6-4 and then use these numbers to plot this firm's demand-for-investment schedule in Figure 6-8.

Table 6-4

Rate of Interest	Demand for Investment
3%	$35
6%	___
10%	___
15%	___

Figure 6-8

   f.   Now suppose that expectations of future business activity take a turn for the worse and that the annual revenue per $1000 for each project is cut in half. Plot a second curve in Figure 6-8 which reflects the new investment demand schedule.

     1.   The demand curve has (**shifted left / shifted right / remained in the same place**) as a result of the perceived change in economic climate.

     2.   Had expectations *improved* and expected revenues doubled, on the other hand, the curve would have (**shifted left / shifted right / remained in the same place**).

9.   This last question explores the relationship between saving and investment. Indicate whether each of the following is true (**T**) or false (**F**):

   a.   Money saved by a family and hidden in a mattress in the family's home is money withdrawn from the income stream; it creates no income or jobs for anyone as long as it remains in the mattress. (**T / F**)

   b.   Money saved by a family and promptly used to buy a new house is money put right back into the income stream. The family's actions would count as both saving and investment. (**T / F**)

   c.   Money saved by a family and promptly used to buy existing or newly issued General Motors stock would count as both saving and investment. (**T / F**)

   d.   Money saved and deposited in a savings account in a bank counts as saving. This is not investment in the economic sense. As long as this money stays deposited, it can potentially be used for investment spending if the bank lends it to a borrower who will use it for investment purposes. (**T / F**)

   e.   Much investment spending is financed by using other people's money, i.e., by borrowing from a bank or by selling bond or stock issues. (**T / F**)

   f.   If business conditions seem particularly uncertain, people with money to spare may hesitate to lend it, feeling that would-be borrowers are likely to get into trouble and be unable to make repayment. Thus, even though there are mechanisms for converting saving into investment, this does not mean that all saved money is automatically transformed into investment. (**T / F**)

VIII. DISCUSSION QUESTIONS

Answer the following questions, making sure that you can explain the work you did to arrive at the answers.

1.   Assume that there are 200 families in a community. Each of these families spends exactly $100 plus one-half its total income each week on consumption. Half (100) of these families are "poor;" they each receive weekly incomes of $200. The other 100 families are "rich;" they receive $400 apiece weekly.

An increase in total consumption spending is desired in this community. To achieve the increase, it is proposed that rich families be taxed $100 apiece weekly and that the tax proceeds be given to poor families to spend. Thus, each and every family would have a net weekly income of $300.

The following justification is given for the tax: Poor families spend 100 percent of their incomes on consumption; they receive $200 in income, and they spend a total of $200. Rich families spend only 75 percent of their incomes; they receive $400, but they spend only $300. So the total consumption spending would be increased by redistribution of income.

   a.   Would such a proposal, if adopted, increase total consumption spending? Explain your answer in terms of the marginal propensity to consume.

   b.   Are there any different circumstances in which such a redistribution-of-income proposal would increase consumption spending? Again answer in terms of the

MPC.

c.   Explain two circumstances in which a redistribution of income through this tax scheme might actually lower consumption spending. (This is a hard question; think beyond the *MPC* notion that was sufficient for answering part **b**.)

2.   Explain why, for most households, the *MPC* decreases with income.

3.   Why does it not make sense for the national *MPC* to be greater than 1?

4.   Briefly discuss the main determinants of investment spending in the economy.

5.   Explain the relationship between saving and economic growth.

IX. ANSWERS TO STUDY GUIDE QUESTIONS

III. Review of Key Concepts

6	Disposable income
13	Dissave
8	Break-even point
11	Consumption function
12	Savings function
4	Marginal
10	Marginal propensity to consume
7	Marginal propensity to save
3	Permanent income
1	Life-cycle hypothesis
9	Wealth effect
5	Accelerator principle
2	Investment demand curve

VI. Multiple Choice Questions

1. D   2. D   3. B   4. A   5. B   6. A
7. C   8. D   9. A 10. B 11. B 12. C
13. E 14. A 15. D 16. D 17. A 18. A
19. D 20. D 21. E 22. D 23. B 24. B
25. D 26. B

VII. Problem Solving

1.   a.

Table 6-1

DI	C	S
$ 0	$100	$-100
100	150	-50
200	200	0
300	250	50
400	300	100
500	350	150

b. and c.

Figure 6-5

d. $200, above, more, below, less
e. $400, $300, $100
f.   save, $50, dissave, $50
g.

Figure 6-6

2.   a.   1.   0.50
          2.   0.50
          3.   0.50
          4.   0.50
     b.   1.   0.64, 0.36
          2.   0.59, 0.41
3.   a. $325
     b. $300
     c.   4
     d.   No.
     e.   fallen
     f.   0.60
     g. $C = 75 + (0.4) DI$

4. a. 2
   b. 3
5. a. D
   b. U
   c. NS
   d. NS
6. a. yes
   b. no
   c. no
   d. no
   e. yes
7. a T
   b. T
   c. T
   d. T
   e. F
   f. T
8. a. 60, 100, 150
   b.

Table 6-3

Annual *Profit* per $1000 at:				
	3%	6%	10%	15%
Project B	$220	$190	$150	$100
Project C	$ 70	$ 40	$ 0	-$ 50
Project D	$ 20	-$ 10	-$ 50	-$100

c. No. No.
d. any interest rate above 10 percent, any interest rate above 5 percent
e. $30, $16, $16. See Figure 6-8.
f. See Figure 6-8.

Figure 6-8

1. shifted left
2. shifted right
9. a. T
   b. T
   c. F
   d. T
   e. T
   f. T

VIII. Discussion Questions

1. a. Total consumption spending would remain unchanged. Since each group has the exact same *MPC*, the transfer of income would probably help the "poor" families provide for themselves, but total spending would not be affected.
   b. If the poorer families had a higher *MPC* than the rich families, the transfer of income would increase consumption spending.
   c. First, if poorer families had a lower *MPC* than the rich, total consumption spending could fall. Second, if the tax on the rich reduces their incentive to work, incomes and thereby consumption spending could decrease.
2. The basic necessities of life—food, clothing, and shelter—must be met by all households, regardless of their income. As incomes increase, households can afford nicer commodities, but once necessities have been met, there is more of an opportunity to think about the future and save.
3. It is impossible for the nation, as a whole, to spend more than it produces. If the change in spending is greater than the change in income, there must be dissaving or borrowing. When there is borrowing, there must be some saving in the economy. If the *MPC* is greater than 1, there would not be any saving.
4. Investment spending is determined by interest rates, business expectations, and the level of GDP itself.
5. Saving can be viewed as the postponement of consumption. This encourages firms to produce less and invest more. Investment leads to greater productive capacity and economic growth.

CHAPTER 7
Business Cycles and the Theory of Aggregate Demand

I. CHAPTER OVERVIEW

Chapter 7 explores business cycles and one of the main economic variables that they influence—aggregate demand. Throughout its economic history the United States and other nations have been subject to fluctuations—upturns and downturns—in economic growth. One of the critical issues facing the economics profession is whether economic policy can be designed to adequately control the adverse effects of the business cycle. Or should policy makers be satisfied with being able to simply dampen the amplitude of cyclical swings?

Aggregate Demand, which can be influenced greatly by business cycle activity, can also have a powerful impact on output, employment, and prices—especially in the short run. This chapter reviews the components of aggregate demand and discusses the overall shape of the aggregate demand curve. In addition, there is a discussion of the factors that can cause the aggregate demand curve to shift. As always, be careful to distinguish between movements *along* the curve and *shifts* in the curve.

II. LEARNING OBJECTIVES

After you have read Chapter 23 in your text and completed the exercises in this *Study Guide* chapter, you should be able to:

1. Outline the business-cycle experience of the United States and the causes behind it.
2. Understand the successive phases of the business cycle.
3. Describe the business-cycle theories that lie behind aggregate supply and aggregate demand.
4. Appreciate the use of econometric modeling in forecasting business-cycle behavior.
5. Explain why the economy's aggregate demand curve is downward-sloping.
6. Understand the differences between *micro*economic and *macro*economic demand.
7. Provide reasons for shifts in the aggregate demand curve.

III. REVIEW OF KEY CONCEPTS

Match the following terms from column A with their definitions in column B.

A	B
__ Business cycle	1. Rapid output growth stimulates investment which in turn, stimulates further economic growth.
__ Recession	2. Variables outside the AS-AD framework.
__ Depression	3. Nominal money supply divided by the price level.
__ Business-cycle phases	4. Swings in total national output usually lasting between 2 and 10 years and marked by widespread expansion or contraction in the economy.
__ Expansion	5. Rooted in the Keynesian tradition, but is more pragmatic in its explanation of movements in aggregate supply and demand.
__ Multiplier-accelerator theory	6. Fiscal and monetary decisionsmade by the government to shift aggregate demand.
__ Demand-induced cycles	7. Phase of the business cycle characterized by economic growth.
__ Aggregate demand	8. A decline in real GDP for at least two consecutive quarters.
__ Real money supply	9 Concentrate primarily on monetary forces in analyzing movements in AD and AS in the economy.
__ Policy variables	10. Business cycles caused by shocks to AD.
__ Exogenous variables	11. Prolonged, cumulative slump in real GDP.
__ Monetarists	12. Total quantity of output that is willingly bought at a given level of prices, other things held constant.

__ Keynesian   13. Peak, trough, expansion, and
    macroeconomics   contraction.

IV. SUMMARY AND CHAPTER OUTLINE

This section summarizes the key concepts from the chapter.

A. Business Cycles

1. Business cycles are all different—and all the same.
Each one has its own cause, its own length of time, its own
degree of severity, and its own trajectory. Despite all these
differences, though, they all seem to follow the same general
pattern: decline into recession (**contraction**); bottom out
(**trough**); climb into recovery and continue into boom
(**expansion**); reach an apex (**peak**); and start all over. The
differences are confounding, but the similarities suggest the
possibility that some general pattern of policy might reduce
the severity of the cycle.

2. There are many possible explanations for the sources of
business cycles, but it may be helpful to classify them into
two categories: external and internal. External sources
include changes that occur outside the economic system.
There are many possibilities here: natural disasters, wars,
new discoveries. Internal mechanisms include the *multiplier-accelerator theory* and *demand-induced cycles*. Recall
from Chapter 22 that the accelerator theory describes a relationship between the rate of (real) GDP growth and investment spending. The multiplier-accelerator theory adds to the
accelerator the relationship between investment and GDP. In
a nutshell, GDP growth generates investment (accelerator),
which in turn, contributes to further GDP growth (multiplier). As Samuelson and Nordhaus indicate, the multiplier will
be explained in greater detail in the next chapter. Hang in
there! The main point behind demand-induced business
cycles is to realize that economic growth or decline can be
caused by rightward of leftward shifts in the aggregate
demand curve.

3. Economists do not fully understand the roots and causes
of business cycles. Appropriately, many different theories
have been developed. Some work better than others; some
work better under different circumstances. Samuelson and
Nordhaus review six different theories. Problem number 6
in section VII. below, reviews these theories.

B. Analytical Foundations of
Aggregate Demand

1. Aggregate demand (*AD*) includes all the desired spending by the different sectors in the economy: consumption
(*C*), private domestic investment (*I*), government purchases
of goods and services (*G*), and net exports (*X*).

2. The primary reason for the downward slope of the *AD*
curve is the **money-supply effect**. As prices in the economy
increase, other things held constant, the **real money supply**

decreases. The real money supply is defined as the *nominal
money supply* divided by the price level. The supply of *real*
money becomes relatively scarce or tight, and therefore, the
price of obtaining money, or the rate of interest, goes up. All
types of spending that rely on borrowed funds—consumption items, investment, even net exports—decline. Hence,
we observe that higher price levels lead to a decrease in the
aggregate demand for goods and services, or a movement up
and along the aggregate demand curve.

3. There are some important differences between microeconomic and macroeconomic demand curves. In *micro*, the
focus is on a particular market for a particular good. When
we construct the demand curve, we allow the price of the
good to vary, while *all other prices and consumer incomes
are held constant*. In *macro*, we attempt to get a picture of
the entire economy, not just one market. The general price
level varies along the vertical axis, and *total output and real
incomes change* as we move along the aggregate demand
curve. The primary reason for the negative slope of the
aggregate demand curve is the money-supply effect; the
main reason for the downward slope of the single market
demand curve is the substitution effect.

4. There are numerous reasons why the aggregate demand
curve might shift. The two main categories of shift variables
are policy variables and exogenous variables. *Policy* variables include changes in either monetary or fiscal policy.

Exogenous variables are variables determined outside
the framework of the model, or beyond the control of policymakers. Examples of exogenous variables include changes
in foreign countries (oil-production decisions, growth rates
abroad), advances in technology, and movements in the stock
market. We are not implying here that the economy and government policies have no bearing on these "outside" variables, only that it is possible for changes to originate in these
areas and that such changes can have an effect on the level of
spending (i.e., aggregate demand) in the economy.

Whether change is due to policy variables or exogenous
variables, the aggregate demand curve will shift (right or
left) in response to these "shocks." There is not universal
agreement among economists about the relative importance
of these factors. Those economists who stress the importance of the role of the money supply are called *monetarists*.
Other economists focus more on the influence of exogenous
variables and fiscal policy. The mainstream of economic
thinking today includes aspects of both the Keynesian and
monetarist points of view.

V. HELPFUL HINTS

1. Several different theories of business cycles are presented in this chapter. You should realize that there are many
unsolved economic problems, and economics cannot *always*
provide exact and clearly defined answers or solutions.

What economic analysis does provide in these circumstances, is a structure and framework for investigating and learning about the economic problem at hand. Once informed, you can argue for, or against, particular theories.

2. Do not forget: The **G** in aggregate demand measures the government's purchases of goods and services. This is not the same thing as the government's budget expenditures which also include transfer payments and interest on the debt.

3. The phrase "other things held constant" is important. In order to clarify specific economic relationships it is desirable to change just one variable at a time. When two or more variables change at once (which in reality happens all the time), it becomes very difficult to isolate causes from effects. For example, when we construct the aggregate demand curve, we vary the price level and hold all other things—including the money supply—constant. And when we analyze the effect of policy or exogenous variables on AD, we change just one variable at a time and hold everything else constant.

4. Models that explain simple economic relationships may teach us a great deal, but may at times, seem removed from the helter-skelter activity of the real world. The price we pay for realism in economic models is complication. Recall Samuelson's and Nordhaus's discussion of business-cycle models that contain systems of equations and thousands of variables.

5. Remember, we use models to understand and explain how the economy functions. You should always be aware of the simplifying assumptions being made.

VI. MULTIPLE CHOICE QUESTIONS

These questions are organized by topic from the chapter outline. Choose the best answer from the options available.

A. Business Cycles

1. Business cycles seem to be caused:
   a. exclusively by external factors.
   b. exclusively by internal factors.
   c. by factors of any type that mostly influence aggregate demand.
   d. by factors that only influence aggregate supply.
   e. all the above.

2. Which of the following would you *not* expect to see during a period of recession?
   a. Lower business investment in durable equipment.
   b. Lower stock prices and lower demand for labor.
   c. Lower tax receipts from corporations and individuals.
   d. Lower corporate profits.
   e. Lower unemployment compensation payments.

3. Which of the following time frames was marked by the most severe period of recession?
   a. 1969-1970.
   b. 1982-1983.
   c. 1974-1975.
   d. 1960-1961.
   e. 1953-1954.

4. Which of the following time frames was marked by the most energetic period of economic boom?
   a. 1983-1984.
   b. 1973-1974.
   c. 1938-1939.
   d. 1955-1956.
   e. 1967-1968.

5. The implication of the theory of political business cycles is that:
   a. anti-inflationary medicine is generally administered early in an administration.
   b. the year after an election is frequently a year of austerity.
   c. the year of an election is frequently a year of growth and prosperity.
   d. the timing of elections can dictate the timing of the business cycle.
   e. all the above are correct.

6. If we look to any particular kind of spending as a key factor in accounting for the business cycle, we find it in:
   a. net investment, specifically spending on inventories.
   b. net investment, specifically spending on durable goods.
   c. consumer spending.
   d. variations in spending by state and local governments.
   e. none of the above, the point stressed being that no single type of spending plays any key role.

7. The role of consumer spending in the business cycle, according to U.S. experience, is best understood by noting that:
   a. changes in consumer durable purchases may occasionally set off an upswing or downturn, and changes in consumer spending will intensify the effect of any disturbance originating outside the consumer sphere, via the multiplier.
   b. consumer spending and investment seem to have approximately equal parts to play in the cycle, although the two are so intermixed that it is difficult to separate one from the other and to analyze the role of either.
   c. changes in consumer spending on nondurables most commonly initiate the downturn in a major business cycle, whereas increases in consumer durable purchases are most likely to start the upturn as replacement of worn-out durable items becomes necessary.
   d. changes in consumer spending are most often the initial disturbing factor, and the impact then spreads to investment, thus intensifying the original disturbance.

e.   consumer spending has no part to play in the cycle, which (except for wartime disturbances) is almost entirely due to changes in investment.

8. Statistically, the widest swings between peak and bottom of the business cycle are to be found in:
    a.   the supply of consumer services.
    b.   the production of inventories.
    c.   the production of durables and capital goods.
    d.   wholesale rather than retail goods.
    e.   export and import goods.

9. The multiplier-accelerator theory focuses on the relationship between:
    a.   taxes, consumer spending, and GDP.
    b.   monetary policy, interest rates, and investment.
    c.   GDP and investment spending.
    d.   GDP and any component of aggregate demand.
    e.   exogenous and policy variables.

10. Which of the following would be considered as a *supply shock* to the economy?
    a.   a sharp increase in foreign oil prices.
    b.   weather-related crop failures.
    c.   a reorganization of the domestic health care industry.
    d.   all of the above.
    e.   none of the above.

11. The index of leading indicators is best described as:
    a.   combination of several statistics that generally give an accurate indication of the direction of economic growth ahead..
    b.   a combination of data on boxcar loadings and steel production.
    c.   a type of econometric forecasting model.
    d.   all of the above.
    e.   choices **a**. and **c**. only.

B. Analytical Foundations of Aggregate Demand

12. Which of the terms below is *not* a component of aggregate demand?
    a.   consumption expenditure.
    b.   government expenditure.
    c.   net exports.
    d.   investment expenditure.
    e.   all of the above terms are part of AD.

13. Which of the following expression is best describes the money-supply effect?
    a.   As the money supply increases, so does inflation.
    b.   As the economy grows, the central bank increases the supply of money.
    c.   Aggregate demand and the money supply are positively related.
    d.   As prices increase, the decline in the real money supply will affect aggregate demand.

e.   Money makes the world go round.

14. Which of the following is a reason why the aggregate demand curve should be drawn downward-sloping?
    a.   Higher prices reduce potential GDP by reducing labor force participation.
    b.   Higher prices cause interest rates to fall, thereby depressing investment.
    c.   Higher prices cause interest rates to rise, thereby depressing investment.
    d.   Higher prices inspire increased labor force participation and therefore increase consumption expenditures.
    e.   None of the above makes any sense in explaining the negative slope of an aggregate demand curve.

15. One of the similarities between microeconomic and macroeconomic demand is that both:
    a.   hold income constant.
    b.   rely on the substitution effect to explain demand.
    c.   rely on the money-supply effect to explain demand.
    d.   vary inversely with price.
    e.   hold the prices of all other goods constant.

16. Which of the following should be expected to shift the aggregate demand curve to the left?
    a.   an increase in government spending.
    b.   a reduction in net exports.
    c.   a reduction in labor force participation.
    d.   the adoption of an improved production technology.
    e.   a reduction in the value of the dollar.

17. Which of the following should be expected to shift the aggregate demand curve to the right?
    a.   an increase in government spending.
    b.   a reduction in net exports.
    c.   a reduction in labor force participation.
    d.   an increase in taxes.
    e.   a decrease in the money supply.

18. According to the money-supply effect, which produces a downward-sloping aggregate demand curve, lower prices in the context of a fixed real money supply should:
    a.   make credit more difficult to obtain.
    b.   increase interest rates and thereby reduce investment.
    c.   depress stock market values and thereby reduce consumption.
    d.   all the above.
    e.   none of the above.

19. According to *monetarists*, the primary determinant of the total dollar of spending in the economy is:
    a.   interest rates.
    b.   the money supply.
    c.   taxes.
    d.   transfer payments.
    e.   the government debt.

VII. PROBLEM SOLVING

The following problems are designed to help you apply the concepts that you learned in the chapter.

A. Business Cycles

1. Record in the spaces provided the business-cycle phase during which you would expect to observe the indicated events; denote contraction by (**C**) and expansion by (**E**):
   ___ a. Business investment increasing
   ___ b. Profits falling
   ___ c. Tax receipts climbing
   ___ d. Demand for labor rising
   ___ e. Stock prices falling
   ___ f. Inflation accelerating
   ___ g. Unemployment-insurance payments increasing
   ___ h. Interest rates falling
2. a. Recessions (or depressions) most commonly arise from a (**drop / rise**) in (**consumption / investment / government spending**).
   b. This initial (**drop / rise**) has magnified consequences because of the multiplier effect; i.e., total spending drops (**even more / somewhat less**) than the initial drop in (**C / I / G**).
   c. Among the following economic variables, the greatest cyclical fluctuation is typically found in (**wholesale prices / production of capital goods / production of basic materials such as petroleum / expenditures on consumer goods**).
3. Play a "what if" game to test your understanding of a few definitions.
   a. If you were to believe that changes in the population were never caused by changes in economic circumstance, then a theory that held that changes in total population caused the business cycle would be (**an external / an internal / a political**) theory of the cycle.
   b. Were you to go to the other extreme, holding that changes in population were exclusively the result of changes in economic circumstance (e.g., you might think that depression increases the number of poor people who cannot have children because they cannot support them), then a theory that proposed a causal relationship between changes in total population and the business cycle would be (**an external / an internal / a political**) theory of the cycle.
   c. The notion that incumbent political parties use the policy tools at their disposal to time recovery and boom for election years and recession and trough for off-election years is (**an external / an internal / a political**) business-cycle theory.
4. Consider Figure 7-1. Suppose that an economic downturn is caused by a shift in aggregate demand.

Figure 7-1

   a. Illustrate this on the diagram.
   b. Give an example of a particular *AD* change that could cause this shift.
   c. What sort of policy change would you recommend to move the economy out of this slump?
5. Now look at Figure 7-2, which is identical to Figure 7-1. Suppose, this time, that an economic downturn is caused by a shift in aggregate supply.

Figure 7-2

   a. Illustrate this on the diagram in Figure 7-2.
   b. Give an example of a particular *AS* change that could cause this shift.
   c. What sort of policy change would you recommend to move the economy out of this slump?
   d. Which type of economic downturn is worse, one caused by a shift in *AD* or one caused by a shift in *AS*? Briefly justify your answer.
6. Samuelson and Nordhaus describe six different theories of the business cycle in this chapter. For each of the theories listed below, match it with the number of its description and the letter of the economist(s) who support it.

__ __ Monetary theories	1. Business cycles caused by shifts in aggregate supply.
__ __ Multiplier-accelerator model	2. Innovations and changes in productivity in one sector can spread to the rest of the economy.
__ __ Political Theories	3. Misperceptions about prices and wages lead people to supply little or too much labor. This leads to cycles in output.
__ __ Equilibrium-business-cycle theories	4. Output growth stimulates investment which generates further growth in output.
__ __ Real business cycle	5. Cyclical swings caused by changes in the money supply and the availability of credit.
__ __ Supply shocks	6. Fluctuations in the business cycle attributed to politically-motivated changes in fiscal and monetary policy.

a. W .Nordhaus and E. Tufte

b. R. Lucas, R. Barro, and T. Sargent

c. J. Schumpeter, E. Prescott, P. Long, and C. Plosser

d. M. Friedman

e. R. J. Gordon

f. P. Samuelson

B. Foundations of Aggregate Demand

7. a. Aggregate demand is generally downward-sloping when drawn against a price index due, in large part, to the (**substitution effect / money-supply effect / income effect**).

b. Higher prices, given a constant real money supply, can be expected to cause interest rates to (**rise / fall / stay the same**), cause stock market prices to (**rise / fall / stay the same**), (**reduce / increase / have no effect on**) the international value of the dollar, and generally make credit (**more difficult / easier**) to obtain.

c. In light of these effects, use the spaces provided below to explain how the values of the components of aggregate demand would change if prices were to fall:

1. Consumption:

2. Investment:

3. Government:

4. Net exports:

8. The first column of Table 7-1 records a series of changes in economic circumstance.

a. Indicate in column (2) the component of aggregate demand (*C, I, G,* or *X*) that would be most directly affected by each change; then note the direction of the effect in column (3) (use + to designate an increase and - to signify a reduction).

b. In column (4) identify whether panel (*a*), (*b*), or (*c*) of Figure 7-3 best illustrates the result graphically as a shift from *AD* to *AD'*.

c. Use column (5) to explain your reasoning. The first row has been completed for you.

d. Look back at column (1) in the table. Circle the letter of those changes in which the effect was generated by a change in a *policy* variable; place a star next to the changes in which the effect was generated by a change in an *exogenous* variable.

9. There is a critical difference between the microeconomic construction of a demand curve for a specific product and the macroeconomic construction of an aggregate demand curve. Indicate whether each of the statements recorded below accurately describes a microeconomic demand curve for a specific product or a macroeconomic aggregate demand curve; use the terms "micro" and "macro."

a. The curve is drawn under the assumption that income is held constant.

b. Total incomes and output vary along this curve.

c. The curve is downward-sloping because consumers can substitute into and out of the consumption of various goods.

d. The curve is downward-sloping because the nominal money supply is fixed.

e. The curve is drawn against a price index even though relative prices may change within that index.

f. The curve is derived from individuals' responses to changes in one price, other prices assumed constant.

Table 7-1

(1) Change	(2) AD Component	(3) Direction	(4) Panel	(5) Explanation
a. Increased population	Consumption	+	(b)	More people mean enlarged consumption.
b. Reduced money supply	__	__	__	_____
c. Increased personal income taxes	__	__	__	_____
d. Severe recession abroad	__	__	__	_____
e. Anticipated recession at home	__	__	__	_____
f. Anticipated recession abroad	__	__	__	_____
g. Rapid escalation in house prices	__	__	__	_____
h. An October stock market crash	__	__	__	_____
i. Diminished defense spending	__	__	__	_____
j. Higher prices abroad	__	__	__	_____

Figure 7-3

VIII. DISCUSSION QUESTIONS

Answer the following questions, making sure that you can explain the work you did to arrive at the answers.

1. Figure 7-4 illustrates how different sectors of the economy were affected by three recessions in the United States. Use the bar chart to discuss how the recessions affected different sectors of the economy in different ways.

2. Figure 23-4 from the text is reproduced here as Figure 7-5. Discuss several reasons why the aggregate demand curve in the economy might shift to the left. For what reasons might policy makers want aggregate demand to shift in this direction?

IX. ANSWERS TO STUDY GUIDE QUESTIONS

III. Review of Key Concepts
4	Business cycle
8	Recession
11	Depression
13	Business-cycle phases
7	Expansion
1	Multiplier-accelerator theory
10	Demand-induced cycles
12	Aggregate demand
3	Real money supply
6	Policy variables
2	Exogenous variables
9	Monetarists
5	Keynesian macroeconomics

Figure 7-4

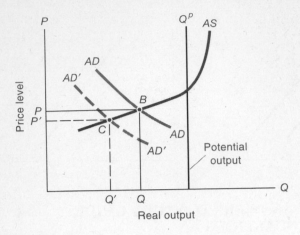

Figure 7-5

VI. Multiple Choice Questions

1. C 2. E 3. B 4. E 5. E 6. B
7. A 8. C 9. C 10. D 11. A 12. E
13. D 14. C 15. D 16. B 17. A 18. E
19. B

VII. Problem Solving

1. a. E
    b. C
    c. E
    d. E
    e. C
    f. E
    g. C
    h. C
2. a. drop, investment
    b. drop, even more, I
    c. production of capital goods
3. a. an external
    b. an internal
    c. a political
4. a.

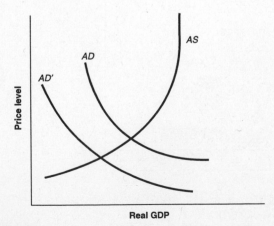

Figure 7-1

b. This shift could be caused by a reduction in consumption, investment, government spending, or net exports. In reality, investment spending is the most volatile of these four possibilities.

c. Stimulative fiscal policy, either a tax cut or an increase in government spending, could be used to get the economy out of the slump. Alternatively, the Fed could pursue an easy monetary policy.

5. a.

Figure 7-2

b. The AS could shift to the left due to an increase in input prices or due to some external shock that raises the price of a commodity that is vital to production in the economy. (The OPEC oil embargo comes to mind.)

c. Usual fiscal or monetary policy measures would have to focus on either the inflation problem or the unemployment problem. It is not possible to alleviate both problems at once. Ideally, the government could use a supply-side policy to shift the aggregate supply curve back to the right.

d. The AS shift is worse since it creates both inflation and unemployment problems.

6. 5 d Monetary theories
    4 f Multiplier-accelerator model
    6 a Political theories
    3 b Equilibrium-business-cycle theories
    2 c Real business cycle
    1 e Supply shocks

7. a. money-supply effect
    b. rise, fall, reduce, more difficult
    c. 1. Spending would increase due to the increase in the real money supply. Consumers would be able to purchase more goods and services with the same income.

    2. Lower interest rates would increase investment spending.

    3. Lower prices would allow the government to purchase more real goods and services with its budget.

4. Lower prices would attract more foreign customers. Net exports would increase.

8. a., b., c.

Table 7-1

(2)	(3)	(4)	(5)
b. Investment	-	(a)	Higher interest rates lower investment.
c. Consumption	-	(a)	Higher taxes reduce disposable income.
d. Net exports	-	(a)	Recession abroad means less foreign demand for goods and services.
e. Investment or Consumption	-	(a)	The fear of lower profits or income reduces spending.
f. Investment	-	(a)	The fear of lower profits in export markets lowers investment.
g. Consumption	+	(b)	Increase in consumer wealth increases spending.
h. Consumption or Investment	-	(a)	Reduced consumer wealth and/or increased cost of raising funds lowers aggregate demand.
i. Government	-	(a)	Reduced government spending lowers aggregate demand.
j. Net exports	+	(b)	Imports are reduced, domestic spending increases.

d. Place a circle around b, c, and i.
Place a star next to the remaining changes.

9. a. micro
   b. macro
   c. micro
   d. macro
   e. macro
   f. micro

VIII. Discussion Questions

1. The recession of 1973-1975 was the most severe for home construction, inventories, and investment. The decline in inventories suggests that firms depleted their inventories rather than produce more products.

The 1981-1982 recession was also felt in the same three sectors, but to a lesser extent. Net foreign trade declined more during this recession than during either of the other two recessions, and consumer spending actually increased. The increased consumer spending may have contributed to the trade deficit. This was not a bad recession for the consumer.

The 1990-1991 recession seems to have been less severe than the other two recessions, but it was the worst one for consumers. It was also more evenly spread throughout the economy.

2. Aggregate demand will shift to the left whenever any of the components *AD* decrease. A decrease in investment spending, an increase in taxes which causes a reduction in consumption spending, or a decrease in net exports would all cause aggregate demand to shift to the left.

If the economy is growing too fast, policy makers, fearing inflation, may want to slow it down. In general, policy makers may want *AD* to shift to the left when inflation is viewed as a problem in the economy.

CHAPTER 8
The Multiplier
Model

I.   CHAPTER OVERVIEW

In the previous four chapters you were introduced to many of the fundamental concepts of macroeconomic analysis: aggregate supply, aggregate demand, GDP, price indexes, consumption, saving, and investment. In this chapter we put the pieces of the puzzle together. The tools and concepts developed here are the essential building blocks for what follows. The completed picture will give you a better understanding of how the macroeconomy works and will enable you to evaluate various governmental economic policy proposals. You will also be ready to formulate your own ideas for economic policies to deal with such problems as high levels of inflation, sluggish periods of high unemployment, or stagnant times marked by unacceptably high levels of both maladies.

In the first section of this chapter, the **multiplier model** is discussed. The multiplier is one of the key building blocks that we will use over and over again. The time you spend now to learn it thoroughly will pay large dividends later.

In the second portion of the chapter, the government sector is added into the analysis. We are especially interested in the relationship between fiscal policy, i.e. government spending and taxes, and the multiplier.

The chapter closes with a review of empirical estimates of the multiplier, and you should not be surprised by the wide range in these estimates. Economists who estimate multipliers face not only the uncertainties of dealing with an enormously complex economy but also the ramifications of different academic and philosophical traditions.

When you have worked through this chapter, you will have a better understanding of the complex interdependencies that frame the contemporary world economy.

II.   LEARNING OBJECTIVES

After you have read Chapter 24 in your text and completed the exercises in this *Study Guide* chapter, you should be able to:

1. Understand the equivalence of the *S* and *I* and *C* + *I* approaches to equilibrium in a *simple* economy.
2. Explain the process by which a simple economy moves toward equilibrium if it is not initially at an equilibrium position.

3. Explain the difference between *planned* and *actual* spending and investment.
4. Derive the value of the *multiplier* from the marginal propensity to consume (*MPC*) and explain how the multiplier is used to determine a new equilibrium position in a simple economy when investment spending changes.
5. Understand how the multiplier model fits into the AS-AD model of the economy.
6. Understand how governmental fiscal policy affects output in the multiplier model.
7. Explain the different effects of taxes and government spending on aggregate demand.
8. Understand how the **tax multiplier** differs from the **expenditure multiplier**.
9. Calculate the equilibrium level of GDP in an economy with government and trade.
10. Relate the multiplier model developed here to the real world and appreciate the complexity of economic research which attempts to measure the value of the multiplier.

III.   REVIEW OF KEY CONCEPTS

Match the following terms from column A with their definitions in column B.

A	B
__ Closed economy	1. Used to show how a dollar change in investment or government spending affects the economy.
__ Actual investment	2. The change in spending on goods and services when disposable income changes by a dollar.
__ Lump-sum taxes	3. Government programs involving spending, transfer payments and taxes.
__ Expenditure multiplier	4. Economy without foreign trade or finance.
__ Tax multiplier	5. Occurs when all *planned* spending in the economy equals what is *actually* spent.
__ Fiscal policy	6. Country which participates in the world economy and is linked

___ Equilibrium

___ Marginal propensity to consume

___ Open economy

with other countries through trade and finance.
7.   Is calculated by multiplying the expenditure multiplier by the MPC.
8.   Money paid to the government which is a constant fixed dollar value and not related to GDP.
9.   Planned investment spending plus any unanticipated changes in inventories.

IV. SUMMARY AND CHAPTER OUTLINE

This section summarizes the key concepts from the chapter.

A. The Basic Multiplier Model

1.   In a simple, closed economy the intersection of the *desired* savings and investment schedules will determine the equilibrium value of GDP. In order to simplify the analysis, Samuelson and Nordhaus (and for that matter, most other principles text authors) make the assumption that investment spending is exogenous. In other words, they treat investment spending as a given that is not determined by GDP. This allows us to plot the investment schedule against GDP as a horizontal line. This is not to say that investment spending cannot change. If investment changes, say, due to a change in interest rates (or any other factor), the investment schedule will simply shift up or down. (Since the investment schedule here is horizontal, we cannot really talk about right and left shifts.) Investment is independent of GDP.

Note to Students *Be sure to note how the axes on diagrams are labeled. We are talking here about the relationship between investment spending and GDP. Investment is plotted on the vertical axis and GDP on the horizontal axis. This presentation and discussion in no way violates or changes the investment demand schedule that we developed Chapter 22. Please refer to Figure 8-1.*

Figure 8-1

When the economy is at equilibrium the *desired* spending and savings of households is equal to the *desired* production and investment of firms. However, if households spend too little, or less than firms thought they would, businesses are left with unsold goods. These unsold goods are added to business inventories and count as part of investment. In this case, *desired* investment will be less than *actual* investment and the economy will not be at an equilibrium position. In subsequent production periods, firms will produce less and lay off workers. GDP falls and the economy moves toward a position where *desired* saving equals *desired* investment.

2.   The equilibrium position in the economy can also be found by comparing the total demand for goods and services ($C + I$) with total output. Figure 24-3 from the text is reproduced here as Figure 8-2. As above, if households spend too little, firms will be left with unplanned additions to their inventories and the economy will contract. Diagrammatically, this approach compares total spending with total output (GDP) and the 45° line is extremely useful in comparing the two terms. When the $C + I$ schedule crosses the 45° line, total spending equals total output, and the economy is at equilibrium. Here, our assumption of fixed or exogenous investment is very helpful. The $C + I$ schedule will have the same slope as the C schedule. The fixed difference between the two lines is the constant level of investment spending. The horizontal investment line has no slope of its own, so the slope of the $C + I$ line is due entirely to the slope of C! Consumption is critically important in this model. This is as it should be—consumption spending accounts for approximately two-thirds of the U.S. aggregate demand.

Figure 8-2 In the Expenditure Approach, Equilibrium GDP Level Is Found at the Intersection of the C+I Schedule with 45° Line.

3. The *multiplier* is also critically linked to consumption. When firms invest more, the workers employed on the investment project will earn more income. The *MPC* determines how much of their extra income they will spend. The recipients of this spending will then turn around and spend more based on the *MPC*. The analysis is simplified by assuming that the same *MPC* applies at all levels of income. Fortunately, in each round marginal spending gets a little smaller (because some of the extra income is saved), and the process converges. The result, however, is that GDP changes by some *multiple* of the initial investment project. The more households spend, the larger that multiple will be. The following formula can be used to calculate the expenditure multiplier:

$$\text{Expenditure multiplier} = \frac{1}{1 - MPC} = \frac{1}{MPS}$$

4. The effectiveness of the multiplier in generating real changes in output depends upon how close the economy is to full employment or potential GDP. If an economy is operating at close to full employment, it will be difficult for a new investment project to generate more employment or output since the economy is close to full employment already. At this point, higher levels of spending will add to the general level of prices (inflation) and comparatively little to real output.

The multiplier model that we are working through can be traced back to Keynes. The focus of Keynes's attention in *The General Theory* (1936) was the Great Depression. Perhaps his development and discussion of the multiplier was not overly concerned with changes in the price level, because inflation, at that point, was hardly a concern for anyone.

5. In the simple model which we consider in the first part of the chapter, only two things could throw an economy out of equilibrium: a decision to change the level of investment up or down and/or a decision to change the level of consumption up or down. Either the *I* line must shift or the *C* line must shift. Without one or the other of these shifts, a Keynesian equilibrium is, in this simple model, eternally durable.

Investment is, of course, inherently volatile. That was one of the lessons of the last chapter. Disturbances to equilibria in simple models like ours are therefore usually cast in terms of sudden, unanticipated changes in *I*, and that is the approach taken here. The consumption function can also shift, to be sure, but the effects of such a shift are similar to the effects of a change in investment, and their coverage is postponed until later.

B. Fiscal Policy in the Multiplier Model

1. The multiplier applies to both external and internal variables that influence and buffet the economy. External changes include wars, the weather, and OPEC oil price changes. Some examples of internal variables that affect the economy via the multiplier are government spending, taxes, and investment. Sometimes these changes are expected, sometimes they are not. Sometimes these changes are very beneficial and help stabilize the economy, and sometimes they do not. The main point here is that a solid understanding of what multipliers are and how they influence the economy is critical to your understanding of macroeconomics. Policymakers must have an appreciation for the working of the multiplier.

2. Economists have long recognized the role the government plays in providing collective or public goods and redistributing income. Keynesian macroeconomic theory further defined the role of government to include stabilizing the economy via active fiscal policy measures. Fiscal policy, when used appropriately, has a significant impact on output, employment, and prices.

3. The government finances its expenditures by taxing (and borrowing). *Lump-sum taxes* are introduced when a fixed sum of money is collected by the government as taxes, regardless of the level of output in the economy. In this case, *DI* is no longer equal to GDP. However, the relationship between the two terms is very direct:

$$DI + T = \text{GDP}$$

4. Government spending (*G*), like investment is treated as exogenous with respect to GDP. The government spending schedule has no slope of its own—it is a horizontal line when plotted against GDP. This is not to say that *G* cannot change. In fact, government spending will change frequently. This is precisely what fiscal policy is all about. A change in *G* means the total spending line will shift up or down. Total spending in the economy now equals *C + I + G*. (The only remaining term to be added is net exports.)

5. If total spending in the economy exceeds the level of output, the economy will expand. Alternatively, if *C + I + G* is less than the level of output, the economy will contract.

6. The effect of a change in G on GDP is *exactly* the same as a change in *I*. It represents a change in spending outside of, or beyond, the consumption function. Therefore, the same *expenditure multiplier* can be used: 1/(1 - *MPC*) = 1/*MPS*.

7. *The tax multiplier equals the expenditure multiplier times MPC.* When the government changes taxes, there will also be a multiplied effect on the economy. However, the tax multiplier will always be smaller than the expenditure multiplier. Here is the reason: When the government raises taxes, households will not pay for the additional tax *entirely* by reducing *C*. They will pay *part* of the tax increase by drawing down *S*. Similarly, when taxes are reduced, households do not typically spend their entire tax cut. Part of the new-found income is saved. Most likely you can appreciate the

importance of the *MPC* in determining the allocation of the tax between *C* and *S*. When taxes change, disposable income changes. The *MPC* determines how much of the *DI* change is spent. This is the logic behind the tax multiplier formula above.

8. This last point should be helpful for those working through problem 9 in the Questions for Discussion section at the end of the chapter in the **textbook**.

Keynes pointed out that if everyone in an economy attempted to save more at the same time, spending in the economy would be reduced. This reduction in spending would cause a contraction in the economy, layoffs would occur, income would fall, and savings would actually decrease—the exact opposite of what people were trying to do.

Remember, Keynes was writing during the Depression. The last thing we needed, Keynes argued, was reduced spending—for whatever reason. During the Depression, firms were cutting back and going out of business. There was just no way businesses were willing or able to increase investment, even if savings had increased.

In a growing economy that is at, or close to, full employment, we can count on firms picking up the slack and investing more when savings increase. When the economy is fully employed, firms have a much greater incentive to add to their capital bases. So, one of the keys to resolving the **paradox of thrift** is knowing the economic health of the nation. The closer the economy is to full employment, the less we have to worry about the paradox.

V. HELPFUL HINTS

1. Do not forget: The *G* in aggregate demand measures the government's purchases of goods and services. This is not the same thing as the government's budget expenditures, which include transfer payments and interest on the debt.

2. The assumption of constant wages and prices when the multiplier model is first introduced allows us to measure its effect on output *only*. The closer the economy is to full employment, the smaller the real change will be and the larger the price increase will be.

3. When the economy is at full employment, we can say it is operating at its potential. *Full employment GDP equals potential GDP.*

4. In a simple economy, without government spending, taxes, trade, or international finance, GDP can be used interchangeably with disposable income (DI).

5. Stimulative fiscal policy works best when there are unemployed resources. The closer an economy is to full employment, the less *real* change there will be in output and the more inflation there will be as a result of stimulative fiscal policy.

6. The terms GDP and *Q* can be used interchangeably. They both represent the output of the economy.

7. Transfers to households are like *negative* taxes. When we talk about taxes we are really talking about *net taxes* or *taxes less transfers*. Taxes themselves are always greater than transfer payments because in addition to redistributing income, the government needs money to purchase goods and services.

8. When lump-sum taxes change, the *C* and hence the *C* + *I* + *G* + *X* lines will *shift*. These lines shift to the *right* by the amount of the tax *increase* and to the *left* the amount of the tax *decrease*. The magnitude of the vertical shift is equal to the change in tax multiplied by the *MPC*.

VI. MULTIPLE CHOICE QUESTIONS

These questions are organized by topic from the chapter outline. Choose the best answer from the options available.

A. The Basic Multiplier Model

1. Suppose that business firms change their plans and increase the total of their spending on new plant and equipment. The basic multiplier model would lead us to expect:
   a. no change in GDP.
   b. GDP and consumer spending to rise.
   c. GDP to rise but consumer spending to be unaffected.
   d. GDP to rise but consumer spending to fall.
   e. GDP to fall but consumer spending to rise.

2. In the simplest Keynesian model with only consumption and investment contributing to aggregate demand, if the value of the marginal propensity to consume is 0.8, then the value of the multiplier must be:
   a. 1.6.
   b. 2.5.
   c. 2.8.
   d. 4.0.
   e. 5.0.

3. If an equilibrium level of GDP were altered by a reduction in planned investment spending, then we would expect to see GDP:
   a. fall but saving (*S*) rise.
   b. fall but no change in *S*.
   c. fall and *S* fall also.
   d. remain unchanged but *S* fall.
   e. none of the preceding.

4. Assume that government spending and net exports are both zero. On a graph that plots spending against GDP, the intersection of the consumption function and a 45° line drawn up from the origin necessarily indicates:
   a. the GDP level at which net investment spending (*I*) first rises above zero.
   b. equality of consumption (*C*) and *I*.
   c. equilibrium GDP.
   d. equality of *C* and saving.

e. none of the above, unless *I* happens to be zero.

5. Consider a simple economy with no government or trade. Actual GDP would then be above its equilibrium level if:

a. the amount that consumers planned to save exceeded the amount that businesses and others planned to invest.

b. the total of planned consumption spending (*C*) exceeded the total of planned *I*.

c. there were no unscheduled or unplanned *I*.

d. GDP had moved temporarily above the break-even point on the consumption function.

e. the total of planned *I* plus the total of planned *C* exceeded the current level of GDP.

6. Which alternative in question 5 would have been correct had that question referred to a GDP below its equilibrium level?

a.
b.
c.
d.
e.

7. Suppose that the current level of GDP is $500 billion and that consumers wish to spend $390 billion of that $500 billion on consumption. Let the total amount of investment spending planned be $120 billion. These figures indicate that GDP is:

a. out of equilibrium and will fall in the future.

b. out of equilibrium and will rise in the future.

c. out of equilibrium, but whether it will rise, fall, or remain at its present level is indeterminate.

d. in equilibrium.

e. none of the above necessarily, since from the information given, GDP may be in equilibrium or out of it.

8. If GDP is in equilibrium, then:

a. consumption must be just equal to investment.

b. business receipts from consumption spending must just equal national income.

c. any increase in spending must result in an inflationary gap.

d. the overall budgets of federal, state, and local governments must be just balanced.

e. none of the above is necessarily correct.

9. Whenever total planned investment exceeds the total of planned saving, then:

a. GDP will fall below potential GDP.

b. GDP will rise above potential GDP.

c. GDP will rise if initially below potential GDP.

d. GDP will fall only if initially at potential GDP.

e. there is no reason to expect any change in GDP, either up or down, or to expect, as a necessary result, any change in potential GDP.

10. When we assume that planned investment spending is independent of GDP, then:

a. when investment is plotted against GDP, it will be a horizontal line.

b. the *C* + *I* spending line will be parallel to, and have the same slope as, the consumption schedule.

c. we assume that GDP has no direct influence on investment.

d. we are making a simplifying assumption about investment to get a better understanding of the basic multiplier model.

e. all the above.

11. When actual investment is greater than planned investment:

a. households are saving less than firms anticipated they would.

b. the economy could still be at an equilibrium position.

c. relative to household consumption plans, firms produced too many goods and services.

d. capital depreciation in the economy must be increasing.

e. the multiplier is getting larger.

12. The basic multiplier model does not work very well when the economy is close to full employment because:

a. it is difficult for the economy to produce more real output.

b. prices tend to become more inflexible as the economy gets closer to potential GDP.

c. potential GDP is a moving target which is nearly impossible to hit with precision.

d. it is not meaningful to talk about full employment in a simple economy.

e. none of the above.

B. Fiscal Policy in the Multiplier Model

13. Lump-sum taxes:

a. equate government spending and taxes.

b. ensure that *DI* will equal GDP.

c. are constant, regardless of GDP.

d. are paid from savings.

e. none of the above.

14. Government spending is plotted as a horizontal line with respect to GDP because:

a. we assume, for simplicity, that *G* is independent of GDP.

b. the tax multiplier is smaller than the expenditure multiplier.

c. government spending has not changed in recent years.

d. all the above.

e. none of the above.

15. The stimulative effect of a tax cut is smaller than an equivalent dollar increase in government spending because:

a. a portion of the tax cut will be saved.

b.   the *MPC* is less than 1.

c.   the vertical shift in the spending line is less for changes in *T* than for changes in *G*.

d.   all the above.

e.   none of the above.

16. When government spending changes, the effect on the economy is:

a.   the same as a change in taxes.

b.   smaller than a change in taxes.

c.   the same as a change in investment.

d.   larger than a change in investment.

e.   greater than a tax change, but smaller than a change in investment.

17. Which expression below best describes the relationship between the *tax multiplier* and the *expenditure multiplier*?

a.   expenditure multiplier = tax multiplier × *MPC*.

b.   tax multiplier = expenditure multiplier × *MPC*.

c.   expenditure multiplier + tax multiplier = 1.

d.   tax multiplier = expenditure multiplier × *MPC*.

e.   expenditure multiplier = tax multiplier / (1-*MPC*).

18. During the Reagan administration:

a.   fiscal policy was rarely used.

b.   the paradox of thrift was resolved.

c.   the economy experienced both recession and prosperity.

d.   exports exceeded imports.

e.   none of the above.

19. If GDP is in equilibrium in an economy with government, then:

a.   consumption must be just equal to investment.

b.   business receipts from consumption spending must just equal national income.

c.   any increase in spending must result in an inflationary gap.

d.   the overall budgets of federal, state, and local governments must be just balanced.

e.   none of the above is necessarily correct.

20. GDP is in equilibrium at its full-employment level. The federal government finds it necessary to increase its expenditures on goods and services by $10 billion. It wants to increase taxes sufficiently so that there will be no more serious threat of inflation; i.e., it wants the net change in the equilibrium level of GDP to be zero. The probable increase in tax collections needed will be:

a.   more than $10 billion.

b. $10 billion.

c.   less than $10 billion, but not zero.

d.   zero.

e.   less than zero; i.e., tax collections can be reduced.

21. There is a small but significant difference between the multiplier effect of an increase of, say, $10 in government spending and that of a decrease of $10 in personal taxes levied. This is because:

a.   government spending, by increasing income earned, increases consumption spending.

b.   a $10 reduction in taxation has a significantly greater effect on the government surplus or deficit than does a $10 increase in government spending.

c.   a tax reduction affects consumer income and spending directly, whereas the effect of an increase in government spending on consumers is only indirect.

d.   a $10 reduction in personal taxes does not produce a $10 increase in consumer spending, since part of this reduction goes into extra saving.

e.   none of the above reasons.

22. Whenever total planned investment exceeds the total of all planned saving in an economy with government, then:

a.   GDP will fall below potential GDP.

b.   GDP will rise above potential GDP.

c.   GDP will rise if initially below potential GDP.

d.   GDP will fall only if initially at potential GDP.

e.   there is no reason to expect any change in GDP, either up or down, or to expect, as a necessary result, any change in potential GDP.

23. Assume that the following conditions hold:

A.   GDP is initially in equilibrium.

B.   The government then increases its total expenditure on goods and services by $2 billion.

C.   There is no increase at all in tax collection.

D.   The marginal propensity to consume is 0.75.

Assuming that there are no price-inflationary consequences in the new equilibrium thus produced, GDP will:

a.   fall by $4 billion.

b.   rise by $2 billion.

c.   rise by $6 billion.

d.   rise by $8 billion.

e.   rise by $4 billion.

24. Which alternative in question 23 would be correct if that question referred to a total reduction of $2 billion in the government's income tax collections, with *no increase* at all in its expenditure on goods and services?

a.

b.

c.

d.

e.

VII.   PROBLEM SOLVING

The following problems are designed to help you apply the concepts that you learned in the chapter.

A. The Basic Multiplier Model

1.   Consider the consumption and investment diagrams in Figure 8-3.

Figure 8-3

Figure 8-4

a., Look first at the solid investment line in the right-hand diagram To draw this line horizontally is to say that investment spending (**rises / remains unchanged / falls**) as GDP increases.

b. The left-hand diagram says that if GDP were equal to 0E, consumption spending would be (*HA / JA / ME / KE*). With GDP at 0E, saving would equal (*HA /JA / MK / KE*).

c. If GDP were to fall to 0A, however, then C spending would equal (*HA /JA / ME / KE*), and S would equal (*HJ / JA / MK / KE*).

d. Saving (*S*) must equal investment (*I*) if GDP is to be in equilibrium. Assume that the same scale of measurement was used to construct both of the diagrams in Figure 8-3. Measure the two levels of saving in the left-hand diagram (*HJ* and *MK*), and compare them with the investment amount indicated along the solid *I* line on the right. The *S* value which would match this *I* value would be (*HJ / MK*). At this point, GDP is equal to (*0A / 0E*).

e. Now suppose that the level of investment spending decreases such that *R*0 rather than *B*0 indicates the level of investment spending in the economy. Again measuring *S* against *I*, it follows that saving would now be (*HJ/ MK*) and GDP would equal (*0A / 0E*).

f. When investment spending drops from *B*0 to *R*0, then C spending (**also drops / remains unchanged / increases**) in the new equilibrium.

2. By now, it should be clear that investment spending plays an important role in determining the level of GDP. We must, therefore, explore more fully what happens when the level of *I* spending changes. For this, we will use Figure 8-4. Assume that GDP is initially at equilibrium at a level of $100, with *I* spending at $30 and C spending at $70. Suppose investment spending then decreases, dropping from $30 to $20. The horizontal *I* line of Figure 8-4 drops to a new and lower position at *I'*. We can follow the move to a new equilibrium in a step-by-step manner, as outlined in the next several paragraphs.

The flow of total spending directed toward producers drops immediately from $100 to $90 because the *I* spending component of this flow has dropped. It will take a little time before consumers begin to feel the impact of this drop. When business was paying out $100 in wages and salaries, interest, and dividend payments, it was simply passing on money it received from the buyers of consumption and investment goods. When (because of the drop in investment spending) this incoming flow drops to $90, the earnings flow (wages and salaries, dividend payments, etc.) must also drop correspondingly. There is no alternative source which could maintain the sum of those payments at the old $100 level. Some workers will be laid off or required to work part-time, and total profits earned by business will fall. Specifically, the flow of earned income reaching consumers must likewise drop from $100 to $90. Not great news, to be sure, but the news gets worse.

a. When income (measured here as GDP) drops, consumption will (**drop / restrain constant / rise**); this is what the consumption function tells us. The question is, by how much? To answer this, we must know the marginal propensity to consume. Suppose, for example, that the *MPC* is 0.6. This would mean that the reduction in consumption prompted by the initial $10 reduction in income would equal (**$0 / $6 / $10**). That is, consumption would equal (**$10 / $64 / $70 / $90 / $100**) instead of $70 if income fell from $100 to $90; saving, meanwhile, would equal (**$0 / $6 / $10 / $26 / $30 / $36**) instead of $30.

b. Investment has fallen to $20. Is *S* equal to *I* after the decrease in C? (**yes / no**) Is GDP at an equilibrium level? (**yes / no**)

We have now reached the point in the analysis at which the notion of "multiplier" must be considered. Although consumption has fallen from $70 to $64 in response to the $10 drop in GDP, we are still nowhere near a new equilibrium GDP level. The fact that GDP is still out of equilibrium is evident from the fact that *S* ($26) is still not equal to *I* ($20). The important point to note here is that the reduction in consumption spending has exactly the same effect on production and on income as the initial drop in investment. So, GDP will continue to fall.

c. When I first decreased, GDP fell by $10. Now, in response to the decrease in C, GDP will fall by an additional (**$3 / $6 / $10**). GDP, which first fell from $100 to $90, will now drop further, to (**$60 / $80 / $84 / $88**).

d. It is not necessary to pursue this repeated sequence of consumption and savings adjustments to its logical conclusion. It should be clear that it will gradually dampen, ending when (with investment at $20) (**GDP has fallen to zero / saving has fallen to zero / saving has fallen to $20**).

This question had two objectives. First, it exercised your understanding of equilibrium. Throughout, in fact, the economy was out of equilibrium. To cement your grasp of why, recall what happened when GDP first fell to $90. By the $S = I$ test, $C = $70 and $I = $20 could not have been in equilibrium because saving was $30. But what of the consumption side of the analysis; did total spending match supply? When GDP fell to $90, C fell to $64, and $C + I$ equaled $84—hardly an equilibrium position.

Second, there was an initial elaboration of the multiplier sequence. Mathematically, this kind of sequence is known as a "convergent geometric progression"—an elegant phrase, useful for impressing your friends (or some of them) on social occasions, if you can manage to work it into the conversation. All you need to know about such a progression is that its sum has a finite limit. That is, GDP does not keep dropping until it collapses to zero or below. The sequence involved here is as follows: $10 + 6 + 3.6 +$ etc. The sum of this sequence, fully extended, is 25, not infinity. The full GDP drop will be $25, and GDP, upon dropping from its original value of $100, will stop when it reaches a new equilibrium at $75.

How do we know that? A straight-line consumption function with an MPC of 0.6 (i.e., a slope of 0.6) which matches a GDP value of $100 with a consumption value of $70 (the original equilibrium position) must have the following equation:

$$C = \$10 + 0.6 \text{ (GDP)}$$

And this means that:

$$S = -\$10 + 0.4 \text{ (GDP)}$$

Try it! GDP = $100 means that $C = $10 + $60 = $70. So what happens when GDP = $75? $C = $10 + $45 = $55, and $S = $75 - $55 = $20. Since I now equals $20, this must be in equilibrium. Also, $C + I = $55 + $20 = $75 =$ GDP.

3. Saving equals investment in equilibrium, so we must be able to use a saving-investment diagram to illustrate equilib-

rium GDP. If we know the consumption function, then we can derive the savings schedule according to $S = $ GDP - C. In Figure 8-5, the SS line is such a savings schedule; it corresponds to the consumption function in Figure 8-4. The solid I line is also replicated from Figure 8-4. The intersection of the SS and I curves, at GDP = $100, indicates the initial equilibrium GDP level, because it is the only GDP level at which S and I are equal.

Figure 8-5

a. The dashed I' line shows what happens if I spending drops from $30 to $20. The new equilibrium GDP must be (**$20 / $30 / $60 / $75 / $90 / $100**), for the same reason as before. If I spending is to be $20, then S must be $20 also; $75 is the only GDP level at which S is $20.

b. Also shown in Figure 8-5 is a dotted I'' line, at $40. If I spending were to rise to this level, the diagram indicates that the resulting GDP equilibrium level would be (**$75 / $100 / $110 / $125 / $150**).

4. In Figure 8-6, the line CC is the same consumption function we have used before. At the GDP level indicated by $0G$ in Figure 8-6, C spending would be DG.

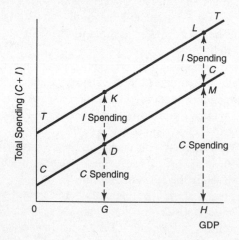

Figure 8-6

For purposes of considering GDP, of course, our interest is in total spending (consumption spending plus investment spending), and there is no reason why investment cannot be added to consumption on a standard diagram to reflect total spending. Simply draw the line TT above CC, and make the vertical distance between these two lines an immediate reflection of investment. The *TT* line thus reflects aggregate demand for any level of GDP.

    a. The vertical distance from any point on *TT* down to the axis line now measures total spending, *C* + *I*. At GDP level *0G*, for example, investment would equal *KD*, consumption would equal *DG*, and total spending, *I* + *C*, would equal *KG*—i.e., *KD* plus *DG*. Similarly, if the GDP level were *0H*, then investment would be indicated by (**LM / DG / MH**) and consumption spending would *equal* (**LM / DG / MH**). Total spending would be measured by (**LM / KG / MH / LH**).

Figure 8-7 is basically the same as Figure 8-6. The same *CC* and *TT* lines appear; in fact, only a 45° line has been added. The fundamental issue, now, is this: Pick any level of GDP at random. Given a consumption function and a level of investment, would that GDP represent an equilibrium?

Figure 8-7

    b. For example, take a GDP of *0G* in Figure 8-7. Total spending, *C* + *I*, would then be *KG*, but point *K* is off the 45° line and *KG* is not equal to *0G*. That is, GDP would not be equal to *C* + *I*. In fact, an equilibrium GDP level can occur only at the point where the total-spending line, *TT*, cuts across the 45° line. This is at point *R*, indicating a GDP of *0E*. Here, total spending of *RE* (**is / is not**) equal to GDP of *0E*.

    c. At any GDP lower than (to the left of) *0E*, *S* would be (**less than / equal to / greater than**) *I*. At any GDP higher than (to the right of) *0E*, *S* would be (**less than / equal to / greater than**) *I*.

5. Any change in *I* spending has a magnified, or "multiplied," effect on the GDP level because it sets off a series of *C* changes (as outlined earlier).

    a. If the multiplier equals 3 and investment increases by $10 billion, then GDP would (**rise / fall**) by (**$10 /**

$20 / $30 / $40 / $50) billion.

    b. If *I* spending rose by $10 billion with a multiplier of 4, then GDP would (**rise / fall**) by (**$10 / $20 / $30 / $40 / $50**) billion.

The multiplier formula in a simple Keynesian model with only consumption (as a function of GDP) and investment is

$$\text{Expenditure multiplier } = \frac{1}{1 - MPC} = \frac{1}{MPS}$$

    c. This means that if the *MPC* is 0.6, the multiplier equals (**1 / 2 / 2.5 / 3 / 3.5 / 4**). If the *MPC* is 0.8, the multiplier equals (**1 / 2 / 2.5 / 3 / 3.5 / 4 / 5**).

    d. Suppose there is a change in investment (either a rise or a fall) of $10. If the *MPC* equals 0.6, then the resulting change in GDP (rise or fall) is (**$10 / $20 / $25 / $30 / $50**) . If the *MPC* equals 0.8, then the resulting change in GDP (rise or fall) is (**$10 / $20 / $25 / $30 / $50**).

(*Note*: The multiplier formula given above holds only in the simplified conditions specified. We will soon incorporate some complications, and the multiplier formula will be changed accordingly.)

6. Table 8-1 describes a simple economy's consumption function.

Table 8-1

GDP	C
130	112
150	126
170	140
190	154
210	168
230	182
250	196
270	210
290	224
310	238

    a. If the amount of investment spending were $60, then equilibrium GDP would equal $_____.

    b. If investment fell to $30, equilibrium GDP would equal $_____.

7. Consult Figure 8-8. The top panel illustrates equilibrium in the consumption-investment geometry of the Keynesian model; the bottom panel presents equilibrium using aggregate supply and aggregate demand. Remember that the top diagram holds prices *fixed*, whereas the bottom diagram has price as a variable on the *Y* axis. Note also that the shape of the aggregate supply curve drawn there is an extreme representation of the shape identified previously. We are assuming here that the highest level of real output that this economy can achieve is $120. This point represents complete full employment of all resources: no more can be produced.

Figure 8-8

a.   Draw, first of all, an aggregate demand curve in the lower panel of Figure 8-8 that would support the same equilibrium level as curve *TT* in the upper panel.

b.   Now let investment increase to *I'* so that *T'T'* becomes the appropriate representation of total spending. Draw a second aggregate demand curve in the bottom panel to illustrate the same new equilibrium. Reading from the vertical and horizontal axes, it appears that the $10 increase in investment has produced a (**$5 / $10 / $15 / $30**) increase in GDP; the multiplier would, therefore, appear to be _____.

c.   Consider, finally, line *T"T"* in the upper panel. It would appear, given the geometry of the upper panel, that the second $10 increase in investment should, by producing *T"T"*, cause GDP to increase by another $_____.

d.   This will, however, not be the case, because *T'T'* has already brought GDP up to its maximum potential. The second increase in *I* will simply cause (**prices / employment / output**) to rise. Show this by drawing a third aggregate demand curve in the lower panel.

8.   Table 24-1 from your text is reproduced here as Table 8-2.

a.   Use the axes in Figures 24-9 and 24-10 to plot these data. In Figure 8-9, plot saving and investment. Indicate the level of equilibrium GDP in the economy.

Figure 8-9

b.   In Figure 8-10, plot *C*, *C + I*, and the 45° line. The equilibrium levels of GDP should line up vertically in the two diagrams.

Table 8-2 Equilibrium Output Can Be Found Arithmetically as the
Level Where Planned Spending Equals GDP
GDP Determination Where Output Equals Planned Spending
(billions of dollars)

(1) Levels of GDP and DI	*(2)* Planned Consumption	*(3)* Planned Saving (3) = (1) - (2)	*(4)* Planned Investment	*(5)* Level of GDP (5) = (1)	*(6)* Total Planned Spending and Investment (6) = (2) + (4)	*(7)* Resulting Tendency of Output
4,200	3 800	400	200	4,200 >	4,000	↓ Contraction
3,900	3 600	300	200	3,900 >	3,800	↓ Contraction
3,600	3,400	200	200	3,600 =		*Equilibrium*
3,300	3,200	100	200	3,300 <	3,400	↑ Expansion
3,000	3,000	0	200	3,000 <	3,200	↑ Expansion
2,700	2,800	-100	200	2,700 <	3,000	↑ Expansion

Figure 8-10

c. What is the value of the *MPC*?

d. What is the value of the *MPS* ?

e. Write down an equation for the consumption schedule. (*Hint*: It should be in the form of:

$$C = \text{intercept} + (MPC \times GDP).)$$

f. What is the value of the multiplier?

g. Assume that there are idle resources and room for expansion in the economy. If investment spending changes by $50, what will be the new equilibrium level of GDP?

h. At the new equilibrium position, *C* = ____, and *S* = ____.

B. Fiscal Policy in the Multiplier Model

9. Consider Figure 8-11. The two consumption schedules illustrate the effect of a *lump-sum tax* on household spending. The solid line, *CC*, represents consumer spending before the tax; the dashed line, *C'C'*, shows consumption after the tax. (Note that the vertical distance between the two consumption schedules is $300 and the rightward shift is equal to $400.)

a. What is the value of the *MPC*? ___

b. How large is the (lump-sum) tax increase? ___

c. When GDP is $4000, what is *DI*? ___

d. What is the value of the *expenditure multiplier*? ___

e. What is the value of the *tax multiplier*? ___

f. What economic problem might the government have been trying to correct when it imposed the tax in the first place?

g. Besides raising taxes, what other fiscal policy action could the government have taken to correct this problem?

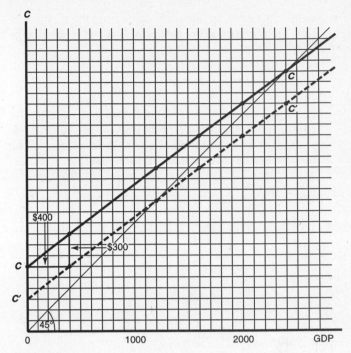

Figure 8-11

10. Needless to say, once we have taxes in our model, we need to include government spending as well. Figure 8-12 includes an after-tax consumption schedule for the economy. Investment is independent of GDP and is equal to $200. Government spending is also assumed to be independent of GDP and is equal to $300.

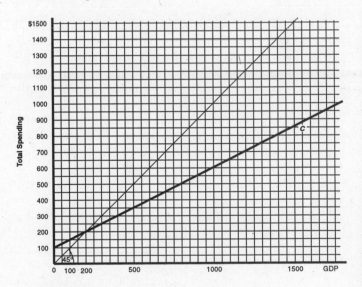

Figure 8-12

a. Plot the *C + I* line on the diagram. What is the value of the intercept? ____

b. Plot the *C + I + G* total-spending line on the diagram. What is the value of its intercept? ____

c.   If government spending increases, the $C + I + G$ line will shift (**up / down / not at all**) due to the change in (C / I / G).

d.   If lump-sum taxes increases, the $C + I + G$ line will shift (**up / down / not at all**) due to the change in (C / I / G).

e.   If the changes in taxes and government spending from parts c and d are of equal magnitude, then (**both shifts will be of equal size / the shift in part c will be larger / the shift in part d will be larger**).

11. Table 8-3 represents an economy that has taxes and government spending but is not yet open to trade.

Table 8-3 Output Determination with Government

(1) GDP	(2) Taxes	(3) DI	(4) C	(5) I	(6) G	(7) C + I + G
1200	200	___	900	200	300	1400
1450	___	___	1100	___	___	___
1700	___	___	1300	___	___	___
1950	___	___	1500	___	___	___
2200	___	___	1700	___	___	___
2450	___	___	1900	___	___	___
2700	___	___	2100	___	___	___

a.   Taxes in the economy are lump-sum, so you can easily complete the rest of column (2).

b.   Investment and government spending are both independent of GDP, so you can fill in the rest of columns (5) and (6) as well.

c.   Complete the disposable income entries in column (3).

d.   Calculate total spending for the economy in column (7).

e.   What is the equilibrium level of GDP in the economy?

f.   When the economy is at equilibrium, what is the level of saving?

When the economy is at equilibrium, investment should equal saving. Now that the government is included, we have to allow for the possibility of government saving. Government saving is equal to $T - G$. (If the difference between T and G is negative, then the government is borrowing, or running a deficit.)

g.   Determine if $I = S + (T - G)$ when the economy is at equilibrium.

h.   What is the value of the *MPC*?

i.   What is the value of the expenditure multiplier?

j.   What is the value of the tax multiplier?

k.   If the government increases spending by $100, what would be the new equilibrium value of GDP?

l.   What economic problem might exist for the government to make this fiscal policy change?

m.   If the government wanted to achieve the same change in GDP as in part **k** by cutting taxes instead, how large would the tax cut have to be?

VIII. DISCUSSION QUESTIONS

Answer the following questions, making sure that you can explain the work you did to arrive at the answers.

1.   Figure 24-2 from the text is reproduced here as Figure 8-13. Explain why point M represents the equilibrium point in this simple economy and explain how this economy would move toward equilibrium if GDP were less than M and I was greater than S.

Figure 8-13

2.   Figure 24-3 from the text is reproduced on page **XXX** as Figure 8-2. Explain why point M represents the equilibrium point in this simple economy and explain how this economy would move toward equilibrium if GDP were greater than M and the level of output was greater than $C + I$.

3.   Explain, in your own words, how an increase in investment spending generates a multiplied effect on GDP.

4.   Why is it that the multiplier model becomes less and less valid as an economy gets closer and closer to full employment?

5.   Explain what the tax multiplier is and why it is less than the expenditure multiplier.

IX. ANSWERS TO STUDY GUIDE QUESTIONS

III. Review of Key Concepts

4   Closed economy
9   Actual investment
8   Lump-sum taxes
1   Expenditure multiplier
7   Tax multiplier
3   Fiscal policy
5   Equilibrium
2   Marginal propensity to consume
6   Open economy

VI. Multiple Choice Questions

1. B   2. E   3. C   4. E   5. A   6. E
7. B   8. E   9. C   10. E   11. C   12. A
13. C   14. A   15. D   16. C   17. B   18. C
19. E   20. A   21. D   22. C   23. D   24. C

VII. Problem Solving

1. a. remains unchanged
   b. *KE, MK*
   c. *JA, HJ*
   d. *MK, 0E*
   e. *HJ, 0A*
   f. also drops
2. a. drop, $6, $64, $26
   b. no, no
   c. $6, $84
   d. saving has fallen to $20
3. a. $75
   b. $125
4. a. *LM, MH, LH*
   b. is
   c. less than, greater than
5. a. rise, $30
   b. rise, $40
   c. 2.5, 5
   d. $25, $50
6. a. $270
   b. $170
7. a. See Figure 8-8 (top of right column).
   b. $30, 3
   c. $30
   d. prices
8. a. See Figure 8-9.

Figure 8-8

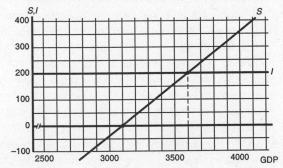

Figure 8-9

   b. See Figure 8-10 (bottom of right column).
   c. 0.67
   d. 0.33
   e. $C = 1000 + (0.67 \times \text{GDP})$
   f. 3
   g. $3,600 + $150 = $3,750
   h. $C = \$3,500, S = \$250$

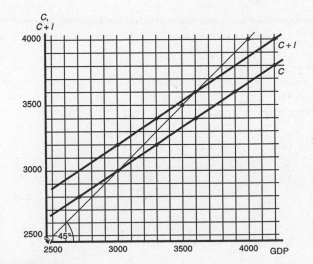

Figure 8-10

9. a. $MPC = 0.75$
   b. $400
   c. $3600

d. 4
e. 3
f. The government may have been trying to decrease inflation in the economy. Alternatively, it could be trying to balance its budget.
g. The government could decrease spending.
10. a. See Figure 8-12. The intercept is 300.

Figure 8-12

b. See Figure 8-12. The intercept is 600.
c. up, *G*
d. down, *C*
e. the shift in part c will be larger
11. a, b, c, d. See Table 8-3.

Table 8-3 Output Determination with Government

(1) GDP	(2) Taxes	(3) DI	(4) C	(5) I	(6) G	(7) C + I + G
1200	200	1000	900	200	300	1400
1450	200	1250	1100	200	300	1600
1700	200	1500	1300	200	300	1800
1950	200	1750	1500	200	300	2000
2200	200	2000	1700	200	300	2200
2450	200	2250	1900	200	300	2400
2700	200	2500	2100	200	300	2600

e. 2200
f. *DI - C* = 300
g. *I* = 200, *S* = 300, *T - G* = - 100. Yes, *I* = *S* + (*T - G*).
h. *MPC* = 200/250 = 0.8
i. 5
j. 4
k. The change in GDP equals $100 × 5 = $500. The new equilibrium value for GDP is $2700.
l. Unemployment may be high and the economy may be in a recession.

m. If the government wants GDP to increase by $500 and the tax multiplier is 4, the tax cut would have to be $125.

VIII. Discussion Questions

1. Saving can be viewed as the portion of disposable income that is not spent. Planned investment spending by firms will exactly offset that reduction in spending when the simple economy is at equilibrium. If GDP is less than *M* and investment is greater than saving, then from the firms' perspective households are spending more and saving less than the firms anticipated. Firms see their inventories being drawn down lower than they would like. Firms respond to this situation by increasing employment and output. Hence, the economy moves toward *M*.
2. At point *M* total spending (*C* + *I*) equals GDP or output. All the goods and services produced are purchased either by households or firms. If GDP is greater than *M*, total spending is less than output. Firms are left with unsold goods and services. In order to reduce their inventories, firms will lay off workers and produce fewer goods and services. The forces of the market will make GDP contract.
3. When investment spending increases, this creates additional employment opportunities for workers. The employees working on the investment project earn income. The *MPC* determines how much of that extra income, they will spend. As labor spends more money, the firms that sell goods and services to the workers earn more income, and they are encouraged to expand. This process continues, but at each subsequent step in the chain the additions to income and GDP get smaller and smaller.
4. As an economy gets closer and closer to full employment, it becomes more and more difficult to increase real output.

Once full employment is reached, the economy cannot produce any more. As certain industries experience an increased demand for their products, this will put upward pressure on prices. The only way an industry can expand is if it bids resources away from other sectors in the economy. The increase in output in one industry will be matched by a decrease in output in another industry, albeit at higher prices.
5. The tax multiplier is used to show the effect of a change in taxes on GDP. When the government raises taxes, households do not reduce their consumption spending by the full amount of the tax increase. Instead, they pay for part of the increase in taxes by reducing saving. Similarly, when taxes are cut, households save part of their increase in disposable income and do not spend it all. Therefore, a tax change has a smaller dollar for dollar impact on the economy than a change in government spending.

CHAPTER 9
Money and
Commercial Banking

I. CHAPTER OVERVIEW

The determination of national output has, up until now, been described with little or no reference to money. It is now time to correct this omission; money is perhaps the most powerful tool of modern stabilization policy, and to continue to ignore its potential would be an enormous mistake. As you progress through the next chapters, it will become clear to you that the omission was a matter of exposition—a recognition that we could not do everything at once. The models that were constructed in earlier chapters can be expanded to include the monetary side of an economy. It therefore made sense to develop them fully before adding a second, *financial* dimension to their stories.

Chapter 25 begins with a discussion of the evolution of money and its associated financial institutions. It is perhaps surprising to note here at the beginning that there is no single, functional definition of "money." Since there are different "near-money" financial instruments available from across a wide spectrum of contemporary financial institutions, it is not possible to write a single all-encompassing definition of money. Economists offer, instead, a list of definitions, each one applying to a slightly different notion and/or application of "money" or "credit."

In this chapter you are also introduced to the demand for and the supply of money. You may begin to suspect that you will shortly see a money market evolve, which could be incorporated into our multiplier model; this will happen in the next chapter. Before that happens, though, we need to learn a little more about money and commercial banking.

The final section explores other types of financial assets. Included here is a discussion of assets that lie outside the technical definitions of M_1 and M_2, but nevertheless are held in great quantities by millions of Americans. There is a brief analysis of the workings of the stock market as well as an introduction to some of the strategies of financial investment.

II. LEARNING OBJECTIVES

After you have read Chapter 25 in your text and completed the exercises in this *Study Guide* chapter, you should be able to:

1 Outline the highlights of the evolution of the monetary system from **barter**, through **commodity money**, and into today's system of **fiat money**.

2. Understand the differences between M_1 and M_2.

3. Discuss the role of interest rates in determining the price of money, and understand the differences between *nominal* and *real* interest rate movements.

4. Describe the three *functions of money* and explain their role in supporting the **transactions demand** and the **assets demand** for money.

5. Outline briefly the evolution of the banking system from a collection of simple goldsmith depositories of wealth into an interconnected array of banks and other financial intermediaries.

6. Describe the process by which a banking system built on **fractional reserves** can create money. Understand the mathematics behind the resulting **money multiplier**, and define the two qualifications upon which its precise computation is dependent.

7. Understand the trade-off between risk and return on financial investments.

8. Discuss some of the historical trends in the U.S. stock market, including the great crash of 1929 and the fall in October, 1987.

9. Understand the basis of the **efficient-market** hypothesis and how it translates into a **random walk** theory of stock market prices.

10. Understand the economic concepts that lie behind the formulation of a rudimentary personal financial strategy.

III. REVIEW OF KEY CONCEPTS

Match the following terms from column A with their definitions in column B.

A	B
__ Money	1. Measures the ease with which an asset can be converted into cash.
__ Barter	2. Money which is used to purchase goods and services—M_1 is considered this.

__ Monetary economy

__ Commodity money

__ Bank money

__ Transactions money

__ Fiat money

__ Broad money

__ Riskless interest rate

__ Liquidity

__ Nominal interest rate

__ Portfolio theory

__ Financial intermediary

__ Reserves

__ Money-supply multiplier

__ Multiple expansion of bank deposits

3. Process by which the banking system transforms reserves into a much larger amount of bank money.

4. Interest rate on money, measured in money terms; also called the money interest rate.

5. Anything that serves as a commonly accepted medium of exchange or means of payment.

6. Sometimes called asset money or near money, it includes M_1 plus savings accounts in banks and similar assets.

7. The exchange of goods for other goods.

8. Value determined by reserve requirements, and measures the number of times each new dollar of deposits is expanded into new money by the banking system.

9. Describes how investors diversify their wealth into different assets.

10. Bank assets held in the form of cash.

11. Checks written on funds deposited in a bank or other financial institution.

12. Particular physical good, with some intrinsic value, that also serves as a medium of exchange.

13. Rate of interest which is paid on loans that have virtually no chance of default or nonpayment.

14. Money that is recognized as the *legally* accepted medium of exchange.

15. Accepts deposits from one group of people and lends them to others.

16. Economic system in which trade takes place through a commonly accepted medium of exchange.

__ Inflation-indexed bonds

__ Transactions demand

__ Asset demand

__ Risk-averse

__ Balance sheet

__ Unit of account

__ Financial intermediary

__ Bank run

__ Bear market

__ Bull market

__ Margin purchases

__ Speculative bubble

__ Stock price index

__ Efficient-market theory

__ Random walk

b. Market prices contain all the available information on the value of a stock.

c. The use of money as a measure of current value or price.

d. Movements of stock prices which, over time, are completely unpredictable.

e. Repayment of the principal on a loan.

f. Occurs when many depositors go to a bank and attempt to withdraw their funds.

g. Price increases based on the market's expectation of further price increases, rather than on actual increases in firm profits or dividends.

h. U.S. government financial asset with interest payments linked to the price level in the economy.

i. Stock market with rising prices.

j. Weighted average of the prices of a group or basket of company stocks.

k. Institutions that take deposits from one group and lend the funds to other groups.

l. Financial statement comparing a company's asset with its liabilities and net worth.

m. The need for money to purchase goods and services.

n. Stock market with falling prices.

o. The desire to avoid taking gambles when making financial investments.

p. The holding of money as a store of value or wealth.

There are so many new terms and expressions in this chapter that we have included another section of matching. To help you keep the two sections separate, the expressions in this section are preceded with letters rather than numbers. Persistence now will pay off!

A

__ Amortization

B

a. Borrowing money to buy stock, using the stock itself for collateral on the loan.

IV. SUMMARY AND CHAPTER OUTLINE

This section summarizes the key concepts from the chapter.

A. Money and Interest Rates

1. The money used in the U.S. economy (and for that matter in most developed economies) has no intrinsic value, but its supply has an enormous effect on the nation's output, employment, and price level. It would be difficult to overstate its importance.

2. Economies based primarily on a **barter** system of transactions do not work very well. Individuals spend too many

precious (and scarce!) resources lining up trading partners and less time producing goods and services.

3. The primary measure of money that we will use in our model of the economy is **transactions money**, or M_1. M_1 includes coin and currency in circulation (i.e., not held by banks), plus demand and other checkable deposits. Our focus on money that is in circulation stems from our concern for money that can be used to facilitate economic transactions. Money held by banks has little influence on the pace of economic activity. The term *demand deposits* is used synonymously with *checking accounts* since you have access to this money anytime and anywhere you are, as long as you have your checkbook. The money is available upon (your) *demand*, as long as the recipient of the money is willing to accept your check. NOW accounts are an example of bother checkable deposits." The acronym stands for "*N*egotiable *O*rder of *W*ithdrawal." These are interest-bearing accounts that allow depositors to write checks.

4. While M_1 is the most appropriate measure of money as a means of payment, a broader monetary aggregate, M_2, is also watched very closely. M_2 includes M_1 plus savings accounts and small time-deposits. Savings accounts and time deposits earn interest and are slightly less liquid than the components of M_1. Over the past 10 years, this broader definition of money has been a more stable indicator of money supply growth than has M_1. This is due, in part, to all the new kinds of checking instruments that have been created by banks.

5. Interest rates are the price of money. If you *save*, you may view the interest you earn as a payment, or return to saving. It can also be considered as the price others (usually banks) are willing to pay you for the use of your money. Similarly, if you *borrow*, you must pay interest to compensate the lender for giving up the opportunity to use the money (that you borrowed) in some alternative use.

There is no one rate of interest for the economy. Other things held constant, the rate of interest will be higher:

    a. The longer the time to maturity of the deposit or loan.

    b. The greater the risk associated with that particular loan or financial investment.

    c. The less liquid the asset is. Liquidity measures the ease with which an asset can be converted into cash.

    d. The higher the administrative costs associated with the loan.

U.S. government securities (or bonds) are among the safest loans a saver can make because the U.S. government is very unlikely to default on its loans. For this reason the U.S. government is able to borrow money at relatively low rates of interest. This rate of interest is often referred to as the "riskless interest rate."

6. Lenders and borrowers alike need to be concerned about the effect of inflation on the value of their financial assets and debt. As inflation increases, the real value, or purchas-

ing power, of money decreases. Suppose you borrow $500 from a bank for one year at an interest rate of 6 percent. When the bank decides to give you a loan, it gives up the opportunity to use that $500 in other ways. In this particular case, let us assume that the bank gave up the opportunity to purchase a new $500 desk for one of its managers. At the end of the year, you must pay the bank back $530 ($500 × 1.06). Suppose further that during the year that you had your loan, inflation in the economy increased by 10 percent. The desk that the bank could have purchased last year now costs $550! When you pay back the loan, the bank cannot use your loan repayment—even with the interest—to purchase the desk. In real, or inflation-adjusted, terms, the bank lost money. *Nominally*, or in dollar terms, the bank earned 6 percent on its loan. However, in *real* terms it *lost* 4 percent! (The bank is now $20 short of the purchase price of the desk; $20 is 4 percent of $500.) You can calculate the real rate of interest very easily:

$$\text{Real rate} = \text{nominal rate} - \text{inflation rate}$$

In 1997 the government introduced *inflation-indexed bonds*. The interest rate on these 10-year bonds is indexed to the general price level. In addition, when the principal is repaid when the bond terminates, its value is also adjusted for inflation in the economy. You should realize that when the government (or any other organization) issues or sells bonds, it is really borrowing money. Buying bonds is a form of saving. Individuals buying government bonds get paid interest for their loan.

7. Money has no usefulness as a commodity. We cannot eat it or wear it or use it for shelter. We demand money so that we can use it to purchase the commodities we need or want. There are three basic functions that money performs. It serves as

    a. a medium of exchange

    b. a unit of account

    c. a store of value

The *medium of exchange* function is the most basic. If people do not universally accept the money (at least within a country) as a means of payment, then we are back to barter. It is that simple.

Unit of account means that whatever we use as money should also be used to measure prices or value. It would be silly to have dollars as our money and then measure prices in terms of apples or donuts or Mexican pesos.

Money serves as a *store of value* in that it does not physically deteriorate over time (this was a problem with some forms of commodity money) or lose its acceptability. Rates of interest on cash are naturally nonexistent, but NOW accounts and the components of M_2 earn interest. While these rates of interest are relatively low, there is also virtually no risk associated with this form of wealth.

8. The cost of holding wealth or assets as money is the for-

gone opportunity to earn higher rates of return or interest on other financial investments.

9. There are two main reasons why people hold wealth as money: (a) transactions demand and (b) asset demand. The transactions demand goes hand in hand with the medium of exchange function of money, while the asset demand matches up with the store of value function. While other assets may pay higher rates of interest, most portfolio managers diversify their wealth among different types of assets.

B. Banking and the Supply of Money

1. Banks hold a portion of their assets in the form of non-interest-earning *reserves*. These reserves are held on hand in the form of cash or are deposited with the central bank. The reserves are held to meet legal reserve requirements and to meet the day-to-day cash needs of the bank.

2. The fractional-reserve banking system enables banks to expand (or contract) the money supply. A portion of each new deposit must be held in the form of idle reserves, but the rest can be loaned out. As the money that is lent out is deposited in other banks, they "pick up the ball" and create additional new loans (money).

Just as the *MPS* was a key component of the expenditure multiplier, the reserve requirement is the key component of the money-supply multiplier.

$$\text{Money-supply multiplier} = \frac{1}{\text{required reserve ratio}}$$

Note that in both cases, the denominator indicates an amount of money that is being withdrawn from the system each time it changes hands. Every time a new deposit is made, the bank must withdraw the required reserves before loaning the rest to a new borrower. Likewise, every time a marginal dollar of income is earned by a household, a portion is saved before the rest is spent on consumption. The multipliers are *not* the same, but their structure is quite similar.

3. In reality, the money creation process will be diminished if banks hold excess reserves or when all of the new money is not deposited in banks.

Banks make loans in order to make profits. If bankers are pessimistic about the economy or the creditworthiness of loan applicants, they will make fewer loans and hold excess reserves. It is preferable to make no money (on reserves) than to lose money on bad loans.

The money creation process assumes that at each step along the way, the newly created money is deposited in someone's checking account. If, instead, the money is held outside of banks (it could even leave the country), then the expansion process will slow down.

C. A Tour of Wall Street

1. *Financial economics* studies how rational investors should allocate their funds to attain their financial objectives.

The word "rational" implies that individuals make use of all the available information in the market place. It does not mean that individuals are infallible or that mistakes never occur. After all, sometimes the information we receive is not entirely accurate. Besides money itself, and savings accounts, the main financial assets that households hold include government bonds and bills, stocks or equities, and pension funds. Generally, there is a trade-off between return and risk on financial assets. Assets with higher risk, or more volatility on their rate of return, usually offer the potential for greater earnings.

2. Millions of Americans have purchased stock in the **stock market**. In recent years, the U.S. stock market has reached one record high after another and new investors may not have learned that there is no guarantee that the market will always rise. While analysts seem to agree that current market increases have been fueled by a strong economy with low inflation and low unemployment, investors need to be wary of *speculative bubbles*. In this case, stock prices increase because people think they are going rise in the future. Such bubbles are not based on actual firm earnings or dividends and invariably pop.

In an **efficient market**, new information affects stock and commodity prices; predictable events have already been incorporated into market prices. Since the new information is unpredictable, prices in the market tend to follow a *random walk*.

V. HELPFUL HINTS

1. Money is like grease or oil for an engine; it makes the economy run more smoothly and efficiently.

2. "Small time-deposits" are savings deposits (at banks) of up to $100,000.

3. There is an example in Chapter 25 dealing with interest rates and monthly payments on a 30-year fixed-interest rate mortgage. If the *annual* rate of interest is 10 percent, you would have to pay one-twelfth of that every *month*. Each month your payment would include one-twelfth of 10 percent or 10/12 percent (or 0.833 percent) of the annual interest on the loan. Note that if the monthly payment is $877.58, over 30 years you would pay a total of $315,928.80, $215,928.80 of which is interest on the $100,000 loan!

4. Whether you lend or borrow, *always* make the effort to get an estimate of the (projected) rate of inflation in the economy. This is precisely why many banks now offer loans with rates of interest that vary over the life of the loan. They are protecting themselves against inflation.

5. There are other definitions of money beyond M_1 and M_2. As you move to "higher" definitions the additional components of money become less and less liquid. Each new broader definition of money includes the components of the lower-numbered definition that precedes it.

6. In recent years there have been many changes in the banking system. Many savings banks now offer checking or demand-deposit accounts, and commercial banks may offer savings-type accounts. While commercial banks are still the primary source of bank money (or checking accounts), the distinction between *commercial* banks and *savings* banks has become blurred.

7. When bankers and portfolio managers use the term *investment* they are probably not using it in our economic sense of the word. To avoid confusion, think of the assets these professionals work with as *financial investments*.

Remember, to economists *investment* means the purchase of something tangible that adds to the productivity capability of the economy. Companies may use the funds they receive from selling stocks and bonds to make investment purchases (new equipment, factories, etc.), but the stocks and bonds themselves are not considered investment. They are part of savings.

VI. MULTIPLE CHOICE QUESTIONS

These questions are organized by topic from the chapter outline. Choose the best answer from the options available.

A. Money and Interest Rates

1. Barter, the first step in the evolution of a monetary system above self-sufficiency, gave way to commodity money because:
   a. barter was an inefficient transaction mechanism involving high transaction cost incurred by the necessity of finding someone willing to trade what you have for what you want.
   b. barter was inconvenient at best.
   c. barter stood in the way of efficient division of labor unless the output was divisible.
   d. barter depended upon a double coincidence of wants that became increasingly unlikely as economies grew more diverse.
   e. all the above.

2. Commodity money was a step toward efficiency, but it was undermined frequently by:
   a. frequent relapse into barter.
   b. the vagaries of supply and demand for the commodity that altered the value of the money.
   c. the inability of communities to agree to one commodity.
   d. the inability of communities to find a commodity that was not perishable.
   e. none of the above.

3. The strictest definition of money, M_1, includes:
   a. coins, currency, and demand deposits.
   b. coins, currency, and time deposits.
   c. coins, currency, and all deposits in a bank.

d. all currencies and near-monies.
e. none of the above.

4. Financial intermediaries are institutions that:
   a. buy and sell all types of goods, including merchandise.
   b. include only international corporations that have large holdings of various types of currency.
   c. accept the deposits of some people and institutions and use that money to support the borrowing needs of others.
   d. are not really necessary in the United States because of the size of the federal debt.
   e. all the above.

5. Commercial banks are the largest category of financial intermediaries; others include:
   a. life insurance companies.
   b. pension funds.
   c. savings and loan institutions.
   d. money market funds.
   e. all the above.

6. The essential difference between money and near-money is that:
   a. money is directly spendable, whereas near-money is not.
   b. near-money includes all deposits in bank accounts, whereas money includes none of these.
   c. the velocity of circulation of money is rapid, while that of near-money is slow.
   d. near-money is fiat money, whereas money is not.
   e. near-money is made up of any and all items that can be marketed for a money price.

7. If you write a check on your bank account, that check:
   a. counts as part of M_1 provided it is a valid check, i.e., there are funds in the bank to support it.
   b. counts as part of M_1 whether valid or not, provided the person to whom it is given accepts it.
   c. counts as part of M_1 if used to buy goods and services, but not otherwise.
   d. does not count as part of M_1, since no bank account is considered part of the money supply.
   e. does not count as part of M_1; to count both it and the deposit account on which it is drawn would be double counting.

8. When money has been deposited in any private financial institution (e.g., a commercial bank, a savings and loan association, etc.), the critical factor in deciding whether that deposit should count as part of M_1 is that:
   a. checks can be freely written against the deposit by its owner.
   b. the deposit has insurance or backing by the government or some public institution.
   c. the institution maintains 100 percent backing or reserve for the deposit—whether the backing is provided by the government or not.

   d. the institution has a legal franchise which permits its deposits to be counted as money.

   e. as long as the money deposited consists of genuine bills or coins, then the deposit within any such institution must be counted as part of the money supply.

9. Money serves as:

   a. a medium of exchange.

   b. a store of value.

   c. a unit of account.

   d. all the above.

   e. none of the above.

10. On the basis of the transactions demand component of the demand for money:

   a. the demand for money climbs as the interest rate climbs.

   b. the demand for money climbs as the interest rate falls.

   c. the demand for money falls as nominal income rises.

   d. the demand for money falls as nominal income falls.

   e. none of the above.

11. Which answer to question 10 would have been correct had that question referred to the assets demand component of the demand for money?

   a.

   b.

   c.

   d.

   e.

12. The "demand for money" means:

   a. the desire to hold securities which can readily be converted into money at a fixed or near-fixed price if necessary.

   b. the amount which businesses will wish to borrow at any given interest rate.

   c. the desire to save more money out of income as protection against the uncertainties of the future.

   d. the same thing as "asset demand for money alone."

   e. the same thing as the sum of "assets and transactions demand for money."

B. Banking and the Supply of Money

13. In a fractional-reserve banking system, such as that of the United States, the required reserve ratios imposed on commercial banks:

   a. are primarily intended to set a limit on the total money supply rather than to serve as adequate protection against bank runs.

   b. are in excess of what is normally required but are sufficient to cover what would be needed if for any reason people became uneasy over the safety of bank deposits.

   c. are essentially an average of the amounts needed to meet the public's demands in good times and bad.

   d. are now obsolete, according to the text, and will shortly be replaced by a 100 percent reserve requirement.

   e. are not correctly described by any of the above.

14. The commercial banking system (all banks taken together) lends money to business firms and consumers, normally by setting up demand deposits which the borrowers may spend. As a result, the money supply:

   a. decreases by the total amount of all coins and bills deposited with the banking system for safe-keeping.

   b. neither increases nor decreases.

   c. increases by an amount somewhat less than the system's total coin-and-bill deposits, owing to the fraction it holds as reserves.

   d. increases by an amount just equal to the system's total coin-and-bill deposits.

   e. increases by an amount considerably greater than the system's total coin-and-bill deposits.

15. The economy's total money supply will increase whenever commercial banks:

   a. increase their deposits with a Federal Reserve Bank.

   b. increase their total loans to the public.

   c. increase their demand deposit liabilities by receiving coins or bills from the public as deposits.

   d. withdraw part of their deposits from a Federal Reserve Bank.

   e. reduce their demand-deposit liabilities by paying out part of these accounts in the form of coins or paper bills.

16. I deposit, in bank X, $10,000 in paper currency which has for a long time been hidden and out of circulation. The legal minimum reserve requirement for banks is 25 percent of deposits. Bank X is one among many banks. Unless bank X is already short on reserves, this deposit would enable the bank, if it wished, to increase its loans by at least:

   a. an undetermined amount.

   b. $7500.

   c. $10,000.

   d. $30,000.

   e. more than $30,000.

17. Assuming that the loan increase does not set off any increase of coins and paper currency in hand-to-hand circulation, the deposit described in question 16 would enable the banking system to increase its loans by a maximum of:

   a. zero.

   b. $7500.

   c. $10,000.

   d. $30,000.

   e. more than $30,000.

18. In the circumstances of questions 16 and 17, if consideration were given to some small increase of coins and paper currency in hand-to-hand circulation, the most probable maximum amount (among the five alternatives listed below) by which the banking system as a whole could increase loans would be:
    a. zero.
    b. less than $5000.
    c. between $20,000 and $30,000.
    d. between $30,000 and $40,000.
    e. more than $40,000.

19. Had bank X been a monopoly bank, with all other circumstances as in question 16 (including zero hand-to-hand circulation leakage), then the maximum amount by which this deposit would have enabled bank X to increase its loans, if so disposed, would be:
    a. zero.
    b. $7500.
    c. $10,000.
    d. $30,000.
    e. more than $30,000.

20. If the required reserve ratio had been 20 percent rather than 25 percent, with all other circumstances as in question 16, the deposit would have enabled bank X to increase its loans, if so disposed, by:
    a. zero.
    b. $2000.
    c. $8000.
    d. $10,000.
    e. $40,000.

21. If the deposit of question 16 (where the reserve requirement equaled 25 percent) had been a $10,000 check drawn on bank Y, then this deposit (considered in isolation from all other deposits or withdrawals) would have enabled bank X to increase its loans, if so disposed, by:
    a. zero.
    b. $7500.
    c. $10,000.
    d. $30,000.
    e. more than $30,000.

22. The deposit of question 21 would enable the entire banking system to increase its loans, if so disposed, by:
    a. zero.
    b. $7500.
    c. $10,000.
    d. $30,000.
    e. more than $30,000.

23. If the legal required reserve ratio is a minimum of 30 percent of the amount of demand deposits, and if the banking system now has excess reserves of $15 million, then (disregarding any resulting increase in hand-to-hand circulation) the banking system could increase demand deposits by a maximum of:
    a. zero.

    b. $10.5 million.
    c. $15 million.
    d. $35 million.
    e. $50 million.

24. The "excess reserves" of a commercial bank consist of:
    a. assets which, although not money, can be quickly converted into money by the bank should the need arise.
    b. money and near-money assets possessed by the bank in excess of 100 percent of the amount of its demand deposits.
    c. cash which must be kept on hand, not because everyday bank needs require it but because of a legal requirement.
    d. money held by the bank in excess of that fraction of its deposits required by law.
    e. the difference between the amount of its money assets and the amount of its demand deposits.

25. The money multiplier is the multiplicative inverse of the required reserve ratio as long as:
    a. currency leakages into circulation and/or foreign markets do not occur.
    b. banks do not maintain excess reserves.
    c. the required reserve ratio is far in excess of the reserves that banks think are prudent given the deposits that they hold.
    d. all the above.
    e. none of the above.

C. A Tour of Wall Street

26. The Dow-Jones Industrial Average:
    a. is an example of a stock-price index.
    b. is used to follow trends in the stock market.
    c. includes some corporations whose stock is traded on the New York Stock Exchange.
    d. is all of the above.
    e. is none of the above.

27. The Standard and Poor 500:
    a. is a package of 500 basic stocks for lower income investors.
    b. includes the 500 most profitable stocks traded on the New York Stock Exchange.
    c. has, on average, been the most profitable Wall Street investment.
    d. was one of the few stock market indexes not to fall during the stock market drop of October 1987.
    e. is a weighted average of the stock prices of the largest 500 American corporations.

28. A speculative bubble:
    a. is compatible with the efficient-market theory.
    b. is more likely to occur during a bear market.
    c. was probably at least partly responsible for the stock market collapse in October 1987.
    d. is a theoretical concept and not likely to be observed in reality.

e.   is none of the above.

29. The essential property of margin buying of a stock is:

a.   participation in stock buying during a period of price rise by inexperienced investors.

b.   trading in a stock in quantities that do not really exist.

c.   any purchase of a stock in anticipation of a rise in its price, provided the stock is held for a short period only.

d.   a stock purchase financed in part by use of borrowed money.

e.   none of the above.

30. The contribution of margin buying to the great stock market crash of 1929 was which of the following?

a.   Owners of stock were forced to sell that stock in order to raise the cash needed to buy the further stock which their margin commitment required them to buy.

b.   The small, or marginal, stock buyers grew panicky and dumped their stock for whatever price they could get.

c.   Margin buying had increased the volume of stock trading and thus intensified the fall in prices, but otherwise it played no special part in the crash.

d.   The lenders of money sold the stock they were holding as collateral security when stock prices began to fall substantially.

e.   Margin buyers made an unsuccessful attempt to stop the decline in stock prices by increasing the amount of their buying.

31. As the result of some favorable news regarding a company, the price of its stock rises. If we were to use supply and demand curves to illustrate the nature of that price rise, we would say that it resulted from:

a.   solely a rightward shift of the demand curve.

b.   solely a leftward shift of the supply curve.

c.   both a rightward demand-curve shift and a leftward supply-curve shift.

d.   principally a rightward shift of the supply curve.

e.   principally a rightward shift of both demand and supply curves.

32. "It is not possible to make profits by looking at old information or at patterns of past price changes. The price movements of a stock over time are completely unpredictable." This statement can best be described as:

a.   chaos theory.

b.   a speculative bubble.

c.   a random walk.

d.   "no news is good news."

e.   utter nonsense.

33. The efficient-market theory:

a.   states that all public information is reflected almost immediately in the price of a share of common stock.

b.   implies that "beating the market" involves predicting unforeseeable events.

c.   implies that stock market prices move in the short run as if they were random numbers.

d.   implies that diversification is a reasonable strategy for investing in the stock market.

e.   all the above.

34. One group of stock market investors buys and holds for the long pull, disregarding short-term price fluctuations. The overall effect that this type of investor has on the market is that he or she:

a.   destabilizes it in that his or her purchases keep tending to push price upward.

b.   stabilizes it by refusing to sell on price declines but destabilizes it by making the market "thinner."

c.   stabilizes it by making it "thinner."

d.   destabilizes it by selling at times which have no relation to the current price of the stock.

e.   does none of these things, since his or her group is not of sufficient importance to have any impact.

VII. PROBLEM SOLVING

The following problems are designed to help you apply the concepts that you learned in the chapter.

A. Money and Interest Rates

1. Money evolved because it was essential for large systems of exchange.

a.   It began as (**fiat money / commodity money / metal money**) when people started to measure the values of various goods and services in terms of so many units of one particular commodity.

b.   Today, all U.S. money is (**fiat money / commodity money / gold-based money**)—legal tender which must be accepted for (**all private and some public / some private and all public / some private and some public / all private and all public**) debts.

2. It has become conventional, in tables listing the money supply, to make the distinction between M_1 and M_2. Items within M_1 are exclusively the three strictly defined money items. The M_2 category takes account of the "very close to being money" items.

a. M_2 consists of the total of (**these "very close" items alone / the "very close" items plus the M_1 items**).

A basic problem with the "very close to being money" idea is, how close is very close? The "official" definition of M_2 includes only time deposits in commercial banks and money market funds. Why not federal government bonds? The market for such bonds is so well organized that ordinarily they can be converted into money very rapidly indeed. If such bonds were included, however, then why not other easily marketed securities? As in all such cases, the decision is necessarily an arbitrary one.

Figure 9-1

b.   Other time deposits and government bonds are lumped into a category called (**convertible money / non-money / near-money / high-grade money**).

c.   Consider the following list of financial "items":

(1) Any deposit in a commercial bank on which checks may be issued

(2) Reserves of a commercial bank

(3) A deposit in a mutual savings account or in a credit union of $130,000

(4) A high-grade corporation bond

(5) A check drawn on a commercial-bank checking account

List the numbers of those items which would be included in M_1:

_____

Now list those items which would be included in M_2:

_____

3.   People (and institutions) are willing to pay interest because borrowed funds allow them to satisfy consumption needs and/or make profitable investments. The rate of interest that is paid is dependent upon a number of factors. The changes listed below should cause the rate of interest paid to rise (R), fall (F), or stay the same (S). Put the appropriate letter in the blank preceding each of the following statements:

___ a.   An increase in the term of the debt

___ b.   A reduction in the risk associated with the debt

___ c.   An increase in the degree of liquidity

___ d.   A reduction in the cost of administering the debt

___ e.   An increase in the rate of inflation

___ f.   A decrease in long-term corporate profits

4.   The demand for money is a result of both the transactions demand and the asset demand.

a.   The transactions demand for money means that the demand for money will (**increase / be unaffected / decrease**) as income climbs.

b.   As interest rates fall, the demand for money should, through its assets demand component, (**fall / remain the same / climb**).

5. The four panels in Figure 9-1 show the quantity of money demanded changing from M to M'. Record in the spaces provided the letter of the panel that best illustrates each of the following changes in economic conditions:

a. An increase in nominal GDP that leaves interest rates fixed

b. An increase in the rate of interest

c. A reduction in prices that is not yet reflected in interest rates

d. A reduction in interest rates that is not yet reflected in a change in aggregate demand

e. A situation in which banks find themselves with excess idle reserves

f. A decrease in the asset demand for money

g. An increase in the transactions demand for money

B. Banking and the Supply of Money

6. In the spaces below, list five types of financial intermediaries:

a. _____
b. _____
c. _____
d. _____
e. _____

7. The questions which follow begin with a situation in which there is no "bank money." They trace the development of such money through lending activity on the part of banks.

These questions concern an isolated community which uses initially only gold coins as money. The local goldsmith has a storage vault for gold. She is prepared to store money for others in this vault, charging a small fee. She chooses to list such deposits as an asset on her balance sheet, matched by a "deposit liability" of equal amount. Her balance sheet, with respect to such deposits, is shown in Table 9-1.

Table 9-1

Assets	Liabilities
Gold coins in vault $10,000	Deposits payable to customers on demand $10,000

a. Jones, a *customer* of the goldsmith, owes her neighbor, Bart, some gold. Bart needs to go shopping and asks if Jones can repay the loan. The goldsmith's shop has already closed for the day, so Jones gives Bart a note reading as follows:

To: Ye Gold Shoppe / Pay Bart $5 from my deposit. (Signed) Jones

What is the name used today for such a note? ___

b. Bart presents the note the next morning, but instead of taking gold coins, he asks the goldsmith to keep the money stored in his name. Is any change necessary in the goldsmith's balance sheet? If so, explain.

_____
_____

8. Observing how convenient it was to settle an account by check, the townspeople adjust their behavior and now handle many transactions by check. Occasionally a depositor withdraws gold to make a payment but the person receiving payment usually deposits it once again, since the vault is the safest place for gold storage and checks can always be drawn against such deposits.

A responsible merchant now asks the goldsmith for a loan of $2000. The goldsmith has no gold free of deposit claims, having only the $10,000 deposited with her. Is there any reason why she should nonetheless consider making the loan? Explain.

_____

9. Assume that the loan is made, and the merchant is given $2000 in gold. Table 9-2 shows the goldsmith's balance sheet after these transactions have been completed.

Table 9-2

Assets	Liabilities
Gold $8,000	Demand deposits $10,000
Loans 2,000	

a. Assume that Ye Gold Shoppe is the only goldsmith in the community . When the merchant gets the loan, he initially deposits it in his account with the goldsmith. Fill in Table 9-3 showing what Ye Gold Shoppe's balance sheet would look like after the merchant makes the deposit.

Table 9-3

Assets	Liabilities
Gold . . . .$___	Demand deposits . . . . .$___
Loans . . . . .___	

b. Has the money supply increased? (**Yes / No**)

c. If so, by how much?

10. Now we are going to change things slightly. Assume that the community holds $2000 in gold for transactions, and the goldsmith has made $20,000 in loans. Table 9-4 reflects this new situation.

Table 9-4

Assets	Liabilities
Gold . . . .$ 8,000	Demand deposits . . .$28,000
Loans 20,000	

a. The total money supply (M_1) is now $___, consisting of $___ in bank money (demand deposits) and $___ in gold held in circulation.

b. Should the $8000 in gold in the goldsmith's vault count as part of M_1? (**Yes / No**) Briefly explain why or why not.

_____
_____

Let us now add three aspects of contemporary realism to the scenario.

(1) Imagine that the institution of goldsmith has evolved into the institution of banker. The balance sheets that will be considered in the questions which follow therefore apply to banks.

(2) Suppose that the gold-based currency system of the previous questions has evolved into a system of fiat money.

(3) Presume that a central financial authority of the government requires that banks maintain reserve stores of currency equal to at least 20 percent of their total demand deposits.

For the time being, however, there is still only one bank (Bank A, grown up from Ye Gold Shoppe) in town.

11. a.   Bank A has $8000 in reserve currency on deposit and is fully "loaned out" against the 20 percent legal reserve requirement. Assume that $2000 in cash and currency is held across the community in transactions demand. Show the bank's balance sheet in Table 9-5.

Table 9-5

Assets	Liabilities
Reserves ....$____	Demand deposits .....$____
Loans ....____	

b.   Given only one bank, the community's total M_1 is at this point $____, consisting of $____ in bank money (again, demand deposits) and $____ in transactions currency.

12. a.   A storekeeper brings $500 in cash into the bank for deposit. Use Table 9-6 to show Bank A's resulting balance sheet, before any new loans are issued.

Table 9-6

Assets	Liabilities
Reserves ....____	Demand deposits .....$____
Loans ....____	

b.   With this deposit, the storekeeper now has enough money on deposit to repay a $1000 loan. His deposit is therefore reduced by $1000, and he is given back his note. Disregarding any interest on the loan, complete a revised balance sheet in Table 9-7.

Table 9-7

Assets	Liabilities
Reserves ....$____	Demand deposits .....$____
Loans ....____	

c.   When the loan is paid off, is the community's M_1 affected? (**Yes / No**) If so, how? If not, why not?

_____

_____

We have assumed, thus far, that there is just one bank in town. Suppose, instead, that there are two banks: the original (Bank A) and a new one (Bank B).

13. a.   The new bank (Bank B) attracts depositors away from Bank A. Perhaps it has a more convenient location or has friendlier tellers. In any event, things finally shake out such that each bank is of equal size and has $4000 in reserves. (The reserve requirement for both banks is still 20 percent.) The townspeople still hold $2000 in currency for transactions. Complete Table 9-8 to show the balance sheet for either bank (remember they are, at this point, identical), assuming that each is fully loaned up against a 20 percent required reserve ratio.

Table 9-8 Bank A or Bank B

Assets	Liabilities
Reserves ....$____	Demand deposits .....$____
Loans ....____	

b.   The community's total M_1 is $____, with $____ in bank money and $____ in circulation.

14. Now suppose that a local woman who has been working abroad returns home with $3000 of new currency. She deposits the cash entirely with Bank B.

a.   Show the balance sheet for Bank B in Table 9-9, assuming that Bank B has not yet had a chance to issue new loans.

Table 9-9 Bank B

Assets	Liabilities
Reserves ....$____	Demand deposits ..$____
Loans ....____	

b.   Now assume that Bank B extends loans to the maximum extent allowed by the 20 percent required reserve ratio. Revise Bank B's balance sheet in Table 9-10, assuming that all the people who receive a loan from Bank B deposit their (new) money in demand deposits in Bank A.

Table 9-10 Bank B after It Makes the Loans

Assets	Liabilities
Reserves ....____	Demand deposits ..$____
Loans ....____	

c.   What is the resulting amount of new loans for Bank B? $____

15. a.   Use Table 9-11 to show the *immediate* change in Bank A when the loan recipients deposit their money.

Table 9-11

Assets	Liabilities
Reserves ....$____	Demand deposits ..$____
Loans ....____	

b.   Now use Table 9-12 to show the balance sheet for Bank A after it meets its reserve requirement.

Table 9-12

Assets	Liabilities
Reserves ....$____	Demand deposits .....$____
Loans ....____	

c   How much in new loans has Bank A loaned out? $____

d.   What is the total amount of new loans in the community after these first two steps in the process have been completed? $____

e.   By how much has M_1 grown? $____

16. Suppose this process continues, back and forth, between the two banks.

a.   What will be the total increase in new loans? $____

b.   What will be the total increase in reserves? $____

c.   What will be the total increase in the money supply? $____

d.   What is the value of the money-supply multiplier? ____.

17. a.   Complete Table 9-13 by recording in column (1) the money multipliers that correspond to the required reserve ratios listed in the left-hand column.

Table 9-13

Required Reserve Ratio (%)	Money Multipliers	
	(1)	(2)
3	____	____
5	____	____
10	____	____
12	____	____
16	____	____

b.   Now complete column (2) under the assumption that banks hedge against the reserve requirement by holding 2 percentage points above and beyond the requirement in "extra reserve." (The notion here is that banks' hedging against being short can turn a required reserve ratio set by the monetary authorities into a functionally stricter requirement and that the actual money multiplier can fall as a result.) Required reserve ratios are, in practice, set higher than necessary so that banks are discouraged from doing too much of this sort of hedging. Why? Because it adds an element of unpredictability to the computation of the money multiplier that the monetary authorities would prefer to live without.

18. The combined balance sheet (billions of dollars) of all the commercial banks in Bancoland appears in Table 9-14. The legal reserve requirement is 10 percent of deposits.

Table 9-14

Assets	Liabilities
Reserves (deposits Federal Reserve and cash in vaults) $30	Demand deposits $100
Loans 70	

a.   These banks thus have excess reserves of (**$0** / **$5** / **$10** / **$15** / **$20** / **$30**) billion.

b.   Show their balance sheet in Table 9-15 after they have taken full advantage of excess reserves to expand loans. Assume that all new money remains as demand deposits.

Table 9-15

Assets	Liabilities
Reserves ....$____	Demand deposits .....$____
Loans ....____	

19. The process of bank-money creation is most easily explained in terms of a deposit of cash in a bank. Bear in mind, though, that once the credit expansion process is completed and banks are fully loaned up, most deposits made with banks do not permit any further loan expansion at all.

Assume that the banking system is fully loaned up in both of the cases which follow. The reserve requirement is 10 percent.

a.   I deposit $1000 in cash in my bank. Which description of this transaction is better?

(1)   This $1000 will permit the banking system to expand loans by $9000.

(2)   Unless the $1000 was a net addition to reserves, no loan expansion by the banking system is possible. The money may have been withdrawn from another bank (or even my bank) a day or two earlier.

b.   I deposit a $1000 salary check in my bank. Again, pick the better description:

(1)   This $1000 will permit the banking system to expand loans by $9000.

(2)   My bank's reserves are increased but at the cost of the reserves of some other bank. There has been no net addition to the entire banking system's reserves.

C. A Tour of Wall Street

20. *Margin buying* on the stock market works as follows: You want to buy XYZ stock, currently selling at $40 per share; you think XYZ will rise to $50 or higher. You have $1000 in cash; this will buy only 25 shares (disregarding the broker's commission and other incidental buying costs) . But with a margin requirement of 25 percent, you can buy a larger number of shares. You do this by borrowing $3000 from your broker or, via the broker, from a bank or other lending agency.

a.   The loan proceeds plus your own cash will buy (**25** / **50** / **100** / **200**) shares.

b.   Of course, you must put up some security against your loan, but you can furnish XYZ stock worth (**$1000** / **$3000** / **$4000**). This is accepted as adequate security for your $3000 loan.

If XYZ does indeed go to 50, you sell your stock, pay off the principal and interest on your loan, and pocket the rest of your profit, happy at having taken an economics course. But if, instead, XYZ should drop below 40 say, to 35—you will get a call from your broker to report that the bank "wants more margin," because the value of the asset you have supplied as collateral is falling.

c. Specifically, if the market price of XYZ is $35, your investment will be worth (**$2500 / $3000 / $3500 / $3750**).

d. With a margin requirement of 25 percent, and assuming that you are still using the stock as collateral, the most you can now borrow is (**$2525 / $2625 / $2725 / $2825**).

e. You must put up some more security or else pay off part of the loan. You have to come up with an additional (**$375 / $400 / $425 / $450**).

If you fail to come across, the bank will sell your XYZ stock. If it sells at close to 30, the entire sale proceeds go to cover your loan, leaving you with the sad reminder that you should first have read beyond Chapter 1 in the text before venturing into the stock market.

f. Note the unstable quality of a market heavily involved with margin buying. If prices begin to fall, this sets off a (**further wave of selling / wave of buying**), as borrowers cannot furnish more margin and lenders sell to protect their loans. This pushes stock prices down even more.

21. a. A "bull" market is one in which most expectations are that stock prices are going to (**rise / fall**). Most people with cash are accordingly inclined to (**buy / refrain from buying**) stocks. Most people holding stocks are inclined to (**continue to hold / sell**) them. The consequence of such expectations is that stock prices general ly (**rise / fall**).

b. A "bear" market is one in which most expectations are that stock prices are going to (**rise / fall**). Most people with cash are accordingly inclined to (**buy / refrain from buying**) stocks. Most people holding stocks are inclined to (**continue to hold / sell**) them. The consequence of such expectations is that stock prices generally (**rise / fall**).

22. Suppose, for the sake of illustration, that you decide that you want to buy a few shares of stock in a firm that has suddenly become more profitable. The firm has just marketed a new product for which demand is unexpectedly high, or just developed a new technology that will dramatically lower its costs and improve its competitive position, or just discovered an enormous oil deposit under its Texas plant.

a. In any case, you are attracted to the stock because future earnings by that firm should be significantly (**higher / lower**) than had originally been expected.

b. You and other investors will want to (**buy / sell**) stock in that firm.

c. People who already own stock in that firm will, on the other hand, want to (**sell / hold onto**) their shares in the expectation that they will soon be worth (**less / more**).

d. The result will be an immediate (**increase / reduction**) in the price of that stock in response to (**higher / lower / unchanged**) demand and (**higher / lower / unchanged**) supply at the original market-clearing price.

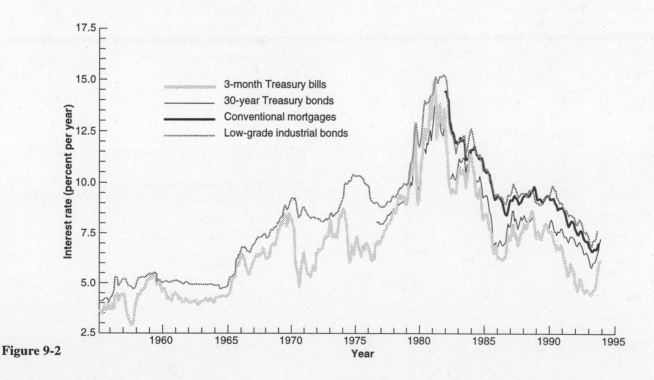

Figure 9-2

By the time you get to the market and find someone who will be willing to sell you the shares that you want, therefore, the price will already include the increment in value of the newly announced profitability that you had hoped to cash in on.

e. The problem is that the efficient-market hypothesis means that the effects of foreseeable events are already included in the prices of stocks before you can get to them. You are therefore left with trying to predict unforeseeable events in your effort to "beat the market." As a result, if you invest in the stock market and accept the hypothesis, then you should (circle one or more):

(1) concentrate your purchases on a small number of stocks.

(2) buy a widely diversified collection of stocks.

(3) keep altering your portfolio—i.e., trade frequently.

(4) stick to your portfolio—i.e., trade infrequently.

VIII. DISCUSSION QUESTIONS

Answer the following questions, making sure that you can explain the work you did to arrive at the answers.

1. Samuelson and Nordhaus write that the barter system "operates under grave disadvantages." Briefly discuss the advantages of a monetary economy.

2. Figure 25-2 (on previous page) from the text is reproduced here as Figure 9-2. Are the interest rates on the vertical axis nominal or real? How do you know?

3. Figure 25-4 from the text is reproduced here as Figure 9-3. Explain what would happen to the transactions demand for money schedule under each of the following situations:

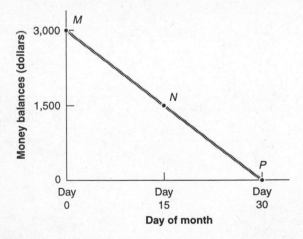

Figure 9-3

a. All prices and incomes double.

b. Real income doubles.

c. Interest rates increase.

4. Explain the difference between the transactions demand and the asset demand for money.

5. What are financial intermediaries and what function do they perform?

6. What sorts of real-world considerations tend to slow down the money creation process and reduce the size of the money-supply multiplier?

7. Briefly explain the *efficient-market* theory. What are the objections to this view of markets?

8. Compare and contrast two significant U.S. stock market crashes this century. How has the banking system changed in the interim years?

9. Explain what is meant by the term *speculative bubble*. What sorts of dynamics does this create in the market?

10. Carefully explain what information is contained in a stock price index. What are the two most common indexes used in the United States?

IX. ANSWERS TO STUDY GUIDE QUESTIONS

III. Review of Key Concepts

5	Money
7	Barter
16	Monetary economy
12	Commodity money
11	Bank money
2	Transactions money
14	Fiat money
6	Broad money
13	Riskless interest rate
1	Liquidity
4	Nominal interest rate
9	Portfolio theory
15	Financial intermediary
10	Reserves
8	Money-supply multiplier
3	Multiple expansion of bank deposits

III. Review of Key Concepts (continued)

e	Amortization
h	Inflation-indexed bonds
m	Transactions demand
p	Asset demand
o	Risk-averse
l	Balance sheet
c	Unit of account
k	Financial intermediary
f	Bank run
n	Bear market
i	Bull market
a	Margin purchases

g   Speculative bubble
j   Stock price index
b   Efficient-market theory
d   Random walk

VI. Multiple Choice Questions

1. E   2. B   3. A   4. C   5. E   6. A
7. E   8. A   9. D 10. D 11. B 12. E
13. A 14. E 15. B 16. B 17. D 18. C
19. D 20. C 21. B 22. A 23. E 24. D
25. D 26. D 27. E 28. C 29. D 30. D
31. C 32. C 33. E 34. B

VII. Problem Solving

1. a. commodity money
    b. fiat money, all private and all public
2. a. the "very close" items plus the M_1 items
    b. near-money
    c. M_1: only (1). (We cannot count (5) because that would be double counting the money in the checking account.) M_2: (1), (3) would count if it were less than $100,000.
3. a. R
    b. F
    c. F
    d. F
    e. R
    f. S
4. a. increase
    b. climb
5. a. (a)
    b. (c)
    c. (d) (due to the decrease in nominal GDP)
    d. (b)
    e. (b)
    f. (d)
    g. (d)
6. a. commercial banks
    b. savings and loans
    c. life insurance funds
    d. pension funds and credit unions
    e. money market funds
7. a. This is a check.
    b. Total deposits in the goldsmith's vault are unchanged. Only the ownership of those deposits has changed. The goldsmith will want to make a record of that.
8. The goldsmith should make the loan. Only a few of the depositors withdraw their gold at any one time. Besides, the gold that is withdrawn is likely to be paid to someone in the community and then redeposited with the goldsmith.

9. a.

Table 9-3

Assets		Liabilities	
Gold	$10,000	Demand deposits	$12,000
Loans	2,000		

    b. Yes
    c. $2,000

10. a. $30,000, $28,000, $2,000
    b. No, The gold must be withdrawn before it can be spent. If and when it is withdrawn, bank liabilities would decrease as well.
11. a.

Table 9-5

Assets		Liabilities	
Reserves	$8,000	Demand deposits	$40,000
Loans	32,000		

    b. $42,000, $40,000, $2,000
12. a.

Table 9-6

Assets		Liabilities	
Reserves	$8,500	Demand deposits	$40,500
Loans	32,000		

    b.

Table 9-7

Assets		Liabilities	
Reserves	$8,500	Demand deposits	$39,500
Loans	31,000		

    c. Yes. Assuming no other changes, M_1 falls by $1000. However, the bank can now loan that money to someone else.
13. a

Table 9-8 Bank A or Bank B

Assets		Liabilities	
Reserves	$4,000	Demand deposits	$20,000
Loans	16,000		

    b. $42,000, $40,000, $2,000
14. a.

Table 9-9 Bank B

Assets		Liabilities	
Reserves	$7,000	Demand deposits	$23,000
Loans	16,000		

b.

Table 9-10 Bank B after it Makes the Loans

Assets		Liabilities	
Reserves	$4,600	Demand deposits	$23,000
Loans	18,400		

c. $2,400

15. a.

Table 9-11

Assets		Liabilities	
Reserves	$6,400	Demand deposits	$22,400
Loans	16,000		

b.

Table 9-12

Assets		Liabilities	
Reserves	$4,480	Demand deposits	$22,400
Loans	17,920		

c. $1920

d. $4320

e. $4320 + 3000 = $7320

16. a. $12,000

b. $3,000

c. $15,000

d. $5

17. a, b.

Table 9-13

Required Reserve Ratio (%)	Money Multipliers	
	(1)	(2)
3	33.33	20.00
5	20.00	14.29
10	10.00	8.33
12	8.33	7.14
16	6.25	5.56

18. a. $20

b.

Table 9-15

Assets		Liabilities	
Reserves	$30	Demand deposits	$300
Loans	270		

19. a.   (2)

b.   (2)

20. a.   100

b. $3000

c. $3500

d. $2625

e. $375

f.   further wave of selling

21. a.   rise, buy, continue to hold, rise

b.   fall, refrain from buying, sell, fall

22. a.   higher

b.   buy

c.   hold onto, more

d.   increase, higher, lower

e.   (2) and (4)

VIII. Discussion Questions

1.   In a monetary economy the pace of economic activity increases dramatically. Once there is a universally accepted currency, people can spend more time producing and far less time looking for trading partners.

2.   The interest rates in the diagram must be nominal. Remember, the real rate equals the nominal rate minus the rate of inflation. The U.S. economy experienced relatively high rates of inflation in the early 1980s. The increase in nominal interest rates reflects this. Besides, real rates of interest of 10 percent or more would be incredibly high.

3.   a.   If all prices and incomes double, the transactions demand for money would double. The curve would look the same, but the entries on the vertical axis would be doubled as well. The household would have $6000 in money balances on day 0 and, as before, have $0 left on day 30.

b.   If real income doubles, the transactions demand for money will increase but will not double. Most households would spend part, but not all, of the increase in real income.

c.   If interest rates increase, households (and especially businesses) become more concerned with cash management. At high rates of interest, it is worthwhile for the household to make more frequent trips to the bank for withdrawals to pay for transactions. Spending patterns may not change. What will change is the amount of cash that the household keeps on hand. The transactions demand schedule will shift to the left.

4.   When people hold some of their wealth in the form of money in order to buy goods and services, this is referred to as the transactions demand for money. Alternatively, most financial analysts suggest that individuals should diversify their wealth into different types of assets with varying degrees of risk. While wealth held in the form of cash earns relatively little or no interest, it is also a good store of value and is relatively risk-free. Wealth held in the form of money is very liquid and enables individuals to respond quickly to changes in the financial marketplace. As the market improves or as new investment possibilities develop, those individuals with liquid assets will be best able to take advantage of new opportunities.

5.   An intermediary is like a middle man. Financial intermediaries (FI) use the money from depositors and then loan it or invest it. Either way, someone else gets to use the money, and they pay interest back to the FI. The FI keeps part of the interest to cover expenses and (hopefully) make a profit, and the rest is paid back to the depositor. For

example, banks use deposits to make loans, and pension funds use deposits for long-term, low-risk investments.

6. When money is created, some of the new money is usually held in the form of cash for transactions purposes. Banks create money when they receive new deposits. If more money is held for transactions and is not deposited in banks, this will slow down the money creation process. Also, if people hoard money, i.e., do not spend it and do not deposit it, the money creation process will slow down. Finally, if money leaves the domestic economy through foreign travel or trade, the process will again slow down.

7. The efficient-market theory states that the price of a stock reflects all the information the market has about that stock.

All new information is quickly understood by market participants and becomes immediately incorporated into market prices. The market does respond to news and surprises, but these are unpredictable events.

Samuelson and Nordhaus discuss four criticisms of the efficient-market theory. (a) If everyone believes the theory and assumes the market automatically adjusts to changes, there will be little or no incentive to trade. If everyone behaved this way, the market would be inefficient.. (b) Those who are quicker, and smarter or who have better advisers may make more money than others. (c) The efficient-market theory does a poor job of explaining why the value of stocks fell so dramatically during the crash of 1987. (d) The efficient-market theory works best when applied to individual stocks. It does a poorer job of explaining fluctuations in the entire market.

8. The crash in 1929 was much longer and more severe. The market eventually lost 85 percent of its value as opposed to 25 percent in 1987. The recovery in 1987 was very quick. Many analysts believe the recovery was due, in large part, to the quick reaction by the Fed. The banking system is much more proactive than in 1929 and has established margin requirements which are much higher.

9. A speculative bubble occurs when stock prices increase based on hopes and dreams and not on any concrete information about the increased profitability of firms. As long as other investors observe the rising prices and purchase stock in an attempt to benefit from the increase in prices, the market will continue to inflate. At some point, investors realize the market and their stocks are way overvalued, so they rush to sell to avoid the plunge. The bubble has just popped!

10. Stock price indexes are weighted averages of the prices of a group of stocks. These indexes are used to track trends in the stock market. The Dow-Jones Industrial Average follows the stocks of 30 large industrial corporations, and the Standard and Poor 500 tracks the 500 largest American firms.

CHAPTER 10
Central Banking and Monetary Policy

I. CHAPTER OVERVIEW

This chapter completes a critical link in our picture of the macroeconomy. The real-world functions of the United States central bank, the Federal Reserve System, are discussed, and the role of money is incorporated into the Keynesian multiplier model of Chapter 24. This chapter builds on the discussion of fractional reserve banking from the last chapter and presents an initial discussion of how changes in the money supply can influence real economic variables Changes in aggregate demand must be translated into increases or decreases in real GDP, prices, and employment.

We begin the chapter by considering how a central-banking system works—first in a domestic and then in an international environment. With particular reference to the Federal Reserve System of the United States, we will see how a variety of tools can be used to adjust monetary policy. Since monetary policy is arguably the most important factor in modern macroeconomic stabilization policy, especially in the short and medium runs, it is essential that you understand not only how each control mechanism works in theory but also how each is managed in the real world of policy-making. This understanding is then expanded by relating changes in these control mechanisms to changes in the real economy.

II. LEARNING OBJECTIVES

After you have read Chapter 26 in your text and completed the exercises in this *Study Guide* chapter, you should be able to:

1. Describe the operating structure of the Federal Reserve System of the United States (the "Fed"), paying close attention to the role of the Board of Governors and the Federal Open Market Committee.
2. Explain precisely how **open-market operations**, changes in the discount rate, and changes in the reserve ratio requirements affect the money supply.
3. Describe the differences between monetary policy variables, intermediate target variables for that policy, and objective variables that help define the intermediate targets.

4. Outline the changes in targets that occurred in October 1979 and after August 1982; show the evolution through those changes to the current policy philosophy of the Fed.
5. Explain the effects of deregulation on the Fed and the banking system.
6. Define "sterilization" of international capital movement, and explain why it is necessary.
7. Describe the link between changes in the supply of money and changes in the nominal interest rate in the money market supply-and-demand diagram.
8. Describe the transmission mechanism link between changes in bank reserves (R) and changes in nominal GDP that works through the money supply (M), the nominal interest rate (i), investment (I) and other spending, and the resulting changes in aggregate demand (AD).
9. Explain how a reduction in the supply of money might cause nominal interest rates to climb in the short run but fall in the (very) long run; and correspondingly, how the long-run effect on real interest rates may be ambiguous.

III. REVIEW OF KEY CONCEPTS

Match the following terms from column A with their definitions in column B.

A	B
__ Board of Governors	1. Asset whose primary purpose is to put funds aside for the future.
__ Federal Open Market Committee	2. Markets where short-term funds are lent and borrowed.
__ Open-market operation	3. A monetary variable that is influenced directly by Federal Reserve policy in its attempt to achieve its ultimate objectives.
__ Discount-rate policy	4. These include open-market operations, the discount rate, and reserve requirements.
__ Reserve requirements policy	5. Seven-member core group of people who control the Fed.

__ Intermediate
targets

__ Ultimate
objectives

__ Transactions
account

__ Non-transactions
account

__ Sterilization

__ Monetary
transmission

mechanism

__ Money markets

__ Neutrality of
money

__ Policy

instruments of
the Fed

6.   Route by which changes in
monetary policy bring about
changes in output, employment,
and prices.
7.   Actions by a central bank
that insulate the domestic money
supply from international reserve
flows.
8.   The inability of money to
affect real or inflation-adjusted
variables in the long run.
9.   Twelve-member group at the
Fed which, among other things,
controls the Fed's decision to buy
and sell bonds.
10.   Changing the legal reserve
ratio requirement on deposits with
banks and other financial institutions.
11.   Goals of monetary policy to
achieve steady growth, low unemployment,
and low inflation.
12.   Setting the interest rate at
which banks can borrow reserves
from the Fed.
13.   Asset whose primary purpose
is to serve as a means of payment.
14.   Fed purchase or sale of government
bonds—the single most
important and frequently used tool
of modern monetary policy.

IV. SUMMARY AND CHAPTER OUTLINE

This section summarizes the key concepts from the chapter.

A. Central Banking and the Federal Reserve System

1.   Monetary policy in the United States is set by the Board of Governors of the Federal Reserve System. The Fed, through decisions made by the board, controls the discount rate (the rate charged by the Fed to banks which borrow from its discount window), open-market operations (through the Open Market Committee), and the reserve requirement (which specifies the maximum benchmark for the money multiplier).

Changes in the discount rate work by clarifying the stance of the Fed; higher (lower) rates suggest tighter (loos-er) monetary policy. Open-market purchases (sales) of gov-ernment securities by the Fed transfer funds to (from) the banking system from (to) the Fed, increase (reduce) reserves,

and set the wheels in motion to affect aggregate demand.
2.   Monetary policy, in essence, is policy designed to make the borrowing of money easier or more difficult, as condi-tions require. Those who borrow money do so in order to spend it. Consequently, if the amount of borrowing can be increased or decreased, so too can the total volume of spend-ing; and as spending goes, so goes GDP. The total of bor-rowing can be manipulated by the Federal Reserve System—the central bank of the United States. The Fed can signifi-cantly influence total borrowing because of the power it can exercise over the reserves of the commercial banks.
3.   Commercial banks do not keep a deposit with the Fed just to demonstrate their faith in the banking system. They do so because they are legally required to keep a reserve against their own customer deposit accounts, and a deposit with the Fed is the most convenient way of keeping most of it. This is particularly true because there are continually accounts to be settled with other banks, and this can be done at a Federal Reserve Bank. Cash on the bank's own premis-es "vault cash," or "till money"—may also be counted as part of this reserve, but the reserve must take one of these two forms: either a deposit with the Fed or cash on hand.
4.   Should the commercial banks happen to have excess reserves when the Fed begins a tighter-money open-market operation, then this operation would simply soak up part of the excess; banks would be under no pressure to reduce their loans and deposits because of a shortage of reserves. The Fed must continue its operation until the banks do come under pressure. The point of specifying high reserve require-ments is to see that this won't happen, because the Fed can assume that banks will operate close to the reserve require-ment.
5.   The U.S. dollar has become something of an internation-al currency. It is widely held by foreign central banks, finan-cial institutions, and business firms. Any flow of these for-eign held dollars back to the United States may increase commercial-bank reserves—and hence the U.S. domestic money supply. An outflow of dollars (caused, say, by an excess of U.S. imports over U.S. exports) may have the reverse effect. This movement of dollars into and out of the United States can look just like a change in the money sup-ply. The Fed sometimes *sterilizes* these flows by enacting changes in its policies to negate their effect.
6.   Today, central banks everywhere seem to be acutely sen-sitive to the charge that they have caused (or contributed sig-nificantly to) past inflation by excessive expansion of the money supply. Central-bank presidents and monetary offi-cials from around the world have responded to this sensitiv-ity by becoming strongly inclined toward tight money. In 1980, the remarkably high interest rates began to reflect this attitude. Blame for the subsequent worldwide recession of 1982 has been laid by many observers squarely on those high interest rates. It is especially revealing to note that most policy officials at the Western economic summit conferences

Figure 10-1

have called on the United States to *lower* its interest rates, not by expanding the money supply but by reducing the size of the federal deficit—but that is a story for another chapter!

B. The Effects of Money on Output and Prices

1. The money supply can change as business firms and families seek to borrow more or to borrow less. The Federal Reserve seeks to control this money supply (and interest rates), having as its goal the maintenance of a reasonably stable price level, the avoidance of recession, and steady economic growth. The money supply can also change with movement in international reserves. While the transactions involved can be exceedingly complex, the elements that need to be grasped for present purposes are relatively simple.

2. The process by which changes in monetary policy affect output, employment, growth, and prices is called the **monetary transmission mechanism**. The steps in the process are summarized as follows:

   a. The Fed takes steps (using one of its three instruments) to change bank reserves.

   b. Each dollar change in bank reserves produces a multiple (via the money-supply multiplier) change in bank deposits and, hence, in the money supply.

   c. The change in the money supply will tend to change interest rates and credit conditions.

   d. Changes in the interest rate affect investment most significantly, but they can also affect consumption behavior, purchases of consumer durables, government spending, and net exports. All of these are components of aggregate demand.

   e. The changes in aggregate demand will ultimately affect output and income, employment, economic growth, and inflation.

Figure 26-3 from the text, reproduced here as Figure 10-1, provides us with a neat summary of this process.

3. The actual link between changes in the money supply and the real economy depends upon two downward-sloping schedules. The first, the demand for money, is downward-

sloping because of the assets demand for money. The second, the demand for investment, is downward-sloping because lower (higher) interest rates make more (fewer) investment projects attractive. The process is illustrated in Figure 10-2.

a. The quantity of money in an economy affects the nominal interest rate and thus the availability of credit. Specifically, the greater the quantity of money available, the lower the interest rate. This relationship is portrayed

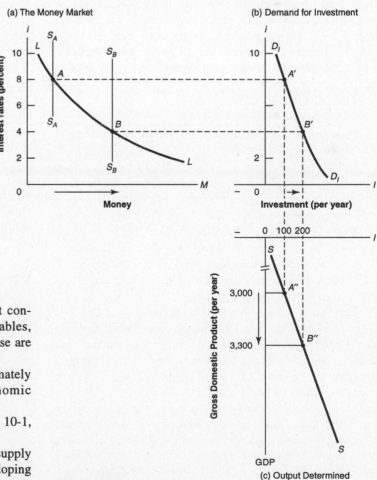

Figure 10-2

in panel (*a*) of Figure 10-2 by movement along curve *LL*—the demand-for-money curve—as the money supply climbs from S_AS_A to S_BS_B.

b   The interest rate influences investment spending in a similar fashion. The lower the interest rate, the more attractive is physical investment in, say, plant and equipment. This is one of the lessons of Chapter 23, and it is portrayed in panel (*b*) of Figure 10-2 by movement along D_ID_I the demand-for-investment curve—from *A'* to *B'* as the interest rate falls from 8 percent to 4 percent.

c.   The level of investment is one of the major determinants of GDP. The saving-investment equality that characterized equilibrium GDP in Chapter 22 is portrayed in panel (*c*) of Figure 10-2. The change in the money supply moves equilibrium out along curve *SS* from *A''* to *B''*.

Should the money supply climb from S_AS_A to S_BS_B, the interest rate would fall from 8 percent to 4 percent, investment would climb from $100 to $200, and nominal GDP would climb from $3000 to $3300. We need to adjust for (possible) changes in the price level to determine the change in *real* GDP.

4.   It is possible that in the long run changes in the money supply lead to proportionate changes in all nominal values but no changes in the real variables of output and employment. This is the so-called **neutrality of money**. It should not be considered as a universal law (like the law of demand) and may be altered by subsequent events in the economy.

V. HELPFUL HINTS

1.   The central bank of the United States, or the Federal Reserve System, is commonly referred to as simply **the Fed**. It would be very difficult to overstate the Fed's importance in the U.S. economy. Few people outside of the fields of economics or finance appreciate the significance of the Fed.

2.   Several times in this chapter Samuelson and Nordhaus refer to the Fed's attempts to influence "real" variables or the "real side" of the economy. The word "real," in this sense, refers to inflation-adjusted measures of output, employment, and growth. (You may recall that economic growth is always measured in real terms.)

3.   The Fed is a bank for banks. It holds their deposits (called *bank reserves)* and lends them money (at the discount rate). Unlike consumers, who may apply for a loan at a bank whenever they like, banks should ask the Fed for loans only when they are in serious financial trouble. The Fed is often called "the lender of last resort."

4.   An open-market *purchase* means that the Fed is *buying bonds* and injecting reserves. The *money supply* should *grow*. An open-market *sale* means that the Fed is *selling bonds* and withdrawing reserves. The *money supply* should *shrink* or at least its rate of growth should slow down.

5.   The terms *treasury bills, government bonds,* and *government securities* can, for our purposes, all be used interchangeably. They are all instruments that the Fed owns, buys, and sells in its attempt to control the money supply. The Fed uses these government bonds because there is a huge supply of them and because they are relatively risk free. The Fed and most other financial institutions hold large portfolios of these bonds.

6.   The Fed does not change reserve requirements often. It is not because this instrument is ineffective, but precisely the opposite! Reserve requirement changes are very powerful, especially when they are increased. If the Fed suddenly increased reserve requirements, many banks would be short reserves. Banks typically lend excess reserves to one another, but in this situation very few banks, if any, would have excess reserves available to lend—they would all be looking to borrow. Interest rates would tend to rise. The Fed also prefers to control the money supply in much more *subtle* ways. The Fed buys and sells securities all the time with a group of different government bond dealers. Most of these transactions are done in order to steady the money supply; only rarely does the Fed undertake policy actions. It is nearly impossible, on any given day, to determine what the Fed's position in the bond market is. Nevertheless, a great deal of people spend a great deal of time and effort "Fed watching" to try to get advance or inside knowledge of changes in monetary policy.

7.   The Fed sets a target for what it thinks the appropriate level of the money supply should be. This target is based on the health of the economy and projections or forecasts of where the economy is headed. Over any given six-month or year-long period the Fed may or may not hit this target precisely; the Fed, after all, cannot control the entire economy and all the possible changes that may occur. Nevertheless, the Fed decides what it thinks the appropriate level of the money supply should be. This is why the money supply curve is drawn as a nearly vertical line. It is not interest rates that determine monetary policy, but the health of the economy.

VI. MULTIPLE CHOICE QUESTIONS

These questions are organized by topic from the chapter outline. Choose the best answer from the options available.

A. Central Banking and the Federal Reserve System

1.   The phrase "open-market operations" refers specifically to:

a.   commercial banks' lending to business firms and to consumers.

b.   the Federal Reserve's making loans to commercial banks.

c. changes in interest rates caused by an increase or a decrease in the total of commercial-bank loans.

d. the operations of the Federal Reserve designed to increase or to decrease the total of member-bank demand deposits.

e. the Federal Reserve's buying or selling government securities.

2. The principal assets on a Federal Reserve balance sheet are:

a. gold certificates and cash, deposits by banks, and deposits by government.

b. Federal Reserve notes, government securities, and loans.

c. gold certificates and cash, bank deposits, and loans.

d. gold certificates and cash, loans, and government securities.

e. Federal Reserve notes, gold certificates and cash, and member-bank deposits.

3. Which among the following combinations constitutes the tools of monetary policy used by the Federal Reserve in its routine operations (i.e., excluding tools that might be employed in exceptional situations)?

a. discount-rate policy, control over stock-buying margin requirements, and moral suasion.

b. moral suasion and legal reserve-requirement changes.

c. open-market operations and discount-rate changes.

d. discount-rate policy and legal reserve-requirement changes.

e. open-market operations, legal reserve-requirement changes, and selective controls over consumer and mortgage credit.

4. The total of Federal Reserve notes held by business and the public appears on the Federal Reserve balance sheet:

a. as a liability, because these notes are IOUs of the Fed.

b. as an asset, since these notes constitute part of the money supply; i.e., they are cash.

c. as a liability, because these notes are part of reserves; i.e., they represent deposits made by commercial banks.

d. within the capital accounts section, since this represents the money by means of which the Federal Reserve is financed.

e. not at all—only notes not held by business or the public appear on this balance sheet.

5. If the Federal Reserve System raises the discount rate, this act should be interpreted as part of a general policy intended primarily to:

a. reduce the total of commercial-bank reserves.

b. increase the amount saved out of income by the public.

c. encourage increased borrowing from the Fed by commercial banks.

d. increase the total of commercial-bank reserves.

e. do none of the preceding.

6. Suppose the Federal Reserve System conducts a large-scale open-market purchase of government securities from the public. Which alternative in question 5 would have correctly identified its primary objective?

a.

b.

c.

d.

e.

7. If a commercial bank deposits a $20 Federal Reserve note with the Federal Reserve, how will the Federal Reserve balance sheet be affected?

a. The asset "discounts and loans" will rise.

b. The liability "commercial-bank demand deposits" will fall.

c. The asset "U.S. government securities" will rise.

d. The liability "Federal Reserve notes" will rise.

e. None of the preceding is correct.

8. One reason why a reduction in the discount rate might have limited effectiveness as a tool of monetary policy is the fact that:

a. the Fed, although it can increase the quantity of money held by the public, cannot force the public to spend that money, which is what is needed to increase GDP.

b. the Fed no longer has the same statutory power it once had to change the discount rate.

c. the Fed cannot control the quantity of discount borrowing, since banks seek to borrow only if and when they choose.

d. such a reduction is likely to be offset by an increase in member-bank reserves.

e. such a reduction is likely to drive down the prices of stocks and bonds.

9. If the Federal Reserve sells a large quantity of U.S. government securities to the public, it would be reasonable to conclude that this action is intended to:

a. increase the total of personal saving.

b. decrease the total of loans made by commercial banks to their customers.

c. increase the total of deposits of member banks with the Federal Reserve.

d. decrease the general level of interest rates.

e. increase the volume of Federal Reserve notes in circulation.

10. If the Federal Reserve buys a large quantity of U.S. government securities from the public, then:

a. the Federal Reserve liability in the form of bank reserve deposits will go up.

b. the commercial-bank liability "demand deposits" will go down.

c. the total quantity of money held by the public will

go down.

d. the Federal Reserve asset "discounts, loans, and acceptances" will go up.

e. the commercial-bank asset "loans and discounts will go down.

11. If the Federal Reserve wants to restrict the growth of the total money supply, its task is made more difficult if:

a. it lacks legal power to reduce the reserve requirements of commercial banks.

b. commercial banks are holding large excess reserves.

c. the amount of personal saving out of income is very high.

d. gold is being exported to other countries in large quantities.

e. business firms and the public are anxious to buy more government bonds than they now hold.

12. The *discount rate,* as this term is used in monetary-policy discussion, means:

a. the degree of reduction in price required by the Federal Reserve when it purchases any government security.

b. the degree of pressure exerted by the Federal Reserve upon commercial banks to reduce their loans to customers.

c. the interest rate charged by the Federal Reserve on loans made to commercial banks.

d. the extent to which the Federal Reserve is acting so as to increase the money supply and the level of GDP.

e. none of the preceding.

13. A large-scale "easier credit" operation conducted by the Federal Reserve through open-market operations will:

a. raise the price of government securities.

b. reduce the total of commercial-bank reserves.

c. lower the level of prices generally.

d. lower the price of government securities.

e. raise the legal reserve requirements imposed upon commercial banks.

14. The Federal Reserve System of the United States is part of:

a. the judicial branch of government.

b. the administrative branch of government.

c. the legislative branch of government.

d. the regulative branch of government.

e. none of the above.

15. The Federal Reserve's objectives include:

a. economic growth.

b. a high level of employment.

c. stable prices.

d. moderate long-term interest rates.

e. all of the above.

16. In which of the following foreign-market activities is the Fed involved?

a. Sterilization.

b. Foreign-exchange-rate intervention.

c. Helping alleviate international financial crises.

d. All of the above.

e. Choices **b**. and **c**. only.

B. The Effects of Money on Output and Prices

17. If the Fed seeks to increase GDP, which of the following is *not* among the steps that link the Fed's action to GDP?

a. Increase investment to raise the level of total spending.

b. Increase interest rates to make lending more attractive to holders of cash.

c. Increase bank reserves to encourage the banks to increase their non-cash assets.

d. Increase demand deposits.

e. Increase the availability of credit.

18. In the "monetarist experiment" of 1979 the Fed decided to:

a. reorganize the operations of the foreign desk.

b. focus primarily on interest rate movements rather than bank reserves and the money supply.

c. focus primarily on bank reserves and the money supply rather than interest rate movements.

d. direct the Treasury to print more money.

e. do none of the above.

19. The bank deregulation of the early 1980s has:

a. reduced the ability of the Fed to control the money supply.

b. begun a process to lift interest rate ceilings from accounts in financial institutions

c. preserved the reserve requirement on transactions accounts.

d. done nothing to undermine the legislative mandate to the Fed that it announce its policy objectives.

e. done all the above.

20. On the basis of the transactions demand component of the demand for money:

a. the demand for money shifts right as the nominal interest rate rises.

b. the demand for money shifts right as the nominal interest rate falls.

c. the demand for money falls as nominal income rises.

d. the demand for money falls as nominal income falls.

e. none of the above occurs.

21. Which answer to question 20 would have been correct had that question referred to the assets demand component of the demand for money?

a.

b.

c.

d.

e.

22. The demand curve for investment:
   a.   parallels the demand curve for money in that high interest rates reduce demand.
   b.   most precisely plots the real rate of interest against quantity of investment funds demanded.
   c.   is negatively sloped because high real interest rates cause marginal investment projects to be rejected.
   d.   is a vital link between changes in the money supply and nominal GDP.
   e.   is described by all the above.

23. A reduction in interest rates engineered by the Federal Reserve can reasonably be expected to:
   a.   encourage investment because it makes the lending of money more profitable to bankers.
   b.   discourage investment because it makes the borrowing of money less attractive.
   c.   have little or no effect on investment, since that is not its purpose—interest rate changes are intended to alter security prices, not investment.
   d.   discourage investment because it makes the lending of money less attractive.
   e.   encourage investment because it makes the borrowing of money more attractive.

24. Monetary policy is made somewhat *less* effective in restraining a period of excessive spending whenever:
   a.   the demand-for-investment schedule is highly elastic.
   b.   dollars held abroad are attracted to higher interest rates in the United States.
   c.   the money demand schedule is highly elastic.
   d.   changes in interest rates tend to bring with them changes in the market value of securities.
   e.   investment spending responds more to changes in credit availability than to changes in interest rates.

25. Because the difference between real and nominal interest rates is the rate of inflation:
   a.   nominal rates can fall, in the long run, in response to tight monetary policy.
   b.   nominal rates must rise, in both the short and the long runs, in response to tight monetary policy.
   c.   there is no difference between the demand for money and the demand for investment.
   d.   the paradox of thrift is less of a concern.
   e.   none of the above is correct.

VII. PROBLEM SOLVING

The following problems are designed to help you apply the concepts that you learned in the chapter.

A. Central Banking and the Federal Reserve System

1.   Suppose, for the sake of illustration, that an open-market operation designed to lower inflation is orchestrated by reducing the level of reserves available to the entire banking system.
   a.   The result would be (**an expansion / a contraction**) in the quantity of bank money supplied to the economy. It should be expected, therefore, that interest rates would (**climb / fall**) and the supply of credit would (**contract / expand**).
   b.   Businesses would therefore find it (**easier / more difficult**) to finance new investment. Individuals would feel (**richer / poorer**) and would therefore (**increase / reduce**) their consumption expenditures. And so on.
   c.   Aggregate demand would, in general, (**climb / fall**) and thus put pressure on GDP to (**climb / fall**), prices to (**climb / fall**), and/or unemployment to (**climb / fall**).

2.   Consider the $247.4 billion liability that appeared on the 1991 Federal Reserve balance sheet under "Federal Reserve notes." Identify which of the following statements are correct by circling the appropriate letters:
   a.   This liability represents the bulk of the paper money circulating in the United States. It is, in fact, all such money except for a few bills of various types (silver certificates, U.S. notes) which date back to earlier generations. (These are still held in small amounts by the public, but they are being withdrawn whenever they come out of hiding and reappear in circulation.)
   b.   This figure of $247.4 billion represents the total of all such Federal Reserve paper money existing outside the Fed itself, i.e., held by commercial banks and by the public.
   c.   This total of paper money is listed as a liability by the Federal Reserve because, in the last analysis, such bills are simply IOUs of the Fed and must be listed on its balance sheet as any such IOU must be.
   d.   If any member commercial bank deposits a $10 Federal Reserve note with the Fed, then on the Fed's balance sheet the liability bank reserves rise by $10 and the liability Federal Reserve notes fall by $10 (since this particular IOU is no longer outstanding).
   e.   If a Federal Reserve employee receives a brand-new $10 Federal Reserve note as part of his or her salary, the Fed's liability Federal Reserve notes must rise by $10.
   f.   If any commercial bank withdraws $10 from its deposit with its Federal Reserve Bank and takes this withdrawal in the form of a $10 Federal Reserve note, then the Fed's liability bank reserves must fall by $10, and its liability Federal Reserve notes must rise by $10.
   g.   Federal Reserve notes held by a commercial bank in its own vaults may be counted as part of its legal reserve.
   h.   The public can increase its holding of Federal Reserve notes simply by withdrawing part of its demand-deposit accounts. This action would decrease the deposit-money total and increase the total of paper money held by the public.

Questions 3 through 7 deal with the operation of monetary policy in terms of Federal Reserve and commercial-bank balance sheets. In these questions, assume that each bank is required to keep a bank reserve of at least 10 percent of its own total demand deposits (owned by its customers). Assume, as well, that the bank tries to keep this reserve as follows: 7.5 percent as a deposit with the Fed and 2.5 percent as cash on its own premises—vault cash.

We start with the balance sheets (in billions of dollars) in Tables 10-1 and 10-2 for the Federal Reserve and the combined commercial banks.

Table 10-1 Federal Reserve

Assets		Liabilities	
Gold certificates $10		Federal Reserve notes ...$15	
Gov't. securities 35		Deposits:	
Loans 5		U.S. Treasury 5	
		Bank reserves 30	

Table 10-2 Combined Commercial Banks

Assets		Liabilities	
Federal Reserve		Demand deposits $400	
deposits ....$ 30			
Vault cash 10			
Loans 360			

3. This question outlines the working of the principal instrument which the Federal Reserve uses in conducting its monetary policy: *open-market operations.* Suppose that the Fed decides (for reasons that will shortly be evident) to buy government securities (i.e., government bonds) from the public. It enters the bond market and buys $10 (billion) of short-term government securities (bidding up the prices of these securities somewhat, if necessary, in order to obtain them). The Fed pays for these bonds by drawing checks on itself. As a consequence of this bond purchase by the Fed, two significant account totals have increased:

a. The public now has an additional $10 in its total demand deposits with commercial banks.

b. The commercial banks likewise have an additional $10 in their deposits With the Federal Reserve.

Write out new balance sheets in Table 10-3 for the Fed and the banks, corresponding to those in Tables 10-1 and 10-2 but showing the changes just described. (As yet, the banks have changed neither their vault cash nor their loans.)

Table 10-3 Federal Reserve

Assets		Liabilities	
Gold certs. ....$____		FR notes ....$____	
		Deposits:	
Gov't. securities ......____		U.S. Treasury ....____	
Loans ....____		Bank reserves ....____	

Combined Commercial Banks

Assets		Liabilities	
FR deposits ....$____		Demand deposits .....$____	
Vault cash ....____			
Loans ....____			

4. a. Commercial banks now (**have excess reserves / are just fully loaned up / are deficient in their total reserve requirement**) . This means that they (**will want to increase / must decrease**) their total loans in order to increase their earnings.

b. Specifically, their total reserves are now (**$10 / $20 / $30 / $40 / $50**), and this is sufficient to maintain demand deposits totaling a maximum of (**$300 / $350 / $400 / $450 / $500 / $550 / $600**).

5. In Table 10-4, show balance sheets for both the Fed and the combined banks after the banks have taken full advantage of this opportunity to increase their loans. Remember that both Fed deposits and vault cash count as reserves and that, by assumption, banks want to keep them in a 3-to-l ratio. Vault cash is increased by withdrawing part of their Fed deposit. Assume that the withdrawal is made in Federal Reserve notes.

Table 10-4 Federal Reserve

Assets		Liabilities	
Gold certs. ....$____		FR notes ....$____	
		Deposits:	
Gov't. securities ......____		U.S. Treasury ....____	
Loans ....____		Bank reserves ....____	

Combined Commercial Banks

Assets		Liabilities	
FR deposits ....$____		Demand deposits .....$____	
Vault cash ....____			
Loans ....____			

6. a. Assuming that the banks do increase their loans to the maximum allowed by the reserve requirement, then the money supply will (**increase / decrease**), altogether by (**$0 / $20 / $40 / $60 / $80 / $100**).

_____

_____

b. How would you expect this to affect the level of GDP? Explain briefly. _____ .

c. In sum, if the Federal Reserve enters the securities market as a buyer, its objective would be to (**raise / restrain**) GDP by making credit (**easier / more difficult**) to obtain.

d. This would be an *easy-money policy.* Interest rates, those on bank loans in particular, should (**rise / fall**) .

7. If the Federal Reserve wanted to reduce credit and to restrain GDP, then it would pursue a *tight-money policy.* It would work the open-market process of the previous questions in reverse.

a.   That is, the Fed would enter the securities markets as a (**buyer / seller**) . If necessary, it would accept a price somewhat (**higher / lower**) than the previously existing market level in order to bring about its (**purchases / sales**) of government securities.

b.   The buyers of these securities (insurance companies, other financial institutions, business corporations, even individuals) would pay for them by means of checks drawn on their commercial bank accounts. The Fed would return these checks to the banks involved and require settlement by (**increasing / reducing**) the reserve deposit which these banks kept at the Fed.

c.   When the reserves of commercial banks decline, then the banks (unless they have excess reserves) must (**increase / decrease**) their loans to customers. The effect of this tighter-money open-market operation is that the totals of commercial bank loans and demand deposits go (**up / down**).

(If you wish, you can work all this out in detail, starting with the same pair of balance sheets in Table 10-4 and with a sale by the Fed of $10 of its government securities. Remember that if a bank has more Federal Reserve notes than needed to cover the 2.5 percent vault-cash requirement, it can return the excess to the Fed, thereby increasing the amount of its reserve deposit.)

8. a.   Notice a difference between easy- and tight-money policies. When an easy-money policy gives them more reserves, the banks (**must / may or may not**) then increase their loans to the fullest possible extent.

If they do not like the credit prospects of the would-be borrowers standing in line, they may decide not to become fully loaned up. The Fed can do nothing to force them to change this decision. Conversely, the Fed can always push a tight-money operation until any excess reserves have been mopped up.

b.   Thereafter, the banks (**do not have any / still have some**) choice. They (**need not necessarily / must**) reduce their loans outstanding.

9.   In a tight-money period, interest rates are generally going to move (**up / down**). In such a period (circle all that apply):

a.   borrowed money is harder to obtain because the total of loans granted may be going down.

b.   the total supply of borrowable money may be smaller.

c.   the total of loans granted may actually be increasing, but not as fast as the demand for such loans; to any borrower, money therefore seems harder to obtain.

10. a.   Consider how an inflow of foreign-held dollars increases U.S. commercial-bank reserves. The effect is the same as it would be if the Federal Reserve had conducted an open-market (**purchase / sale**) of securities. However, the Fed did not initiate this action, and it may decide to undertake offsetting action; i.e., it can *sterilize* the increase in reserves by means of an open-market

(**purchase / sale**).

To illustrate this matter of international reserve movements more fully, consider a different example, one arising out of foreign trade. Suppose that the Bavarian Motor Works and Audi-Volkswagen have sold $100 million worth of their automobiles in the United States. These sales are not matched by U.S. sales abroad, so the United States has imported $100 million more than it has exported. The two German companies accordingly have $100 million in deposits in U.S. commercial banks. These companies, being German-based, want to convert their dollars into deutsche marks, so they sell their dollar accounts to the West German central bank, the Bundesbank, receiving the marks that they want in exchange.

The Bundesbank in turn sells these dollar accounts to the Federal Reserve. It doesn't matter here how the Fed makes payment to the Bundesbank; that is a matter of international settlements, a topic discussed later in the text. The point is that the Fed now owns the U.S. commercial-bank deposit accounts worth $100 million.

b.   In this respect, it is in exactly the same position as it would have been if it had conducted an open-market operation, (**buying / selling**) U.S. government securities. It has an increased claim on these banks.

c.   If the Fed wishes, it can ask the banks to settle up. This will cause them to (**lose / gain**) reserves. In effect, the Fed would have conducted a (**tight- / easy-**) money operation.

d.   Of course, if the Fed considers that policy undesirable in the light of domestic conditions, it can keep the commercial-bank deposit accounts or it can conduct a sterilizing, or offsetting, (**tight- / easy-**) money operation.

11. The political independence of the Federal Reserve is an issue of enormous importance. As it stands now, the Fed belongs to (**the administrative / the legislative / the judicial / no single**) branch of government. It reports directly to (**Congress / the President**), hears advice and criticism from (**Congress / the President / everyone**), but makes up its own mind about the direction of policy actions. This may or may not be consistent with fiscal policy.

12. Another issue of potentially extreme consequence is the effect of recent deregulation on the ability of the Fed to control the money supply. Two significant acts of Congress in 1980 and 1982 greatly diminished the Fed's power.

a.   Non-transactions accounts were (**totally / partially**) deregulated, and thus, by 1986, there were (**no / higher / lower**) interest rate ceilings and (**higher and substantial / lower and minimal**) reserve requirements applied to those accounts. These non-transactions accounts include (**savings / checking / store-based credit**) accounts.

b.   Transactions accounts were (**totally / partially**) deregulated, as well, with interest rate ceilings (**lapsing / being raised / being lowered**) by 1986, but with substantial reserve requirements remaining.

B. The Effects of Money on Output and Prices

13. The *LL* curve drawn as it is in panel *(a)* of Figure 10-3 suggests that if the interest rate were to go up, some people would decide they ought to (**use some of their "idle" money to buy securities / sell some of their securities and hold money as an asset instead**). Alternatively, the total quantity of money which people would want to hold as an *asset* would (**increase / decrease**) if the interest rate were to fall.

In sum, interest is the reward paid to you for parting with money (parting with liquidity). If the interest rate falls, that reward is less, and the attractiveness of parting with money decreases; i.e., the demand to hold money becomes a stronger force.

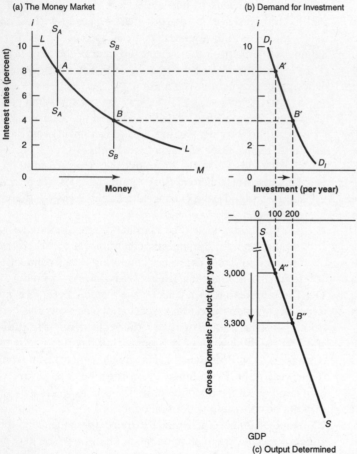

Figure 10-3

14. Figure 10-3 shows how the Fed would try to use an increase in the money supply to push an economy out of a recession; i.e., the ultimate policy goal here is to increase nominal GDP. Start at point *A*. The policy step is to increase the money supply from $S_A S_A$ to $S_B S_B$; it can be accomplished by a large open-market operation.

The Fed would simply enter the securities market and (**buy / sell**) government securities—bidding (**up / down**)

their prices to the extent necessary to make supply and demand match. Equilibrium in the money market therefore moves from point *A* to point *B*. with the nominal rate of interest lower than before. Therefore, with (**lower / higher**) interest rates and easier credit conditions, borrowers with real investment projects in mind are (**discouraged / encouraged**) to undertake them.

15. a. Look once again at the *LL* curve in Figure 10-3 Suppose it was much steeper (closer to being vertical). Compared with the one drawn, a steeper curve would mean that any given change in interest rates—say, the indicated reduction from 8 percent to 4 percent—would produce a (**larger / smaller**) change in the demand for money. Starting from point *A* but with a steeper *LL* curve than the one shown, the Fed would have to pump a (**smaller / larger**) amount of extra money into the economy to get the interest rate down from 8 to 4 percent.

b. Conversely, if the *LL* curve were flatter (closer to being horizontal), then the Fed's task (for any desired reduction in interest rates) would be (**easier / more difficult**). If the *LL* curve were flatter, it would mean that asset holders were highly sensitive to interest rate changes. Even a fairly modest reduction in interest rates would "turn them off" to securities; they would want to sell securities in large quantities and to hold money instead.

16. Figure 10-3 depends, in its final panel, on our multiplier model that determines GDP by the equality of saving and investment. Figure 10-4 portrays the increase in investment that was depicted in panel *(b)* of Figure 10-3 as an increase in aggregate demand.

a. In panel *(a)* of Figure 10-4 (top of next page), the story told by Figure 10-3 is repeated; the higher investment causes real GDP to climb because output was initially (**well below / almost equal to / far above**) potential GDP.

b. In panel *(b)*, though, the higher investment causes only nominal GDP to climb, because (**real GDP / only prices**) **climb(s)**. The key here, of course, is that GDP was initially (**far below / almost equal to / well above**) potential.

17. a. The difference between the nominal interest rate and the real interest rate is the _____.

b. In the long run, a reduction in the money supply can cause nominal interest rates to (**fall / climb**), even though they may (**fall / climb**) in the short run.

c. Initially, as the money supply contracts, (**the nominal / the real / both**) interest rate(s) climb(s), causing investment to fall, aggregate demand to fall, and, eventually, price inflation to slow down.

d. As a direct result of the slowdown in inflation, though, the (**nominal / real**) rate will fall. This change is supported by the slower growth in nominal GDP that

(a) Real GDP   (b) Real GDP

Figure 10-4

causes the demand for money to shift (**to the right / nowhere / to the left**), where it can intersect an even smaller money supply at a lower nominal rate of interest.

e. One problem with this scenario is, though, that (**it may happen too fast for people to keep up / it may happen too slowly to avoid the costs of high unemployment**).

VIII. DISCUSSION QUESTIONS

Answer the following questions, making sure that you can explain the work you did to arrive at the answers.
1. Explain in words how the Fed uses open-market operations to control the money supply. Do not use any numbers or balance sheets—just words.
2. Explain why it is in the Fed's interest to set reserve requirements above what bankers would willingly hold by themselves.
3. Explain why changes in reserve requirements (especially increases) are so drastic. What is a better way to control the money supply?
4. What happened when the Fed began targeting M_1, M_2, and bank reserves in October 1979? How has the Fed modified this policy since 1982?
5. Is the Fed too independent? Argue pro and con.
6. Briefly discuss the reason why dollars might be held abroad.
7. Discuss the long-term effects of monetary policy on the economy and the neutrality of money.

IX. ANSWERS TO STUDY GUIDE QUESTIONS

III. Review of Key Concepts

5	Board of Governors
9	Federal Open Market Committee
14	Open-market operation
12	Discount-rate policy
10	Reserve requirements policy
3	Intermediate targets
11	Ultimate objectives
13	Transactions account
1	Non-transactions account
7	Sterilization
6	Monetary transmission mechanism
2	Money markets
8	Neutrality of money
4	Policy instruments of the Fed

VI. Multiple Choice Questions

1. E 2. D 3. C 4. A 5. A 6. D
7. E 8. C 9. B 10. A 11. B 12. C
13. A 14. E 15. E 16. D 17. B 18. C
19. E 20. D 21. E 22. E 23. E 24. C
25. A

VII. Problem Solving

1. a. a contraction, climb, contract
    b. more difficult, poorer, reduce
    c. fall, fall, fall, climb

2.   All the statements are correct.

3.

Table 10-3 Federal Reserve

Assets		Liabilities	
Gold certs.	$10	FR notes	$15
		Deposits:	
Gov't. securities	45	U.S. Treasury	5
Loans	5	Bank reserves	40

Combined Commercial Banks

Assets		Liabilities	
FR deposits	$ 40	Demand deposits	$410
Vault cash	10		
Loans	360		

4   a.   have excess reserves, will want to increase
    b. $50, $500

5.

Table 10-4 Federal Reserve

Assets		Liabilities	
Gold certs	$10	FR notes	$17.5
		Deposits:	
Gov't. securities	45	U.S. Treasury	5.0
Loans	5	Bank reserves	37.5

Combined Commercial Banks

Assets		Liabilities	
FR deposits	$37.5	Demand deposits	$500
Vault cash	12.5		
Loans	450.0		

6.   a.   increase, $100
     b.   Increased lending by banks means that people are borrowing and spending more. GDP will increase.
     c.   raise, easier
     d.   fall
7.   a.   seller, lower, sales
     b.   reducing
     c.   decrease, down
8.   a.   may or may not
     b.   do not have any, must
9.   up, All the choices are possible.
10. a.   purchase, sale
     b.   selling
     c.   lose, tight
     d.   easyk
11. no single, Congress, everyone
12. a.   totally, no, lower and minimal, savings
     b.   partially, lapsing
13. use some of their "idle" money to buy securities, increase
14. buy, up, lower, encouraged
15. a.   smaller, smaller
     b.   more difficult
16. a.   well below

     b.   only prices, almost equal to
17. a.   rate of inflation
     b.   fall, climb
     c.   both
     d.   nominal, to the left
     e.   it may happen too slowly to avoid the costs of high unemployment

VIII. Discussion Questions

1.   Open-market operations refer to the Fed's purchase and sale of U.S. government securities or bonds. When the Fed sells a bond, the buyer of the bond (bank, business, individual) pays for it with money, usually a check. When the Fed presents the check to the bond purchaser's bank for payment, the bank loses demand deposits and reserves. This reduces the bank's ability to make loans and will ultimately affect other banks in the economy since they will no longer be receiving deposits from the first bank's loan recipients.
When the Fed buys bonds, it injects liquidity or reserves into the system. When the bond seller (whoever it is) deposits the payment from the Fed in the bank, the bank finds itself with excess reserves. This increases the bank's ability to make loans, and the money supply increases. As loan recipients spend their borrowings, other banks find themselves with excess reserves and the process continues.

2.   If bankers willingly hold reserves beyond the Fed's requirements, this reduces the Fed's ability to use reserve requirements as a policy tool. If the Fed reduces reserve requirements to encourage lending, this may have a minimal effect since banks already had excess reserves that they chose not to lend. Alternatively, if the Fed increases reserves to slow down the money creation process, it may have little impact since banks may already have enough (excess) reserves to meet the new requirement.

3.   When the Fed increases reserve requirements, many banks are likely to be short of reserves. (Even the most conservative banker knows that idle reserves earn no interest, so there is an incentive to keep reserves down to the legal minimum.) As the banking system as a whole tries to meet the new reserve requirement, there would be few available lenders. The "announcement effect" of this change in policy could be dramatic. The Fed prefers to conduct its business in much more subtle ways. Open-market operations are more discreet and much less disruptive.

4.   When the Fed focused its attention on the money supply, it had to give up its ability to control interest rates. Remember, interest rates are the price of money. When the Fed reduced the growth rate of the supply of money, it had to realize that interest rates would rise. (There is no way that the producer of a good can restrict its supply and also keep its price from rising.) While the Fed's strict attention to the money supply dramatically reduced inflation in the economy, many analysts believe it also pushed the economy into a recession. As the banking industry developed new types of

money instruments, M_1—and to some extent M_2—became less reliable predictors of movements in aggregate demand. As a result, the Fed has recently paid closer attention *to real rates of interest* in the economy.

5. *Pro*: The Board of Governors is not elected. Fourteen-year term of office is too long. Bankers may be more concerned with the profits of fellow bankers and less with the health of the economy. *Con:* Bankers and economists are more likely to do a better job managing the money supply than politicians. Independence of the Fed insulates it from political pressure and enables monetary policy to counterbalance fiscal policy.

6. The dollar is recognized around the globe as a safe and stable currency. Foreign investors and those who trade with the United States hold dollars. Dollars are held for speculation, investing, and trade.

7. First of all, we should keep in mind that the long term here may be many decades. Research results suggest that in the long run the effects of changes in the money supply will be shown primarily as changes in the price level. Eventually prices, wages, and interest rates will all adjust to changes in the money supply, and there will be minimal impact on real output and employment in the economy.

CHAPTER 11
The Process of Economic Growth

I. CHAPTER OVERVIEW

Most of our attention thus far has focused on short- to medium-term changes in economic conditions associated with the business cycle. The focus here is on longer patterns of growth and the associated level of aggregate output in the economy. The approach used here is similar to the other models we have constructed in that it seeks to help explain another facet of the macroeconomy.

Economic growth, by definition, deals with changes in the level of *real* output, or GDP, in the economy. Without growth economies eventually stagnate and fade away. The chapter is divided into two parts: the first discusses several theories and trends in economic growth, the second part focuses on an analysis of economic growth in the United States.

II. LEARNING OBJECTIVES

After you have read Chapter 27 in your text and completed the exercises in this *Study Guide* chapter, you should be able to:

1. Discuss the four basic elements/factors in economic growth.
2. Trace the evolution of thought about economic growth from Smith and Malthus to the **neoclassical growth model** developed in large measure by Robert Solow.
3. Define **capital deepening** and explain why it tends to increase the real wage paid to labor and reduce the return earned by capital. Understand how and why reductions in the return to capital, in the absence of technological change, can bring capital deepening to a halt in a long-run **steady state.**
4. Explain how and why **technological change** can push a factor-price frontier out, thereby illustrating how a relatively high return to capital can be maintained even as continued capital deepening drives the capital-labor ratio upward.
5. Summarize briefly the (seven) basic trends in the economic development of advanced economies.
6. Understand the equations of **growth accounting,** and use that approach to identify the major sources of growth in per capita output in the United States.
7. Explain how technological change itself can be viewed as an output, produced by the economy.
8. Discuss the explanations of the productivity slowdown in the United States.

III. REVIEW OF KEY CONCEPTS

Match the following terms from column A with their definitions in column B.

A	B
___ Economic growth	1. Process by which the quantity of capital per worker (or the K/L ratio) increases over time.
___ Social overhead capital	2. An invention or innovation which has no major effect on relative demand for, or returns to, different factors.
___ Technological change	3. An invention or innovation that reduces the capital requirement more than the labor requirement. This raises wages relative to profits.
___ Neoclassical growth model	4. Level of real GDP the economy would produce if unemployment were at the "natural rate."
___ Capital-labor ratio	5. An invention or innovation that reduces the need for labor and increases the demand for capital. This increases profits relative to wages.
___ Capital deepening	6. Equals the growth of output minus the growth of the weighted-sum of all inputs. (This is another expression for *technological change*, but do *not* put this number with that term.)

133

___ Aggregate production function

___ Long-run steady state

___ Labor-saving invention

___ Capital-saving invention

___ Neutral invention

___ Growth accounting

___ Total factor productivity

___ Potential GDP

7. The expansion of a country's real potential GDP or output.

8. Total dollar value of capital goods divided by the number of workers, or the quantity of capital per worker.

9. A way of separating out the contributions of the different ingredients driving observed trends in growth.

10. Change in the processes of production or the introduction of new products such that more or improved output can be obtained from the same bundle of inputs.

11. Assuming technology is held constant, this describes a long run equilibrium position in which there is a cessation of capital deepening and constant capital returns, real wages, and interest rates.

12. Investments in a nation's infrastructure undertaken by the government, that precede and lay the framework for a thriving private sector.

13. Model in which a single homogeneous output is produced with two inputs: capital and labor.

14. Relates total national output to technology and all of a country's inputs.

IV. SUMMARY AND CHAPTER OUTLINE

This section summarizes the key concepts from the chapter.

A. Theories of Economic Growth

1. Economic growth ponders the processes by which the American standard of living has improved so dramatically and by which the stock of American capital has grown so large. These are not merely topics of academic curiosity. This topic is paramount when policymakers and economic theorists question, for example, the sources of the recent slowdown in American productivity and search for remedies that can revitalize economic growth. It is also a topic that needs to be understood if we are to be able to assist developing economies in their attempts to improve the lots of their citizens. Economic growth is the single most important factor in the economic success of nations in the long run.

2. The perspective of Chapter 27 is admittedly long-term,

and the analysis might appear at first blush to be a bit more complex than that found in other chapters of the text. It may help to point out that most models of economic growth are explained almost exclusively in terms of the interplay between the diminishing marginal productivity of the factors of production and technological change. The three factors of production—human resources (or labor), natural resources (or land), and capital—along with technology are the four main elements of economic growth.

The aggregate production function relates total national output to all of the economy's inputs and technology. It is written as:

$$Q = A \, F(K, L, R)$$

where Q is national output of GDP, A is the level of technological know-how in the economy and K, L, and R are the capital, labor, and natural resource inputs in the economy. The production function itself simply says that national output is some function of a combination of the inputs, weighted by the level of technology.

3. Each new stage in the interplay between diminishing marginal productivity and technology affects the distribution of income between labor and capital. It is important to understand that input proportions can change as economic growth occurs. Furthermore, diminishing returns can apply even when the supplies of all inputs are increasing—if they are not increasing at the same rate.

4. Consider a production function depending upon just two inputs, *capital* and *labor*. The input with the slower rate of growth (usually thought to be labor in a developed economy) can, for purposes of studying growth, be considered to be the (relatively) fixed input, while the other is viewed as the (relatively) variable input. Since the payment offered to the variable input (capital, in this simple illustration) depends upon its marginal product, and that marginal product should decline as the supply of capital increases relative to labor, diminishing returns work against the well-being of the owners of capital. In the extreme, in fact, diminishing returns might drive the marginal product of capital to zero, so the competitive return earned by capital would also move to zero. It is, of course, unlikely that this circumstance would come to pass; investment is likely to stop increasing the capital stock well before the zero-payment level is reached.

Early (i.e., pre-industrial revolution) discussions of economic growth were also based on two inputs, but in those approaches *land* was viewed as the fixed factor and *labor* was variable. With the emphasis on diminishing returns, it was inevitable that economists like Malthus should conclude that labor's future looked gloomy.

In more recent discussions, labor has been the fixed input and capital the variable one (because the stock of capital is growing faster than population). Now the shoe is on the other foot. Capital, it would seem, is the input that is vulnerable to the ravages of diminishing returns; but capital has another card to play: *technological progress.*

The diminishing-returns effect, which continually works against the return to the owners of capital, is more or less continually being offset by technological advance.

5. **Capital deepening** occurs when the stock of capital grows more rapidly than the labor force. When we hold other factors constant, this accounts for the positive (though declining) slope of the aggregate production function (*APF*) in Figure 27-4 from your textbook (reproduced here as Figure 11-1). When **technology** changes, as in Figure 27-5 from your textbook (here, Figure 11-2), the entire *APF* schedule will shift. Capital and technology are the basic ingredients in the **neoclassical growth model.**

Figure 11-1 Economic Growth Through Capital Deepening

Figure 11-2 Technological Advance Shifts up the Production Possibilities

6. Recent theories of economic growth suggest that technological change may itself be an output of the economic system. Rather than assuming that technology is a "given" or determined exogenously (i.e., outside the economic system), newer economic models investigate how the private market and public policy contribute to technological progress.

Many aspects of technological change should also be viewed as public or "nonrival" goods. While new technologies may be expensive to develop, they tend to be rather inexpensive to reproduce. Further, once developed, many people and producers can use or share the same technology simultaneously without using it up. These public good attributes of technology suggest that the private market would tend to underproduce technology and that the government or public agency should be more involved in its development.

B. The Patterns of Growth in the United States

1. Aggregate U.S. statistics describe the following pattern of growth since 1900:

   a. The annual growth rate of labor and employment has been consistently smaller than the annual growth rate of capital. This is called capital deepening.

   b. For the most of this century, the real wage paid to labor has increased.

   c. The share of GDP paid to labor has increased only slightly, and been nearly constant for the last 20 years.

   d. There have been large fluctuations in both rates of profit and real interest rates and no discernible trends either up or down.

   e. The capital-output ratio has actually declined since 1990.

   f. The savings rate and the investment-output ratio has held stable, for the most part, except for a sharp decrease in the national savings rate since 1980.

   g. National output has grown at an average rate of about three percent per year. The weighted average annual growth rate of the three inputs (K, L, and R) has been less than three percent. This suggests that technology (or other factors) has played a key role in economic growth.

2. For those who read through the section on the **growth-accounting approach,** we offer the following explanation of equations (1) and (2) presented there. Samuelson and Nordhaus begin with:

$$(1) \ \% \ Q \text{ growth} = 0.75 \times (\% \ L \text{ growth}) + 0.25 \\ \times (\% \ K \text{ growth}) + T.C.$$

The 0.75 and 0.25 represent the relative contributions of labor and capital, respectively, to economic growth.

There are a couple of intermediate steps between equations (1) and (2). First, subtract (% *L* growth) from both sides of the equation. Since the right-hand side of equation (1) already has $0.75 \times (\% L$ growth) in it, we are left with negative one-quarter of $(\% L$ growth) on the right-hand side. This leaves:

$$\text{(1a)} \quad \% Q \text{ growth} - \% L \text{ growth} =$$
$$0.25 \times (\% K \text{ growth}) - 0.25 \times (\% L \text{ growth}) + T.C.$$

We can combine the capital and labor growth terms on the right-hand side of equation (la) since they are both premultiplied by 0.25.

$$\text{(1b)} \quad \% Q \text{ growth} - \% L \text{ growth} =$$
$$0.25 \times (\% K \text{ growth} - \% L \text{ growth}) + T.C.$$

Finally, when you calculate percentage changes, and two terms are subtracted, you can first form them into a ratio or fraction and then calculate the percentage change.
For example, let:

$$Q_1 = 100 \text{ and } Q_2 = 105$$
$$L_1 = 200 \text{ and } L_2 = 202.$$

The percentage change in Q is 5 percent, and the percentage change in L is 1 percent. So, we could write:

$$\% Q \text{ growth} - \% L \text{ growth} = 5\% - 1\% = 4\%$$

Alternatively, we could first form the terms above into an output-labor ratio, and then calculate the percentage change in that ratio.

$$(Q/L)_1 = 100/200 \text{ and } (Q/L)_2 = 105/202$$
$$(Q/L)_1 = 0.5000 \text{ and } (Q/L)_2 = 0.5198$$

The percentage change in the ratio is 0.0396. (If the changes are very small, or if we calculate the change using the midpoint of the range, rather than the initial value as the base, then the two answers would be identical!)

This all leads to Samuelson's and Nordhaus's second equation:

$$\text{(2)} \quad \% Q/L \text{ growth} = 0.25 \times (\% K/L \text{ growth}) + T.C.$$

About 60 percent of the growth in output in the United States can be attributed to increases in capital and labor. The rest is a residual factor and can, in large part, be attributed to technology and factors related to it: research and development, innovation, economies of scale, scientific advances, and education.
3. When compared with the period from 1948 to 1973, the rate of productivity growth in the United States has slowed dramatically since 1973. While no clear-cut explanation for the **productivity slowdown** exists, studies point to several factors that have become more prevalent since the early

1970s. Stricter environmental regulations, the sharp increase in energy prices, a deterioration in labor quality, and a disproportionate share of research and development dollars (when compared to other industrialized economies) allocated to national defense and space exploration have all been proposed as contributing factors to the productivity slowdown.

V. HELPFUL HINTS

1. It has been mentioned previously that economic growth is always measured in *real* terms. Growth is also usually measured in *percent* per time period.
2. It may be helpful to keep in mind that when economists talk about the **steady state,** the level of technology is held constant. As long as technology keeps changing, an economy cannot be in a steady state position.
3. As we move along the aggregate production function *(APF)* in Figure 11-1, we add more capital per worker, holding all other factors constant. This is **capital deepening**.
4. The *APF* schedule will shift if there is a change in technology or natural resources.
5. If an invention or innovation is capital-saving, the firm will demand more labor relative to capital. Correspondingly, the amount of money paid in wages relative to profits will increase.
6. The classical approach to economics includes, for the most part, ideas that were developed in the eighteenth and nineteenth centuries. Economists of that time did not consider themselves as "classicals"—that is just what we call them now. Some of their ideas are very powerful and relevant today.
   Neoclassical models are modern (twentieth-century) refinements of classical ideas.

VI. MULTIPLE CHOICE QUESTIONS

These questions are organized by topic from the chapter outline. Choose the best answer from the options available.

A. Theories of Economic Growth

1. Suppose agricultural output requires only two inputs, labor and land. The quantity of land available is fixed; the quantity of labor is variable. Then, as labor quantity is increased in order to increase output quantity, the law of diminishing returns will begin to operate, and:
   a. the ratio of labor to land will increase, but the ratio of land to output will fall.
   b. both the labor-land ratio and the land-output ratio will fall.
   c. both the labor-land ratio and the land-output ratio will increase.
   d. the labor-land ratio will fall, but the land-output ratio will not change.

e.   the labor-land ratio will increase, but the land-output ratio will not change.

2. In the simple labor theory of value, demand for goods plays the following role:

a.   It interacts with supply to determine price, as in any other case.

b.   It dominates over supply in the determination of price but does not influence quantities produced and consumed.

c.   It settles quantities produced and consumed but has no influence on price.

d.   It has no influence either on quantities produced and consumed or on price.

e.   It dominates over supply in determining not only the price but also the quantities produced and consumed.

3. The most important single factor accounting for increased productivity and growth in the American economy thus far appears to have been:

a.   a deepening of the capital stock.

b.   technological change.

c.   a widening of the capital stock.

d.   the use of growth-encouraging monetary and fiscal policy.

e.   the increase in skills of the labor force.

4. If the amount of capital employed increased while the amount of labor and other inputs stayed approximately fixed, and if the capital-output ratio remained constant, then:

a.   the capital-labor ratio must have fallen.

b.   the price of capital must have fallen.

c.   the law of diminishing returns must have been in operation.

d.   technological improvements must have been made.

e.   total output must have fallen.

5. A deepening of capital must, in the absence of technological change, eventually:

a.   increase the capital-output ratio.

b.   decrease the capital-output ratio.

c.   increase output by an amount that is more than proportionate to the increase in capital.

d.   increase output in proportion to the increase in capital.

e.   increase the share of capital-owners in the total of output.

6. "Deepening of capital" means:

a.   an increase in the stock of capital relative to the size of the labor force.

b.   the introduction of new capital goods which embody technological change.

c.   a change in either productivity or amount of capital which increases the share of capital-owners in total product.

d.   an increase in the productivity of capital which reduces, or at least does not increase, the total of the capital stock.

e.   none of the above.

7. If capital is considered to be the only variable input, then diminishing returns (without technological change) suggest that:

a.   the share of capital-owners in total output must increase as output is increased.

b.   the capital-output ratio must decrease as output is increased.

c.   the share of capital-owners in total output must decrease as output is increased.

d.   the capital-output ratio must increase as output is increased.

e.   the capital-output ratio must, by definition, remain constant as output is increased.

8. If a nation's capital-output ratio gradually increases over time despite capital deepening, then:

a.   the share of capital-owners in total output is increasing.

b.   the diminishing-returns stage has not yet been reached with respect to capital.

c.   the marginal physical product of capital must have reached zero.

d.   technological progress must be improving the productivity of capital.

e.   the law of diminishing returns is operating with respect to capital's productivity.

9. In economics, "capital formation" specifically refers to:

a.   the purchase of any new commodity.

b.   net investment.

c.   the borrowing of money.

d.   the sale of any new stock issue.

e.   none of these activities.

10. Which of the following have been presented as negative side effects of too much economic growth?

a.   Global warming.

b.   Deforestation.

c.   Species extinction.

d.   All of the above.

e.   Choices **a** and **b** only.

11. The neoclassical growth model developed by Robert Solow:

a.   analyzes the growth of potential output.

b.   assumes the economy is basically competitive.

c.   expands earlier growth models by including capital growth and technological change.

d.   includes all of the above.

e.   includes none of the above.

12. What role does technological change have in Solow's neoclassical growth model?

a.   Technological change is most important when capital deepening does not occur.

b.   Technological change is not very important, only capital deepening matters.

c. Without technological change, incomes and wages end up stagnating.

d. Technological change is more important in Malthus's model.

e. Technological change has no role in the neoclassical growth model.

13. Recent models of economic growth have suggested that technological change:

a. is not as important as in previous time periods.

b. may be exogenous.

c. increases capital productivity more than labor productivity.

d. is an output of the economic system.

e. is all of the above.

B. The Patterns of Growth in the United States

14. Which of the following is *not* considered a trend in the recent economic growth of industrialized countries?

a. Average national product growth of about three percent per year.

b. Capital deepening.

c. Swings in real interest rates, especially during business cycles.

d. A decline in the share of wages and salaries in national income.

e. A decline in the capital-output ratio.

15. The **productivity slowdown** can be attributed to:

a. the depreciation of the capital stock.

b. an increase in energy prices.

c. stricter environmental regulations.

d. all of the above.

e. choices **b** and **c** only.

16. Since 1900, the stock of capital in the United States has increased:

a. eightfold, and operation of the diminishing-returns law has significantly reduced the capital-output ratio.

b. tenfold, and operation of the diminishing-returns law has significantly increased the capital-output ratio.

c. by an amount exactly proportionate to the increase in the labor force, so the diminishing-returns law has had no application.

d. threefold, and operation of the diminishing-returns law has significantly reduced the capital-output ratio.

e. eightfold, but the capital-output ratio has not increased significantly despite the diminishing-returns law.

17. Since 1900, the share of wages and salaries in national income:

a. has significantly increased.

b. has remained about constant, showing only a very slight upward trend.

c. has significantly fallen, except for a period during and immediately after World War II.

d. rose fairly steadily until about 1930 and remained constant until 1945 (excluding World War II), but has fallen perceptibly since then.

e. is not correctly described by any of the above.

VII. PROBLEM SOLVING

The following problems are designed to help you apply the concepts that you learned in the chapter.

A. Theories of Economic Growth

1. In very early attempts to construct economic theory (e.g., in Adam Smith's work), the discussion was often conducted as if production were exclusively a matter of labor cost. With only one input to consider, there could not be any conflict over the division of the output. Soon, however, it became evident (and this drew major emphasis in the work of Malthus) that land was likewise a productive input, one that was scarce or limited in supply. Moreover, there was no comparable limit to the size of population that might ultimately appear. "The law of diminishing returns" evolved, bringing along the need to ponder the distribution of output between the two input categories.

a. In the Malthus approach to diminishing returns, (**land / labor / capital**) was the fixed input, and (**land / labor / capital**) was the variable one. Malthus felt that a final "equilibrium" would be reached when labor had (**increased / decreased**) sufficiently to make the wage per worker just equal to the minimum-subsistence level.

b. This wage per worker would be labor's (**marginal / total**) product. The remainder of total product, after these wages were paid, would go to landowners.

2. The two ingredients in Malthus's diminishing-returns analysis were land and labor, with labor as the variable and increasing element. In modern growth theory, the participants have changed.

a. The fixed input is considered to be (**land / labor / capital**), while the variable input is (**land / labor / capital**). When this variable input is increased relative to the fixed input, the condition is described by economists as capital (**widening / deepening / maintenance**).

If the stock of capital (i.e., machinery tools, and other such equipment) were to increase gradually over time, then we would expect to see at least some accompanied technological improvement, i.e., the appearance of different and more efficient capital goods. Suppose, for the sake of illustration, though, that we assume that this type of technological change is absent.

b. An increase in capital with labor or population fixed—or more generally, an increase in the ratio of total capital to total labor—would lead to (**an increase / a decrease**) in the return to each unit of capital and (**an increase / a decrease**) in the wage paid to labor.

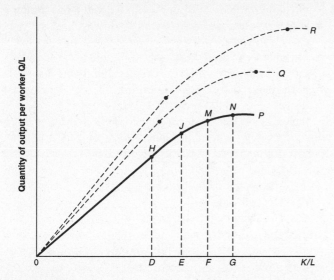

Figure 11-3

3. Consider the process indicated in question 2 in more detail. Designate the variable input capital as K, the fixed input labor as L, and quantity of total output as Q. Then, with no technological progress, the following results should be expected if K were increased relative to L:

a. The capital-labor ratio K/L should (**increase / decrease**).

b. The capital-output ratio K/Q should (**increase / decrease**). When the law of diminishing returns is operating, any increase in the variable input yields an increase in output Q that is (**less than / exactly / more than**) proportionate to the increase in K.

c. The interest or profit rate (price of K per unit) should (**increase / decrease**), and the wage rate (price of L) should (**increase / decrease**) as the K/L ratio increases.

d. The fractional or percentage share of total output going to K owners (**must increase / might increase / must decrease**).

B. The Patterns of Growth in the United States

4. In the United States, over the past century the stock of capital has grown more or less steadily and has grown more rapidly than population or the labor force. But what about technological progress, which improves the performance of K (capital) and which was specifically ruled out in the last question? In terms of Figure 11-3 (where the variable input

Figure 11-4

is now *K per worker*), technological progress lifts the output curve from 0*P* to 0*Q* and from 0*Q* to 0*R*. (The first black dot on the 0*Q* and 0*R* lines marks the point at which curvature begins [the line begins to get flatter]—i.e., the point at which the influence of diminishing returns first begins to set in.)

a.   Thus even though *K is* increasing, the shift in position of the *APF* curve means that the marginal product of *K* will (**increase / decrease**). The rate of interest or profit (per unit of capital) will thus (**fall / rise**) relative to labor's wage rate.

b.   Combining the two effects (diminishing returns and technological progress), we see that the increase in the capital stock (**raises / lowers**) total output.

c.   Technological progress (**raises / lowers**) total output. The increase in the capital stock (disregarding technological progress) (**raises / lowers**) the demand for labor. Hence we would expect labor's wage or price to (**increase / decrease**).

d.   Moving against this trend is technological progress, which (**increases / decreases**) the interest or profit rate and tends to (**increase / decrease**) the demand for labor.

5.   The facts of economic growth in the United States are summarized below. Refer to Figure 27-6 from the text, which has been reproduced here as Figure 11-4 (on previous page), to deduce the answers.

a.   Since 1900, the labor force has (**remained roughly constant / nearly doubled / approximately tripled / increased more than sixfold**). The stock of capital has, meanwhile, (**remained roughly constant / nearly doubled / increased nearly fourfold / increased approximately eightfold / increased by more than elevenfold**). That is to say, the capital stock, in proportion to the labor force, has (**increased / decreased**) by a factor of approximately (**1 / 2 / 3 / 6**). There (**has / has not**) been a (**small / significant**) deepening of capital.

b.   Disregarding technological change, if both capital and labor had increased eightfold, then we would have expected to see output increase by a factor of 8. With labor only tripled, though, we would expect to see output increase by (**more / less**) than 8 times its value in 1900.

c.   In fact, however, output has increased by a factor of approximately (**3 / 8 / 11**). This means that the ratio of the capital stock to annual output has (**increased / remained about constant / decreased slightly**). Things (**have / have not**) worked out as the simple law of diminishing returns would indicate, the reason evidently being (**that the law has been incorrectly set out / the effects of technological change / the higher real wage paid to labor**).

d.   Real wages (**have risen / have fallen / show no clear trend either up or down**). The interest or profit rate—the "price of capital"—(**has risen / has fallen / shows no clear trend either up or down**).

e.   Output per worker-hour, or *Q/L*, has (**risen / remained constant / fallen**). The increase in the wage rate (**has significantly exceeded / has been approximately equal to / has fallen behind**) the (**increase / decrease**) in output per worker-hour.

6.   Seven basic trends in major economic variables have been typical of growth in the United States as well as in most developed countries. Indicate the direction of each in the spaces provided below:

a.   The capital-labor ratio has _____.

b.   The real wage has _____.

c.   The share paid to labor has _____.

d.   The real rate of interest has _____.

e.   After _____ from 1920 through 1945, the capital-output ratio has _____ since 1950.

f.   The savings-output ratio has _____.

g.   Output has _____.

7.   a.   Trend **f**, combined with a small level of net foreign investment, implies that the investment-output ratio has (**risen / remained steady / fallen**).

b.   Trends **a** and **b** are consistent with the neoclassical model of growth (**only when technological change is introduced / even without technological change**).

c.   Trends **d** and **e** (**do / do not**) depend on technological change because no progress would always combine with a deepening capital stock to predict (**higher / lower**) real interest rates and (**higher / lower**) capital-output ratios.

8.   Complete Table 11-1 on the basis of the growth-accounting procedures presented in the text.

Table 11-1

	Case I	Case II	Case III
Rate of growth of labor (%)	1	0	1
Rate of growth of capital (%)	4	4	5
Rate of technological change (%)	2	2	2
Rate of growth of output (%)	—	—	—
Rate of growth of output per worker (%)	—	—	—

VIII. DISCUSSION QUESTIONS

Answer the following questions, making sure that you can explain the work you did to arrive at the answers.

1.   Briefly describe Smith's and Malthus's approaches to economic growth.

2.   How does Solow's neoclassical growth model differ from the classical approach to growth? How is it similar?

3.   According to Table 27-1 in the text, Turkey and India both experienced greater annual growths of output per person than the United States during the period from 1973 to 1993. Nevertheless, citizens in the United States are much

wealthier than people in either of these other two countries. How do you reconcile these two disparate facts?

4. Briefly explain the role of technology in the neoclassical growth model.

IX. ANSWERS TO STUDY GUIDE QUESTIONS

III. Review of Key Concepts

7	Economic growth
12	Social overhead capital
10	Technological change
13	Neoclassical growth model
8	Capital-labor ratio
1	Capital deepening
14	Aggregate production function
11	Long-run steady state
5	Labor-saving invention
3	Capital-saving invention
2	Neutral invention
9	Growth accounting
6	Total factor productivity
4	Potential GDP

VI. Multiple Choice Questions

1. A   2. C   3. B   4. D   5. A   6. A
7. D   8. E   9. B   10. D   11. D   12. C
13. D   14. D   15. E   16. E   17. B

VII. Problem Solving

1. a. land, labor, increased
   b. marginal
2. a. labor, capital, deepening
   b. a decrease, an increase
3. a. increase
   b. increase, less than
   c. decrease, increase
   d. must decrease
4. a. increase, rise
   b. raises
   c. raises, raises, increase
   d. increases, decrease
5. a. approximately tripled, increased approximately eightfold, increased, 3, has, significant
   b. less
   c. 11, decreased slightly, have not, the effects of technological change
   d. have risen, shows no clear trend either up or down

e. risen, has been approximately equal to, increase
6. a. risen
   b. risen
   c. risen very slightly
   d. been trendless
   e. falling, remained constant
   f. been stable
   g. increased (at about 3 to 4 percent per year)
7. a. remained steady
   b. even without technological change
   c. do, lower, higher
8.

Table 11-1

	Case I	Case II	Case III
Rate of growth of output (%)	3.75	3.00	4.00
Rate of growth of output per worker (So)	2.75	3.00	3.00

VIII. Discussion Questions

1. Both Smith and Malthus stressed the importance of land in economic growth. Smith viewed land as an abundantly free resource; therefore, the value of all production belonged to, and would be returned to, labor. Malthus pointed out that land was fixed; therefore, the returns to labor would eventually have to decrease. As the population grew, and more and more labor was applied to the fixed supply of land, the marginal product of labor would fall and wages would be pushed to a subsistence level.

2. Solow's model is also based on two inputs: one variable and one fixed. In Solow's model, however, labor is the fixed input and capital is the variable. Indeed, capital has grown much more rapidly than labor in the twentieth century. Solow resolves Malthus's dilemma by recognizing the role of capital and technology in economic growth.

3. This question tempts the reader to confuse stocks and flows. The wealth of a nation and its citizens is a stock variable—it is measured at a particular point in time. Annual economic growth is a flow variable—it measures how a nation's output (or wealth) is changing. India and Turkey may have higher rates of growth, but their respective stocks of wealth are still far below that of the United States.

4. Technology is an important component of the neoclassical growth model. Technological change means that more output can be produced with a given amount of capital and labor. Technological change counterbalances the law of diminishing marginal returns (to capital) and helps keep the real wage of labor from falling.

CHAPTER 12
The Challenge of Economic Development

I. CHAPTER OVERVIEW

"Of the 5 billion people on this planet, perhaps 1 billion live in absolute poverty—barely able to survive from day to day." So begins Chapter 28 in your text. There exists, across the globe, a disparity in standards of living that boggles the mind; and it is this observation that raises a litany of questions which could turn out to be *the* critical questions for survival through the twenty-first century. What, first of all, could possibly be the source of this disparity? Second, what can be done by the developing countries to correct it? And finally, what does the future hold for further changes in economic development? Without some attempt to answer these questions, the growing gap between the wealthy and the poor nations of the world could foster economic, political, and military conflict that could wreak havoc across the planet.

In the first part of this chapter, Samuelson and Nordhaus document the characteristics of a developing nation. They discuss various issues in economic development and strategies for its eradication. In the second part of the chapter, alternative models of economic development are discussed. Particular attention is given to the economies of Asia and the former Soviet Union.

Only if we understand the sources of inequity between nations can we begin to work to correct it, and only if we sort out false strategies from productive strategies will progress be made. The major objective of the chapter is, therefore, an understanding of the dimension of the economic development problem.

II. LEARNING OBJECTIVES

After you have read Chapter 28 in your text and completed the exercises in this *Study Guide* chapter, you should be able to:

1. Discuss the aspects of life in developing countries.
2. Identify the four "wheels of development" and explain the problems faced by less developed countries in getting any one of them "rolling uphill."
3. Describe the vicious cycle of underdevelopment, and identify the means by which it might be broken.
4. Explain the backwardness hypothesis.
5. Discuss the pros and cons of each of the following

issues in economic development: (a) industrialization vs. agriculture, (b) inward vs. outward orientation, and (c) state vs. market control.
6. Explain the approach used in the **newly industrialized** countries of Southeast Asia.
7. Discuss the various aspects of socialism.
8. Understand the historical underpinnings of Marx's radical theory and his contribution to economic thought.
9. Understand the economic history of the Soviet Union as it evolved from a czarist regime, to communism, to a newborn market economy.

III. REVIEW OF KEY CONCEPTS

Match the following terms from column A with their definitions in column B.

A	B
__ Developing country	1. Controlled prices which are artificially held below market clearing levels and which result in shortages.
__ Newly industrialized country (NIC)	2. Encompasses a wide variety of economic approaches ranging from democratic welfare states with nationalized industries to deregulation and privatization of the market.
__ Demographic transition	3. Strategy for development in which countries attempt to be self-sufficient and replace imports with domestic production.
__ Brain drain	4. Advocates a complete and quick transition from a command to a market-based system.
__ Infrastructure	5. An industry that is owned and operated by the state.
__ Vicious cycle of poverty	6. The less developed a country is, relative to other nations, the more advantages it has to develop.
__ Backwardness hypothesis	7. A country with low real per capita income relative to industrialized nations; also known as an LDC (less developed country).

___ Import substitution

___ Outward orientation

___ Free-market absolutism

___ Communism

___ The Asian managed-market approach

___ Socialism

___ Command economy

___ Nationalized industry

___ Forced-draft industrialization

___ Repressed inflation

___ Soft budget constraints

___ Step-by-step reform

___ Shock-therapy approach

8. Advocates a gradual and cautious transition to a market economy.

9. The questions of *how, what,* and *for whom* are determined by the government bureaucracy.

10. The transformation from high birth and death rates and a growing population to low birth and death rates and a stable population.

11. This establishes state-planned priorities for industrial development.

12. This country was a "developing country," but it has recently experienced significant and successful growth.

13. Social overhead capital.

14. In a controlled economy, operating losses may be covered by state subsidies and therefore not lead to bankruptcy.

15. Specific type of totalitarian, collectivized economic system withgovernment ownership of land and capital.

16. Laissez-faire economy with minimal government involvement.

17. Economic system with both strong government oversight and powerful market forces.

18. Reinforcing obstacles of low income, low saving, low capital growth, and low productivity that keep a nation poor.

19. Strategy for development in which countries pay for imports by improving efficiency and competitiveness, by developing foreign markets, and by giving incentives for exports.

20. Intelligent citizens of LDCs are attracted to industrialized countries for education and training. When they do not return home after completing their education, this occurs.

IV. SUMMARY AND CHAPTER OUTLINE

This section summarizes the key concepts from the chapter.

A. Economic Growth in Poor Countries

1. Human resources, natural resources, capital formation, and technological advance are the four driving forces of development. Less developed countries typically have difficulty in exploiting all four.

2. Investments in the labor force (i.e., human capital) are critical to economic development. While the other factors of production can be imported if need be, labor is homegrown. Education, training, health, and nutrition are vital to the development of this resource and the economy.

The United Nations has developed a Human Development Index (HDI) which combines four different demographic, social, and economic statistics: life expectancy at birth, school enrollment, adult literacy, and real GDP per capita. The relationship between HDI and per capita output is strong and positive for most countries.

3. The vicious cycle of underdevelopment runs from low saving and investment to low capital accumulation, low productivity, and low incomes, and back again. It applies to many situations, but its general applicability varies from country to country depending upon the country's population, technology, resources, and capital base.

4. The **backwardness hypothesis** suggests that today's developing economies may have an advantage over countries in the 19th century simply because they can learn from and use technologies and supplies from more advanced economies. The key here is that some countries are backward, *relative* to others. As low-income countries learn and grow, economic *convergence* is expected to occur.

5. Strategies for promoting economic development abound. Some emphasize export goods; some emphasize import-competing goods; still others emphasize borrowing new technologies. Each has merit somewhere in the world, but none is universally applicable, especially in a world in which development must proceed with a cautious eye cast at its environmental consequences.

B. Alternative Models for Development

1. All societies are faced with the basic economic problem of scarce resources and unlimited wants. All societies need to determine *how* to produce goods and services, *what* to produce, and how to distribute them (i.e., *for whom*). The spectrum of alternative economic systems includes **market economies** at one end and **command economies** at the other. A market economy is based on voluntary decisions, and prices are determined by the interaction between buyers and sellers in the marketplace. In a command economy, the questions of *what, how,* and *for whom* are made by a government bureaucracy.

2. Some of the economies of eastern Asia (Japan, South Korea, Singapore, Hong Kong, Thailand) have experienced impressive rates of economic growth during the last few decades. There are several common threads to their success:

a. All are market-oriented economies, albeit with differing levels of government involvement.

b. All have above-average rates of investment.

c. In each economy, macroeconomic policy has attempted to keep inflation rates low and investment rates high.

d. Each economy is **outward-oriented**. These countries have encouraged exports and attempted to replicate the best technological advances of the high-income countries.

e. Rather than relying entirely on the market, governments in some of these economies have organized non-market contests to allocate resources. After identifying strategic areas for development, the government, in these countries, sets up an internal contest among domestic firms to stimulate competition and promote efficiency.

3. China has enjoyed rapid economic growth during the past decade. The Chinese government has gradually decentralized some areas of economic decision making and established several special economic zones in which private and foreign-owned firms are permitted. There has, however, been limited political reform in China during this time period.

4. Karl Marx (1818-1883) said that the value of all commodities was determined by the amount of labor effort required to produce them. The value of commodities produced mainly by capital equipment was derived from the labor required to produce the capital. The profits received by the owners of the companies were viewed by Marx as "unearned income" since there was no productive labor embodied in their efforts. As the industrial revolution progressed and production became more capital intensive, Marx envisioned that the marginal product and rate of return on capital would fall and the unemployment rate would rise. As the masses of unemployed grew, discontent would spread and eventually the workers would rise up and overthrow the owners. One possible explanation as to why all of this did not occur can be found in the previous chapter. Technological change helped maintain the productivity of capital, increased the demand for labor, and contributed to economic growth!

5. Socialism, which was developed by Marx and others, lies between market and central-planned systems. Socialism encompasses a wide variety of alternative economic approaches ranging from democratic welfare states with nationalized industries to deregulation and privatization of the market. Nevertheless, there are some common threads running through most socialist economies:

a. Government ownership of productive resources.

b. Coordinated planning rather than "chaotic" market allocations.

c. Redistribution of income.

d. Control via peaceful, gradual, democratic evolution.

6. Central planning worked, more or less, in the Soviet Union for 70 years, but then the economy, and the union, fell apart. While researchers are still studying the collapse, it is clear that the Soviet planners paid much too little attention to their consumers. Emphasis was placed instead on the military, space exploration, and certain key industries. It also proved impossible to determine optimal production methods, product quality, and the distribution of goods and services by relying exclusively on centralized top-to-bottom decision making.

7. Most of the nations of the former Soviet Union are finding that the transition to market-based economies is both slow and painful. Economic hardships abound, and the obstacles are numerous. While each country is unique, they share some common economic problems.

a. All resources and means of production must be released by the government and turned over to private ownership. Corporations must be developed, stock markets *created,* and banking and credit institutions modernized and greatly expanded.

b. Prices must be determined by the forces of supply and demand in the marketplace. Government controls and subsidies must be removed.

c. Individuals need to learn how to live in a market economy based on individual choice.

V. HELPFUL HINTS

1. The citizens of industrialized countries may be tempted to think of their economically poorer neighbors as slow or backward. This would be a grave mistake. Remember, GDP is not necessarily an accurate indicator of happiness or well-being. While not rich by industrialized standards, these nations have a wealth of culture, tradition, and history. Differences in lifestyle and/or values do not necessarily reflect impoverishment.

2. Duplication of Western technology in developing countries may or may not be successful. Production techniques need to be changed to fit the available supply of resources. Countries that are predominantly agricultural may be better served by trying to improve productivity in that area rather than industrializing the economy.

3. As we will see when we study international trade (Chapter 35), even the richest of nations can benefit by trading with less developed partners.

VI. MULTIPLE CHOICE QUESTIONS

These questions are organized by topic from the chapter outline. Choose the best answer from the options available.

A. Economic Growth in Poor Countries

1. One area of economic development in which the country's government must take the initiative and also participate relates to:

a.   maintaining balanced growth.

b.   promoting heavy industry.

c.   transferring resources needed in the shift from agricultural predominance to industrial predominance.

d.   providing social overhead capital.

e.   none of the above, because there are no areas in which such government involvement is always needed.

2. The main reason population growth has spurted ahead so rapidly in many less developed countries in recent years is that:

a.   birth rates have increased sharply with improvements in nutrition.

b.   great strides have been made in keeping older people alive an extra 5 or 10 years.

c.   infant mortality and mortality due to epidemics have been drastically lowered.

d.   large-scale immigration has occurred into many countries since World War II.

e.   birth rates have risen markedly as the natural result of widespread reductions in the customary age of marriage.

3. Four of the following five statements identify a problem of economic development. Which one does *not*?

a.   Developing economies often have reasonable prospects of looking to "increasing returns to scale" as they expand their total output.

b.   Ordinarily, individual firms cannot undertake investment in social overhead capital, no matter how important such projects may be.

c.   Entrepreneurship and innovation are vital for the success of any developing economy.

d.   The principle of protecting import-competing industries is not necessarily a wise one for a developing nation to follow.

e.   In a probable majority of the less developed nations, excess saving is a significant problem.

4. As a country develops economically and builds its own industry, one of the following usually does *not* occur. Which one?

a.   It imports less and less from other developed and industrialized countries.

b.   Its total exports tend to rise.

c.   It imports more and more from other industrialized, highly developed countries.

d.   It imports more from less developed countries.

e.   Its total imports tend to rise.

5. "Social overhead capital" is:

a.   the money investment required before any return is obtainable from a particular natural resource.

b.   typically financed by foreign countries.

c.   investment in those projects considered to have the highest net productivity.

d.   projects which must be financed by the nation itself, as distinct from those financed by private corporations.

e.   any capital investment whose amount does not vary as the quantity of national output is increased.

6. An example of "social overhead capital" would be:

a.   a rural electrification project.

b.   state-financed hospitals and schools.

c.   the development of a domestic transportation system.

d.   all of the above.

e.   **a** and **c** above, but not **b**.

7. An absolute precondition for growth is the:

a.   development of some excess of income over consumption.

b.   creation of a surplus labor force for employment in manufacturing.

c.   discovery and exploitation of some internal economies.

d.   cultural acceptance of free enterprise principles of economic behavior.

e.   development of manufacturing to the point where it can begin to supplant agriculture.

8. Four of the following five statements identify a problem of economic development. Which one does *not*?

a.   In some less developed countries, considerable investment takes place but goes into items that are of low priority or even are undesirable from the standpoint of national economic development.

b.   The development of adequate social overhead capital is usually essential if there is to be much economic development.

c.   Historically, political revolutions have often taken place after some economic progress has been achieved.

d.   Most of the less developed countries are known to have substantial unexploited natural resources, if only the capital needed to bring them into effective use were available.

e.   In poor countries, especially rural ones, often a large part of the labor pool does almost nothing because there is nothing for it to do.

9. Less developed countries have lower per capita incomes than developed countries. Over the past several decades, that gap has been:

a   diminishing between the "free enterprise" less developed countries but widening with respect to the socialist-oriented ones.

b.   almost impossible to measure because of differences in cultures, tastes, and climates.

c.   perceptibly diminishing, evidently as the result of foreign-aid programs.

d.   diminishing with respect to those countries which have concentrated their investment upon social overhead capital.

e.   essentially stable, and in some areas may even be widening.

10. The human development index:

a. combines economic and social indicators in an assessment of human conditions.

b. has a strong negative correlation with per capita output.

c. has been criticized by economists.

d. is all of the above.

e. is none of the above.

B. Alternative Models for Development

11. In "free-market absolutism:"
    a. the government has complete or absolute control.
    b. all goods and services are free.
    c. consumers have free choice in the marketplace, but jobs are assigned by the state.
    d. government has a very limited role in the economy.
    e. none of the above.

12. The "Asian managed-market approach:"
    a. has been used successfully in mainland China.
    b. coexists with communism in several nations.
    c. developed from socialism.
    d. all the above.
    e. none of the above.

13. In socialist economies:
    a. industries may be nationalized.
    b. tax rates tend to be higher and more progressive.
    c. the free market may be critically important to the nation's economic health.
    d. all the above.
    e. a and b only, not c.

14. The most impressive economic growth during the last 50 years has occurred in:
    a. Western Europe.
    b. North America.
    c. East Asia.
    d. Latin America.
    e. South America.

15. Investment is critical for economic growth because it:
    a. allows firms to focus less on current production and more on the development of new technology and the acquisition of capital.
    b. attracts foreign financial capital.
    c. encourages consumer spending on new products.
    d. raises tax revenues which are used to finance expenditures on social overhead capital.
    e. increases competition among firms.

16. The Chinese government has:
    a. successfully organized nonmarket contests between firms to encourage efficiency and growth.
    b. instituted political reforms since the Tiananmen Square incident in 1989.
    c. allowed foreign firms to operate alongside state-owned firms.
    d. a large trade deficit with the United States.

e. restricted the operation of "special economic zones."

17. Marx's labor theory of value suggests that:
    a. the value of all goods and services is derived from the labor effort that went into making them.
    b. the profits of factory owners really belong to the workers.
    c. there is labor value even in capital equipment.
    d. all the above.
    e. a and b only, not c.

18. The "soft budget constraints" in the Soviet-style brand of communism can best be described as:
    a. an example of repressed inflation.
    b. subsidies from the government to cover operating losses of firms.
    c. cost restrictions on nontangible commodities such as services.
    d. budget restrictions on all sectors of the economy, except the military.
    e. none of the above.

19. Which statement below about the former Soviet Union is most accurate?
    a. While reform has been gradual, most of the citizens of Russia are economically better off now than they were under communism.
    b. Step-by-step reform has worked much better in the (former) satellite countries than has the shock-therapy approach.
    c. Economic reform in Russia has been more difficult than in the (former) satellite countries.
    d. All these statements are accurate.
    e. None of these statements is accurate.

20. Recent declines in socialist approaches to economic development have been attributed to:
    a. the overall decline in communism.
    b. stagnation in many European economies where socialism was popular.
    c. the successes of market-dominated economies.
    d. all of the above.
    e. choices b and c only.

VII. PROBLEM SOLVING

The following problems are designed to help you apply the concepts that you learned in the chapter.

A. Economic Growth in Poor Countries

1. The world's less developed countries are characterized by per capita income levels that are well below the world-wide average. Associated with low incomes are, moreover, human problems like poor health, widespread illiteracy, poor housing, poor diets, and demoralizing underemployment.

Table 12-1 Important Indicators for Different Groups of Countries

Country Group	Population, 1990 (million)	Gross Domestic Product			Adult Illiteracy, 1990 (%)	Life Expectancy at Birth (years)
		Total, 1990 ($,billion)	Per Capita			
			Level, 1990 ($)	Growth, 1965-1990 (% per year)		
Low-income economies:						
China and India	1,983	619	360	3.7	37	65
Other	1,075	307	320	1.7	45	55
Lower-middle-income economies (e.g., Chile, Philippines, Malaysia)	629	930	1,530	1.5	25	65
Upper-middle-income economies (e.g., Brazil, Korea, Mexico)	458	1,520	3,410	2.8	16	68
High-income economies (e.g., United States, Japan, France)	816	16,316	19,590	2.4	4	77

Countries are grouped by the World Bank into four major categories depending upon their per capita incomes. In each, a number of important indicators of economic development are shown. Note that low-income countries tend to have highly illiteracy and low life expectancy.

[Source: World Bank, *World Development Report,* 1992 (World Bank, Washington, D.C., 1992).]

This question asks you to record quantitative measures of these problems. Table 28-1 from your text, and reproduced here also as Table 12-1, analyzes country groups according to key indicators.

The data show that, compared with the high-income market economies, low-income countries display the following characteristics:

a. Per capita levels of GDP that are (**about 50 percent lower / about 90 percent lower / over 90 percent lower**).

b. Per capita GDP growth rates that are (**lower / higher / higher in China and India, but otherwise lower**).

c. Adult illiteracy rates that are (**25 percent higher / nearly 50 percent higher / over 75 percent higher**).

d. Life expectancies that are approximately (**20 percent lower / 33 percent lower / 50 percent lower**).

e. Total population that is (**twice as great / between 3 and 4 times as great / 5 times as great**) as in high-income economies. (Note that more people live in low-income countries than in the other three groups *combined*.)

2. Economists have identified four economic fundamentals which drive economic development: population, natural resources, capital formation, and technology.

a. Focusing for a moment on *natural resources,* which of the following statements or questions accurately describe a resources-related issue? (Circle neither, one, or both.)

(1) Many less developed countries appear to be resource-poor. How then are they to develop?

(2) Land reform is necessary for development in many countries, since individual holdings are too small to be used to their best advantage.

b. Turning now to *capital formation,* circle the numbers of all the statements that accurately record a development issue:

(1) Less developed nations find it very difficult to save (to refrain from consumption) in order to free resources for investment activity.

(2) The social customs in some less developed countries encourage rich people to hoard their saving or use them in nonproductive ways; they are not used to finance investment projects that would raise the national product.

3) The desire for development and the example of the developed nations have noticeably increased the amount of saving out of income in many less developed countries.

(4) In many poor countries, investment expenditure tends to go heavily into housing, an investment form which does not have the highest priority in development.

(5) The amount of private lending for financing investment activity by citizens in developed areas is greater than it was in the nineteenth century, both absolutely and relatively; in less developed countries, it is not.

c. Finally, repeat the process one more time for the role of *technology*:

(1) Less developed countries have the advantage that imitation of techniques already worked out is easier than development of new and sometimes sophisticated techniques.

(2) Efforts by developed countries to export advanced "technological know-how" are frequently unsuccessful.

(3) Some advanced technologies are "capital-saving," and these are likely to be particularly well suited to adoption in less developed countries.

3. Figure 12-1 illustrates the vicious cycle of underdevelopment. Identify the boxes of the cycle in the spaces provided. Box C is already identified for the purpose of providing perspective.

A: _____

B: _____

C: Low productivity _____

D: _____

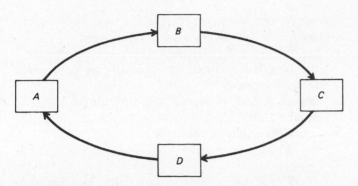

Figure 12-1

4. a. Higher saving will be useless and productive investment will not take place in any country unless it has a class of vigorous, creative _____.

b. Sometimes it is said that the recurring problem with which a developed country must cope during recession is that of (**too much / too little**) saving and hence (**too much / too little**) demand for consumption.

c. By contrast, the problem of the less developed country is that of (**too much / too little**) saving and hence (**too much / too little**) demand for consumption.

5. Strategies for development must confront and answer at least three general questions if they are to be successful.

First, is it more worthwhile to concentrate on industry or agriculture in initiating growth?

a. Investment in industry might provide a few high-paying jobs, but investment in agriculture might support industrialization by (**increasing the productivity of city workers / increasing the productivity of the farms and thereby releasing labor for industrial jobs / creating large agricultural surpluses that can replace imports**).

Second, it is important to decide whether to promote exports to generate growth supported by the worldwide marketplace or to protect import-competing industries to generate growth in domestic markets.

b. Care should be taken in considering the second alternative because protection can (**increase / decrease**) domestic prices, (**increase / decrease**) real incomes, and (**stimulate / retard**) investment at home and from abroad.

Third, many developing countries find themselves over-specialized and vulnerable to the whims of the world market for the few goods in which they have a comparative advantage.

c. The key to avoiding this difficulty is (**specialization / diversification**).

6. A less developed country is undertaking a large-scale development program and asks you to supply information on the points listed in parts **a** through **c**. What will you advise? (In each part, circle the number of the statement which you think furnishes the most likely scenario.)

a. Capital-formation policy:

(1) In view of the post-World War II experience, primary reliance can be placed on borrowing and aid from abroad.

(2) The primary problem will be achieving a better allocation of existing saving rather than increasing total saving.

(3) Historical experience suggests that the percentage of national product put into personal saving and into capital formation will have to be increased.

(4) Borrowing technology" will enable development at existing levels of saving.

b. Investment allocation:

(1) The government should make sure that it is undertaking adequate investment in social overhead capital.

(2) Private entrepreneurs can be relied upon to properly allocate available saving.

(3) Although inflation tends ultimately to discourage saving, it also tends to better allocate available saving.

(4) Modern technology makes heavy use of capital in production and hence should be avoided.

c. Change in foreign trade:

(1) Imports are likely to fall as domestic manufactures replace foreign manufactures.

(2) Imports are likely to rise because of the need for foreign capital goods and possibly for food and fuel.

(3) Exports of primary products should be pushed, since this is where comparative advantage must lie.

(4) Exports should fall as the demand of developed countries for raw materials continues to decline.

B. Alternative Models for Development

7. Throughout Chapter 28 Samuelson and Nordhaus discuss the theories of many different writers and economic philosophers. Some of these theories of economic development are very broad and general, while others relate to specific aspects of growth. Match each of the individuals in column A with "their" theory, as briefly described in column B.

A	B
__ Francis Hackett	1. Advocated the shock-therapy approach with a more rapid move from a command to a market-based economy.

__ Thomas Malthus

__ Max Weber

__ Mancur Olson

__ Alexander Gerschenkron

__ Karl Marx

__ Josef Stalin

__ Jerry Sachs

__ Yegor Gaidar

2.   Said that the relative backwardness of a country may actually aid in its development.

3.   Led a group of economists who opted for more rapid economic changes rather than gradual reform in their country.

4.   Instituted programs of collectivized agriculture and forced draft industrialization.

5.   Argued that the value of all commodities is derived from the efforts of labor embodied in them. Also saw capitalism as inevitably leading to socialism.

6.   Argued that a nation's population growth would exceed its ability to produce more and more food.

7.   Argued that a nation begins to decline when its decision making structure becomes inflexible and obstacles arise against further social and economic change.

8.   Believed in materialism and felt that the benefits of it should all be available for everyone.

9.   Emphasized the "Protestant ethic" as a driving force behind capitalism.

8. It is clear that a wide range of economic development exists across the countries of the world. Furthermore, different approaches and strategies of economic development have been tried in various countries. Match each country in column A with the descriptions in column B.

A   **B**

__ South Korea

__ India

__ Italy

__ Bolivia

__ China
__ Poland

1.   In 1990, Sachs persuaded this country's government to adopt a shock therapy approach to economic reform.

2.   In the 1980s this country needed all of its export earnings just to pay the *interest* on its foreign debt.

3.   Newly industrialized country with an outward orientation.

4.   Has tried both step-by-step and shock-therapy approaches to economic reform. This country continues to face serious economic hardships.

5.   Industrialized country.
6.   Low-income country.

__ Russia

7.   Has established "special economic zones" and allowed alternative forms of property ownership.

VIII. DISCUSSION QUESTIONS

Answer the following questions, making sure that you can explain the work you did to arrive at the answers.
1. a. Why is saving so important for economic growth?
    b. Why is it so difficult, especially for developing countries, to save?
2. Why is it both important and difficult for LDCs to acquire capital?
3. a. What is infrastructure?
    b. Why is infrastructure necessary for economic development?
    c. Why is it typically necessary for the government to finance infrastructure projects?
4. Briefly describe some of the common factors contributing to the rapid economic development of the Asian dragons."
5. List and briefly describe three factors that contributed to the economic collapse of the Soviet Union.
6. List and briefly describe three problems that Russia must grapple with as it attempts to transform its economy from one that is command- to one that is market-based.
7. Why did Marx view the profits received by capitalists as "unearned income?"

IX. ANSWERS TO STUDY GUIDE QUESTIONS

III. Review of Key Concepts

7	Developing country
12	Newly industrialized country (NIC)
10	Demographic transition
20	Brain drain
13	Infrastructure
18	Vicious cycle of poverty
6	Backwardness hypothesis
3	Import substitution
19	Outward orientation
16	Free-market absolutism
15	Communism
17	The Asian managed-market approach
2	Socialism
9	Command economy
5	Nationalized industry
11	Forced-draft industrialization
1	Repressed inflation
14	Soft budget constraints
8	Step-by-step reform
4	Shock-therapy approach

VI. Multiple Choice Questions

1. D   2. C   3. E   4. A   5. D   6. D
7. A   8. E   9. E   10. A   11. D   12. E
13. D   14. C   15. A   16. C   17. D   18. B
19. C   20. D

VII. Problem Solving

1. a. over 90 percent lower
   b. higher in China and India, but otherwise lower
   c. over 75 percent higher
   d. 20 percent lower
   e. between 3 and 4 times as great
2. a. (1), (2)
   b. (1), (2), (4)
   c. (1), (2), (3)
3. a. Low saving and investment
   b. Low pace of capital accumulation
   c. Low productivity
   d. Low average incomes
4. a. entrepreneurs
   b. too much, too little
   c. too little, too much
5. a. increasing the productivity of the farms and thereby releasing labor for industrial jobs
   b. increase, decrease, retard
   c. diversification
6. a. (3)
   b. (1)
   c. (2)
7. 8 Francis Hackett
   6 Thomas Malthus
   9 Max Weber
   7 Mancur Olson
   2 Alexander Gerschenkron
   5 Karl Marx
   4 Josef Stalin
   1 Jeffrey Sachs
   3 Yegor Gaidar
8. 3 South Korea
   6 India
   5 Italy
   2 Bolivia
   7 China
   1 Poland
   4 Russia

VIII. Discussion Questions

1. a. Saving is important for economic growth for (at least) two reasons. First, it sends a signal to producers that consumers will want more goods and services in the future and less now. So producers need to postpone some current production and retool for the future. Second, saving provides the financial resources, via the credit market, that firms need to borrow to finance their investment projects. Other things held constant, the more households save, the greater the availability of funds in the credit market and the lower the interest rates will be.

   b. Developing countries have great difficulty saving because such a large proportion of their resources, time, and effort must be devoted to providing the basic necessities of food, clothing, and shelter for their citizens.

2. The acquisition of capital and investment are needed to improve the productive base in LDCs and raise productivity. LDCs, however, have not always proved to be good credit risks. Some LDCs have defaulted on loan payments, and lending institutions and nations have lost money on their loans.

3. a. Infrastructure, or social overhead capital, refers to the economic environment of a country and its ability to support and sustain economic growth. Infrastructure includes a nation's transportation system, communication industries, utilities, schools and hospitals.

   b. Once we see what infrastructure includes, its relationship to economic development is obvious.

   c. Many of the benefits of improved infrastructure accrue to the nation as a whole and not solely to private individuals. We all benefit from better highways, clean water, and telephone service, and it would be very difficult (not to mention impractical) to provide these commodities for just a few people and not everyone. The private market often has a difficult time providing these public types of goods, so the government taxes its citizens and provides these products for all.

4. First, the "Asian dragons" have had very high rates of investment. This has helped develop infrastructure and modernize production. Second, these nations have used their macroeconomic policies to keep inflation rates low and investment rates high. These governments have also spent a great deal on education and the development of human capital. Third, the "Asian dragons" have had an outward orientation to promote exports and adjust to external changes in technology. Finally, in some countries the government has sponsored competitions among firms, in certain industries, to encourage efficiency.

5. First, in the Soviet-style command economy it was decided to allocate resources to the military and investment. Consumers always received what was left over, and there was never enough. Second, it proved too difficult to centrally control such a huge and complex economy. Managers were not given proper incentives to produce quality output. Finally, the political and economic repression that was necessary to have central control proved too unbearable for the citizens to take.

6. Russia faces many problems. First, prices need to be determined by the forces of supply and demand. Market-based economies change prices all the time and markets

adjust, sometimes with hardly a notice. In Russia, prices have always been set by someone else. Grappling for *market-clearing* and *profit-maximizing* prices is a new challenge. Second, entrepreneurs must now realize that inefficiency can no longer be supported by the government. Profits are the reward for taking risk. Finally, the means of production have to be turned over to private hands. Stock markets need to be developed and credit markets created to finance business expansion. This is a huge adjustment that has to be made.

7.   In Marx's model the only productive contributors to the production process are the workers. Even the machinery and capital equipment used to produce goods and services were first made by labor. Since labor contributes all the effort and value, they should receive all the rewards.

CHAPTER 13
Unemployment and the
Foundations of Aggregate Supply

I. CHAPTER OVERVIEW

Chapters 11 and 12 focused on economic growth and development. In the first part of this chapter we study the foundations of aggregate supply. While the concept of aggregate supply (AS) was first introduced in Chapter 4, after working through Chapter 13 you should have a deeper understanding of both national output and the underpinnings of economic growth. Obviously, without output there can be neither growth nor development.

Unemployment is, to some, a major macroeconomic issue, especially when growth and development stagnate. To others, it is simply a measure of how many people do not want to work at the going wage. Chapter 13 explores both of these points. A precise definition of unemployment is presented, in terms of both economic content and statistical expedience. The social costs of unemployment are also discussed at some length. Interpretation of the scope of involuntary *unemployment* will command some of our attention, as will the effect of unemployment on various subgroups of the population.

The focus here is not on macroeconomic policies that might help reduce unemployment by pushing output higher; those are the topics of past and future chapters. Instead, some of the micro-based sources of unemployment are discussed along with some of the policies that might be designed specifically to alleviate this problem.

II. LEARNING OBJECTIVES

After you have read Chapter 29 in your text and completed the exercises in this *Study Guide* chapter, you should be able to:

1. Describe the two fundamental sets of forces behind the **aggregate supply** schedule.
2. Explain the difference between the *classical* view and the *Keynesian* view of the aggregate supply curve.
3. Explain the difference between the short-run shape and the long-run shape of aggregate supply.
4. Understand the meaning, significance, and empirical validation of **Okun's Law**.
5. Understand the dimension of the economic and social consequences of unemployment: forgone GDP, forgone investment, increased stress, heightened illness, and lost skills.
6. Explain how the **unemployment rate** is calculated and discuss the problems associated with the measurement procedure.
7. Differentiate between **frictional, structural**, and **cyclical** unemployment.
8. Differentiate between **voluntary** and **involuntary** unemployment. Understand the role of wage stickiness in explaining the existence of involuntary unemployment.
9. Recognize that unemployment is distributed unevenly over different classifications of workers.
10. Understand the reasons for the recent increase in unemployment rates in Europe.

111. REVIEW OF KEY CONCEPTS

Match the following terms from column A with their definitions in column B.

A	B
___ Aggregate supply curve	1. Unemployment that exists because people seek employment at wage rates above the prevailing market wage rate.
___ Potential output	2. The number of people unemployed divided by the total labor force.
___ Employed	3. Highly organized and competitive market where price floats up or down to balance supply and demand.
___ Unemployed	4. Unemployment that exists because more people seek work at the prevailing market wage than there are jobs available.
___ Not in labor force	5. Unemployment due to a mismatch between the type of job openings and the skills or type of job seekers.

__ Labor force

__ Unemployment rate

__ Frictional unemployment

__ Structural unemployment

__ Cyclical unemployment

__ Voluntary unemployment

__ Involuntary unemployment

__ Non-clearing labor market

__ Auction market

__ Administered market

__ Okun's Law

6. For every 2 percent shortfall between actual GDP and potential GDP, the unemployment rate increases by 1 percent.

7. Maximum output that the economy can produce without triggering rising inflationary pressures.

8. Unemployment due to a decline in the *overall* demand for labor. This corresponds to a downturn in the business cycle.

9. Schedule showing the level of total national output that will be produced at each possible price level other things equal.

10. Labor market in which the *prevailing* market wage is different from the market-clearing equilibrium wage.

11. People who perform any paid work and those who have jobs but are absent due to illness, strikes, or vacation.

12. Market in which prices are set according to some scale or predetermined criteria.

13. Unemployment due to the movement of people between jobs or geographical locations (considered as *voluntary* unemployment, but do not put this number in that space).

14. Not working in the market place and not looking for work.

15. People who are not employed but who are actively seeking work or waiting to return to work.

16. Includes the employed and the unemployed.

IV. SUMMARY AND CHAPTER OUTLINE

This section summarizes the key concepts from the chapter.

A. The Foundations of Aggregate Supply

1. The level of **aggregate supply** in the economy is determined by the economy's *potential* to produce goods and services and the behavior of wages and prices in the economy.

2. The classical view of the world envisions wages and prices responding so quickly that an economy's performance is determined almost exclusively by its potential GDP. In the arena of aggregate supply and demand, this view is represented by a vertical aggregate supply curve at potential GDP.

3. The Keynesian view of the world envisions wages and prices responding slowly such that an economy can be in equilibrium well below its potential. In terms of aggregate supply and demand, this view is represented by an aggregate supply curve which is horizontal or very flat, at least to the left of potential GDP.

B. Unemployment

1. **Okun's Law** is one of the miracles of statistics—a simple rule that fits reality. It tells us that every 2 percent reduction in actual GDP relative to potential GDP causes unemployment to *increase* by 1 percentage point. If real GDP simply grows at the same rate as potential GDP (which does tend to increase marginally every year), the unemployment rate would remain unchanged.

2. The unemployed (U) are people without jobs who are actively looking for work. The employed (E) are people who work for pay in the marketplace. The labor force (LF) includes both the employed and the unemployed (U + E). The unemployment rate (measured as a percent) is the proportion of people in the labor force who are unemployed.

$$\frac{\text{Unemployment}}{\text{rate}} = \frac{U}{U + E} \times 100\% = \frac{U}{\text{labor force}} \times 100\%$$

People who work outside the labor force (e.g., at home taking care of a family) are not in the labor force. As far as the government unemployment statistics are concerned, they are neither employed nor unemployed!

3. Economists have, after decades of study, identified three different sources of unemployment. **Frictional unemployment**, caused by the usual turnover of some workers, reentry of others, and migration by still others, is the first major category. It is generally viewed as a lubricant for the overall labor market because it improves that market's economic efficiency. It can, however, be taken to an extreme. Teenagers typically change jobs frequently, and their unemployment rate is among the highest in the country.

Structural unemployment, meanwhile, arises from the contraction of some industries whose time has come and is now going. Even in a growing economy, some industries contract as the demand for their products contracts, and they must therefore lay workers off.

Finally, **cyclical unemployment** is the natural manifestation of the business cycle in the labor market; an overall contraction in business activity means that fewer people are required to produce the desired level of output, and employment must therefore fall.

4. In another attempt to understand unemployment and the reasons behind it, economists have made a distinction between **voluntary unemployment** (people who choose not

to work at the offered wage) and **involuntary unemployment** (people who would gladly work at the offered wage but who cannot find work). Involuntary unemployment is the result of *sticky* wages which do not fall in response to excess supply in the labor market.

5. Different types of unemployment suggest different policy responses. Frictional and/or voluntary unemployment is perhaps not very troublesome. Cyclical unemployment can be reduced by policies which smooth out the troughs of the business cycle. Structural unemployment requires more than that; the structurally unemployed frequently need retraining to acquire new skills.

6. Recessions, and the unemployment they create, affect different types of people differently; but nearly every demographic category suffers. The unemployment rate in every category generally rises (the rise is often proportionate across categories), and the duration of unemployment for each rises as well.

7. Recently, unemployment rates in Europe have surpassed those in the United States. The German economy is the strongest on the European continent and the other European countries have tied their monetary policies to those of Germany. The Bundesbank, Germany's central bank, has (logically) been more concerned with economic conditions in Germany than in Europe as a whole. The Bundesbank's efforts to control inflation in Germany after the 1990 reunification, thereby contributed to higher unemployment rates in the rest of Europe. Another factor contributing to European unemployment rates is an increase in the rate of structural unemployment as compared with the United States. This is related to both philosophical and actual differences in unemployment benefits between the U.S. and European nations.

V. HELPFUL HINTS

1. To be counted as unemployed, you must be looking for work. Full-time students, household caregivers, and retirees are generally not looking for work—they are not unemployed, and they are not in the labor force. Once you look, though, you should be counted, and you become part of the labor force, whether you have a job or not.

2. All part-time workers are counted as employed. These individuals may want to work longer hours *and* they may actually be seeking more work, but they are nonetheless counted as employed. To the extent that this problem exists, the unemployment rate is an *under*estimate of the true unemployment problem.

3. The individuals without work may not know, nor particularly care, what category of unemployment they fall into. However, from a policy perspective it is very important to know whether people are frictionally, structurally, or cyclically unemployed. For example:

    a. Frictionally unemployed workers do not need a

government-financed retraining program, but the structurally unemployed may.

    b. Structurally unemployed workers will not be helped very much by a general tax cut, but the cyclically unemployed may be.

4. The unemployment rate is an average measure of unemployment for the entire labor force. Pay careful attention to the different rates of unemployment for various subgroups of the population. The national unemployment rate may be 6 percent, but the individual seeking a job may consider his or her *personal* rate of unemployment to be 100 percent!

VI. MULTIPLE CHOICE QUESTIONS

These questions are organized by topic from the chapter outline. Choose the best answer from the options available.

A. The Foundations of Aggregate Supply

1. Which of the following should be expected to shift the aggregate supply curve out to the right?
    a. an increase in government spending.
    b. a reduction in net exports.
    c. a reduction in labor force participation.
    d. the adoption of an improved production technology.
    e. a reduction in the value of the dollar.

2. Suppose that government spending rises. Assuming that the economy is operating at potential GDP, the long-run effect of this policy change should be:
    a. higher prices with no change in output.
    b. higher prices with higher output.
    c. higher prices with lower output.
    d. lower prices with higher output.
    e. lower prices with no change in output.

3. Which answer to question 2 would have been correct had that question referred to the short-run effect with output close to but beneath potential GDP?
    a.
    b.
    c.
    d.
    e.

4. Which answer would have been correct if question 2 had referred to the long-run effect expected from the Keynesian perspective?
    a.
    b.
    c.
    d.
    e.

5. Which answer to question 2 would have been correct had that question referred to the long-run effect expected from the classical perspective of improved technological productivity?

a.

b.

c.

d.

e.

6. Which answer to question 2 would have been correct if that question had referred to the long-run effect expected from the Keynesian perspective and there was a simultaneous contraction in available inputs?

a.

b.

c.

d.

e.

7. In the short run, "sticky elements of cost" contribute to:

a.   firms' ability to make profits.

b.   a willingness to produce more as prices rise.

c.   the positive slope of the short-run aggregate supply curve.

d.   all of the above.

e.   none of the above.

B. Unemployment

8. According to Okun's Law, if potential GDP rose by 9 percent between 1979 and 1982 but actual GDP did *not* change, then unemployment should have climbed from 5.8 percent in 1979 to:

a.   6.1 percent.

b.   10.3 percent.

c.   11.2 percent.

d.   8.8 percent.

e.   9.7 percent.

9. A computation of forgone output of the 1975-1984 period of high unemployment estimated the loss at:

a. $2100 billion.

b. $40 billion.

c. $1333 billion.

d. $3000 billion.

e.   an amount roughly comparable to the deadweight loss created by the abuse of market power.

10. Psychological studies indicate that being fired from a job is:

a.   a positive factor in an individual's labor-market experience.

b.   something everyone should experience, at least once.

c.   generally as upsetting as the death of a close friend.

d.   on average, neither harmful nor beneficial to most individuals.

e.   both **a** and **b**.

11. A person who is waiting to be recalled to a job would be classified as:

a.   employed.

b.   unemployed.

c.   not in the labor force.

d.   underemployed.

e.   a discouraged worker.

12. Which answer to question 11 would have been correct had that question asked for the classification of a person who was too sick to work?

a.

b.

c.

d.

e.

13. Suppose a college graduate starts work in a family business the day after graduation. As a result, we should expect the unemployment rate:

a.   not to change at all.

b.   to go up slightly.

c.   to go down slightly.

d.   to fluctuate slightly, first up and then down.

e.   none of the above—more information is needed.

14. The existence of involuntary unemployment:

a.   depends critically on the Keynesian assumption that wages do not rise in response to excess demand in the labor market.

b.   depends critically upon the Keynesian assumption that wages do not fall in response to excess supply in the labor market.

c.   is accepted even by classical economists.

d.   plays a small role in the overall unemployment statistics.

e.   is described by none of the above.

15. Which of the following statements is accurate?

a.   Unemployment rates are generally different for different demographic categories of people.

b.   Unemployment rates tend to move in parallel as the economy proceeds through the business cycle.

c.   The duration of unemployment tends to increase during recession.

d.   An increase in frictional unemployment is not necessarily bad.

e.   All the above are accurate.

16. Someone who loses his or her job because of a recession would fall into the category of:

a.   frictionally unemployed.

b.   structurally unemployed.

c.   cyclically unemployed.

d.   permanently unemployed.

e.   none of the above.

17. Which of the answers to question 16 would have been correct if the person in question became unemployed because of the decline of the U.S. steel industry?

a.

b.

c.

d.

e.

18. Which of the answers to question 16 would have been correct if the person in question had just entered the labor force but had not yet found a job?
   a.
   b.
   c.
   d.
   e.

19. The recent increase in unemployment rates in Europe can be attributed in part to:
   a.   a world-wide recession.
   b.   the elections in France and the political business cycle.
   c.   the slow down in growth in the United States.
   d.   the monetary policies of the Federal Reserve System.
   e.   the monetary policies of the Bundesbank.

VII. PROBLEM SOLVING

The following problems are designed to help you apply the concepts that you learned in the chapter.

A. The Foundations of Aggregate Supply

1.   a.   The two major determinants of aggregate supply are categorized as _____ and _____.
   b.   Table 13-1 lists a series of changes in economic circumstances. For each change, indicate in column (2) which of the aggregate supply determinants from part **a** is involved.
   c.   Use column (3) to designate whether panel (a), (b), or (c) of Figure 13-1 best illustrates the effect graphically as a shift from AS to AS', and explain your reasoning in column (4). The first row has been completed for your reference.

2.   A number of events are listed below. For each one, determine what a Keynesian and a classicist would expect in terms of the event's effect on GDP and prices. In the spaces provided in Table 13-2 indicate only the direction of the expected effect by recording **U** for "up," and **D** "down," **0** for "no change," and **?** for an ambiguous effect. It may be useful (as it always seems to be) to represent the event on a graph with the appropriate aggregate supply curve drawn beforehand. Use Figures 29-2 and 29-3 (top of next page) to help you with your answers.
   a.   An increase in potential output
   b.   A large increase in aggregate demand
   c.   An increase in interest rates that depresses aggregate demand
   d.   A dramatic reduction in foreign oil suppliers which increases oil prices, depresses the demand for domestic goods and services, and increases overall input prices
   e   A major catastrophe that reduces potential output by 25 percent

(a)

(b)

(c)

Figure 13-1

Table 13-1

	(1) Change	(2) AS Category	(3) Panel	(4) Explanation
a.	Population increase	Potential output	(a)	More inputs available
b.	Higher wage rates	____	—	_____
c.	Higher input prices	____	—	_____
d.	Improved production technology	____	—	_____
e.	Destructive earthquake	____	—	_____
f.	Increase in consumption	____	—	_____

Figure 13-2

Figure 13-3

Table 13-2

Case	Keynesian		Classicist	
	Price	Output	Price	Output
a.	—	—	—	—
b.	—	—	—	—
c.	—	—	—	—
d.	—	—	—	—
e.	—	—	—	—

3. A "pure" Keynesian model might envision a perfectly horizontal aggregate supply curve, at least for GDP less than potential.

    a. As a result, any stimulus to aggregate demand created in that region by an adjustment in either taxes or government spending produces (**no / a positive / a negative**) effect on GDP and (**no / a positive / a negative**) effect on prices.

    b. At the other extreme, the classical view holds that stimulative fiscal policy will produce (**no / a positive / a negative**) effect on GDP and (**no / a positive / a negative**) effect on prices.

    c. In between these two extremes, changes in fiscal policy can be expected to affect (**both prices and GDP / only GDP / only prices**).

4. Fill in the spaces provided in Table 13-3 with the expected effects of the policy changes indicated. As before, use **U** for "up," **D** for "down," and **0** for "no change." Take care to note that you must answer according to the specified philosophy.

Table 13-3

Case	Keynesian View		Classical View	
	Price	Output	Price	Output
a. Increase in taxes	—	—	—	—
b. Increase in government spending	—	—	—	—
c. Reduction in taxes	—	—	—	—
d. Reduction in government spending	—	—	—	—

B. Unemployment

5. Consider Table 13-4. Record your prediction for the actual unemployment rate for the years indicated by applying Okun's Law to the data provided. For purposes of comparison, the actual unemployment rates are listed in Table 13-5.

Table 13-4

Calendar Year	Annual Growth Rates		Unemployment Rates	
	Potential GDP (%)	Actual GDP (%)	Initial (%)	Predicted (%)
1960	3.3	2.2	5.5	___
1965	3.3	6.0	4.8	___
1970	3.3	- 0.2	3.5	___
1975	3.3	- 1.1	5.6	___
1980	2.7	- 1.3	7.5	___

Table 13-5

Year	Actual Unemployment Rate (%)
1960	6.7
1965	3.8
1970	4.9
1975	8.5
1980	9.8

6. To bring the unemployment rate down, actual GDP must grow faster than potential GDP. Assume that potential GDP is growing at 2 percent per year and the current rate of unemployment is 9 percent. Suppose Congress wants the unemployment rate to fall to 6 percent in three years. According to Okun's Law, what must be the annual growth rate in real actual GDP to achieve this objective? __

7. a. The unemployment rate is measured every month by sampling across (**10,000 / 30,000 / 60,000**) households to determine their employment status.

   b. There are three categories: employed, unemployed, and not in the labor force. In the spaces provided, indicate the category into which the people in the following circumstances would be classified; designate employed by (**E**), unemployed by (**U**), and not in the labor force by (**N**):

   ___ (1) A laid-off autoworker looking for work

   ___ (2) A laid-off autoworker employed part-time at Wendy's

   ___ (3) A lawyer too sick to work

   ___ (4) An unemployed steelworker too discouraged to look for a job

   ___ (5) A full-time college student

   ___ (6) A car mechanic going to college at night

   ___ (7) An executive on leave to go to law school

   ___ (8) A housewife who works full-time at home

   ___ (9) A housewife who works part-time at the library

   ___ (10) A housewife who volunteers part-time at the library

8. For each person listed below, identify the type of unemployment that his or her situation most closely exemplifies; denote structural unemployment by (**S**), frictional unemployment by (**F**), and cyclical unemployment by (**C**):

   ___ a. A graduating senior who cannot find a job

   ___ b. A steelworker who loses his job because of permanent foreign competition

   ___ c. An autoworker who loses her job in a recession

   ___ d. An executive who loses her job because higher oil prices cause aggregate demand to fall

   ___ e. An executive who loses his job because higher oil prices cause the demand for oil burners to fall

   ___ f. A spouse who quits a job because the family has to move

   ___ g. A member of the garment union who loses his job because union wages refuse to fall when faced with inexpensive foreign labor

9. To explore the distinction between voluntary and involuntary unemployment, consider Figure 13-4. Curve *SS* represents a typical supply schedule for labor. Let the size of the available labor force be 1000 workers. Curve *DD* reflects the demand for labor.

   a. The equilibrium wage is $___, with ___ people desiring and finding employment and ___ people choosing not to work.

   b. Therefore, the number of people voluntarily unemployed is ___, and the number of people involuntarily unemployed is ___.

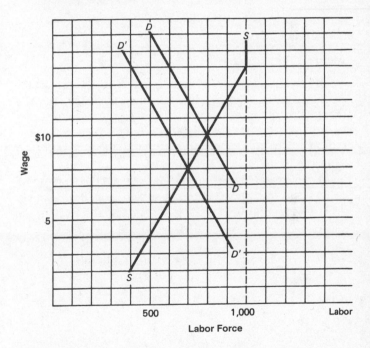

Figure 13-4

Suppose, however, that demand conditions deteriorate so that *D'D'* now represents the demand for labor.

   c. If the wage could fall, then the new equilibrium wage would be $___, and total employment would be ___.

   d. Total involuntary unemployment would be ___ and total voluntary unemployment would be ___.

   e. If the wage could not fall, though, then total employment would be ___, total involuntary unemployment would be ___, and total voluntary unemployment would be ___.

(a) Flexible Wages

(b) Inflexible Wages

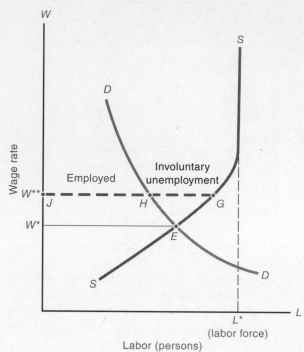

Figure 13-6

The important point to note from this exercise is that the existence of involuntary unemployment depends critically upon the inability of the wage to fall in response to excess supply in the labor market. Quite simply, no one who wanted to work at the going wage would be unable to do so if wages were sufficiently flexible.

f.   This (**is / is not**) to say that total employment would not fall if the demand for labor were to fall; it is simply

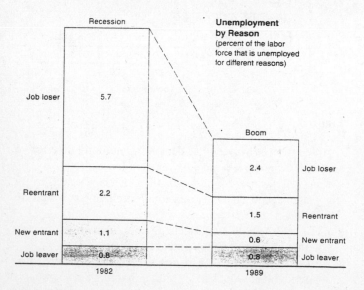

Figure 13-5

a statement about the ability of people to find a job if they want to work even at the lower wage.

10. a.   Figure 29-8 from the text is reproduced here as Figure 13-5. This diagram shows us that recession tends to increase the unemployment rate by increasing the percentage of those in the labor force who are unemployed because they have (**reentered the labor market / lost their jobs / left their jobs voluntarily / entered the labor market for the first time**).

b.   The unemployment rate in 1982 was ___ percent, and in 1989 it was ___ percent.

c.   According to Figure 13-6, there are four main reasons why people are unemployed. Complete Table 13-6 by calculating the percent of unemployment in each year that is attributable to each of the reasons. (The first entry is already filled in for 1973.)

Table 13-6

Reason	Percent of Unemployment In 1982	Percent of Unemployment An 1989
Job loser	58.2	___
Reentrant	___	___
New entrant	___	___
Job leaver	___	___

d.   In which year are entrants (both "New" and "Re") a larger percent of the total? ___

e.   In which year are job losers a larger percent of the total? ___

Labor market group	Unemployment rate of different groups (% of labor force)		Distribution of total unemployment across different groups (% of total unemployed)	
	Recession (1982)	Boom (1989)	Recession (1982)	Boom (1989)
By age:				
16–19 years	23.2	14.7	18.5	17.7
20 years and older	8.6	4.6	81.5	82.3
By race:				
White	8.6	4.6	77.2	74.5
Black and other	17.3	9.4	22.8	25.5
By sex (adults only):				
Male	8.8	4.3	58.5	51.1
Female	8.3	5.0	41.5	48.9
All workers	**9.7**	**5.3**	**100.0**	**100.0**

Figure 13-7

f. Reconcile your answers to parts **d** and **e** with what you have learned about patterns of unemployment during the business cycle.

g. During which year are workers more likely to leave their jobs and search for something better? Please explain briefly.

VIII. DISCUSSION QUESTIONS

Answer the following questions, making sure that you can explain the work you did to arrive at the answers.

1. Explain the differences between the short-run and long-run aggregate supply curves.

2. Explain the differences between the Keynesian and classical views of aggregate supply.

3. Figure 29-4 from the text is reproduced here as Figure 13-7. Note that for men, the proportion employed increases with each age group—at least until the age of 65. For women however, there is no difference in employment patterns between the ages of 20 and 65. How would you explain this?

4. Table 29-3 from the text is reproduced here as Table 13-7. Teenage unemployment in the boom year of 1989 accounted for **x.x** percent of all the unemployment in that year. However, in the recession year of 1982, teenage unemployment was only 18.5 percent of the total. How would you explain the decrease?

TABLE 13-7 Unemployment by Demographic Group

Labor Market Group	Unemployment Rate of Different Groups (% of labor force)		Distribution of Total Unemployment Across Different Groups (% of total unemployed)	
	Recession (1982)	Boom (1989)	Recession (1982)	Boom (1989)
By age:				
16-19 years	23.2	0	18.5	0
20 years and older	8.6	0	81.5	
By race:				
White	8.6	0	77.2	0
Black and other	17.3	0	22.8	0
By sex (adults only):				
Male	8.8	0	58.5	0
Female	8.3	0	41.5	0
All workers	9.7	0	100.0	100.0

IX. ANSWERS TO STUDY GUIDE QUESTIONS

III. Review of Key Concepts

9	Aggregate Supply Curve
7	Potential output
11	Employed
15	Unemployed
14	Not in labor force
16	Labor force
2	Unemployment rate
13	Frictional unemployment
5	Structural unemployment
8	Cyclical unemployment
1	Voluntary unemployment
4	Involuntary unemployment
10	Non-clearing labor market

3	Auction market
12	Administered market
6	Okun's Law

VI. Multiple Choice Questions

1. D   2. A   3. B   4. A   5. D   6. C
7. D   8. B   9. A   10. C   11. B   12. C
13. C   14. B   15. E   16. C   17. B   18. A
19. E

VII. Problem Solving

1. a.   wages and costs, potential output
    b. and c.

Table 13-1

(1)	(2)	(3)	(4)
b.	wages and costs	(b)	increased costs shift AS left
c.	wages and costs	(b)	increased costs shift AS left
d.	potential output	(a)	greater Q at every price level
e.	potential output	(b)	inputs and resources are destroyed
f.	neither	(c)	consumption affects AD

2.

Table 13-2

Case	Keynesian Price	Keynesian Output	Classicist Price	Classicist Output
a.	D	U	D	U
b.	U	U	U	0
c.	D	D	D	0
d.	?	D	?	D
e.	U	D	U	D

3. a.   a positive, no
    b.   no, a negative
    c.   both prices and GDP

4.

Table 13-3

Case	Keynesian View Price	Keynesian View Output	Classical View Price	Classical View Output
a. Increase in taxes	0	D	D	0
b. Increase in government spending	0	U	U	0
c. Reduction in taxes	0	U	U	0
d. Reduction in government spending	0	D	D	0

5.   6.05 percent, 3.45 percent, 5.25 percent, 7.80 percent, 9.50 percent

6.   4 percent (If actual GDP grows 2 percent faster than potential GDP for a year, the unemployment rate will fall 1 percent. If this continues for three years, the unemployment rate will fall 3 percent.)

7. a.   60,000
    b.   (1) U
        (2) E
        (3) N
        (4) N
        (5) N
        (6) E
        (7) N
        (8) N
        (9) E
        (10) N

8. a.   F
    b.   S
    c.   C
    d.   C
    e.   S
    f.   F
    g.   S

9. a. $10, 800, 200
    b.   200, 0
    c. $8, 700
    d.   0, 300
    e.   600, 200, 200
    f.   is not

10. a.   lost their jobs
    b.   9.8 percent, 5.3 percent
    c.

Table 13-6

Reason	Percent of Unemployment In 1982	Percent of Unemployment In 1989
Job loser	58.2	45.3
Reentrant	22.4	28.3
New entrant	11.2	11.3
Job leaver	8.2	15.1

    d.   1989
    e.   1982
    f.   In boom years more entrants are attracted into the labor force. In recession years the unemployment rate swells with job losers. The data in the table support this.
    g.   1989. When the economy is growing, new job opportunities abound. Workers are more apt to leave their job and search for something better.

VIII. Discussion Questions

1. The short-run aggregate supply curve is positively sloped. Higher prices are associated with increases in output. In the long run, however, aggregate supply is determined by the level of potential output in the economy. Potential output is in turn determined by population growth, technological advances, and other factors, but not the price level. So the long run aggregate supply curve is drawn as a vertical line.

2. Keynes, focusing on the Great Depression, viewed the aggregate supply curve as a horizontal line. Keynes looked at the economy and saw massive unemployment and idle resources. Hence, in his eyes, it was possible for real GDP to increase substantially without exerting any upward pressure on prices. Classical economists, on the other hand, thought the economy would always adjust to any disturbances (like unemployment) and return to a position of long-run equilibrium. For them, the aggregate supply curve was a vertical line right at potential GDP.

3. During child-bearing years women are more likely than men to have interrupted labor force participation. The consistency of the data for women—across all ages—suggests that women are no longer leaving the labor market when they have children. Overall, employment rates for women are catching up with those of men, though employment rates for men are still somewhat higher.

4. A number of factors could account for the reduced percentage. Perhaps during the recession more teens become discouraged and stop looking for work. Alternatively, so many prime-age workers could lose employment during the recession that their increased numbers make the teen rates fall in comparison. The number of unemployed teens could stay the same or even increase. The teen numbers just become swamped by the adult unemployment numbers.

CHAPTER 14
Ensuring Price Stability

I. CHAPTER OVERVIEW

We have seen the terms **inflation** and **price** mentioned in nearly every previous chapter in the text. It is time that we devoted an entire chapter to these critically important topics. Earlier chapters have concentrated your attention on how changes in economic conditions can move real GDP up or down. Previous chapters have conducted analyses of these changes in the context of both the aggregate supply-and-demand model of macroeconomics and the total-spending construction of the basic Keynesian model. Most recently, Okun's Law has been used to translate changes in actual real GDP into changes in employment. It is now time to extend our field of vision to include changes in the price level. It is time, more specifically, to ponder the sources and costs of inflation.

As you work through this material, you will confront some of the fundamental economic issues of today (and yesterday and tomorrow). Why has history recorded an occasional episode of hyperinflation, and what can be done to guard against its recurrence? What are the costs of inflation, and how are those costs dependent upon economic circumstance? Are there different strains of inflation that are more or less costly than others?

We also need to explore the purported tradeoff between unemployment and inflation. Is an economy forever doomed to endure high levels of one or the other, or can fiscal and monetary policies be employed to reduce the severity of the tradeoff? Can some type of incomes policies be employed to lower inflation without creating intolerable levels of unemployment? And, finally, can the cost of reducing inflation by enduring high levels of unemployment be assessed in either the short or the long run?

As you can see, we have a great deal of new ground to cover.

II. LEARNING OBJECTIVES

After you have read Chapter 30 in your text and completed the exercises in this *Study Guide* chapter, you should be able to:

1. Describe the means by which inflation is measured, and understand the distinction between **inflation, deflation**, and **disinflation.**
2. Outline the history of inflation for the United States (and, to some degree, for other countries).
3. Delineate the differences between *moderate* inflation, *galloping* inflation, and *hyper* inflation.
4. Relate how inflation has an economic impact on the distribution of wealth, the allocation of resources, and relative prices.
5. Decipher the distinction between **anticipated** and **unanticipated** inflation, on the one hand, and **balanced** and **unbalanced** inflation, on the other.
6. Differentiate between **inertial** inflation, **demand-pull** inflation, and **cost-push** inflation. Relate how shocks to an economy can contribute to increases in the inertial rate of inflation.
7. Illustrate each type of inflation in the context of graphs of aggregate supply and demand.
8. Outline the role of inertial inflation in short- and long-run **Phillips curves.**
9. Define the **lowest sustainable unemployment rate** (LSUR) and explain some of the challenges of lowering it.
10. Use both the short-run and the long-run Phillips curve constructions to derive the spiral patterns of unemployment and inflation combinations that describe the U.S. experience of the 1970s and 1980s.
11. Understand how **indexing** to inflation can lead to greater instability in prices.

III. REVIEW OF KEY CONCEPTS

Match the following terms from column A with their definitions in column B.

A	B
__ Inflation	1. Nominal or money wage divided by consumer prices.
__ Price index	2. A way of adapting to inflation, in which wages, prices, and contracts are partially or wholly

___ Real wages

___ Inertial rate of inflation

___ Demand-pull inflation

___ Cost-push Inflation

___ Stagflation

___ Philips curve

___ Lowest sustainable unemployment rate

___ Indexing

___ Disinflation

___ Income policies

compensated for changes in the general price level.
3.   High inflation in periods of high unemployment.
4.   A reduction in the *rate of increase* in the price index.
5.   Occurs when *AD* rises more rapidly than the economy's productive potential.
6.   Represents the highest sustainable level of employment at which the inflation rate is stable—also corresponds to potential GDP.
7.   An increase in the general level of prices.
8.   Rate of inflation that is expected and built into contracts and informal arrangements—also called the core, underlying, or expected inflation rate.
9.   Government actions that attempt to moderate inflation by direct steps, whether by verbal persuasion, legal controls, or other incentives.
10   Inflation resulting from rising costs during periods of high unemployment and slack resource utilization—also known as supply-shock inflation.
11.   A weighted average of the prices of a group of goods and services.
12.   Illustrates the "tradeoff" theory of inflation—inflation is the tradeoff for low levels of unemployment.

IV. SUMMARY AND CHAPTER OUTLINE

This section summarizes the key concepts from the chapter.

A. Nature and Impacts of Inflation

1.   Inflation is measured as a rate of change in a price index from one period (e.g., 1 year) to the next. If P_1 represents the price index recorded in year 1 and P_2 represents the index recorded in year 2, then inflation between years 1 and 2 would be:

$$\frac{P_2 - P_1}{P_1} \times 100\%$$

A major issue, therefore, is how the price indexes are constructed. *Inflation* is not an increase in all prices. It is, instead, an increase in the *general* level of prices and costs.
2.   Despite the occasional occurrence of hyperinflation throughout history, it is happy news that even galloping inflation does not necessarily accelerate to unmanageable levels in the absence of heroic anti-inflationary policy measures. Moderate inflation, meanwhile, does not seem to be terribly troublesome because relative prices are not terribly distorted, people do not spend too much time and energy in managing their money balances to avoid losses in real purchasing power, and inflationary expectations are fairly stable and predictable. Expectations of moderate inflation can, in fact, be self-fulfilling prophesies if they generate moderate wage settlements.
3.   Balanced inflation affects the prices of all goods or most goods (roughly) proportionately. Unbalanced inflation focuses its effects on specific goods or categories of goods. Unbalanced inflation can breed inefficiency by causing people to spend more time managing their money (recall the example of "shoe leather" costs from the chapter) and by eroding the informational content of prices.
4.   Anticipated inflation can be handled by advance planning. Unanticipated inflation can cause distributional effects (from lenders to borrowers, for example) which breed potentially costly hedging strategies. The most damaging inflation is unbalanced and unanticipated.
5.   Most economists agree that stable prices, with only a small annual increase, are the best prescription for an economy. While it may be politically unpopular to fight inflation (because of resulting unemployment), the central banks of most of the industrialized economies are ardent inflation fighters.

B. Modern Inflation Theory

1.   **Demand-pull** inflation is the result of excessive aggregate demand and can be associated with higher levels of real as well as nominal GDP. (If an economy is operating at its potential, then the increase in GDP will be entirely nominal.) **Cost-push** inflation is caused by increased costs which push aggregate supply up; it is therefore associated with lower levels of real GDP, so nominal GDP can be higher or lower.
2.   The "rate of inertial inflation" is a bit of a misnomer. The inflation rate itself has some inertia—that is, a tendency not to move unless pushed—only because prices have a consistent momentum that translates into a stable rate of increase. **Inertial inflation** therefore reflects an internal rate of inflation with which an economy seems to be comfortable. Individuals expect it, and the expectations tend to become self-fulfilling prophesies. Policies are written in acceptance of those expectations; interest rates include premiums to accommodate those expectations; transfer payments are amended to keep up with those expectations; and so on.

Either demand-pull or cost-push inflation can contribute to inertial inflation, the best reflection of which is a simultaneous shifting up of both the aggregate supply curve and the aggregate demand curve.

3. Due to the dynamic nature of the economy, we should never expect unemployment to be completely eradicated. People are constantly searching for new jobs (frictional) and new industries are continually emerging from the ashes of old ones (structural). In order to provide employment, at acceptable pay levels to *all* workers, the wage rate would have to higher than what many firms are otherwise willing to pay. The upward pressure on inflation in the economy would be very great. The LSUR is the lowest sustainable unemployment rate. This is as low as we can realistically expect the unemployment rate to get without putting a great deal of upward pressure on the inflation rate in the economy. The evidence suggests that the declining influence of American labor unions and the strengthening of competition in the economy have contributed to a decline in the LSUR during the last ten years.

4. The **Phillips curve** displays an inverse relationship between inflation and unemployment. It is anchored by the LSUR and the inertial rate of inflation. Moving unemployment below (above) the LSUR can, in particular, be expected to move inflation above (below) the inertial rate in the short run and contribute to an increase in the inertial rate in the long run. The short-run Phillips curve can, therefore, shift around.

5. Modern theory suggests that there is no tradeoff between inflation and unemployment in the long run; the long-run Phillips curve is therefore vertical at the LSUR..

C. Dilemmas of Anti-inflation Policy

1. An economy can, to some extent, insulate itself from the effects of inflation. This insulation would, in particular, include such things as the indexing of transfer payments like social security and the adjustment of nominal interest rates to preserve the desired real rate. If 10 percent inflation were expected, for example, then banks that wanted a 3 percent real return would charge 13 percent.

2. To reduce the rate of inertial inflation, an economy must be willing to accept an economic slowdown and higher unemployment. It is estimated that it would cost the United States about $304 billion (in 1996 prices) in lost jobs and output to reduce the inflation rate by 1 percentage point. Other tools have been suggested: wage and price controls, voluntary guidelines, and tax-based incomes policies. No economy has yet managed to maintain full employment over long periods of time with completely stable prices and free markets.

V. HELPFUL HINTS

1. Sometimes it is not easy to identify the cause of inflation as being strictly demand-pull or cost-push. Suppose, for example, workers demand higher wages in response to an increase in prices that were caused by an increase in government spending. If we focus our attention solely on the workers, this *looks like* cost-push inflation. However, all labor is doing is reacting to higher prices—which were caused by an increase in aggregate demand. If we are going to point a finger here, we need to back up and collect all the relevant information. The root problem, in this example, would be demand-pull inflation, not cost-push inflation.

2. If you try to push the unemployment rate beneath the LSUR without changing the underlying structure of the economy, you are asking for inflationary trouble.

3. The analysis of shifts in the AS and AD curves in Figure 14-6 (and others) assumes "...that potential output is constant..." (p.589). You should realize that in a growing economy more real goods and services can be produced and that inflation does not *necessarily* have to increase.

4. Historically, wage and price controls have not done a very good job in reducing inflation. Wage and price controls are similar to placing a lid on a boiling kettle of soup to keep it from boiling over. However, nothing is done to lower the heat, or in this case, the inflationary pressure in the economy. Occasionally, when wage and price controls have been left on for a long period of time, they have been successful in lowering inflationary expectations and thereby inflationary pressure in an economy.

VI. MULTIPLE CHOICE QUESTIONS

These questions are organized by topic from the chapter outline. Choose the best answer from the options available.

A Nature and Impacts of Inflation

1. Prices in the United States:
   a. became less volatile after World War II.
   b. have stabilized since the Depression.
   c. have increased faster than wages since World War II.
   d. have increased since World War II only because of the Vietnam war and the OPEC oil shock.
   e. have done none of the above.

2. Moderate inflation:
   a. is characterized by less than double-digit rates.
   b. is characterized by relatively stable relative prices.
   c. does not seem to cause people to spend excessive amounts of time and energy managing their account balances.
   d. creates fairly stable inflationary expectations.
   e. is described by all the above.

3. Inflation can be associated with:
   a. only increasing nominal GDP.
   b. increasing or decreasing real GDP, depending upon its source.
   c. only decreasing real GDP.

d.   only increasing nominal GDP when the economy is operating past its full potential.

e.   none of the above.

4.   One of the potential costs of unanticipated inflation is:

a.   the redistribution of wealth from lenders to debtors.

b.   the redistribution of wealth from debtors to lenders.

c.   the redistribution of wealth from the government to those who have helped finance its debt.

d.   the indexing of transfer payments to inflation.

e.   the elimination of variable-rate mortgages.

5.   In response to increased risk of unanticipated inflation, you should expect:

a.   that banks will charge a risk premium on loans that they write.

b.   that socially motivated governments will try to index transfer payments to people on fixed incomes.

c.   that banks will try to sell variable-rate mortgages to home buyers.

d.   that people will look for assets whose value is insulated from inflation.

e.   all the above.

6.   Unbalanced and unanticipated inflation usually causes:

a.   no harm.

b.   efficiency losses.

c.   the redistribution of income and wealth.

d.   efficiency losses accompanied by a redistribution of income and wealth.

e.   none of the above.

7.   One potential cost of anticipated and balanced inflation is:

a.   the lost resources devoted to the management of money.

b.   the loss of employment required to raise the inflation rate for political reasons.

c.   the excessive inflation of real estate prices.

d.   a reduction in the flow of imports into the country.

e.   none of the above.

8.   Which of the following is a hedge that you might expect to see an individual pursue in an effort to protect *only* himself or herself from the risk of unanticipated inflation?

a   Negotiate a cost-of-living clause in a long-term wage contract.

b.   Accept an adjustable-rate mortgage whose rate of interest would be expected to climb with inflation.

c.   Offer a friend a loan at a rate of interest lower than that charged by a hedging bank.

d.   Start a new business with cash withdrawn from a variable-rate savings account.

e.   All the above.

9.   Two common features associated with most hyperinflations are:

a.   a decline in the real demand for money and a decrease in the stability of relative prices.

b.   an increase in the real demand for money and a decrease in the stability of relative prices.

c.   a decline in the real demand for money and an increase in the stability of relative prices.

d.   an increase in the real demand for money and an increase in the stability of relative prices.

e.   an increase in the overall savings rate.

10. Recently, in the United States, the most vigorous and successful fighter of inflation has been:

a.   the President.

b.   Congress.

c.   the Federal Reserve.

d.   the Fortune 500 companies.

e.   organized labor.

11. The lowest sustainable unemployment rate (LSUR) is the rate at which:

a.   upward and downward forces on price and wage inflation are in balance.

b.   inflation is stable.

c.   the economy has the lowest level of unemployment that can be maintained without upward pressure on inflation.

d.   all of the above.

e.   choices **b**. and **c**. only.

B. Modern Inflation Theory

12. Inertial inflation:

a   can usually be traced to some sort of supply-side price shock.

b.   can usually be traced to some sort of increase in aggregate demand.

c.   reflects an expected rate of inflation to which the major institutions of an economy have adjusted.

d.   is highly volatile and unpredictable at best.

e.   is described by none of the above.

13. Which answer to question 12 would have been correct had that question referred to cost-push inflation?

a.

b.

c.

d.

e.

14. Which answer to question 12 would have been correct had that question referred to demand-pull inflation?

a.

b.

c.

d.

e.

15. The inertial rate of inflation is reflected in:

a.   interest rates.

b.   wage settlements.

c.   long-term price specifications.

d.   federal macroeconomic-policy specifications.

e.   all the above.

16. In Figure 14-1 AS_1 and AS_2 represent aggregate supply curves for two successive years; AD_1 and AD_2 depict the corresponding aggregate demand curves. In moving from year 1 to year 2, then:
   a.   prices climb in classic illustration of cost-push inflation.
   b.   prices climb, illustrating inertial inflation.
   c.   prices are stable, but real GDP falls.
   d.   prices climb in illustration of demand-pull inflation.
   e.   prices are stable, but real GDP falls in response to lower aggregate demand.

Real GDP

Figure 14-1

17. The occurrence of stagflation can be explained as a consequence of:
   a.   a cost-push inflationary episode caused by a supply shock.
   b.   an increase in the rate of inertial inflation.
   c.   a demand-pull inflationary episode caused by an increase in aggregate demand.
   d.   all the above.
   e.   none of the above.

18. Which of the following correctly states the correlation between the LSUR and the rate of inertial inflation?
   a.   Any inertial rate of inflation can be maintained at the LSUR as long as nonlabor costs increase at the same rate as labor costs.
   b.   If the rate of unemployment falls below the LSUR, then the inertial rate of inflation can be expected to climb, and vice versa.
   c.   If the rate of unemployment is driven above the LSUR, then the inertial rate of inflation can be expected to climb, and vice versa.
   d.   Answers **a** and **b**.
   e.   Answers **a** and **c**.

Use Figure 14-2 to answer questions 19 through 22. Assume that the LSUR is 5 percent and the dots correspond to successive years (i.e., dot 1 to year 1, dot 2 to year 2, etc.).

Figure 14-2

19. This figure illustrates:
   a.   an austerity cycle.
   b.   a boom cycle.
   c.   a complete business cycle.
   d.   a supply-side price shock.
   e.   none of the above.

20. Movement from dot 1 to dot 2 represents:
   a.   movement along a short-run Phillips curve toward higher levels of unemployment.
   b.   a shift in Phillips curves caused by increased supplies.
   c.   a shift in Phillips curves caused by a reduction in the rate of inertial inflation.
   d.   movement along a short-term Phillips curve toward lower levels of unemployment.
   e.   movement along a long-run Phillips curve.

21. Which answer to question 20 would have been correct had that question referred to movement from dot 2 to dot 3?
   a.
   b.
   c.
   d.
   e.

22. Which answer to question 20 would have been correct if the question had referred to movement from dot 3 to dot 4?
   a.
   b.
   c.
   d.
   e.

C. Dilemmas of Anti-Inflation Policy

23. The short-run Phillips-curve tradeoff might be made more favorable by:

    a. a policy that lowers export competition.

    b. an incomes policy that reduces inertial inflation.

    c. a trade policy that deflects inflationary price shocks from abroad.

    d. a constitutional amendment mandating that the fraction of GDP supported by government spending cannot climb.

    e. none of the above.

24. The point of an incomes policy would be to:

    a. lower inertial inflation without the country's suffering a period of high unemployment.

    b. simultaneously moderate the wage demands of as many workers as possible.

    c. lower the inflationary expectations of bankers so that the inflationary premiums built into interest rates might fall.

    d. facilitate a monetary policy designed to support a lower rate of inflation without creating unemployment.

    e. do all the above.

25. Among the paradoxes of the study of inflation is (are):

    a. that lower unemployment is sometimes associated with higher inflation and sometimes not.

    b. that indexing an economy to protect it from inflation may tend to make inflation worse.

    c. that inflationary expectations are sometimes as important as actual events in the economy.

    d. that foreign trade is affected by rates of domestic inflation.

    e. all the above.

VII. PROBLEM SOLVING

The following problems are designed to help you apply the concepts that you learned in the chapter.

A. Nature and Impacts of Inflation

1. a. Three "strains" of inflation, distinguished by their virulence, have been identified; they are:

(1) _____

(2) _____

(3) _____

b. Use Figure 14-3 to diagnose the strain infecting the countries listed in Table 14-1 during the years indicated. For each country, record the approximate rate of inflation in the first blank and identify the strain in the second blank.

Table 14-1

Country/Period	Inflation Rate(%)	Strain
1. United States (1970s)	___	___
2. Germany (1922)	___	___
3. Germany (1923)	___	___
4. Israel (1980s)	___	___
5. Germany (1960s)	___	___
6. Brazil (1970s)	___	___
7. Poland (1923)	___	___

2. a. Consider the impact of inflation on GDP. In the top three panels of Figure 14-4 (top of next page), draw a new aggregate demand curve that illustrates the potential that higher demand (caused by, e.g., higher government spending or a tax cut) might cause inflation; label the new curve *AD'*. In each case, *AS* indicates the aggregate supply curve and *AD* represents aggregate demand before the increase.

b. It is clear from this analysis that higher aggregate demand is most likely to produce higher prices when equilibrium GDP is (**nearly equal to / far above / far below**) potential GDP.

c. Moreover, real GDP can be expected to (**rise / fall / hold roughly constant**) when the economy is close to its potential.

d. When a moderate increase in prices is expected, though, real GDP might actually (**fall / rise**).

e. In the bottom three panels of Figure 14-4, record the change in aggregate supply that might produce inflation as the result of an outside price shock that leaves potential GDP fixed. Label the new curve AS.

f. In each of these three cases, real GDP can be expected to (**fall / rise**).

Figure 14-3

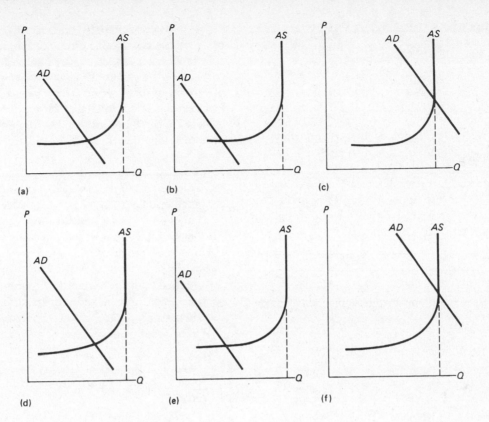

Figure 14-4

3. Inflation can cause two general types of effects. The first surrounds the distribution of wealth and income; the second concerns the efficiency of relative prices and the information that they contain. The incidence of these effects can be expected to depend critically upon whether or not the inflation is (a) anticipated or unanticipated and (b) balanced or unbalanced.

     a. If all prices were to increase at the same rate, for example, then the resulting inflation would be _____.

     b. If it were anticipated, then it (**would also / would not**) be expected to produce "winners and losers" depending upon what types of goods and services individuals and institutions purchased or produced. There (**would / would not**), in other words, be troublesome efficiency losses created by the inflation.

     c. If the prices of some goods rose disproportionately, though, then some people could win at the expense of others. People might therefore spend (**more / less**) time managing their money to avoid becoming locked into a disadvantageous financial position.

     d. In extreme cases, the information contained in relative prices could be (**increased / distorted**), because they would change so quickly that nobody could keep up.

     e. If balanced inflation were fully anticipated, then there would be (**almost no / surely a significant**) cost.

The inflation would look like a situation of stable prices to all those people who could insulate themselves from the rising prices.

     f. If the inflation were unanticipated, then (**distributional / governmental**) effects would be expected even if it were balanced. Borrowers would, for instance, be (**worse off / better off / unaffected**) because they could pay off their debts with currency that was (**worth more / worth less**). Lenders would experience the opposite effect. Under conditions of high inflationary risk, therefore, lenders can be expected to hedge against unanticipated inflation by charging (**higher / lower / exactly the same**) interest rates on new loans.

     g. Alternatively, they might try to shift the risk to the borrower through (**policy lobbying / offering no loans / offering adjustable-rate loans**).

4. Summarize the potential costs of inflation in Table 14-2 by noting the appropriate cost that is associated with each type of inflation. Put the letters of the costs below in the boxes of the table. (There is one letter for each box.)

<u>Costs</u>
a. Essentially costless
b. Efficiency losses
c. Distribution losses
d. Both efficiency and distribution losses

Table 14-2

	Balanced Inflation	Unbalanced Inflation
Anticipated inflation		
Unanticipated inflation		

5. a. Fill in the inflation rates for the years noted in the spaces provided in Table 14-3.

b. Notice that high rates of inflation seem to be associated with high nominal rates of interest. Do you see any evidence that interest rates in the 1980s included a hedge against the possibility that inflation might be unexpectedly rekindled? Explain.

_____

_____

Table 14-3

Year	CPI (1967 = 100)	Inflation Rate (%)	Nominal Rate of Interest (%)
1977	181.5		5.5
1978	195.4	___	7.6
1979	217.4	___	10.0
1980	246.8	___	11.4
1981	272.4	___	13.8
1982	289.1	___	11.1
1983	298.4	___	8.8
1984	312.7	___	9.8

B. Modern Inflation Theory

6. Suppose that labor is the only productive factor available to an economy, so it has only one type of production cost—the wage paid to the labor that it employs. Let the rate of *growth of labor productivity* be zero, and assume that labor expects prices to climb over the next year at a rate of 5 percent. When the workers negotiate their contracts for that year, therefore, they should demand and receive a 5 percent raise.

a. The result must be a ___ percent increase in the average cost of production, a ___ percent increase in the price of output, and thus a ___ percent rate of inflation. Labor's inflationary expectations are thereby (**exceeded / met exactly / found to be excessive**).

b. Reinforced by this experience, labor should be expected to demand a second-year raise that would be (**higher than / identical to / lower than**) the first-year raise that initiated the process. (**Declining / Stable / Increasing**) price and wage inflation could therefore be perpetuated in the absence of any outside shocks.

Now suppose that the economy suffers an outside shock that produces an additional 5 percent increase in prices, so the overall rate of inflation in year 2 is 10 percent.

c. If labor expects year 2 inflation to continue into year 3, then labor would demand a (**5 / 10 / 15**) percent raise for year 3, which would support a (**5 / 10 / 15**)

(a): _____

(b): _____

(c): _____

Figure 14-5

percent wage-based inflation rate in year 3 even without another outside shock. Once again, labor's expectations would be (**exceeded / met exactly / found to be excessive**), and the inertial rate of inflation would have (**increased / remained the same / decreased**).

7. a. Use the spaces provided in the three panels of Figure 14-5 to label each one according to the type of inflation that it illustrates.

b. On the basis of that labeling, it appears that cost-push inflation can occur when the economy is operating (**above / at / below**) its potential and causes (**an increase / no change / a reduction**) in real GDP. (**Cost-push / Demand-pull**) inflation can, therefore, be identified as one source of stagflation.

Turn now to the specific sources of inflation, and indicate in the spaces provided which type of inflation each of the following is more likely to create; denote cost-push with a (**C**), demand-pull with a (**D**), and inertial inflation with an (**I**).

___ c. A dramatic increase in oil prices

___ d. A dramatic increase in government expenditure to finance a war

___ e. An automatic wage increase produced by a cost-of-living clause that follows inflation closely

___ f. A sudden reduction in the saving of an entire population

___ g. A wage settlement that increases the cost of steel

___ h. A sudden and large reduction in personal income taxes

8. Refer now to Figure 14-6. Three aggregate supply curves are drawn there. AS_1 represents aggregate supply at the beginning of year 1; AS_2 represents aggregate supply at the beginning of year 2; and AS_3 represents aggregate supply at the beginning of year 3. The corresponding aggregate demand curves are indicated by AD_1, AD_2, and AD_3.

a. The rate of inflation during year 1 was ___ percent, while the rate of inflation during year 2 was ___ percent.

b. If potential GDP were growing at 4 percent per year throughout this two-year period, then an initial unemployment rate of 6 percent would, by application of Okun's Law, (**grow / fall**) to ___ percent by the end of year 1 and ___ percent by the end of year 2.

9. The geometry of the Phillips curve can be displayed with either price inflation or wage inflation on the vertical axis.

a. This arithmetic equivalence can be supported by a markup theory of pricing that equates the difference between the rate of wage inflation and the rate of price inflation with (**a constant 2.45 percent / the rate of growth of labor productivity / the rate of conservation of scarce energy resources**).

b. On the basis of this equality, complete Table 14-4.

Figure 14-6

Table 14-4

Rate of Wage Inflation (%)	Rate of Price Inflation (%)	Rate of Productivity Growth (%)
10	___	3
10	___	0
3	5	___
___	7	2
___	150	0

10. Assume that labor has a long-term contract guaranteeing that wages will climb by 80 percent of the rate of increase of prices during the previous year. Using the equation that you employed in question 9 (namely, that the rate of inflation equals the rate of wage increase minus the rate of productivity growth), complete Table 14-5 given a constant rate of growth of labor productivity of 2 percent per year and an initial rate of price inflation of 20 percent.

Table 14-5

Year	Rate of Wage Inflation (%)	Rate of Price Inflation (%)
1	___	___
2	___	___
3	___	___
4	___	___

The rate of growth of labor productivity acts as a buffer between wage and price inflation that can serve to reduce inertial inflation over periods of time in an economy. Note too that no indexation scheme in the world will allow the standard of living to increase faster than real output—the rate of growth of labor productivity in this question.

C. Dilemmas of Anti-inflation Policy

11. Figure 14-7 shows five panels. Among the set are portraits of *a boom cycle, an austerity cycle, an inflationary*

Figure 14-7

supply shock, and *a complete political business cycle.* The 5 percent level indicates the LSUR, and the dots along the schedules indicate years (dot 1 for year 1, dot 2 for year 2, etc.).

Match each cycle with its most appropriate portrait; write your answers in the spaces provided in the graphs. (*Note*: One of your responses should be "none of the above.")

12. Suppose that a tiny economy has only 1000 workers. In the absence of any growth in their productivity and any outside shocks, suppose further that any wage increase that they all receive is passed on, percentage point for percentage point, to the price of the economy's output. Thus, an X percent rate of wage inflation would always be translated into an X percent rate of price inflation.

If these workers expected inflation to be 10 percent in the following year, then they would demand a 10 percent wage increase to preserve their real standard of living.

a.   That would, of course, produce a ____ percent rate of inflation.

If one worker were to realize that his or her wage increase would contribute to inflation, then he or she could,

of course, refuse the offer of a 10 percent wage increase in the interest of being a "good citizen."

b.   In that case, his or her real wage would (**rise / fall / remain the same**) by ____ percent, but the rate of inflation would (**rise / fall dramatically / remain almost exactly the same**) because the increase in the average cost of production would (**rise / fall dramatically / fall ever so slightly**).

c.   If, by way of contrast, everyone were to realize that his or her wage settlement contributed to inflation and were to demand only a 5 percent wage increase, then inflation would be ____ percent. If all the workers agreed to no wage increase, in fact, then inflation in this simple economy would be ____ percent.

The key, therefore, is to get everyone to adjust his or her wage demand at the same time. Nobody would want to be alone in taking a lower wage settlement, but something that would encourage everyone to react in the same moderating way could have a moderating effect on price inflation. It would be the purpose of an incomes policy to provide the incentive for everyone to behave in that way.

VIII. DISCUSSION QUESTIONS

Answer the following questions, making sure that you can explain the work you did to arrive at the answers.

1. Briefly discuss three features common to different hyperinflations.

2. Explain why workers should be more concerned about their real wage than their nominal wage. Are most labor contracts written in real or nominal terms?

3. Explain how wealth gets redistributed by inflation.

4. What reasons can be given for the recent decline in the LSUR? What sorts of policies could be pursued to lower the LSUR?

IX. ANSWERS TO STUDY GUIDE QUESTIONS

III. Review of Key Concepts

7	Inflation
11	Price index
1	Real wages
8	Inertial rate of inflation
5	Demand-pull inflation
10	Cost-push inflation
3	Stagflation
12	Phillips curve
6	Lowest sustainable unemployment rate
2	Indexing
4	Disinflation
9	Incomes policies

VI. Multiple Choice Questions

1. A	2. E	3. B	4. A	5. E	6. D
7. A	8. A	9. A	10. C	11. D	12. C
13. A	14. B	15. E	16. B	17. A	18. D
19. A	20. A	21. C	22. D	23. B	24. E
25. B					

VII. Problem Soaring

1. a. (1) moderate inflation
      (2) galloping inflation
      (3) hyperinflation
   b.

Table 14-1

Country/Period	Inflation Rate (%)	Strain
1. United States (1970s)	7	moderate
2. Germany (1922)	> 1000	hyperinflation
3. Germany (1923)	> 1 bil	hyperinflation
4. Israel (1980s)	> 100	galloping
5. Germany (1960s)	4	moderate
6. Brazil (1970s)	45	galloping
7. Poland (1923)	> 1000	hyperinflation

2. a. See Figure 14-4 (top panels).
   b. nearly equal to
   c. hold roughly constant
   d. rise
   e. See Figure 14-4 (bottom panels).
   f. fall
3. a. balanced
   b. would not, would not

Figure 14-4

c.   more
d.   distorted
e.   almost no
f.   distributional, better off, worth less, higher
g.   offering adjustable-rate loans

4.

Table 14-2

	Balanced	Unbalanced
Anticipated	a	b
Unanticipated	c	d

5.   a.   The inflation rates in Table 14-3 are 7.7, 11.3, 13.5, 10.4, 6.1, 3.2, 4.8.

b.   Inflation decreased dramatically after 1981. Nevertheless, nominal (and real) rates of interest remained high in 1982, 1983, and 1984.

6.   a.   5 percent, 5 percent, 5 percent, met exactly
b.   identical to, Stable
c.   10 percent, 10 percent, met exactly, increased

7.   a.   (a) cost-push, (b) inertial, (c) demand-pull
b.   below, a reduction, cost-push
c.   C
d.   D
e.   I
f.   D
g.   C
h.   D

8.   a.   10 percent, 8 percent (The price index in year 2 increased from 110 to 119.)
b.   grow, 8 percent, 10 percent

9.   a.   the rate of growth of labor productivity
b.   Reading across each row in Table 14-4, the entries are: 7, 10, -2, 9, 150

Table 14-4

Wage (%)	Price (%)	Growth (%)
10	7	3
10	10	0
3	5	-2
9	7	2
150	150	0

10.

Table 14-5

Year	Rate of Way Inflation (%)	Rate of Price Inflation (%)
1	16.0 (20 × .8)	14.0 (16 - 2)
2	11.2	9.2
3	7.4	5.4
4	4.3	2.3

11. (a) austerity cycle, (b) complete political business cycle, (c) inflationary supply shock, (d) none of the above, (e) boom cycle

12. a   10 percent
b.   fall, 10 percent, remain almost exactly the same, fall ever so slightly
c.   5 percent, 0 percent

VIII. Discussion Questions

1.   Three features common to all hyperinflations are: (1) a dramatic decrease in the demand for real money, (2) the distortion and destabilizing of relative prices, and (3) a very significant alteration of the distribution of wealth.

2.   Workers should be concerned with the cost of purchasing goods and services. A nominal wage increase of 10 percent that just equals an inflation increase of 10 percent amounts to a real wage increase of 0 percent! Many workers have automatic cost-of-living adjustments (COLAs) written into their contracts. This was a much greater concern during the early 1980s when inflation was much higher.

3.   Unanticipated inflation redistributes wealth from lenders to borrowers. People and institutions (like the government) that borrow get to pay back their loans with cheaper dollars. Furthermore, everyone with saving is made poorer by inflation. The purchasing power of saving is reduced as prices increase. The German hyperinflation wiped out decades of saving by German citizens.

4.   Part of the decline in the LSUR could be attributable to the decreased power of American labor unions. The percent of the labor force that is unionized has been declining and with it, the ability of organized labor to dictate conditions of employment or pay. Hence the wage rate has become more responsive to changes in the market place. As the economy has become more competitive, both internally and through trade and immigration, there has been a further downward pressure on the LSUR.

To lower the LSUR, efforts could be made to increase labor market information. Better information could bridge the gap between job seekers and job openings. Improved training programs could decrease structural unemployment and a general revamping of government programs could help send the appropriate signals to (potential) labor market participants.

CHAPTER 15
Open-Economy Macroeconomics

I. CHAPTER OVERVIEW

Chapter 15 returns to our multiplier model of Chapter 8 and incorporates foreign trade into the analysis. Not only does the inclusion of a foreign sector change the composition of aggregate demand, but the overall effects of changes in fiscal policy and investment are altered when imports are sensitive to changes in GDP. Adding a foreign sector also brings questions of exchange-rate effects and international policy coordination to the fore, and these are discussed as well.

The last section of the chapter focuses on the increased interdependence among nations in the global economy and returns to the concept of economic growth in an open environment. Of critical importance here will be the relationships between saving and investment, and national and global interest rates.

II. LEARNING OBJECTIVES

After you have read Chapter 31 in your text and completed the exercises in this *Study Guide* chapter, you should be able to:

1. Appreciate the importance of foreign trade and finance in the contemporary world economy.
2. Understand the bearing that flexible and fixed exchange rates have on international trade and trade policy.
3. Understand how trade is incorporated into an **open model** of the economy.
4. Calculate the **marginal propensity to import** and the **open-economy multiplier**.
5. Discuss recent trends in net exports in the United States.
6. Understand how domestic economic growth can be affected by international trade and economic circumstances abroad.
7. Understand the relationship between saving and investment in an open economy.
8. Discuss the strategies for promoting growth in an open economy.

III. REVIEW OF KEY CONCEPTS

Match the following terms from column A with their definitions in column B.

A	B
__ Open economy	1. Occurs when the value of a nation's currency increases, relative to the currency of other nations.
__ Closed economy	2. Financial market policies that allow easy and inexpensive transactions in the foreign-currency market.
__ Net exports	3. Price at which one nation's currency exchanges for another nation's currency.
__ Domestic demand	4. Economy without foreign trade or finance.
__ Foreign exchange rate	5. Occurs when financial capital can flow easily among countries.
__ Marginal propensity to import	6. Occurs when the value of a nation's currency falls, relative to the currency of other nations.
__ Merchandise trade	7. Country which participates in the world economy and is linked with other countries through trade and finance.
__ Net foreign investment	8. Includes human capital and other types of nonphysical capital.
__ Depreciation	9. Trade in goods like foodstuffs and manufacturing.
__ Appreciation	10. Total spending on goods and services in a closed economy, i.e., C+I+G, or GDP-X.
__ High capital mobility	11. The change in spending on imports for each dollar change in GDP.
__ Intangible capital	12. Value of imported goods and services subtracted from the value of exports.

__ Convertibility

13. Denotes net saving or investment abroad and is approximately equal to the value of net exports.

IV. SUMMARY AND CHAPTER OUTLINE

This section summarizes the key concepts from the chapter.

A. Foreign Trade and Economic Activity

1. Our model of total spending or aggregate demand in the economy becomes complete when we include trade in the analysis.

$$\text{Total aggregate demand} = \text{GDP} = C + I + G + X$$

2. Net exports (X), are the difference between a nation's exports (*Ex*) and imports (*Im*):

$$X = Ex - Im$$

Imports and exports are determined primarily by incomes, relative price differences, and foreign exchange rates. When a nation's exchange rate rises, the prices of imported goods fall while its exports become more expensive to foreigners.

3. There are two basic exchange rate systems: **flexible** and **fixed exchange rates**. With flexible exchange rates, the market forces of supply and demand determine the rate at which currencies are traded. Under a fixed exchange rate system, the government specifies the rate at which its nation's currency will be traded for other currencies.

4. When trade is included in our macroeconomic model, we need to adjust the *I* and *G* expenditure multiplier because some of that spending typically leaks out to the rest of the world.

Exports are treated as an exogenous variable since they are determined largely by factors outside the domestic economy, such as foreign incomes, prices abroad, and exchange rates. Imports also depend on exogenous foreign variables, but they vary directly with (domestic) GDP as well. As income and GDP increase, other things held constant, so does spending on foreign goods and services, such as coffee, bananas, and kiwi fruit.

When net exports are included in the model, the equilibrium level of GDP may be higher, lower, or unchanged.

5. Recall our earlier discussion of the relationship between the terms *margin* and *change*. The *marginal propensity to import, Mpm*, measures the *changes* in spending on imports for each dollar *change* in GDP. We can write this as:

$$Mpm = \frac{\text{change in } m}{\text{change in GDP}}$$

We now have an additional factor influencing the slope of the C + *I* + *G* + *X* or total spending line. The slope is

determined by both the *MPC* and the *Mpm*. Other things held constant, as GDP increases, so too will spending on *foreign* goods and services. Therefore, the *Mpm* represents a drain or leakage on the economy and, as such, will reduce the slope of the total spending line.

In the example in the text, the *MPC* is 0.67 and the *Mpm* is given as 0.10. If GDP increases by $300, C will increase by $200 ($300 × 0.67) and imports will increase by $30 ($300 × 0.10). Remember, this increase in imports means that there is a $30 increase in spending on foreign goods and services—this is $30 that is no longer spent at home. The total change in spending (C and m combined) is $170 ($200-$30). Since slope is a measure of margin or change, we can write:

$$\frac{\text{Slope of total}}{\text{spending line}} = \frac{\text{total change in spending}}{\text{change in GDP}} = \frac{170}{300}$$
$$= 0.567$$

Given the assumptions made in this model, in a *closed* economy, the slope of total spending is the *MPC*. In an open economy, the slope of total spending is flatter due to the leakage of spending on imports. Changes in **exports** will shift the entire spending line up or down, just like changes in *I* and *G*.

6. The *open-economy multiplier* is less than the closed economy expenditure multiplier.

$$\text{Open-economy multiplier} = \frac{1}{MPS + Mpm}$$

(As the denominator of a fraction increases, the value of the expression decreases.)

7. When two countries pursue a policy of fixed exchange rates, they must make sure that their interest rates move in tandem. If there is a divergence in interest rates speculators will have an incentive to move financial capital into the country with higher rates. In essence, the smaller of the two countries can no longer follow an independent monetary policy—its monetary policy must be devoted to aligning its interest rates with its fixed-exchange-rate partner.

8. Under a system of flexible exchange rates, monetary policy may become more effective. In the early 1980s the Fed raised interest rates in the United States to fight inflation and slow down the economy. On the international market, the higher interest rates attracted foreign financial capital, increased the demand for the dollar, which then appreciated in value and subsequently reduced exports and increased imports. This helped to slow the economy further!

B. Interdependence in the Global Economy

1. In a closed economy, deficit spending by the government tends to lower savings and investment. As government saving, T - G, decreases, this tends to reduce the overall level of saving in the economy. At any given interest rate, there is

less saving available for lending, so this tends to push the equilibrium real interest rate up.

2.   In an open economy, real interest rates are determined in world capital markets. If domestic saving and investment are not in balance exchange rates will move to ensure that the appropriate level of net exports is reached. It is important to realize that net exports will be the same as net foreign investment. If a country has a trade surplus, i.e., Ex > Im, then foreigners are purchasing more of the country's goods and services than its citizens are purchasing abroad. Therefore, the country will be left with a surplus of foreign currency. Whether this is invested abroad or not, this can be considered as *net foreign investment*.

3.   There are several policies that a nation can pursue to promote economic growth in an open system. In order to encourage foreign investment countries need to strive to select the best technological processes. Care needs to be exercised here. What works well in Country A may not succeed in Country B. Differences in resources as well educational and cultural dissimilarities may make it difficult to adapt to new technology. Nevertheless, foreign investors need to be assured that their investments are secure. Trade policies need to be open and competition needs to be encouraged. Countries also need to invest in their *human* as well as their physical capital.

V. HELPFUL HINTS

1.   Remember, the *open*-economy expenditure multiplier is less than the *closed*-economy expenditure multiplier. This is because imports (a leakage) increase as income or GDP rises. Exports are primarily determined by the economic health of other countries and are treated as exogenous.

2.   We have talked at length in previous chapters about the importance of saving and investment for economic growth. The discussion in this chapter should reinforce this point.

3.   Keep in mind that when Samuelson and Nordhaus refer to "capital mobility" in this chapter, they are referring to financial capital, not the physical capital which we consider a factor of production.

4.   The quote from de Toqueville at the very beginning of the chapter speaks eloquently about the advantages of international trade. Take this advice to heart. We return to trade issues in Chapter 34.

VI. MULTIPLE CHOICE QUESTIONS

These questions are organized by topic from the chapter outline. Choose the best answer from the options available.

A. Foreign Trade and Economic Activity

1.   Assume that the following conditions hold:
   A.   GDP is initially in equilibrium.

B.   The government then increases its total expenditure on goods and services by $2 billion.

E.   There is no increase at all in tax collection.

D.   The marginal propensity to consume is 0.75.

E.   The marginal propensity to import is 0.25.

Assuming that there is no price-inflationary consequences in the new equilibrium thus produced, GDP will:

a.   fall by $4 billion.

b.   rise by $2 billion.

c.   rise by $6 billion.

d.   rise by $8 billion.

e.   rise by $4 billion.

2.   Which answer to question 1 would be correct if instead of the increase in government spending, exports respond to a depreciation in the value of domestic currency and increase by $2 billion?

a.

b.

c.

d.

e.

3.   Which answer to question 1 would be correct if instead of the increase in government spending, exports respond to an appreciation in the value of domestic currency and decrease by $2 billion?

a.

b.

c.

d.

e.

4.   Over most of the twentieth century:

a.   the United States pursued isolationist policies.

b.   the United States ran a trade surplus.

c.   the volume of trade between the United States and Canada declined.

d.   all the above.

e.   none of the above.

5.   The difference between national output and domestic expenditure is:

a.   net imports.

b.   exports minus imports.

c.   imports minus exports.

d.   saving.

e.   none of the above.

6.   Assume that the exchange rate of Japanese yen to U.S. dollars falls. Which of the following statements is true?

a.   It will now take more dollars to purchase the same amount of yen.

b.   Other things held constant, Americans will probably purchase fewer Japanese goods and services.

c.   Other things held constant, the Japanese will probably purchase more American goods and services.

d.   We would say that, relative to the yen, the dollar has depreciated in value.

e.   All of the statements above are true.

7.   When we move from a closed to an open model of the economy:

a.   GDP increases.

b.   the expenditure multiplier increases.

c.   lump-sum taxes will not change.

d.   the slope of the total spending line does not change.

e.   exports and imports will have the same *absolute* impact on the economy, just the *direction* of the change will be different.

8.   The open-economy multiplier:

a.   is linked to the slope of the total spending line.

b.   equals the expenditure multiplier multiplied by the *MPC*.

c.   is equal to 1/*Mpm*.

d.   will decrease when imports exceed exports.

e.   is none of the above.

9.   The key feature of countries with fixed exchange rates and high capital mobility is that:

a.   except for capital, their economies must be closed.

b.   they should trade primarily with each other.

c.   their interest rates must basically be the same.

d.   they must be on the gold standard.

e.   all of the above.

10. The United States adopted a policy of flexible exchange rates in:

a.   1962.

b.   1973.

c.   1979.

d.   1987.

e.   None of the above, the United States follows a system of fixed exchange rates.

11. When the dollar appreciates in value:

a.   imports tend to increase.

b.   exports tend to increase.

c.   monetary policy is used to counteract the appreciation.

d.   the government budget deficit tends to decrease.

e.   the marginal propensity to import tends to decline.

B. Interdependence in the Global Economy

12. Developing a program of economic growth entails:

a.   encouraging saving.

b.   expanding capital.

c.   developing appropriate trade policies.

d.   adopting the best technological advances.

e.   all of the above.

13. High domestic interest rates tend to:

a.   attract funds from abroad.

b.   contribute to an appreciation of the domestic currency.

c.   lead to a reduction in exports.

d.   lead to an increase in imports.

e.   contribute to all of the above.

14. A country's foreign trade balance is primarily determined by:

a.   domestic saving.

b.   domestic investment.

c.   its level of productivity.

d.   all of the above.

e.   choices **a**. and **b**. only.

15. Over the long run, the single most important way of increasing per capita output and living standards in a country is to:

a.   increase the savings rate.

b.   increase foreign investment.

d.   increase domestic investment.

d.   adopt the best possible technological advances in production.

e.   lower per capita tax rates.

16. When there is a gap between savings and investment, the gap tends to be offset:

a.   by changes in net exports.

b.   by changes in the world interest rate.

c.   when the country adopts a policy of fixed exchange rates.

d.   when monetary policy intervenes.

e.   in the long run.

17. When world interest rates exceed domestic rates:

a.   the domestic currency appreciates in value.

b.   saving tends to flow abroad.

c.   imports will exceed exports.

d.   all of the above.

e.   none of the above.

18. *Intangible capital*:

a.   is hidden in the underground economy.

b.   includes investment in the service sector of the economy.

c.   includes capital investment in off-shore corporations.

d.   includes investment in human capital.

e.   is composed primarily of investments in less developed countries.

19. The risk premium:

a.   equilibrates interest rates between countries.

b.   is paid by the United States to other countries.

c.   is usually negative.

d.   is, in most cases, the same as the real rate.

e.   tends to raise domestic interest rates far above the world rate.

VII. PROBLEM SOLVING

The following problems are designed to help you apply the concepts that you learned in the chapter.

A. Foreign Trade and Economic Activity

1. Consider the open economy defined in Table 15-1.

Table 15-1

GDP	C	I	G	T	Ex	Im
900	340	200	500	500	250	90
950	370	200	500	500	250	95
1,000	400	200	500	500	250	100
1,050	430	200	500	500	250	105
1,100	460	200	500	500	250	110
1,150	490	200	500	500	250	115
1,200	520	200	500	500	250	120
1,250	550	200	500	500	250	125
1,300	580	200	500	500	250	130
1,350	610	200	500	500	250	135
1,400	640	200	500	500	250	140
1,450	670	200	500	500	250	145
1,500	700	200	500	500	250	150
1,550	730	200	500	500	250	155
1,600	760	200	500	500	250	160
1,650	790	200	500	500	250	165
1,700	820	200	500	500	250	170
1,750	850	200	500	500	250	175
1,800	880	200	500	500	250	180
1,850	910	200	500	500	250	185
1,900	940	200	500	500	250	190
1,950	970	200	500	500	250	195
2,000	1,000	200	500	500	250	200
2,050	1,030	200	500	500	250	205

a. Solve GDP = $G + I + G + X$ to compute the equilibrium level of GDP for the open economy. The equilibrium level of GDP or GDP* = $___.

b. Record the values assumed by the following variables at GDP*:
- (1) I = $__
- (2) S = $__
- (3) $T - G$ = $__
- (4) $Im - Ex$ = $__

When the economy is at equilibrium, investment should again be equal to all saving. Just as we added government saving in the last problem, we must, in addition, include foreign saving here. A positive figure for foreign saving will occur when imports are greater that exports. ("Foreign saving" means that U.S. buyers are spending more on foreign goods and services than foreigners are spending on U.S. products.) So, we need to include the *Im—Ex* term above as part of saving.

c. At GDP* the sum of private saving, government saving, and foreign saving is $__; this (**matches / falls short of / exceeds**) investment at GDP*.

d. If this economy were closed, and thus exports and imports were both zero, then equilibrium GDP would be $__.

e. Opening the economy according to the data provided in Table 15-1 therefore (**increases / has no effect on / decreases**) GDP by ___ percent.

Opening an economy can distort the Keynesian multipliers because the level of imports can change with the level of domestic economic activity; and if imports change while exports hold constant, then net exports must change.

One measure of the sensitivity of imports to GDP is the *marginal propensity to impost (Mpm)*. Given any change in GDP, the *Mpm* is defined as the ratio of the resulting change in imports to the change in GDP.

f. The import schedule displayed in Table 15-1 exhibits a marginal propensity to import of ___.

Given any marginal propensity to import, the expenditure multiplier for a change in government spending and/or a change in domestic investment is no longer 1/*MPS*. It is, instead:

$$\frac{1}{(MPS + Mpm)}$$

g. As long as the *Mpm* is greater than zero, the open-economy multiplier is (**larger than / equal to / smaller than**) the closed-economy multiplier.

Changes in either investment or government spending therefore have a smaller effect on GDP in an open economy than in a closed economy. Why? Because any stimulus that might be created by an increase in investment or government spending in an open economy is partially vented abroad.

h. Compute the marginal propensity to consume exhibited by the consumption function in Table 15-1; *MPC* equals ___.

i. The closed-economy multiplier would then be ___, but the open-economy multiplier is ___.

2. Use Table 15-1 to answer the following questions.

a. Suppose that investment increases by $250 billion. If the economy were *closed*, you would expect GDP to (**increase by / hold steady at / decrease by**) $___.

b. In the *open* economy illustrated in Table 15-1, though, GDP should (**increase by / stay the same at / fall by**) $___.

c. Verify your second calculation using the investment equals saving approach:
- (1) GDP** = $___.
- (2) I = $___.
- (3) S = $___.
- (4) $T - G$ = $___.
- (5) $Im - Ex$ = $___.

d. Suppose that the trading partner of the economy depicted in Table 15-1 follows a "beggar thy neighbor" trade policy by prohibiting our economy's exporting of any product; i.e., let x fall to $0. Equilibrium CDP would (**rise / fall**) to $___.

e. Now suppose that a change in the exchange rate makes imports more expensive, causing exports to rise by $100 and the import schedule to fall by $30 at every level of GDP. The economy's currency must, therefore, have (**appreciated / depreciated**). Equilibrium GDP would (**rise / fall**).

3. This problem is based on Table 31-1 in the text. Table 15-2 here is identical to the one in the text, *except* exports have been changed from 250 to 350.

Table 15-2: Output Determination with Trade

(1) Initial GDP	(2) Domestic Demand C+I+G	(3) Exports Ex	(4) Imports Im	(5) Net Exports X=Ex-Im	(6) Total Spending C+I+G+X
4100	4000	350	410	___	___
3800	3800	350	380	___	___
3500	3600	350	350	___	___
3200	3400	350	320	___	___
2900	3200	350	290	___	___

a. Complete columns (5) and (6) in the table and estimate the new equilibrium of GDP in the economy. (Your answer at this point may not be exact because the GDP numbers in the table always change by 300. The exact answer lies in between two of the numbers.) GDP is (approximately) equal to $ _____.

b. The *MPC* = _____.

c. The *Mpm* = _____.

d. The open-economy expenditure multiplier = _____.

e. The change in exports was 100. If you multiply that change by the open-economy multiplier, you get $

_____, which is precisely the change in GDP! The new equilibrium level of GDP is $ _____.

f. Figure 31-2 from the text is reproduced here as Figure 15-1. Add the new spending line to this diagram.

B. Interdependence in the Global Economy

4. Figure 15-2 illustrates the relationship between saving and investment in a closed economy. Recall that *S* includes total private saving by households and businesses, and public saving is the difference between government tax receipts (T) and expenditures (G). The economy begins at equilibrium at point *A*. Suppose now, other things held constant, that the government increases taxes.

a. As a result, the government budget deficit should (**increase / decrease / remain the same**).

b. Draw a new line in Figure 15-2 which includes the change in taxes.

c. At the new equilibrium point in the economy, the real interest rate is (**lower / higher / unchanged**) and the level of investment spending in the economy has (**decreased / increased / remained the same**).

d. Why do you think the government decided to raise taxes in the first place?

5. Figure 15-3 shows the relationship between saving and investment in an open economy, which is too little to influence the world interest rate, r^W. Recall that an open economy has alternative sources of investment and alternative

(a) Monetarist Approach

(b) Keynesian Approach

Figure 15-1: Adding Net Exports to Domestic Demand Gives Equilibrium GDP in the Open Economy

Figure 15-2: Saving and Investment in the Closed Economy

outlets for saving. Initially, total national savings equals total national investment and the economy is at equilibrium at point A.

    a.   Suppose there is an increase in national frugality and the savings rate increases. Illustrate this change on the diagram. Label the new line S-S.

    b.   As a result domestic interest rates will (**increase /**

decrease/ remain unchanged) relative to the world rate, and foreign investment will (**increase / decrease/ remain unchanged**).

    c.   In turn, the domestic currency will (**appreciate / depreciate / remain the same**) in value, and exports will (**increase / decrease / remain unchanged**).

    d.   Suppose instead, that world interest rates increase

Figure 15-3: Saving and Investment in an Open Economy

relative to rates in the domestic economy. As a result, domestic investment will (**increase / decrease / remain unchanged**) and domestic interest rates will (**increase / decrease / remain unchanged**).

e.   This will lead to a/an (**increase / decrease / no change**) in domestic saving. Since people are saving (**more / less / the same**), spending will (**decrease / increase / remain the same**) and the domestic currency will   (**appreciate / depreciate / remain the same**) in value.

f.   Finally, net exports and foreign investment will (**increase / decrease / remain unchanged**) and equilibrium will be restored.

g.   Illustrate the changes that occur in Figure 15-3.

VIII. DISCUSSION QUESTIONS

Answer the following questions, making sure that you can explain the work you did to arrive at the answers.
1.   Discuss some of the important economic linkages that exist between the United States and other countries.
2.   Briefly discuss the primary determinants of imports and exports in an economy.
3.   Explain why the slope of the total-spending line is flatter in an open economy than a closed economy.
4.   Figure 31-3 from the text is reproduced here as Figure 15-4. What caused the large drop in net exports in the early 1980s and its recovery since then?

IX. ANSWERS TO STUDY GUIDE QUESTIONS

III. Review of Key Concepts
7   Open economy
4   Closed economy

12   Net exports
10   Domestic demand
3   Foreign exchange rate
11   Marginal propensity to import
9   Merchandise trade
13   Net foreign investment
6   Depreciation
1   Appreciation
5   High capital mobility
8   Intangible capital
2   Convertibility

VI. Multiple Choice Questions
1.   E   2.   E   3.   A   4.   B   5.   B   6.   E
7.   C   8.   A   9.   C   10. D   11. A   12. E
13. E   14. C   15. D   16. A   17. A   18. D
19. E

VII. Problem Solving
1.   a.   GDP* = $1500
     b.   (1) $I = 200
          (2) $S = 300
          (3) $T - G = 0
          (4) $m - e = -$100$
     c. $200, matches
     d. $1250
     e.   increases, 20
     f.   5/50 = 0.10
     g.   smaller than
     h.   30/50 = 0.60, $C = 100 + (0.6 ¥ DI)$
     i.   2.5, 2.0
2.   a.   increase by, $250 × 2.5 = $625
     b.   increase by, $250 × 2.0 = $500
     c.   (1) GDP** = $1500 + 500 = $2000
          (2) $I = $200 + 250 = $450

Figure 15-4: **Real Net Exports Added to Depth of Recession of Early 1980s**

(3) $S = \$500$

(4) $T - G = \$0$

(5) $m - e = -\$50$

d. fall, $\$250 \times 2 = \$500$, GDP*** $= \$2000 - 500 =$ $\$1500$. To check your answer, compare investment with all savings: $I = \$450$, $S = \$300$, $T - G = \$0$, $m - e = \$150$

e. depreciated, rise

3. a.

Table 15-2: Output Determination with Trade

(1) Initial GDP	(2) Domestic Demand C+I+G	(3) Exports Ex	(4) Imports Im	(5) Net Exports X=Ex-Im	(6) Total Spending C+I+G+X
4100	4000	350	410	-60	3940
3800	3800	350	380	-30	3770
3500	3600	350	350	0	3600
3200	3400	350	320	30	3430
2900	3200	350	290	60	3260

GDP is approximately equal to $3700.

b. 0.67

c. 0.10

d. 1/0.43 = 2.33

e. $233, $3733

f.

4   a.   decrease

b.

c.   lower, increased

d. Taxes were probably increased to fight inflation and slow the economy down. Alternatively, taxes may have been increased to finance a new spending project.

5. a.

b. decrease, decrease

c. depreciate, increase

d. decrease, increase

e. increase, more, decrease, depreciate

f. increase

g. The world interest rate is $r^{w'}$. BC indicates exports or foreign investment.

VIII. Discussion Questions

1. There are several important economic linkages between the United States and other countries. The most obvious is through trade. The United States sells its goods and services abroad, and its citizens import goods and services from other countries. There are financial linkages as well. Foreigners invest a great deal of money in the United States, and the United States, and its citizens have many investments abroad. U.S. banks also provide financial services for many foreign nations and corporations. Finally, we should recognize the growing importance of the multinational corporation. More and more corporations are establishing factories and bases of production in more than one country.

2. Imports and exports are influenced by the economic health of the country: whether it is growing, the extent of inflation, the extent of unemployment. This is important for

Figure 15-1: Adding Net Exports to Domestic Demand Gives Equilibriium GDP in the Open Economy

Figure 15-2 Saving and Investment in the Closed Economy

both trading partners. In addition, foreign exchange rates are an important determinant of trade. If a nation's currency is appreciating, it is able to import goods and services more cheaply, and its products become relatively more expensive for foreigners.

3. In an open economy, imports are related to the level of GDP in the domestic economy. When income increases, some of that income will be spent on foreign goods and services. Likewise, when income falls, domestic spending will not bear the full brunt of the decline since citizens will cut

back on their imports as well. As a result, the slope of the spending line and the multiplier are reduced.

4. After the 1982 recession the U.S. economy experienced strong growth relative to most of its major trading partners. This led to an increase in U.S. imports and a decline in U.S. exports. Analysts also point out that an over-valuation of the dollar also contributed to the decline in net exports. The declining value of the dollar and the recovery of foreign economies has helped increase the trade deficit in recent years.

Figure 15-3: Saving and Investment in an Open Economy

CHAPTER 16
The Warring Schools of Macroeconomics

I. CHAPTER OVERVIEW

You have spent a great deal of time and effort learning the basics of the macroeconomy. You have learned about fiscal policy and the Keynesian multiplier. You have learned about monetary policy and the Federal Reserve System. You have learned about the problems of unemployment and inflation and the various approaches used to deal with each malady. While there is general agreement among economists about what the fundamental economic problems are, there is much less agreement about the methods used to solve these problems.

Economists, like other scientists, have different backgrounds and different philosophical points of view. Moreover, the solutions proposed by alternative schools of thought often seem to be more contradictory than supportive of each other. We must keep in mind that economics does not exist in a vacuum or in a controlled laboratory. Policymakers do not have the luxury of first trying new ideas out in a controlled environment to see how they will work.

In Chapter 32, Samuelson and Nordhaus discuss five different schools of economic thought. The first two, **classical economics** and **Keynesianism**, are already somewhat familiar to you. The other three—**monetarism, the new classical economics**, and **supply-side economics**—are new, but they rely to a considerable extent on concepts you already know. For example, throughout the analysis, Samuelson and Nordhaus employ the aggregate demand-aggregate supply diagram and the Phillips curve to explain the differing philosophical viewpoints. Your general objective is to develop sufficient "feel" for the various schools of thought to enable you to sort through their similarities and differences.

II. LEARNING OBJECTIVES

After you have read Chapter 32 in your text and completed the exercises in this *Study Guide* chapter, you should be able to:

1. Understand that the **classical** view of the world envisions wages and prices responding so quickly that an economy's performance is determined almost exclusively by its potential GDP.

2. Understand that the **Keynesian** view of the world envisions wages and prices responding so slowly that an economy can be in equilibrium well below its potential.

3. Define the **income velocity of money** and explain its role in (a) the classical **quantity theory** and (b) the modern **monetarist** view of macroeconomic policy.

4. Relate the lessons of the **monetarist experiment** in the United States during the early 1980s.

5. Understand the **new classical economics** and the two fundamental assumptions of **rational expectations**.

6. Discuss the criticisms leveled against rational expectations, and explain the responses of its proponents to the criticisms.

7. Recall the "**Lucas critique**" of monetarist rules and the new classical economics.

8. Explain and appraise the **supply-side** approach to economic policy.

III. REVIEW OF KEY CONCEPTS

Match the following terms from column A with their definitions in column B.

A	B
__ Classical theory	1. People incorporate all available information into their economic decision making. Since they anticipate predictable changes in policy and react accordingly, the policy action itself becomes less effective.
__ Say's Law	2. Monetary policy that sets the growth of the money supply at a fixed rate and holds to that rate through *all* economic conditions.
__ Crowding out	3. Emphasizes *incentives* for people to work and save more, thereby stimulating output and lowering prices.
__ Keynesian revolution	4. Dramatic change in Fed operating procedure in the late 1970s in which the Fed decided to

__ Monetarism

__ Income velocity
of money

__ Quantity theory
of money and
prices

__ Monetary rule

__ Monetarist
experiment

__ New classical
macroeconomics

__ Rational-
expectations
hypothesis

__ Real business-
cycle theory

__ Policy
ineffectiveness
theorem

__ Lucas critique

__ Adaptive
expectations

__ Supply-side
economics

stop focusing on interest rates and instead endeavored to keep bank reserves and the money supply on predetermined growth paths.

5. With rational expectations and flexible prices and wages, anticipated government policy can not affect real output or unemployment.

6. Approach to macroeconomics that emphasizes the powerful self-correcting forces in an economy due primarily to flexible wages and prices.

7. People form their expectations simply and mechanically on the basis of *past* information.

8. When the government increases its spending, production of private goods and services will be displaced.

9. Explains business cycles purely as shifts in *AS*, without any reference to monetary or other demand-side forces.

10. Supply creates its own demand—overproduction is impossible by its very nature.

11. Dramatic change in economic thought that overthrew the classical model of macroeconomics

12. Maintains that prices move in proportion with the supply of money.

13. Maintains that the money supply is the major determinant of short-run movements in nominal GDP and of long-run movements in prices.

14. Emphasizes the role of flexible wages and prices but adds rational expectations as well.

15. Measures the rate at which the stock of money turns over or gets spent relative to the total output of the nation—the ratio of nominal GDP to the stock of money.

16. Criticizes the fixed rules of monetarism and the new classical economics because people may change their behavior when policy changes.

IV. SUMMARY AND CHAPTER OUTLINE

This section summarizes the key concepts from the chapter.

A. Classical Stirrings and Keynesian Revolution

1. The most straightforward summary of the classical model is contained in Say's Law of Markets, which states that "Supply creates its own demand," or, in today's jargon, "Supply rules!" Say lived in the very early 1800s, at the dawn of the industrial revolution, long before the birth of huge conglomerates and multinational corporations. In such a competitive economy with flexible wages and prices, resources were more likely to be allocated efficiently, and the income that labor earned could be used to purchase the commodities produced. Think back to the circular-flow model of the economy in which households provide the factors of production and get paid wages, rent, interest, and profits. Any unemployment that exists, in this view, is temporary and more *micro* in nature. Workers could be moving between jobs or may temporarily demand above-market wages.

There is no need or role for *macro*economic policy (either fiscal or monetary) here. The price flexibility that is assumed to exist in all markets assures us that full employment equilibrium will be achieved. Government interference in markets is unnecessary and impacts only the price level. Since the economy always adjusts and moves to full employment, the aggregate supply curve is a vertical line at potential GDP.

2. The Keynesian view of the world envisions slower wage and price adjustments, so the aggregate supply curve is thought to be positively sloped, not vertical, in the short run. Demand-side manipulation is therefore expected to have some ability to alter the level of GDP in the short run. Potential GDP nonetheless defines a vertical long-run aggregate supply curve.

One critical difference in the classical-vs.-Keynesian debate concerns prolonged periods of unemployment. Keynesians think that *equilibrium* can be sustained, at least for a period of time, *below* potential GDP and thus can be accompanied by prolonged unemployment. (Remember, Keynes was writing during the Depression.) This is because wages and prices respond slowly to changes in the economy especially during contractions, when firms are initially reluctant to lower prices and workers are adamant about refusing cuts in pay. Of course, during recessions, when prices are falling, labor's *nominal* wage could be constant, but the *real wage* could be rising. The problem is that most workers are not immediately aware of this.

Note, too, Keynes's emphasis on demand. In the Keynesian view, fiscal and monetary policies can be both helpful *and* necessary to move an economy to its potential.

B. The Monetarist Approach

1. Keynes recognized the importance of money in an economy, but **monetarism** holds that the money supply is *the major* policy variable. Modern monetarism rests on three major propositions: (a) growth in the money supply is the primary determinant of growth in nominal GDP; (b) prices and wages are quite flexible in response to excess supply and/or demand; and (c) the private economy is very stable. Derived from these propositions are beliefs that (a) macroeconomic fluctuation is caused by erratic money-supply growth; (b) active government intervention into economies should be avoided; and (c) stable money growth at 3 to 5 percent per year should painlessly produce stable prices and steady growth.

2. The **income velocity of money** is one of two factors in the **quantity theory of money** which strict monetarists hold as constant. The other constant term is real GDP (equal to potential GDP, since the economy has flexible wages and prices and will thereby self-adjust to full employment). Velocity measures the rate at which the stock of money turns over or gets spent. It can be defined as:

$$V = \frac{GDP}{M} = \frac{PQ}{M}$$

This can be rewritten as follows:

$$VM = PQ$$

$$P = \frac{VM}{Q}$$

$$P = kM$$

where k, the ratio of V to Q, is constant, or close to it in the short run. In this view, money has no *real* effect on the economy, just on prices.

3. In what has come to be known as the *monetarist experiment* of the early 1980s, the Fed stopped focusing on interest rates and instead endeavored to keep the money supply on a predetermined and rigid growth path. The Fed's determined adherence to this tight policy taught us that (a) money *is* a powerful determinant of aggregate demand; (b) the money supply can be an effective inflation fighter; and (c) anti-inflationary tight monetary policy is not appreciably less expensive (in terms of lost employment and output) than alternative macroeconomic tools.

C. The New Classical Economics

1. The **new classical economics**, like the classicals and monetarists, emphasizes the role of flexible wages and prices; however, the new classical economics adds a new feature called **rational expectations**. Believers in rational expectations hold that individuals efficiently and rationally use the available information in the economy to form their expectations of what will happen in the future. It follows that any predictable policy designed to move aggregate demand will be ineffective because the people will see through its mechanism and undermine its power, thereby keeping GDP at its potential. For example, a tax cut would be undermined by people who, realizing that the resulting deficit would have to be repaid with interest in the future, would save the proceeds in anticipation of the "bill's coming due." It follows that policy rules are better than discretionary changes in policy.

2. Critics of the theory of rational expectations are particularly quick to point out that it falls short of explaining prolonged periods of unemployment.

3. The **real business cycle (RBC) theory** explains business cycles purely as shifts in aggregate supply. Shifts in the long run (vertical) aggregate supply curve are independent of aggregate demand and cause changes in real output. Proponents of the RBC theory argue that these shifts in AS may give the appearance of a short-run Phillips curve.

4. The efficiency-wage theory brings together parts of both classical and Keynesian economics. It suggests that firms may increase wages above market-clearing levels to increase labor productivity. As workers compete for these high paying jobs, the labor market may not clear and involuntary unemployment may persist over the long term. Proponents of the efficiency wage theory argue that long-term increases in the LSUR may be due to a worsening in efficiency-wage attributes in the labor market.

D. Ultra-Classicism: Supply-side Economics

The **supply-side** policies of the Reagan and Thatcher administrations emphasized the role of fiscal policy in the determination of economic growth and aggregate supply. They provided *incentives,* in the form of large tax cuts to consumers and businesses, to encourage work effort, saving, and investment. They believed that even though tax rates were lower, the increased growth and output in the economy could generate more tax revenue.

The U.S. economy did grow strongly throughout most of the 1980s, but many economists believe the rightward shift in aggregate demand was much more influential than any changes in aggregate supply. Furthermore, national saving did not increase as the supply siders expected, and the tax cuts produced enormous federal budget deficits that still hinder the economy today.

V. HELPFUL HINTS

1. To keep track of these models, it might be helpful to view them in historical context.
   a. The classical model was developed at the beginning of the industrial revolution. England and other

European countries experienced unprecedented economic growth. It is no wonder that this model called for limited government involvement.

b.   Keynes was reacting to the Great Depression and the inability of the classical model to deal with it.

c.   Monetarism, the new classical economics, and supply-side economics are all related to the classical model. The inability of the Keynesian model to deal with some of the macroeconomic problems of the 1970s encouraged their development.

2.   The term *new classical* should not be confused with the "neoclassical growth model" of Chapter 27. They are different models and address different issues.

3.   Monetarists adhere to a fixed growth rate of the money supply. This is not because they view money as unimportant, but rather that they view discretionary swings in the money supply as potentially upsetting to the economy and doing more harm than good.

4.   In footnote number 5 in this chapter of your text, Samuelson and Nordhaus describe the aggregate demand curve, in the monetarist view, as a rectangular hyperbola. This is illustrated in panel *(a)* of Figure 32-4, which is reproduced here as Figure 16-1. Recall that the quantity theory of money states that $MV = PQ$. So if V is constant (as monetarists contend) and the money supply does not change, then the multiplication of P and Q must remain constant as well. This is precisely the characteristic of a rectangular hyperbola—the area underneath the curve is the same at every point along the curve. We have drawn two rectangles underneath the *AD* curve, one touching at point *A* and another touching at point *B*. The area of each rectangle (P times Q) is identical.

5.   During a year's time every dollar in the economy is spent several times. This is what velocity measures. Get a dollar bill out of your wallet (any denomination will do). On the front of the bill, to the left of the picture, is a capital letter (A through L). The letter, and the seal around it, represent one of the twelve Federal Reserve district banks. A is Boston, D is Cleveland, L is San Francisco, and so on. (You can find the name of the Federal Reserve Bank, written in small letters, in the seal around the big letter.) Chances are, most of the money in your wallet is from the Federal Reserve Bank(s) in your area. But some bills may be from far away. This money has changed hands many times before it found its way into your wallet. Money that is spent does not go out of circulation. It continues to be turned over and spent again.

VI. MULTIPLE CHOICE QUESTIONS

These questions are organized by topic from the chapter outline. Choose the best answer from the options available.

A. Classical Stirrings and Keynesian Revolution

1.   Which of the following economists would *not* be considered a classical economist?
a.   John Stuart Mill
b.   Adam Smith
c.   David Ricardo
d.   A. C. Pigou
e.   They are all considered classicals.

(a) Monetarist Approach

(b) Keynesian Approach

Figure 16-1

2. Why do classical economists contend that the economy moves to its long-run equilibrium position very quickly?
   a. People process information efficiently and respond accordingly.
   b. Fiscal policy is effective in shifting *AD*.
   c. The money supply grows at a fixed rate.
   d. Prices and wages are flexible.
   e. The short run is too short to be meaningful.
3. Stimulative aggregate demand policies are ineffective in the classical model because:
   a. the economy is already at, or moving toward, potential GDP.
   b. they will only drive up prices.
   c. unemployment is more of a short-run micro problem.
   d. all the above.
   e. none of the above.
4. Keynes argued that:
   a. the economy would tend to move toward potential GDP in the long run.
   b. the AS curve had shifted to the left during the Depression.
   c. demand creates its own supply.
   d. workers respond quickly to changes in *real* wages but not to changes in *nominal wages*.
   e. none of the above.
5. Keynesian economics contends that the aggregate supply curve:
   a. is flat or upward-sloping when output is beneath potential GDP.
   b. is flat or upward-sloping throughout.
   c. is no longer relevant—only aggregate demand matters.
   d. shifts when the unemployment rate changes.
   e. shifts when the government cuts taxes.
6. The retreat from Keynesianism came in part from:
   a. the failed fiscal policies of the 1960s.
   b. its overemphasis on incentives for long-run growth.
   c. Richard Nixon's declaring, "We are all Keynesians now."
   d. its overemphasis on wage and price rigidity.
   e. none of the above.
7. In terms of the saving-investment diagram used extensively in earlier chapters, the introduction of a tight-money policy by the Federal Reserve would be intended to:
   a. lower both the investment (*I*) and savings (*S*) schedules and hence lower GDP.
   b. raise the *I* schedule and hence lower GDP.
   c. raise the *I* schedule and hence raise GDP.
   d. lower the *S* schedule and hence raise GDP.
   e. lower the *I* schedule and hence lower GDP.

B. The Monetarist Approach

8. The quantity theory of money assumes:
   a. that both *V* and nominal GDP are fixed.
   b. that both *V* and real GDP are fixed.
   c. that only *V* is fixed.
   d. that *V* and the price level are fixed.
   e. none of the above.
9. Monetarists believe:
   a. that the money supply determines nominal GDP in the short run.
   b. that the money supply determines prices in the long run.
   c. that fiscal policy is essentially ineffective.
   d. that market forces will maintain potential GDP in the long run.
   e. all the above.
10. The lessons of the past decade or so include which of the following?
    a. Strict adherence to money-supply growth targets can cause substantial unemployment.
    b. The Keynesian view is entirely wrong.
    c. There is nothing to the monetarist view of the world that should be accepted in constructing policy.
    d. Money matters, but so does fiscal policy.
    e. Answers **a** and **d**.
11. The **monetary rule** states that:
    a. the economy should grow at a fixed rate and that money supply growth should vary.
    b. the money supply should grow at a fixed rate, regardless of economic conditions.
    c. monetary policy should maintain a steady trend in real interest rates.
    d. the Federal Reserve should fight inflation.
    e. the money supply should grow more during recessions.

C. The New Classical Economics

12. The basic assumptions of rational-expectations macroeconomics include:
    a. a presumption that people form their expectations about the future efficiently and rationally.
    b. a presumption that prices are extremely flexible in both directions.
    c. a presumption that wages are extremely flexible in both directions.
    d. all the above.
    e. answers **a** and **c** only.
13. It follows from the assumptions of rational expectations that:
    a. most unemployment is voluntary.
    b. monetary policy can work in the short run but not in the long run.

c. fiscal policy can affect the long term but not the short term because of delays in Congress.
d. any policy might work, independent of the circumstance.
e. none of the above.

14. It follows from the assumptions of rational expectations that a reduction in taxes to stimulate consumption:
a. would work as advertised.
b. would not work unless accompanied by accommodating monetary policy.
c. would not work because people would save their tax break in anticipation of future higher taxes.
d. might work unless there were substantial leakages into foreign markets.
e. would involve none of the above.

15. According to rational-expectations macroeconomics, the short-run Phillips curve is effectively:
a. horizontal.
b. positively sloped.
c. vertical.
d. negatively sloped.
e. sloped in either direction depending upon conditions.

16. Should an economy attempt to move up its short-run Phillips curve to reduce unemployment below the natural rate, the rational-expectations macroeconomist would expect that:
a. people would not be fooled, and only inflation would result.
b. people would gradually find out that real wages had climbed, turning the curve vertical in the long run.
c. the economy would be successful in the short term, but successful in the long term only if there were substantial economic growth.
d. the natural rate would indeed fall as potential output grew.
e. none of the above would occur.

17. The policy prescription of rational-expectations macroeconomics includes:
a. the notion that stable monetary-policy rules should be constructed and followed so that changes in velocity can maintain equilibrium at potential GDP.
b. the notion that discretionary policy should be avoided.
c. the notion that no policy adjustment would be required to help an economy overcome an oil crisis like the one that occurred in 1973.
d. the notion that fiscal policy should determine the mix of public and private spending once and for all and then leave it alone.
e. all the above.

18. The existence of periods of prolonged unemployment in our history does damage to:
a. the expectations assumption of rational expectations only.

b. the flexibility assumption of rational expectations only.
c. both assumptions of the rational-expectations theory.
d. either assumption of rational expectations, depending upon conditions.
e. neither assumption of rational expectations in any circumstance.

19. Without the flexibility (of prices) assumption of rational expectations:
a. periods of unemployment could exist.
b. the short-run Phillips curve would have some negative slope.
c. policy could be used to exploit the short-run trade-off.
d. the expectations hypothesis would be damaged but not necessarily destroyed.
e. all the above would be true.

20. A policy mix that targets monetary policy at inflation and fiscal policy at unemployment seems to produce high-consumption, low-investment, high-deficit economies because:
a. monetary policy is ineffectual against inflation.
b. fiscal stimulus during recession is never turned off, so monetary policy must become increasingly contractionary over time.
c. Congress never writes fiscal policy fast enough to avoid a recession.
d. fiscal policy is ineffective in stimulating an economy past its potential GDP.
e. none of the above.

21. The real business cycle theory (RBC) theory:
a. also relies on rational expectations and competitive markets.
b. explains business cycles purely as shifts in AS.
c. contends that changes in the unemployment rate are the result of movements in the LSUR.
d. is all of the above.
e. is none of the above.

22. The efficiency wage theory:
a. argues that the LSUR should fall over time.
b. offers an explanation for the rigidity of real wages and the existence of involuntary unemployment.
c. says there is little or no relationship between wage rates and worker productivity.
d. was first developed by Keynes.
e. says more about production and output than it does about wages.

D. Ultra-Classicism: Supply-side Economics

23. Which of the following statements is (are) true about the supply-side program for economic recovery offered by the Reagan administration in 1981?

a.   It represented a retreat from belief in the Keynesian model of macroeconomic behavior.

b.   It represented a belief that price and wage adjustments would keep any recession short.

c.   It included a prescription to increase potential output that depended upon a nearly vertical aggregate supply curve to be most effective.

d.   It attempted to increase aggregate demand by cutting personal taxes.

e.   All the above.

24. The supply-side approach placed a key role on incentives to:

a.   save.

b.   invest.

c.   increase production.

d.   work harder.

e.   all the above.

25. The Reagan tax cuts of the 1980s:

a.   pushed the economy into recession.

b.   actually generated more revenue for the government via the Laffer curve.

c.   probably stimulated *AD* more than *AS*.

d.   all the above.

e.   none of the above.

VII. PROBLEM SOLVING

The following problems are designed to help you apply the concepts that you learned in the chapter.

A. Classical Stirrings and Keynesian Revolution

1.   a.   The (**Keynesian / classical**) view holds that a reduction in aggregate demand will cause no significant change in GDP because there will be (**an immediate / some / no significant**) change in prices. The appropriate representation of the aggregate supply curve is therefore (**a horizontal line up to / a positively sloped line through / a vertical line directly above**) potential output.

b   The (**Keynesian / classical**) view, meanwhile, holds that a reduction in aggregate demand will cause GDP to fall by more than the initial reduction in demand because there will be (**an immediate / some / no significant**) change in prices. The appropriate representation of the aggregate supply curve is therefore (**a horizontal line up to / a positively sloped line up to / a vertical line directly above**) potential output.

2.   The classical view of the economic world is based upon the immediate responsiveness of wages and prices to disequilibrium.

a.   Belief in this responsiveness was dealt a severe blow by (**World War II / the stock market crash of 1989 / the**

Great Depression). A persistent unemployment rate of about (**8 / 25 / 34**) percent during the early 1930s cast serious doubt on the ability of wages to fall in response to excess supply of labor.

b.   Even today, there are many reasons why wages appear to be sticky. Use the spaces below to list four:

(1) _____

(2) _____

(3) _____

(4) _____

c.   If you accept the stickiness of wages, as the Keynesians do, then it (**is / is not**) possible for an equilibrium to persist with a high rate of unemployment of not only labor but also other productive resources. In response to this situation, a Keynesian would prescribe (**nothing, because nothing would work / some kind of increase in aggregate demand / some kind of reduction in aggregate demand**) that would increase equilibrium GDP and thus employment.

d.   A classicist, on the other hand, would prescribe (**nothing, because nothing is required / some sort of increase in aggregate demand / some sort of reduction in aggregate supply**); he or she would remark either that the existing unemployment was voluntary or that artificial barriers had prevented the necessary movement of wages down to equilibrium.

e.   List three possible policies that a Keynesian might suggest to reduce unemployment:

(1) _____

(2) _____

(3) _____

B. The Monetarist Approach

3.   a.   In the space provided, record the quantity exchange equation: _____

b.   According to the quantity theory, velocity and real GDP are assumed to (**vary proportionately / be fixed / be wildly variable**). The result is, according to the theory, that any change in the money supply will be immediately reflected in (**prices / output / investment**).

c.   While this is a reasonable explanation of (**recession / hyperinflation / hyperventilation**), it is not very satisfactory in a world where the velocity of money has been (**climbing / falling**) for the past three decades and was quite variable during the monetarist experiment of 1980, 1981, and much of 1982.

4.   The problems with the crude theory aside, modern monetarists use a fairly stable velocity and the quantity theory of money to make their points. Their first proposition is that the money supply determines nominal GDP in the short run.

a.   If *V* is fixed in the short run, then any change in the money supply will, by application of the quantity equation, be (**proportionately / progressively**) reflected in (**nominal / real**) GDP.

Their second proposition is that the money supply determines prices in the long run.

   b   This follows from the quantity theory and their (**conservative political views / belief in the market responsiveness of wages and prices / belief in the proportional variation of velocity**). In particular, market clearing sets real GDP at its (**potential / nominal level / second-best optimum**), so the quantity equation has, in effect, (**one / two / three**) constants, namely _____.

Any change in the money supply is therefore translated directly and proportionately into changes in prices.

As an aside, the quantity theory of modern monetarism still precludes the effectiveness of fiscal policy to move GDP around. There is, quite simply, no place in the quantity equation for either government spending or taxes to appear. The only role for fiscal policy is to determine the mix of spending between the public and private sectors.

5. a.   The Fed conducted a monetarist experiment in the United States from (give month and year) _____ through _____ under the leadership of Chairman Paul Volcker.

   b.   During this time, it stopped trying to (**maintain stable interest rates / maintain stable exchange rates / keep bank reserves and the money supply moving along predetermined growth paths**) and focused instead on (**smoothing interest rates / maintaining stable exchange rates / keeping bank reserves and the money supply moving along predetermined grown paths**).

   c.   Which of the following statements accurately describe the lessons that were learned from the experiment? (Circle the number of each accurate statement.)

   (1) The velocity of money proved to be quite stable in the context of firm monetary policy.

   (2) The short-run effects of tight money were felt more in prices than they were in output.

   (3) Money proved to be relatively impotent in determining aggregate demand.

   (4) Firm monetary policy proved to be a relatively inexpensive way to curb high rates of inflation.

6. The effectiveness of monetary policy is still an issue of current debate. Consult Figure 16-2. There, initial equilibrium is given by E and is supported by long-run aggregate supply AS and aggregate demand AD. Short-run aggregate supply below equilibrium is shown by AS'.

   a   A contraction in the money supply should move aggregate demand to (**AD'/ AD"**). In the short run, output should fall to (**0B / C0 / F0 / 0G**) . In the long run, prices should fall to (**0B / C0 / F0 / 0G**).

   b.   Figure 16-2 can therefore be used to explain why the effect of monetary policy seems to be felt more in (**output / prices**) in the short run and more in (**output /**

prices) in the long run.

Figure 16-2
Because potential GDP determines output in the long run, contractionary monetary policy eventually produces lower prices (deflation); it does not, however, avoid the cost of recession required to initiate the process.

C. The New Classical Economics

7. a.   Proponents of rational expectations contend that most unemployment that is observed during a recession is (**voluntary / involuntary**).

Consider the supply and demand curves representing a labor market in Figure 16-3; SS represents the supply curve, and *DD* represents an initial demand curve.

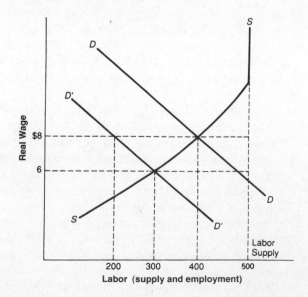

Figure 16-3

b. The initial equilibrium wage is $\_\_\_$, with $\_\_\_$ people voluntarily unemployed; i.e., they (**are / are not**) willing to work for the going wage because (**it is too low / they cannot find a job**).

c. If the demand curve were to fall to $D'D'$, the rational expectations theory would predict (**an immediate / a slow and tortured**) decline in wage to $\_\_\_$ with $\_\_\_$ people in voluntary unemployment and $\_\_\_$ people in involuntary unemployment.

d. If the wage did not fall, though, $\_\_\_$ people would be employed and $\_\_\_$ people would be out of work—$\_\_\_$ voluntarily and $\_\_\_$ involuntarily.

8. The proponents of rational-expectations macroeconomics hold that the observed slope in the short-run Phillips curve is a source of confusion and misperception. Consult Figure 16-4.

Figure 16-4

a. Beginning at point A, wage inflation would be running at $\_\_\_$ percent, with unemployment holding at the natural rate of 6 percent.

Suppose, now, that government policy is initiated to try to stimulate employment and to move the economy along the short-run Phillips curve to a point like B.

b. Rational-expectations theory states that unemployed workers would (**have to be offered higher real wage increases / have to be tricked into thinking that higher nominal wage increases were higher real wage increases**) to accomplish that move. Only if labor thought that the (**nominal / real**) wage were rising would the workers be attracted to work (remember, the 6 percent natural rate includes a significant number of voluntarily unemployed workers), and the unemployment rate would fall.

c. The $\_\_\_$ percent wage increase noted at point B

would, according to the theory, be exhausted by price inflation, so the increase in the real wage would be (**the expected positive increment / zero / actually negative**) and those who were voluntarily unemployed at point A would again leave the labor force.

d. As a result, the economy would have moved to point (**C / D / E**) instead of B.

Even in the short run, because labor would not have been so fooled in the first place, the policy stimulus would have been vented entirely in price and wage inflation and not in the intended reduction in the rate of unemployment.

e. Notice that it (**does / does not**) matter whether the stimulus was the result of a change in monetary policy or of a change in fiscal policy; the result (**would / would not**) be the same in either case—a short-run Phillips curve that is unstable and, for policy purposes, effectively (**vertical / horizontal**) in the region directly above the (**current rate / natural rate**) of unemployment.

9. a. If employment policy can (a) always be immediately undone and (b) create bad things like inflation, then it follows that discretionary changes in policy (**should nonetheless be allowed because they are currently expected / should be discontinued because they are only harmful**) .

b. The money supply should increase at a (**targeted / variable**) rate with the clear understanding that the velocity of money will (**be fixed / vary to preserve potential GDP**).

D. Ultra-Classicism: Supply-side Economics

10. There were three components of the supply-side recovery packages enacted in the early 1980s by the Reagan administration in the United States and the Thatcher administration in the United Kingdom. The *first* was a retreat from the short-run stabilization prescriptions of the Keynesian model, turning attention instead to the medium run.

a. This retreat was supported by a view that the aggregate supply curve was (**nearly vertical / nearly horizontal**), so any recession that might be forthcoming would be short and mild.

b. Prices and wages would, in particular, (**quickly / slowly**) adjust to any excess supply in the labor market, and changes in aggregate demand would have a (**large / little**) effect on GDP.

The *second* was a set of tax incentives designed to move the aggregate supply curve up and (mostly) out by boosting potential GDP, as shown in Figure 16-5 by the shift from AS to AS'. The effectiveness of this policy also depends upon the shape of the aggregate supply curve.

c. If the curve were vertical (or if the economy were represented by AD_1 on the vertical portion of the AS curve), then the shift would be effective in (**increasing / reducing**) actual GDP and (**lowering / increasing**) prices.

Figure 16-5

d.   If the curve were closer to horizontal in slope (or the economy represented by AD_2 on the flat portion of AS), though, then the supply shift would (**increase actual GDP slightly / reduce actual GDP slightly / still be effective in increasing GDP substantially**) and actually (**increase / reduce**) prices.

Again, support for the program was based upon a rejection of either the sloped or the horizontal AS curve of the Keynesian model. The *third* arm of the program was a substantial reduction in personal income taxes.

e.   The effect of this reduction would, of course, influence (**aggregate demand / aggregate supply**). As such, one should have expected that it would increase actual GDP with stable prices only if the aggregate supply schedule were (**nearly vertical / nearly horizontal**).

f.   Otherwise, the increase in aggregate demand would be vented almost exclusively in (**prices / potential GDP / output**).

In supporting this final component of the program, it would appear that the architects of the program were not ready to discard Keynes entirely. Indeed, the Reagan people campaigned for the program by comparing it favorably with the Kennedy round of tax cuts of the early 1960s—the beginning of the high point for Keynesians in making federal policy.

11. The record of the supply-side experiment in the United States ran its course over two presidential terms.

a.   The 1981 Economic Recovery Program forecast annual growth rates for real GDP averaging 4.8 percent into the middle of the 1980s; actual experience showed growth (**significantly greater than / roughly equal to / significantly lower than**) the forecast.

The program aimed to support this growth by significant increases in saving, investment, and productivity.

b.   Over the course of the 1980s, in fact, the national savings rate (**rose significantly / held roughly constant / fell significantly**). Investment was (**down / stable / up**), and productivity growth (**increased / held steady / declined**).

The record was not what was hoped.

VIII. DISCUSSION QUESTIONS

Answer the following questions, making sure that you can explain the work you did to arrive at the answers.

1.   Why did velocity in the United States become unstable in the early 1980s? What did this do to monetarism?

2.   Both monetarists and new classical economists call for fixed rules. Explain the role of fixed rules in each of these approaches.

3.   Given your expanding knowledge of economics and the macroeconomy, which of the schools of thought presented in this chapter do you think is most accurate right now? Which is least accurate?

4.   Explain the major components of supply-side economic policy.

5.   Discuss the results of the Reagan supply-side package in the early 1980s.

IX. ANSWERS TO STUDY GUIDE QUESTIONS

III. Review of Key Concepts

6	Classical theory
10	Say's Law
8	Crowding out
11	Keynesian revolution
13	Monetarism
15	Income velocity of money
12	Quantity theory of money and prices
2	Monetary rule
4	Monetarist experiment
14	New classical macroeconomics
1	Rational expectations hypothesis
9	Real business-cycle theory
5	Policy ineffectiveness theorem
16	Lucas critique
7	Adaptive expectations
3	Supply-side economics

VI. Multiple Choice Questions

1. E   2. D   3. D   4. C   5. A   6. E
7. E   8. B   9. E   10. E   11. B   12. D
13. A   14. C   15. C   16. A   17. E   18. C
19. E   20. B   21. D   22. B   23. E   24. E
25. C

VII. Problem Solving

1. a.   classical, an immediate, a vertical line directly above
    b.   Keynesian, some, a positively sloped line up to
2. a   the Great Depression, 25 percent
    b.   (1) multiyear-labor contracts
         (2) cost-of-living clauses
         (3) regulated prices
         (4) inertia of prices charged by large corporations
    c.   is, some kind of increase in aggregate demand
    d.   nothing, because nothing is required
    e.   (1) increase in government spending
         (2) a reduction in taxes
         (3) an increase in the money supply
3. a. $MV = PQ$
    b.   be fixed, prices
    c.   hyperinflation, climbing
4. a.   proportionately, nominal
    b.   belief in the market responsiveness of wages and prices, potential, two, potential real GDP and velocity
5. a.   October 1979, August 1982
    b.   maintain stable interest rates, keeping bank reserves and the money supply moving along predetermined growth paths
    c.   All the statements are inaccurate.
6. a. AD', $0B$, $C0$
    b.   output, prices
7. a.   voluntary
    b. $8, 100, are not, it is too low
    c.   an immediate, $6, 200, 0
    d.   200, 300, 100, 200
8. a.   8 percent
    b.   have to be tricked into thinking that higher nominal wage increases were higher real wage increases, real
    c.   10 percent, zero
    d. D
    e.   does not, would, vertical, natural rate
9. a.   should be discontinued because they are only harmful
    b.   targeted, vary to preserve potential GDP

10. a.   nearly vertical
    b.   quickly, little
    c.   increasing, lowering
    d.   reduce actual GDP slightly, increase
    e.   aggregate demand, nearly horizontal
    f.   prices
11. a   significantly lower than
    b.   fell significantly, down, declined

VIII. Discussion Questions

1. The high interest rates of the early 1980s encouraged financial innovation and the development of interest-bearing checking accounts. These new types of money contributed to the instability of velocity. It has also been suggested that the heavy reliance on monetary policy itself contributed to the increase in velocity. The instability of velocity diminished the linkage between the money supply and both prices and nominal GDP.

2. The private economy is viewed as being stable, and government policies tend to destabilize the economy. Classical economists contend that changes in the money supply affect only prices, while monetarists believe that money affects output only after long and variable lags. Consequently, both approaches call for a fixed rate of growth of the money supply.

3. Your choice. Do a great job!

4. There were three components of the Reagan supply-side approach. First, more attention was paid to the medium run rather than the short run. Second, individuals were given incentives to work harder, produce more, and invest more. Third, it was expected that tax cuts would influence aggregate supply more than aggregate demand. The increased productivity and output generated by the tax cut was expected to increase tax revenues.

5. During the 1980s the savings rate fell and economic growth slowed. Investment and productivity growth both declined. While other factors may have contributed to these changes, supply siders certainly did not observe the results they had hoped for.

CHAPTER 17
Policies for Growth and Stability

I.   CHAPTER OVERVIEW

Several chapters ago, you were introduced to the concept of economic growth (see Chapters 27 and 28). Samuelson and Nordhaus discussed trends in economic growth and examined several economic growth models. You have also learned about the business cycle (Chapter 23) and the problems of unemployment (Chapter 29) and inflation (Chapter 30). By now, you can also appreciate that there are different points of view, especially among economists, about how to deal with these problems (Chapter 32).

With all of this new information in hand, the focus in this chapter becomes more applied and policy-oriented. In the first section we confront one of the most controversial political and economic issues of our time: what to do about the federal deficit and the resulting federal debt. Are deficits recession-induced or policy-induced? Are there burdens associated with deficits that should cause us to avoid them at all cost? In the second section, Samuelson and Nordhaus consider the possibility of fiscal and monetary policy working together to provide stability and growth for the economy. In the final section, the discussion moves to long-term growth alternatives for increasing saving, investment, and productivity.

II. LEARNING OBJECTIVES

After you have read Chapter 33 in your text and completed the exercises in this *Study Guide* chapter, you should be able to:

1.   Differentiate between the **structural budget** and the **cyclical budget**.

2.   Explain why there is a **crowding out** (of investment) controversy and discuss its relationship to monetary policy.

3.   Differentiate between **internal** and **external** debt and discuss the relationship between the national debt and the foreign trade deficit.

4.   Explain how the burden of the debt is affected by efficiency losses from taxation and the potential displacement of capital.

5.   Evaluate the relative effectiveness of fiscal and monetary policy in managing aggregate demand.

6.   Form an educated opinion on the appropriate **fiscal-monetary mix** for the economy.

7.   Understand the two sides of the *fixed-rules-vs.-discretion* debate.

8. Discuss the components of the **national savings rate** and explain the long-term decline in saving in the United States.

9.   Understand the 1993 Budget Act and discuss its main features.

10. Point out the components of **total national wealth** and discuss the relative importance of each.

11. Appreciate the spirit of enterprise in the U.S. market-based economy.

III. REVIEW OF KEY CONCEPTS

Match the following terms from column A with their definitions in column B.

A	B
__ Budget	1. As the government debt grows, people will accumulate government debt instead of private capital, and the nation's private capital stock will be displaced by the public debt.
__ Budget surplus	2. Calculates what government revenue, expenditures, and deficit would be if the economy were operating at potential output.
__ Budget deficit	3. To pay interest on the debt, the government has to raise taxes; these tax increases may cause people to work less or save less.
__ Balanced budget	4. Shows, for a given year, the planned expenditures and expected revenues of the government.
__ Government debt	5. Debt owed by a nation to its own citizens—occurs when U.S.

__ Fiscal policy

__ Discretionary fiscal policy

__ Structural budget

__ Cyclical budget

__ Crowding out

__ Internal debt

__ External debt

__ Displacement of capital

__ Distortion from taxation

__ Demand management

__ Fiscal-monetary mix

__ Gramm-Rudman Act

__ Pay-as-you-go provision

__ Purchasing-power parity

__ National savings rate

citizens purchase U.S. government bonds.

6. Increases in the structural deficit through tax cuts or higher government spending; tends to raise interest rates and thereby reduce investment.

7. Occurs when expenditures exceed taxes and other revenues.

8. Government taxation and spending programs.

9. Consists of the total or accumulated borrowings by the government; also called the public debt or national debt.

10. Debt owed by a nation to foreigners; occurs when foreigners buy U.S. government bonds.

11. Occurs when expenditures and all revenues are equal.

12. Exists when the government *changes* tax rates or spending programs, usually by new legislation.

13. Difference between the actual budget and the structural budget; it measures the impact of the business cycle on the budget.

14. Occurs when all taxes and other revenues exceed government expenditures for a year; this does not happen very often in the United States.

15. Measure of technological change which measures total output per unit of all inputs.

16. Total saving, both private and public, divided by net domestic product (NDP).

17. Includes reproducible capital, capital, human capital, technological and land resources.

18. Attempt to increase national saving by raising rates of return on saving or investment by lowering taxes on capital gains and rewarding investment with investment tax credits.

19. The use of monetary and l fisca policy to set AD at a desired level.

20. Attempt to increase national saving by lowering government dissaving and private consump-

__ Income-oriented approaches

__ Price-oriented approaches

__ Total factor productivity

__ Total national wealth

tion while stimulating investment through lower interest rates.

21. Refers to the relative strength of fiscal and monetary policies and their effect on different components of output.

22. Requires that Congress find the necessary revenue before enacting any new spending program.

23. Method of comparing living standards across countries by measuring the quantity of goods and services that can be purchased.

24. Congressional bill passed in 1985 which required the deficit to be reduced by a specified dollar amount each year and balanced in 1991.

IV. SUMMARY AND CHAPTER OUTLINE

This section summarizes the key concepts from the chapter.

A. The Economic Consequences of the Debt

1. The **structural** component of the budget reflects what the government would collect and spend if it were operating at its full potential; it is the measure which best indicates the impact of fiscal policy. The **cyclical** component reflects the effect of the business cycle on what the government collects and spends. When the economy is contracting or in a recession, the government brings in less revenue in the form of tax receipts and pays out more money in the form of transfer programs (unemployment compensation, food stamps, etc.). In such years, the *structural* budget may actually be balanced, but the *actual* budget may show a large deficit due to the large cyclical component.

Cyclical budget + structural budget = actual budget

Actual budget deficits during these "lean" years are not as problematic as deficits during years of prosperity and strong economic growth. In "good" years, the positive cyclical component should help push the actual budget into a surplus. This did not happen during the mid- and late 1980s, a period of prolonged economic growth in the United States.

2. Concern is often voiced that government deficits **crowd out** private investment by driving up interest rates. The strict monetarist view of the world holds, in fact, that crowding out would be immediate and complete as government dissaving shrinks the pool of available financing. Others look for considerably less than 100 percent crowding out in the short run, particularly during periods of recession.

3. The nominal level of the federal debt has been growing steadily since World War II, but it exploded in the early 1980s. The Reagan structural deficit, combined with enormous cyclical components, brought in government revenues more than $200 billion short of government expenditures.

4. There are some serious sources of concern about the burden of the debt which cannot be overlooked in using deficit spending as an arm of fiscal policy:

    a. the cost of servicing external debt

    b. the distortions created by the taxes required to service even internal debt

    c. the potential crowding out of capital

    d. the possibility that the cost of servicing the debt may grow more quickly than GDP

B. Stabilizing the Economy

1. In addition to determining the appropriate level of output and growth for an economy, policymakers must also decide on the mix or combination of fiscal and monetary tools to use to achieve their objectives. For example, to achieve high investment (which is crucial for economic growth), the budget should be balanced or have a surplus (to reduce the possibility of crowding out) and monetary policy should be expansionary or loose to help keep interest rates low. Until recently the federal government budget has been running very high deficits because the government either spends "too" much or taxes "too" little; and monetary policy has been relatively tight to keep the lid on inflation and inflationary expectations.

2. Fiscal policy, at least in the United States, has become the "weak sister" when it comes to providing stabilization for the economy. Timing lags delay the responsiveness of fiscal policy to swings in the business cycle. It takes time to recognize problems; debate appropriate policy responses and pass new legislation; and then (via the multiplier) affect output, employment, and income. By the time an impact is felt on the real side of the economy, it is possible for the economic winds to have changed and be blowing in the opposite direction. What was to have been a beneficial policy response may thus become the wrong medicine for the economy.

3. Monetary policy operates more indirectly than fiscal policy. It affects spending through changes in interest rates, credit conditions, and exchange rates. Nevertheless, the Fed has become a more effective stabilizer in the U.S. economy. Empirical results indicate that money-supply changes have their primary impact on output in the short run. Over longer time spans, more of the changes in nominal GDP are manifested instead in prices and wages.

C. Increasing Long-term Growth

1. There are several reasons for the slowdown in labor productivity in the United States since the 1970s:

    a. Environmental and health-and-safety regulations may have improved the quality of life, but they have had no positive impact on output.

    b. Large increases in the cost of energy encouraged firms to substitute labor and capital for it. As these other factors of production were used more intensively, their productivities declined.

    c. There has been a large infusion of inexperienced, low-wage workers into the labor force.

2. The decline in the national savings rate in the United States has been dramatic. All the components of national saving—government saving, business saving, and personal saving—have declined.

3. The nation's total wealth includes more than just its tangible assets and physical capital. In today's global economy with highly mobile resources, a nation's labor force and the human capital embodied in it are key to long-term prosperity. Consider the economic recovery of Japan with few natural resources, small size, and a capital base that was in large part destroyed by the Second World War.

V. HELPFUL HINTS

1. The government *debt is* the *accumulation of* all the yearly budget *deficits*. Every year that the government does not balance its budget, it borrows more money to pay its bills. This adds to the debt. If the government runs $200-billion-dollar deficits five years in a row, this would add $1 trillion to the national debt! In fiscal year 1995, approximately 14 percent of the federal government's expenditures were being used just to pay the interest on the debt. These payments do nothing to reduce the principal of this huge loan, which grows larger every year.

2. When the government borrows money it sells bonds. The government sells bonds because it does not bring in enough revenue, in the form of taxes, to pay for all of the programs that it wants to fund. Selling bonds is viewed as politically less costly than raising taxes or cutting spending, which are the only alternatives to selling bonds.

3. As an economy grows, a nation can handle more debt. This is analogous to individuals' being able to borrow more money as their income increases. Unlike individuals, the federal government does not, at least at the present time, seem to worry about paying the debt off. Creditors do not seem to be overly concerned about this either. This is partly because the federal government, unlike an individual, does not age or become less inclined to saddle itself with long-term debt as the years go by. U.S. government bonds continue to be one of the safest, most secure instruments in the world for financial investment.

4. Whether or not crowding out occurs depends upon several different factors: slack in the economy, monetary policy, business expectations. Keep an open mind and try to collect

as much information as possible before forming an opinion about this important issue.

5. There exists a relationship between the national debt and the balance of trade.

   a. As the government borrows more, this puts upward pressure on interest rates.

   b. Higher interest rates in the United States attract more foreign financial capital.

   c. The demand for dollars increases in the foreign exchange markets. (The United States sells bonds to get money, i.e., *dollars*. If foreigners want to buy U.S. bonds, they must first convert their currency into dollars.)

   d. The dollar appreciates in value.

   e. U.S. goods and services become more expensive to foreigners, and foreign goods and services become cheaper to U.S. citizens.

   f. Result: The United States exports less and imports more.

6. Before screaming that the government is running up yet another budget deficit, look at the state of the economy. Is the business cycle in contraction or expansion? Look for the *structural* budget.

7. One of the key points of this chapter is that getting the economy to a particular place with regard to output, employment, and growth is only part of the problem. How the economy gets there and the mix of monetary and fiscal policy tools used are also very important.

8. The Federal Open Market Committee (the key policy-making arm of the Fed) meets often: 10 times a year. These frequent meetings in addition to the Fed's political independence—help it to maintain its focus.

9. While there is controversy over the appropriateness of establishing fixed budgets and policy rules for legislatures and the Fed, *credibility is* the most important attribute of an effective policy.

VI. MULTIPLE CHOICE QUESTIONS

These questions are organized by topic from the chapter outline. Choose the best answer from the options available.

A. The Economic Consequences of the Debt

1. Structural deficits:

   a. vary in size with changes in discretionary fiscal policy.

   b. vary in size with the sensitivity of the tax revenues to upswings in the economy.

   c. vary in size depending upon the latitude of welfare entitlement programs during economic downturns.

   d. are reflections of the degree of stimulus embodied in monetary policy.

   e. are described by none of the above.

2. Cyclical deficits are:

   a the products of discretionary fiscal policy.

   b. the appropriate reflection of the stimulative character of fiscal policy.

   c. dependent in part on the unemployment rate in the economy.

   d. never considered until strict monetary control raises the specter of crowding out.

   e. none of the above.

3. A $50 billion increase in defense spending is an example of:

   a. monetary policy directed at reducing inflation.

   b. fiscal policy directed at reducing inflation.

   c. fiscal policy that would contribute directly to increasing the structural deficit.

   d. fiscal policy that would contribute directly to increasing the cyclical deficit.

   e. none of the above.

4. Which answer to question 3 would have been correct had that question asked about an increase in tax revenues caused by a growing economy and a progressive income tax?

   a.

   b.

   c.

   d.

   e.

5. Which answer to question 3 would have been correct if the question had asked about an open-market operation that purchased bonds?

   a.

   b.

   c.

   d.

   e.

6. Discretionary fiscal policy:

   a. is more effective in fighting recessions.

   b. is more effective in fighting inflation.

   c. would include a new public-works project.

   d. must be approved by Congress.

   e. none of the above.

7. Monetary policy:

   a. can typically be changed more quickly than fiscal policy.

   b. has a limited discretionary component.

   c. has been relatively ineffective in fighting inflation.

   d. is conducted by an independent agency and therefore cannot be coordinated with fiscal policy.

   e. is changed only when the Board of Governors meets.

8. Deficits in the early 1980s were enormous, in part because the Reagan administration:

   a. pursued expansionary fiscal policy with high structural deficits.

b. received the tight monetary policy that it wanted.

c. suffered a recession that enlarged the cyclical deficit.

d. did all the above.

e. did none of the above.

9. In the face of a stagnant economy, a government should:

a. spend more, tax less, and/or pursue a contractionary monetary policy.

b. spend less, tax less, and/or pursue an expansionary monetary policy.

c. spend more, tax less, and/or pursue an expansionary monetary policy.

d. spend less, tax more, and/or pursue an expansionary monetary policy.

e. do nothing and rely on the ability of the economy to rapidly return to potential GDP just as it did in the 1983 recovery.

10. The linkage between government spending that could lead to the crowding out of private investment is best outlined by a causal connection from spending growth to:

a. output growth, to an increase in the assets demand for money, and eventually to higher interest rates, which cause reduced investment.

b. output contraction, to an increase in the transactions demand for money, to a lower assets demand for money, and finally to lower interest rates, which encourage more investment.

c. output growth, to an increase in the transactions demand for money, to a lower assets demand for money, and finally to higher interest rates, which cause reduced investment.

d. output growth and to higher investment with higher transactions and assets demands for money.

e. none of the above.

11. Strict monetarists believe in a vertical aggregate supply schedule. They believe, as a result, that every increase in government spending of one dollar should cause private investment to fall by:

a. 50 cents.

b. 75 cents.

c. 90 cents.

d. $1.

e. none of the above.

12. Which of the following is a valid reason for being concerned about the size of the federal debt?

a. It has grown, in the recent past, as a proportion of GDP.

b. It has grown, in the recent past, so much that interest payments are growing faster than GDP.

c. High deficits may displace capital by distorting the financial markets.

d. The taxes required to pay the interest result in losses in efficiency.

e. All the above.

13. Which of the following statements about the relationship between the federal budget deficit and the government debt is true?

a. If the debt is getting smaller, the budget must have a surplus.

b. Large *cyclical budget* surpluses could reduce the debt.

c. Every single-year deficit adds more to the debt.

d. All these statements are true.

e. These statements are all false.

14. Internal debt:

a. is owed by a nation to its own citizens.

b. can result in efficiency losses due to the taxes required to pay the interest.

c. can redistribute wealth from taxpayers to bondholders.

d. is all of the above.

e. is just **a** and **b**.

15. A displacement of capital can occur when:

a. foreigners own more of the debt.

b. interest rates are rising.

c. people start to save less.

d. people accumulate more government bonds and less private capital.

e. all the above.

B. Stabilizing the Economy

16. To revive a lagging economy, the government can:

a. manage aggregate demand by raising monetary growth.

b. manage aggregate demand by cutting taxes.

c. manage aggregate demand by increasing the structural deficit.

d. both **a** and **b**.

e. all the above.

17. The *biggest* current impediment to effective fiscal policy is:

a. the size of the federal deficit.

b. tight monetary policy.

c. the foreign trade deficit.

d. disagreements between the White House and Congress.

e. the decline in labor productivity.

18. Other things held constant, when interest rates increase, this tends to:

a. decrease investment and decrease imports.

b. increase investment and increase imports.

c. decrease investment and decrease exports.

d. decrease investment and increase *net* exports.

e. decrease investment but have no predictable impact on trade.

19. How was the Reagan administration able to have a large defense buildup without inflation?

a.   The administration raised taxes to finance the increased expenditures on defense.

b.   An increase in personal saving financed the buildup.

c.   The administration's goal was helped by the Fed's tight-money policy.

d.   Wage and price controls were used to keep inflation down.

e.   Private investment was increasing and the subsequent economic growth helped finance the increased defense expenditures.

20.   If policymakers are concerned about the low national savings rate they can:

a.   cut taxes and the growth rate of the money supply.

b.   raise taxes and interest rates.

c.   "tax and spend" more.

d.   remove interest rate ceilings.

e.   balance the budget.

21.   Partly as a result of the Gramm-Rudman bill:

a.   the government debt decreased.

b.   the federal government deficit decreased.

c.   the national savings rate increased.

d.   all the above.

e.   none of the above.

22.   Data from the Federal Reserve Board and the U.S. Department of Commerce indicate that:

a.   the variability of M_2 exceeds the variability of M_1.

b.   the variability of M_1 is less than the variability of nominal GDP.

c.   nominal GDP is more variable than either measure of the money supply.

d.   a fixed monetary growth rule may not work.

e.   none of the above.

C. Increasing Long-term Growth

23.   During the past 15 years, which component of national saving has decreased the most?

a.   government saving.

b.   business saving.

c.   personal saving.

d.   They have all fallen by about the same amount.

e.   The data are not precise enough to measure this.

24.   The decline in business saving is due primarily to:

a.   increased corporate mergers.

b.   the increase in multinational firms operating in the United States.

c.   the trade deficit.

d.   high real interest rates.

e.   the declining share of corporate profits in the total economy.

25.   Which of the following has contributed to the decline in personal saving?

a.   the slowdown in the growth of incomes.

b.   declining imperfections in capital markets.

c.   the increase in government transfer programs.

d.   all the above.

e.   none of the above.

26.   The 1993 Budget Act:

a.   hoped to eliminate the deficit by 1998.

b.   hoped to reduce the deficit by approximately $144 billion by 1998.

c.   continued the cycle of "tax and spend."

d.   was not passed by Congress

e.   none of the above.

27.   In addition to reproducible capital, the country's total wealth includes:

a.   human capital.

b.   technological capital.

c.   renewable land resources.

d.   all the above.

e.   **a** and **b** only.

VII. PROBLEM SOLVING

The following problems are designed to help you apply the concepts that you learned in the chapter.

A. The Economic Consequences of the Debt

1.   In the spaces provided, record whether the following policies would affect the structural budget (**S**), the cyclical budget (**C**), or neither (**N**).

___ a.   A reduction of 25 percent in tax rates

___ b.   An increase in unemployment compensation during recession

___ c.   An increase of $50 billion in defense spending

___ d.   A reduction in social security tax rates

___ e.   An expansion of the money supply

___ f.   An expansion in tax receipts during an economic upswing

__ g.   A reduction in funding for Head Start and other welfare programs

2.   A number of changes in economic condition are listed in Table 17-1. In the spaces provided in the table, indicate the likely short-term effects of each change on the structural and cyclical deficits. Denote a reduction with (**-**), an increase with (**+**), and no change with (**0**).

Table 17-1

	Change In Condition or Policy	Structural Deficit	Cyclical Deficit
a.	A permanent tax cut	___	___
b.	A sharp increase in private investment	___	___
c.	Tighter monetary policy	___	___
d.	A corn blight	___	___
e.	An increase in welfare payments	___	___
f.	An increase in tax evasion	___	___

3. a. From 1979 through 1982, the actual budget deficit (**fell / rose**) in response to (**active fiscal policy / passive fiscal policy**). The result was actually (**an increase / a reduction**) in the (**structural / cyclical**) deficit that signaled (**more stimulative / no change in the degree of stimulus applied by / less stimulative**) fiscal policy.

b. In 1982, though, the supply-side tax cuts and the massive defense buildup of the Reagan administration came on line. The result was fiscal (**stimulus / contraction**), reflected by a dramatic increase in the (**structural / cyclical**) deficit. In fact, from 1982 through 1986 the cyclical deficit (**fell / rose**) while the structural deficit (**fell / rose**).

Numbers supporting your answers to these questions can be found in Table 17-2 (use this table to answer the questions that follow).

c. The federal government ran an actual deficit of $___ in 1986. This was up $___ from 1979 and $___ from 1982.

d. A deep recession in 1982 increased the cyclical deficit by $___ from 1979, but that increase fell to $___ by 1986.

e. The structural deficit, meanwhile, climbed by only $___ through 1982, but by $___ through 1986.

Table 17-2 The Source of Rising Federal Deficits

Deficit or Contributing Factor	1979	1982	1986
A. Budget deficit:			
Actual	$16	$146	$204
Cyclical	0	91	26
Structural	16	55	178
B. Increase in budget deficit from 1979:			
Actual	0	130	188
Cyclical	0	91	26
Structural	0	39	162
C. Contributing factor:			
Decreased share of taxes	0	5	26
Increased share of defense	0	40	72
Increased transfer payments	0	58	44
Increased interest payments	0	31	64
Total, Contributing Factors	0	134	206

Source: U.S. Department of Commerce.

f. It is clear, therefore, that fiscal policy was (**stimulative / contractionary**) over the second period.

g. Under "Contributing Factors," it is important to note that higher interest payments added $___ to the actual deficit from 1979 through 1986.

Why? Certainly because the government borrowed a lot more money, but that is not the only reason. The federal government turns over the equivalent of its entire debt every three or four years; large increases in current interest rates can therefore have large effects on the cyclical deficit. Also notice that the combined effect of the listed contributing factors sums to more than the increase in the actual deficit (i.e., $206 billion, which is greater than $188 billion). How is that possible? Other items in the spending budget were slashed by the difference ($18 billion) .

4. Suppose, in the face of stagnation, the President wants to stimulate recovery without adjusting monetary policy.

a. You, as adviser to the President, should recommend a policy that would (**increase / decrease**) government spending and/or (**increase / decrease**) federal taxes.

b. The immediate result of your recommendation would be (**a reduction / an increase**) in the size of the (**structural / cyclical**) deficit.

c. If your policies were implemented and worked to stimulate recovery, the ultimate result would be (**a reduction / an increase**) in the (**structural / cyclical**) deficit.

d. To bring the actual deficit down, though, you would have to also recommend (**the eventual cancellation of the active policy / no further change**).

Facing the opposite problem, of course, you would recommend the opposite policies.

e. If you were free to suggest changes in monetary policy to support the stimulus package that you proposed above, though, you should recommend (**a reduction / an increase**) in the money supply, probably instituted by (**an open-market operation / a reduction in the reserve requirement / an increase in the discount rate**).

f. The desired result would be (**an increase / a decrease**) in investment because of (**higher / lower**) interest rates and perhaps induced investment (crowding in).

5. The Reagan Economic Recovery Program instituted in January 1981 called for (a) substantial cuts in personal taxes, (b) substantial cuts in business taxes, (c) substantial increases in defense spending, and (d) moderate cuts in social spending. President Reagan also asked the Fed to pursue fairly tight monetary policy.

a The ultimate result was (**stimulative / contractionary**) fiscal policy, reflected halfway through his first term by an increase in the (**cyclical / structural**) deficit but also by lower investment caused by high interest rates.

Some contend that the recession of 1982 was caused in large part by the high interest rates.

The Carter administration had tried to stimulate investment in the late 1970s by (a) increasing taxes, (b) maintaining government spending, and (c) encouraging expansionary monetary policy.

b. The idea was to (**increase / reduce**) the structural deficit and thereby (**increase / decrease**) public saving, lower interest rates, and promote investment.

Monetary policy turned out to be too tight, though, and investment did not climb.

c.   Combined with the oil shock of the Iran-Iraq war, a recession developed because the change in the (**structural / cyclical**) deficit actually signaled a move toward more (**contractionary / expansionary**) fiscal policy.

6.   The basic mechanism behind the concern that increased government spending "crowds out" private investment can be traced through expected changes in interest rates.

a.   An increase in government spending initially causes GDP to (**rise / fall**). As a result, the transactions demand for money (**rises / falls**), so interest rates must (**rise / fall**) to engineer the change in the assets demand for money that is required to cancel the change in transactions demand.

And because interest rates respond, investment must decline. The problem is particularly acute in the monetarist view of the world, in which GDP does not increase with G because government spending replaces investment spending, dollar for dollar. The economy is, by assumption, at its potential, and further increases in GDP are impossible. An increase in aggregate demand caused by an increase in government spending must, therefore, be matched by an equal reduction in investment.

The evidence on crowding out is mixed. The expansionary fiscal policy of the early 1960s did not cause any substantial crowding out.

b.   However, that was not really a fair test because during the 1960s, (**the natural rate of unemployment was lower / the Fed accommodated fiscal policy to keep interest rates constant / the Keynesian model was widely accepted**).

c.   The empirical evidence suggests that (**25 / 50 / 75**) percent of the stimulative effects of increases in government spending are canceled in the short term and that (**75 / 90 / 100**) percent of the effects may disappear in the long term. This is because the long run aggregate supply curve is (**horizontal / vertical**) over potential GDP.

d.   Even in the long term, though, crowding out appears to be a problem associated only with the (**cyclical / structural**) deficit.

There is reason to believe that an increase in government spending caused by automatic stabilizers during a recession might actually increase investment.

e.   If the spending does in fact promote recovery, then GDP will begin to rise, and (**higher / lower**) investment might be induced by the prospect of a more vigorous economy. By the time the potential for crowding out appears (i.e., by the time the economy approaches its level of potential GDP), the cyclical spending will have (**disappeared / accelerated**) and there will be (**nothing left / even more spending**) to do the crowding.

7.   Indicate which of the following arguments for or against large budget deficits are valid (**V**) and which are invalid (**I**).

___ a.   I can't run a deficit forever, so neither can the government.

___ b.   The debt is internally held, so there is no problem.

___ c.   There are efficiency losses associated with the taxes required to pay the interest.

___ d.   Private debt is high, too, and that is not a source of concern.

___ e.   There is a significant likelihood that large deficits displace capital from private borrowers to public ones.

___ f.   If interest payments grow faster than GDP, then increasingly large proportions of GDP will have to be taxed away to pay for the debt service.

___ g.   Other things held constant, the more debt that is owned by foreigners, the larger will be the trade surplus.

B. Stabilizing the Economy

8.   Table 33-4 from the text is reproduced here as Table 17-3.

Table 17-3 Money, Output, and Prices

Affected Variable	Response of Affected Variable to 4 Percent Change in Money Supply (% change in affected variable from baseline path)				
	Year 1	Year 2	Year 3	Year 4	Year 5
Real GDP	0.9	1.1	1.2	1.1	0.8
Consumer prices	0.2	0.7	1.1	1.5	1.8
Nominal GDP	1.1	1.8	2.3	2.5	2.7

A survey studied the impact of a change in monetary policy in eight different econometric models. in each case, a baseline run of the model was "shocked" by adding 4 percent to the money supply in year 1 and holding the money supply 4 percent above the baseline in all years thereafter. Estimates in the table show the average calculated response of the models.

Note an initial response of real output to a monetary-policy shift, with the peak response coming in year 3. The impact upon the price level builds up gradually because of the inertial response of price and wage behavior. Note that the impact on nominal GDP is less than proportional to the money growth even after 5 years. [Source: Ralph C. Bryant, Peter Hooper, and Gerald Holtham, "Consensus and Diversity in the Model Simulations," in Ralph Bryant et al. (ads.), *Empirical Macroeconomics for Interdependent Economies* (Brookings, Washington, D.C., 1988).]

a.   Why does the percentage change in real GDP increase and then decrease?

_____

_____

b.   Why does the percentage change in nominal GDP get larger and larger?

_____

c.   What does it mean if the percentage change in nominal GDP is increasing while the percentage change in real GDP is falling? When does this occur?

_____

_____

d.   Given the material you have read in this chapter, what do you think the results of this study would have been if fiscal policy had been changed instead?

_____
_____
_____

C. Increasing Long-term Growth

9.   Two alternatives which have been suggested to increase national saving are the *income-oriented* and *price-oriented* approaches. For each of the following policy options, write **I** if the proposal is income-oriented and **P** if it is price-oriented.

___ a.   Lowering government dissaving
___ b.   Raising the real rate of return to saving
___ c.   Lowering taxes on capital income
___ d.   Increasing taxes to reduce the deficit
___ e.   Increasing capital depreciation allowances

10. Figure 33-4 from the text is reproduced here as Figure 17-1.

a.   What reasons lie behind the fall in the personal savings rate? _____
b.   To what do you attribute the decrease in the overall national savings rate? _____

VIII. DISCUSSION QUESTIONS

Answer the following questions, making sure that you can explain the work you did to arrive at the answers.

1.   Explain why it may be difficult to get a clear picture of what the structural budget actually is.
2.   When is crowding out most likely to occur?
3.   Briefly discuss some of the problems associated with a government debt that is entirely *internal*.
4.   How may the foreign inflow of financial capital in the 1980s have helped reduce the crowding out that was caused by the increasing federal budget deficits?
5.   Briefly discuss the long-run impact of the government debt on economic growth.
6.   Briefly explain the essence of the "rules vs. discretion" debate.
7.   Explain the fall in the national savings rate from 8 percent of net domestic product to less than 2 percent in the early 1990s.
8.   What did Congress do when it could not meet the deficit-reduction targets established by the Gramm-Rudman bill?
9.   Give several examples of public investments and explain how they would increase total national wealth.
10. What can an economy do to encourage new technology?

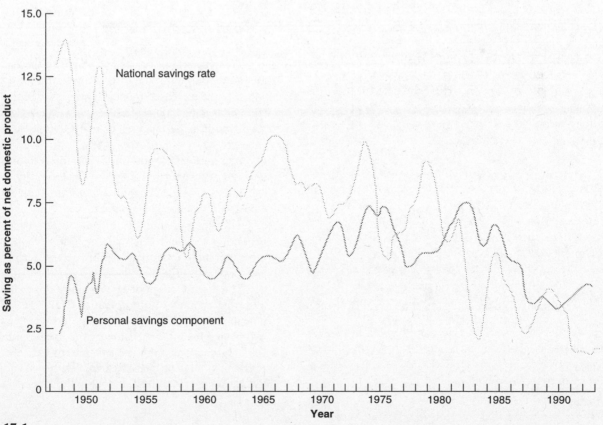

Figure 17-1

IX. ANSWERS TO STUDY GUIDE QUESTIONS

III. Review of Key Concepts

4	Budget
14	Budget surplus
7	Budget deficit
11	Balanced budget
9	Government debt
8	Fiscal policy
12	Discretionary fiscal policy
2	Structural budget
13	Cyclical budget
6	Crowding out
5	Internal debt
10	External debt
1	Displacement of capital
3	Distortion from taxation
19	Demand management
21	Fiscal-monetary mix
24	Gramm-Rudman Act
22	Pay-as-you-go provision
23	Purchasing-power parity
16	National savings rate
20	Income-oriented approaches
18	Price-oriented approaches
15	Total factor productivity
17	Total national wealth

VI. Multiple Choice Questions

1. A   2. C   3. C   4. E   5. E   6. C
7. A   8. D   9. C   10. C   11. D   12. E
13. D   14. D   15. D   16. E   17. A   18. C
19. C   20. E   21. E   22. D   23. A   24. E
25. D   26. B   27 D

VII. Problem Solving

1. a. S
   b. C
   c. S
   d. S
   e. N
   f. C
   g. S
2. a. +, - (perhaps 0, depending on the stimulus of the cut)
   b. 0, -
   c. 0, +
   d. 0, +
   e. +, - (perhaps 0, depending on the stimulus of the payments)
   f. +, 0 (assuming that evasion is not related to the business cycle)

3. a. rose, passive fiscal policy, an increase, cyclical, no change in the degree of stimulus applied by
   b. stimulus, structural, fell, rose
   c. $204, $188, $58
   d. $91, $26
   e. $39, $162
   f. stimulative
   g. $64
4. a. increase, decrease
   b. an increase, structural
   c. a reduction, cyclical
   d. the eventual cancellation of the active policy
   e. an increase, an open-market operation
   f. an increase, lower
5. a. stimulative, structural
   b. reduce, increase
   c. structural, contractionary
6. a. rise, rises, rise
   b. the Fed accommodated fiscal policy to keep interest rates constant
   c. 50 percent, 100 percent, vertical
   d. structural
   e. higher, disappeared, nothing left
7. a. I
   b. I
   c. V
   d. I
   e. V
   f. V
   g. V
8. a. The response of prices and wages to the increase in the money supply is sluggish. It takes time for them to adjust to the increased money supply. So, initially there is a larger impact on real GDP. However, as prices and wages adjust, the changes in real GDP peak and then taper off.
   b. As prices and wages react and adjust, nominal GDP changes accordingly. There is some rigidity to prices and wages, and they cannot respond immediately to the increase in the money supply.
   c. This means that the effect on the economy is becoming less and less real (in terms of output) and more and more inflationary. This occurs during years 4 and 5 in Table 17-3.
   d. The effectiveness of fiscal policy depends on how close the economy is to potential GDP. The closer to potential the economy is, the more crowding out there will be and the more inflationary the fiscal policy stimulus. Given the size of the national debt, many economists believe that fiscal policy can no longer be used as a major stabilization tool in the United States.
9. a. I
   b. P
   c. P

d.   I

e.   P

10. a.   The personal savings rate has fallen due to a decrease in the rate of income growth, the increased growth of government transfer programs (like social security), and the deregulation of the banking industry, which has made it easier for consumers to borrow.

b.   The national savings rate is made up of three components: government, business, and personal saving. The huge federal budget deficits during the past decade are the single biggest reason for the decline in the national savings rate. Due to a declining share of corporate profits in the economy, business saving has fallen as well.

VIII. DISCUSSION QUESTIONS

1.   The economy is always in some phase of the business cycle, and it is only with hindsight that we can determine the economic climate with precision. While we observe the actual budget, it is difficult to separate that into structural and cyclical components.

2.   Crowding out is most likely to occur when the economy is not in a recession. During recessions, the demand for money and interest rates fall, so there is apt to be less of an influence of government borrowing on interest rates. If interest rates do not respond to the government's increase in borrowing, there will be less crowding out. If the economy is at potential GDP, crowding out should be greatest.

3.   If the debt is held internally, there would be a redistribution of wealth from taxpayers to bondholders (who are owed interest for lending money to the government) . If the government needs to raise taxes to make interest payments, this will have an effect on patterns of work and saving. The greater the debt, the more the government has to use its (finite) budget to service the debt rather than provide programs for its citizens.

4.   To the extent that foreigners willingly purchased U.S. government bonds, the funds from domestic saving were still available to private industry without pushing interest rates higher.

5.   As the government borrows more and more, people will acquire more public debt (government bonds) and less private debt. As the funds for private investment dry up, there will be less investment spending and less expansion of capital and thereby less growth in the nation's ability to produce goods and services. Private investment spending is a vital component of economic growth.

6.   Proponents of discretion argue that the Fed needs to have flexibility in setting monetary policy so that it can react to economic shocks and disturbances. A good example is the Fed's immediate response to the stock market crash of October 1987. Proponents of fixed rules state that a predetermined monetary growth path is needed to remove uncertainty from the financial markets and enhance the Fed's credibility as an inflation fighter.

7.   The primary reason for the fall in the national savings rate has been the ballooning of the national debt. The structural deficits of the Reagan administration added over a trillion dollars to the national debt. Lower economic growth rates and the recession of 1990-1991 contributed to the decline in saving as well.

8.   Congress has amended the Gramm-Rudman bill several times when it became clear that its guidelines for deficit reduction could not be met. In 1993, Congress did pass a pay-as-you-go provision that required that any new spending programs be fully funded before being put into place. This by itself will do nothing to reduce the deficit, but it will at least help prevent the deficit from getting bigger.

9.   Government programs to repair and improve the nation's infrastructure can facilitate economic growth and increase national wealth. Examples include highways, airports, utilities, and even the information superhighway. Additionally, the government can invest in the nation's human capital by providing funds for higher education and training programs to help labor adapt to the structural changes occurring in the economy.

10. A free marketplace seems to be the best setting for the development of new ideas and technology. Competition brings out the best in both individuals and industry. In this market setting, the government needs to encourage and support research and development by private industry. The government can also encourage foreign investment and technology to do business with, and in, the U.S. economy.

CHAPTER 18
International Trade and Exchange Rates

I. CHAPTER OVERVIEW

Chapter 18 begins a three-chapter excursion into the fundamentals of international economics—the issues surrounding the conduct of international trade and finance. The first two chapters introduce the real factors involved in trade and describe how differences in resource endowments, tastes, and technology can generate the potential for all parties to receive substantial welfare benefits from trade. In this chapter, Samuelson and Nordhaus discuss trends in foreign trade and explain the role of the **foreign exchange market.** The chapter concludes with an explanation of **international balance-of-payments accounts.**

The formal economic model of international trade, based on the principal of **comparative advantage,** is developed in the next chapter. The problems associated with trade and the restraint of its proliferation by tariffs and quotas are also central to the discussion in Chapter 35.

In the final chapter, Samuelson and Nordhaus discuss the details of the monetary mechanisms that have been developed to support international trade; the authors also point out some of the complexities of managing the global economy.

The details of international economics *are* complex, and an introductory course can only scratch the surface of these issues. Nevertheless, the fundamental welfare implications of international trade are easily presented and understood.

II. LEARNING OBJECTIVES

After you have read Chapter 34 in your text and completed the exercises in this *Study Guide* chapter, you should be able to:

1. Discuss some of the recent trends in foreign trade and understand the economic factors that lie behind international trade patterns.
2. Define what is meant by a **foreign exchange rate,** and describe the supply-and-demand framework through which exchange rates are determined.
3. Differentiate between the terms **depreciation** and **devaluation** and between **appreciation** and **revaluation.**

4. Explain the **purchasing-power-parity theory of exchange rates.**
5. Outline the basic accounting procedure that is used to keep track of the **international balance of payments.** Define the four components of balance-of-payments accounting.
6. Trace the evolution from young debtor nation to mature creditor nation.

III. REVIEW OF KEY CONCEPTS

Match the following terms from column A with their definitions in column B.

A	B
__ Open economy	1. In a world with free trade and no transportation costs, exchange rates will move until the cost of buying a given bundle of goods and services is the same in all markets.
__ Foreign exchange rate	2. Contains data on a nation's exports and imports of goods and services.
__ Depreciation	3. Item in a country's international balance-of-payments account that involves spending foreign currency.
__ Appreciation	4. Item recorded in the balance-of-payments accounts when a country intervenes in the foreign exchange market.
__ Devaluation	5. Systematic statement of all economic transactions between a country and the rest of the world.
__ Revaluation	6. Contains data on financial flows (lendings and borrowings) into and out of a country.
__ Purchasing-power parity theory exchange rates	7. An economy that engages in of international trade.

__ Balance of international payments

8. Item in a country's international balance-of-payments account that earns foreign currency.

__ Credit

9. Deals with the *official* lowering of a country's foreign exchange rate in terms of other currencies or gold.

__ Debit

10. The price of a unit of foreign currency in terms of the domestic currency.

__ Current account

11. A *market-determined* rise in the price of one currency in terms of others.

__ Capital account

12. A *market-determined* fall in the price of one currency in terms of others.

__ Official settlements

13. Deals with the official raising of a country's foreign exchange rate in terms of other currencies or gold.

__ Law of one price

14. In the long run, exchange rates tend to move with changes in *relative* prices of different countries. This doctrine also holds that countries with high inflation rates will tend to have depreciating currencies.

IV. SUMMARY AND CHAPTER OUTLINE

This section summarizes the key concepts from the chapter.

A. Economic Basis for International Trade

1. The fundamental point of these three chapters is that foreign trade can improve the welfare (i.e., the standard of living) of most nations, even if they are the most productive in producing everything.

2. There are several differences between international trade and domestic trade. When a country moves into the international arena, it:

    a. enjoys a much richer menu of products to choose from.

    b. must deal with the laws and regulations of another sovereign nation.

    c. must trade its currency in foreign exchange markets.

3. While there are numerous reasons why nations may find it beneficial to engage in international trade, there are three main economic considerations:

    a. diversity in conditions of production.

    b. economies of scale and decreasing average costs.

    c. differences in tastes.

B. The Determination of Foreign Exchange Rates

1. When producers in Country A sell their products to people in other countries, they prefer to be paid in their own currency. Therefore, before the people in Country B can purchase products from Country A, they must acquire some of Country A's currency. They purchase Country A's currency with their own currency in a **foreign exchange market.**

2. An exchange rate is simply the price of some currency, A, in terms of some other currency, B. It is determined by the interaction of supply and demand in the foreign exchange market.

3. In free markets, with relatively low transportation costs, a nation's exchange rate will move to equalize the cost of buying traded goods and services at home with the cost of buying those goods abroad. This known as *the law of one price* and it leads to **the purchasing-power-parity (PPP) theory of exchange rates.** In the long run, according to PPP theory, exchange rates will tend to move with changes in relative prices of different countries.

4. When market exchange rates are used, many poor countries appear to have very small national output. Many of the goods and services in these countries which are *not* traded in international markets are relatively labor-intensive and therefore very *in*expensive. When PPP exchange rates are used to evaluate output, it raises the per capita GDP of low-income countries.

C. The Balance of International Payments

1. There are four components in the **balance-of-payments accounts:**

    a. the *current account* (for goods and services)

    b. the *capital account* (for capital goods and services)

    c *official settlements*

    d. *statistical discrepancy* (a catchall category)

Any transaction which requires foreign currency (e.g., the purchase of a commodity produced in another country) is recorded as a debit; any transaction which generates foreign currency (e.g., the sale of a domestic product in a foreign country) is recorded as a credit.

2. Countries usually evolve through several stages in their balance-of-payments histories:

    a. young debtor nation

    b. mature debtor nation

    c. new creditor nation

    d. mature creditor nation

A less developed nation is typically one which borrows abroad to the full extent of its line of credit. A mature, developed nation is typically one which lends to other countries. As a nation develops over a long time period, it may change from borrower to lender, and this shift will affect its balance-of-payments position. The four-stage sequence, outlined above, is an attempt to describe the likely balance-of-payments changes involved.

3.   Some economists suggest that during the 1980s the United States may have entered a fifth stage of development, namely that of "senile debtor nation." Greatly diminished saving has caused heavy U.S. borrowing and turned the world's biggest creditor into the world's biggest debtor.

V. HELPFUL HINTS

1.   As with all diagrams, pay careful attention to how the axes are labeled when working with diagrams depicting foreign exchange markets. Like any supply-and-demand diagram, price is measured on the vertical axis and quantity on the horizontal axis. In this case, the *quantity* will always be the amount of some currency: French francs, German deutsche marks, Japanese yen, whatever. If we are considering the cost of these currencies from the U.S. perspective, the *price* (on the vertical axis) will measure how many dollars are needed to purchase each unit of the foreign currency. So in the foreign exchange market for Japanese yen, the price would be dollars per yen, or $/Y. (Note: Regardless of which currency market you are studying, the currency which is measured on the *horizontal* axis will always be in the denominator of the price on the *vertical* axis.)

Consider Figure 18-1. Panel *(a)* illustrates the market for yen. Note how the axes are labeled. When people demand yen, they will pay for them with dollars. The suppliers of yen will sell them for dollars.

Panel *(b)* illustrates the mirror image of panel *(a)*. The suppliers of yen (from panel [*a*]) are now the demanders of dollars, and the folks supplying dollars are demanding yen for dollars back in panel *(a)*.

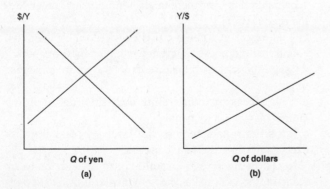

Figure 18-1

2.   Samuelson and Nordhaus point out that "a rise in the price of a currency in terms of another currency is called an 'appreciation.'" The key phrase here is "in terms of." Suppose that a dollar, *in terms of* deutsche marks (DM), costs 2 DM. For purposes of example, assume that a year later that same dollar now costs 3 DM. *In terms of* DM, the dollar is now more expensive—it costs more DM to get

dollars. We would say that, at least relative to DM, the dollar has appreciated in value.

3.   A **devaluation** occurs when a country or government *intervenes* in the foreign exchange market to lower the value of its currency vis-à-vis other currencies. The result is similar to a **depreciation,** but that comes about via the forces of supply and demand in the market place.

4.   In the balance-of-payments account, the **current account** refers to the difference between exported and imported goods and services. This is the trade deficit that in recent years has been mentioned frequently on U.S. television news. Keep in mind that balance-of-payments accounts are only half the picture. Equally important are the flows of financial capital that are measured in the **capital account.**

5.   If a transaction earns foreign currency, it is called a **credit.** Exports earn foreign currency because foreigners who want to purchase goods and services from county A must sell their currency to buy some of Country A's currency. Borrowings, in the capital account, are also counted as credits, because when a country lends to Country A, it gives up some of its currency, again through the foreign exchange market, to Country A.

6.   Surpluses or deficits that exist in the current account must be financed or offset by lendings or borrowings in the capital account.

7.   The PPP exchange rate calculations in Table 34-2 in your text make China's GDP, and that of other low-income countries, much higher. Many of the products which are not traded internationally are labor-intensive services. These are very inexpensive, even in low-income countries. Therefore, when market exchange rates are used to evaluate output, GDP in low-income countries tends to be underestimated. Keep in mind, however, that the numbers in this table are "gross" and not "per capita." China remains the most populated nation on thc earth.

VI. MULTIPLE CHOICE QUESTIONS

These questions are organized by topic from the chapter outline. Choose the best answer from the options available.

A.   Economic Basis for International Trade
1.   Countries engage in international trade to:
     a.   take advantage of economies of scale.
     b.   acquire additional resources.
     c.   satisfy the tastes of their citizens.
     d.   all the above.
     e.   **a** and **b** only.
2.   One of the big differences between domestic trade and international trade is that:
     a.   the distances, and hence the transportation costs, are greater.
     b.   foreigners are harder to deal with.

c.   currencies must be exchanged.

d.   all the above.

e.   none of the above.

B. The Determination of Foreign Exchange Rates

3.   If we say that a country's currency has been devalued, we mean that:

a.   it has gone off the gold standard.

b.   the domestic purchasing power of its currency unit has increased.

c.   its government has increased the price it will pay for gold.

d.   it is experiencing an unfavorable balance of trade.

e.   the prices of at least some foreign currencies, as expressed in that country's domestic currency, have fallen.

4.   In a stable exchange-rate situation, if the price of the French franc were 25 U.S. cents and the price of the U.S. dollar were 600 Italian lire, then the price of the French franc in Italian lire would be:

a.   90 lire.

b.   150 lire.

c.   200 lire.

d.   300 lire.

e.   600 lire.

5.   If the price of French francs in terms of U.S. dollars is 25 cents, then the price of dollars in terms of French francs is:

a.   2 francs.

b.   3 francs.

c.   4 francs.

d.   5 francs.

e.   cannot be determined from the information given.

6.   If the British pound appreciates in value in terms of the Mexican peso, we can say that:

a.   there are now more pesos to the pound.

b.   there are now fewer pounds to the peso.

c.   other things held constant, British goods now cost more in Mexico.

d.   all the above.

e.   **a** and **c** only.

7.   If the market exchange rate between Swiss francs and U.S. dollars were to change from Sfr. 4 to the dollar to Sfr. 3 to the dollar, then the franc's price must have:

a.   risen from 25 cents to 33 cents, and the dollar has appreciated relative to the franc.

b.   fallen from 33 cents to 25 cents, and the dollar has depreciated relative to the franc.

c.   risen from 25 cents to 33 cents, and the dollar has, been devalued relative to the franc.

d.   risen from 25 cents to 33 cents, and the dollar has depreciated relative to the franc.

e.   fallen from 33 cents to 25 cents, and the dollar has appreciated relative to the franc.

8.   A substantial fall in the price of the dollar in foreign currencies could be expected to affect physical quantities of exports from the United States and imports into the United States in which of the following ways?

a.   It would increase both exports and imports.

b.   It would increase exports and decrease imports.

c.   It would decrease both exports and imports.

d.   It would decrease exports and increase imports.

e.   It would have no perceptible effect on either imports or exports.

9.   If a country depreciates the foreign exchange value of its currency, the results will typically be that:

a.   its imports will seem cheaper (from the viewpoint of its own citizens), and its exports will seem more expensive (from the viewpoint of foreigners).

b.   its imports will seem more expensive (from the viewpoint of its own citizens), and its exports will seem cheaper (from the viewpoint of foreigners).

c.   both its imports and its exports will seem cheaper (from the viewpoint of both its own citizens and foreigners).

d.   both its imports and its exports will seem more expensive (from the viewpoint of both its own citizens and foreigners).

e.   none of the above will occur, since there is no reason why the prices of either imports or exports should be affected.

C. The Balance of international Payments

10.   A "favorable balance of trade" means:

a.   an excess of merchandise exports and other capital account credits over merchandise imports and other capital account debits.

b.   an excess of foreign currency received by the home country over domestic currency received by foreigners.

c.   an excess of merchandise exports over merchandise imports.

d.   an excess of total credits over total debits in the entire balance of payments

e.   a situation in which the value of total imports exceeds the value of total exports.

11.   The following five transactions are all entries to be made on the U.S. balance of payments. For balance-of-payments purposes, four of the five are fundamentally similar. Which one is different?

a.   The Federal Reserve Bank of New York sells dollars in the foreign exchange market.

b.   An American tourist on vacation spends francs in Paris.

c.   A South American country sells coffee in New York.

d.   A British shipping firm is paid to carry an American export commodity abroad.

e.   An American computer company receives an order for software programs from Germany.

12. A mature debtor nation is one whose balance of trade is:
a.   unfavorable, the import surplus being paid for by borrowing.
b.   unfavorable, thanks to the interest which is received from abroad.
c.   favorable, the interest on past borrowing being paid out of the surplus of exports.
d.   favorable, being made so by interest received from abroad.
e.   not correctly identified by any of these descriptions.

13. The **trade balance** consists of:
a.   the difference between the capital account and the current account.
b.   the difference between foreign investment and foreign saving.
c.   imports or exports of merchandise.
d.   a comparison of international exchange rates.
e.   none of the above.

VII. PROBLEM SOLVING

The following problems are designed to help you apply the concepts that you learned in the chapter.

A. Economic Basis for International Trade

1. a.   As shown in Figure 18-2, the trend in the United States over the past half-century has been to (**open / dose**) its economy to foreign trade.
b.   The usual measure of openness, the ratio of ___ and/or ___ to GDP has, in fact, (**risen / fallen**) over time.
c.   The percentage of U.S. GDP that is related to trade is (**higher / lower**) than the percent which characterizes most of the economies of Europe.

Figure 18-2

B. The Determination of Foreign Exchange Rates

2. For each of the following statements, indicate whether its effect would be to increase (**I**) or to decrease (**D**) the dollar's price in foreign-currency terms. Use the supply-demand framework reflected in Figure 18-3 to inform and illustrate your answers.
___ a.   American demand for imports increases.
___ b.   Foreign demand for U.S. goods decreases.
___ c.   A recession in the United States results in falling GDP, employment, and imports.
___ d.   The rate of inflation in foreign countries is more rapid than that in the United States.
___ e.   Americans decide to invest less abroad— i.e., their demand for foreign assets decreases.
___ f.   Foreign firms increase their dividend payments, and some of the shareholders are Americans.
___ g.   Foreigners decide to hold fewer U.S. dollars.

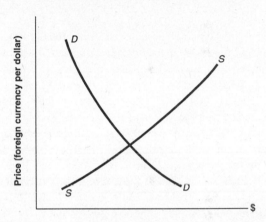

Figure 18-3

3. A demand schedule for francs, at various dollars-and-cents prices, is outlined in Table 18-1.

Table 18-1

P of Franc (in $)	Q of Francs Demanded	P of Dollar (in francs)	Q of Dollars Supplied
1.00	0	___	___
0.90	100	___	___
0.80	200	___	___
0.70	300	___	___
0.60	400	___	___
0.50	500	___	___
0.40	600	___	___
0.30	700	___	___
0.20	800	___	___
0.10	900	___	___

a.   Convert the table into a supply schedule for dollars, at various franc prices.

$/Franc

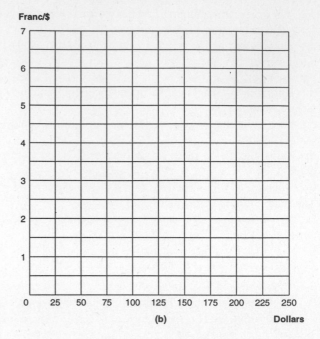

Franc/$

(a)   Francs

(b)   Dollars

Figure 18-4

Hint: A "straight-line" demand schedule results in a supply schedule of quite unexpected shape. Convert in this way: If the price of 1 franc is 90 cents, then 1 franc = 90 cents, and so $1 = 100/0.90 franc (i.e., the price of $1 is about 1.1 francs). The schedule in Table 18-1 says that 100 francs will be demanded when the price of the franc is 90 cents; i.e., $90 will be supplied to buy them. In sum, then, $90 will be supplied when the dollar's price is 1.1 francs. Work out other points on the supply schedule similarly.

b. Plot both curves in the appropriate panels of Figure 18-4. The demand schedule goes in panel (*a*) and the mirror-image supply schedule goes in panel (*b*).

4. What effect, if any, is each of the following events likely to have on the price of the franc in dollars? For each statement below, put (**U**) in the blank if the effect should be to push the price of the franc (in terms of dollars) up, (**D**) if it should push the price down, and (**N**) if there is no reason why the price of the franc should be affected at all.

___ a. French corporations have a large interest payment to make, in dollars, to American bondholders.

___ b. French corporations have a large interest payment to make, in francs, to American bondholders.

___ c. France emerges from a recession, and with this increase in incomes, the French people want to buy more American merchandise.

___ d. American residents decide to buy French bonds.

___ e. French corporations sell bonds to Americans, borrowing in dollars in New York because the interest rate is lower there. The proceeds of the bond issue are to be spent on French labor and materials.

___ f. Foreign exchange speculators decide that the price of the dollar in francs is going to fall.

___ g. The taste of American gourmets for French wine is replaced by a taste for California wine.

___ h. The French government decides that American movies are immoral and refuses to admit them into France.

___ i. An American citizen sends a package of merchandise to her French relatives as a gift.

___ j. An American citizen sends a remittance of dollars to his French relatives as a gift.

___ k. A French bank, in possession of a dollar bank account, decides to convert the dollars into francs.

5. Canada relies heavily on exports to, and imports from, the United States. Suppose that the Canadian authorities (to whom the exchange rate is consequently important) decide that it would be desirable for trading purposes to keep the price of the U.S. dollar at $(Can.) 1.15.

a. If the price of the U.S. dollar begins to drift below this figure, then Canada could enter the foreign exchange market and support the price by (**selling / buying**) U.S. dollars.

b. It would, for this purpose, supply (sell) (**Canadian / American**) dollars.

c. If the U.S. dollar's price started to move above $(Can.) 1.15, on the other hand, Canada could (**buy / sell**) U.S. dollars.

Alternatively, Canada might choose a modified version of the same plan, keeping the price of the U.S. dollar within a "band" of, say, $(Can.) 1.12 and $(Can.) 1.18. Canada could not, of course, keep the exchange rate indefinitely at a level not justified by supply and demand.

d. If the price of the U.S. dollar kept trying to push above $(Can.) 1.18, then Canada would (**accumulate too many / run out of**) U.S. dollars.

6. The word "devaluation" goes back to the days of the gold standard, in which the currency unit allegedly had a "gold content" and gold consequently had an "official price" per ounce.

a. Devaluation meant a government-decreed (**reduction / increase**) in that gold content—i.e., (**a reduction / an increase**) in the official price of gold.

b. President Roosevelt's 1933 declaration that the dollar's gold content would be reduced from 1/21 to 1/35 of an ounce (**was / was not**) an instance of devaluation.

Depreciation, in the context of foreign exchange, refers to a reduction in the price of a currency relative to other monies.

c. Suppose that the price of the Canadian dollar is 90 U.S. cents. If this price were to drop to 85 U.S. cents, then the Canadian dollar would be worth, in U.S. funds, (**more / less**); this would be an instance of depreciation.

d. If the price were to rise from 90 U.S. cents to 95 U.S. cents, on the other hand, this would indicate (**a depreciation / an appreciation**) of the Canadian dollar.

e. Any depreciation of a foreign currency (relative to the U.S. dollar) makes that foreign country's goods appear (**cheaper / more expensive**) to Americans. To residents in that other country, in terms of their own currency, American goods appear (**cheaper / more expensive**).

f. When a country's currency is depreciated, therefore, this move tends to (**increase / decrease**) the volume of its exports and to (**increase / decrease**) the volume of its imports.

C. The Balance of International Payments

7. A country's balance of payments is the official record of all its transactions with foreign countries for some specified period of time, usually 1 year. There are four main categories; list them in the spaces provided:

a. _____
b. _____
c. _____
d. _____

The key to entries in any of these categories is the effect that the transaction has on domestic holdings of foreign currencies.

e. If a transaction generates foreign currency, then it is recorded as a (**debit / credit**); if it costs currency because a foreign citizen (or institution) requires payment in his or her (or its) own currency, then it is a (**debit / credit**).

8. A less developed nation is likely to try to build up its stock of capital goods through sales of its IOUs to more developed countries.

a. On its balance of payments, these security sales will be recorded as a (**credit / debit**).

b. The import of capital equipment or other goods

purchased with security-sale proceeds will appear on the merchandise line as a (**credit / debit**).

c. This country has (**a favorable / an unfavorable**) balance of trade.

These facts make it a "young debtor" nation.

As time passes, the country ceases to borrow, or borrows in smaller quantities. It still pays interest and dividends on earlier years of bond and stock financing, but its exporting capacity has increased.

d. It now shows a surplus of merchandise exports over imports, or an excess of (**credits over debits / debits over credits**).

e. This (**favorable / unfavorable**) balance of trade is matched, or approximately so, by a surplus of debits on the investment income line of the balance of payments.

The "mature debtor" stage has been reached.

Further down the road, the country may begin not only to repay its own earlier borrowings but also to lend to other countries.

f. This means a surplus of (**credits over debits / debits over credits**) in the balance-of-payments capital account.

If this is matched, or approximately so, by a surplus of merchandise exports over imports, the "knew creditor" stage has been reached.

Ultimately, the "mature creditor" stage may be attained. At this point, the country may still be lending capital abroad, but its inflow of interest and dividend payments is more than sufficient to offset this lending.

g. In the balance-of-payments merchandise account, therefore, there is a surplus of (**credits over debits / debits over credits**), and the balance of trade is (**favorable / unfavorable**).

h. This balance is supported by the (**debit / credit**) balance in the investment income account.

VIII. DISCUSSION QUESTIONS

Answer the following questions, making sure that you can explain the work you did to arrive at the answers.

1. Why does the use of PPP exchange rates, as opposed to market exchange rates, increase the value of GDP in low-income countries?

2. According to the PPP doctrine, why do countries with high inflation rates tend to have depreciating currencies?

IX. ANSWERS TO STUDY GUIDE QUESTIONS

III. Review of Key Concepts

7   Open economy
10   Foreign exchange rate
12   Depreciation

11	Appreciation
9	Devaluation
13	Revaluation
14	Purchasing-power-parity theory of exchange rates
5	Balance of international payments
8	Credit
3	Debit
2	Current account
6	Capital account
4	Official settlements
1	Law of one price

VI. Multiple Choice Questions

1. D 2. C 3. C 4. B 5. C 6. D
7. D 8. B 9. B 10. D 11. E 12. C
13. C

VII. Problem Solving

1. a. open
   b. imports, exports, risen
   c. lower
2. a. D
   b. D
   c. I
   d. I
   e. I
   f. I
   g. D
   See Figure 18-3 for the appropriate shifts.

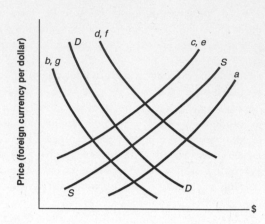

Figure 18-3

3. a.

Table 18-1

P of Franc (in $)	Q of Francs Demanded	P of Dollar (In francs)	Q of Dollars Supplied
1.00	0	1.00	0
0.90	100	1.11	90
0.80	200	1 25	160
0.70	300	1 43	210
0.60	400	1 67	240
0.50	500	2.00	250
0.40	600	2 50	240
0.30	700	3.33	210
0.20	800	5.00	160
0.10	900	10.00	90

(a)   Francs

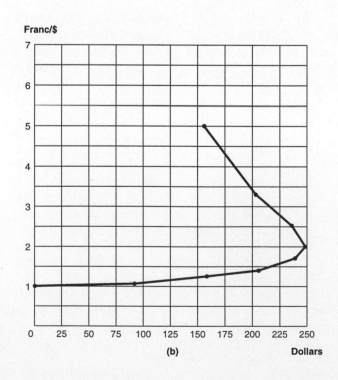

(b)   Dollars

Figure 18-4

b.

4. a. D
    b. D
    c. D
    d. U
    e. U
    f. U
    g. D
    h. U
    i. N
    j. U
    k. U

5. a. buying
    b. Canadian
    c. sell
    d. run out of

6. a. reduction, an increase
    b. was
    c. less
    d. an appreciation
    e. cheaper, more expensive
    f. increase, decrease

7. a. current account
    b. capital account
    c. official settlements
    d. statistical discrepancy

    e. credit, debit
8. a. credit
    b. debit
    c. an unfavorable
    d. credits over debits
    e. favorable
    f. debits over credits
    g. debits over credits, unfavorable
    h. credit

VIII. DISCUSSION QUESTIONS

1. Low-income countries tend to have large, low-income, labor-intensive service sectors. The output from these sectors tends, by its nature, not to be traded in international markets. The use of market-established exchange rates is an accurate way to establish a common value for traded goods, but it is less accurate in assessing the value of nontraded products. PPP exchange rates may more accurately reflect the true value of a nation's output when there are different products and means of production across countries.

2. Countries with relatively high rates of inflation will experience higher prices. Higher prices hurt exports, and the demand for the nation's currency on the foreign exchange markets will fall. In other words, the country's currency will depreciate in value.

CHAPTER 19
Comparative Advantage and Protectionism

I. CHAPTER OVERVIEW

In this chapter, Samuelson and Nordhaus present the basic economic model of trade. The fundamental point is that foreign trade can improve welfare (i.e., the standard of living) of most nations, even if they already are the most productive in producing everything. Part of David Ricardo's great contribution to the study of international trade was to show that inefficiency in all lines of production would make a country poor, but it would not cause its trading opportunities to totally evaporate. Relatively efficient and inefficient countries can still trade to mutual advantage, provided there are some differences in their relative costs of production. The first part of the chapter explains Ricardo's innovative view of trade.

Once the case for free trade is made, Samuelson and Nordhaus turn the coin over to look at its opposite side—protectionism. If free trade is so beneficial, why do we see so many barriers to free trade in the real world? To answer this question, it is essential to see how trade barriers work. Only then can their effects be delineated and their merits evaluated. The second section of Chapter 35 tends to this task. With the effects of protectionism firmly in hand, the various arguments for and against protection are then critically reviewed.

II. LEARNING OBJECTIVES

After you have read Chapter 35 in your text and completed the exercises in this *Study Guide* chapter, you should be able to:

1. Distinguish between **absolute advantage** and **comparative advantage**.
2. Explain, using a simple two-commodity model, how a country can increase its real income by specializing (for the purpose of export) in the commodity in which it has a comparative advantage and importing the commodity in which it has a comparative disadvantage.
3. Understand that the Ricardo model is easily extended to include multinational trading arrangements.

4. Use supply-and-demand analysis to outline the economic effects of protection. Show that opening trade in a good drives its domestic price toward equality with its world price. Show that a tariff can be expected to generate welfare losses.
5. Outline the economic as well as the noneconomic arguments for trade restriction and evaluate their validity.
6. List a few nontariff barriers to trade that have been employed by the United States in the past few years and explain how they work.

III. REVIEW OF KEY CONCEPTS

Match the following terms from column A with their definitions in column B.

A	B
__ Principle of comparative advantage	1 Occurs when a firm from Country B sells its product in Country A at a price beneath its average cost, or at a price lower than the existing domestic price in Country B.
__ Absolute advantage	2. Illustrates pre- and post-trade production and consumption, and trade alternatives for a country.
__ Comparative advantage	3. Program or policy which protects the domestic economy at the expense of other countries.
__ Terms of trade	4. Tariff that maximizes a country's domestic real income by shifting the terms of trade in its favor.
__ Consumption-possibility curve	5. Each country will specialize in the production and export of those goods that it can produce at *relatively* low cost and import those which it produces at *relatively* high cost.

___ Multilateral trade

___ Tariff

___ Quota

___ Mercantilism

___ Dumping

___ Optimal tariff

___ Infant industry tariff

___ "Beggar thy neighbor" policy

6.   Tariff which is used to protect a new domestic industry from powerful fully developed international competitors.

7.   Exists when a country can produce a commodity at lower *relative* cost.

8.   Exists when a country can produce a commodity with greater *absolute* efficiency or lower resource cost.

9.   The exchange of goods and services among a multitude of nations.

10.   A ratio of export prices to import prices which defines the upper and lower price boundaries for goods traded between countries.

11.   Pre-Ricardian economic philosophy that espoused the benefits of trade surpluses and the acquisition of gold.

12.   A tax on imported goods and services.

13.   A limit on the quantity of imports.

IV. SUMMARY AND CHAPTER OUTLINE

This section summarizes the key concepts from the chapter.

A. The Principle of Comparative Advantage

1.   If the United States had no domestic sources of tin, then it would surely have to import the tin it needed. What is not so obvious is why the United States, or any other country for that matter, should import a commodity which it could and does produce. The basic message of this chapter is that a nation should import some goods which it is capable of producing at home if it wants to use its resources to the best advantage. Each country should move toward specializing in the production of those commodities it is best equipped to make, given its own resources and those available to other countries. It should export part of what it has produced, receiving in exchange other goods (imports) which it is less equipped to make.

2.   Before trying to understand why certain frequently held notions about international trade are incorrect, you must first grasp the basic notion of **comparative advantage**; it alone explains why, in terms of real income, it pays each nation to move toward specializing in the production of a specific good or goods, to export those goods, and to use the

proceeds of that export trade to finance the import of other goods. A country has an **absolute advantage** in the production of any good X if it can produce X at a smaller cost than a potential trading partner. It has a **comparative advantage** in the production of X if it can produce X *relatively* less expensively than it can produce some other tradable commodity.

3.   The potential gains from trade are derived from comparative advantage. A country can collect these gains by concentrating its production efforts on goods in which it has a comparative advantage, exporting some or all of its output in exchange for goods in which it has a comparative disadvantage. A country with absolute advantages in the production of all goods can therefore still improve its welfare through trade if it concentrates on the production of goods in which its absolute advantage is largest.

4.   The Ricardo model, which first described comparative advantage and the potential gains from trade, is a classical, full-employment model. Adjustment in the product mix designed to take full advantage of the potential can, however, be marked painfully by the short- to medium-term unemployment of displaced factors of production. Even when long-run equilibrium has been achieved with full employment, moreover, some people may be worse off than before. The idea is only that *aggregate* welfare has been improved.

5.   The *mercantilist* philosophy was that a nation ought to apply the same principles of prudence appropriate for a family. It is prudent for a family to try to save part of its income. The nation, mercantilists said, is just the family on a larger scale. And they equated saving, at the national level, with the accumulation of gold.

The argument is not totally fallacious. Any nation will find it desirable to have reserves of gold (or foreign exchange) to cope with changing events which may produce balance-of-payments deficits. Even at the family level, though, the argument for "prudence" is wrong if interpreted as meaning that all families must hoard their money. Saving which is not allowed to flow into investment spending leads only to depression and to a fall in saving.

B. Protectionism

1.   Three principal reasons, often working together, explain the rationale behind most of the actual or proposed restraints of foreign trade:

a.   A country fears unemployment and regards import competition as a potential source of that unemployment.

b.   A country is short of foreign exchange reserves and sees increased tariffs as a potential source of new revenue.

c.   The groups within a country who would benefit most directly from protection bring political pressure to bear for its imposition.

2.   In a period of heavy unemployment, it is hard to preach comparative advantage and free trade to legislators and

business people. They will argue that a reduction in imports would raise domestic employment at the expense of lower aggregate demand and correspondingly higher unemployment abroad, and so they might advocate an increase in protective tariffs. Such an attempt to "export unemployment" could, of course, be negated when other countries retaliate with similar tariff increases.

3. It would be wrong to insist that import restrictions can never reduce unemployment. The proper objection is that fiscal and monetary policies can be far more effective. Moreover, these policies avoid the dubious ethics of trying to foist off domestic unemployment onto other nations, and they do not incur the danger of retaliation.

4. Given reasonable assurance that unemployment can be handled by methods other than protection, many people in developed countries find it fairly easy to accept the free-trade principle; but people living in less developed countries tend to be more hesitant. They look at the world's most prosperous nations and hope that their own country might someday enjoy equally high standards of production and income. They wonder if some restriction on imports may be needed in order to widen production and employment opportunities and to foster their nation's industrial growth.

5. Simple supply-and-demand analysis can be employed to show that protection strategies increase domestic prices and generate welfare losses by (a) promoting inefficient domestic production and (b) reducing consumption.

6. Unless the protection is prohibitive, it can generate revenue for the government (tariff collections or import license auctions can be equivalent in this regard).

7. Noneconomic arguments for protection are sometimes made: national interest and/or security, cultural and/or regional integrity, and so on. Domestic subsidies can be more effective in these instances.

8. Other economic arguments are false: protecting domestic employment, special-interest protection, and mercantilistic pursuit of favorable terms of trade. Alternative domestic policies can be more effective in these instances.

9. Dynamic arguments for protection are more attractive, but they can be risky. Optimal tariff barriers and infant-industry protection run the risk of retaliation, for example.

V. HELPFUL HINTS

1   *Absolute advantage* means lower resource cost, or more efficient use of resources. *Comparative advantage* means lower relative cost, that is, relative to what has to be given up.

Consider the following example. There are two countries: Annastasia and Bobbyland, or A and B. Prior to trade, they each produce two goods: robots (R) and xylophones (X). Table 19-1 shows the labor cost (assuming labor is the only factor of production) of producing a unit of each good.

Table 19-1 Labor Hours Needed to Produce One Unit

	A	B
R	1 hour	10 hours
X	3 hours	20 hours

Annastasia has an absolute advantage in the production of *both* goods. It can produce them with fewer resources. To evaluate comparative advantage, we need to measure the *relative* cost of producing each commodity within each country.

In Annastasia, the relative cost of producing one robot is 0.33 xylophones. Here is why: When Annastasia decides to produce robots, it costs 1 hour of labor for each one. If that hour of labor had been used in the manufacture of xylophones, it could have produced *one-third* of a xylophone instead.

In Bobbyland, the relative cost of R is 0.50X. Relatively speaking, or relative to what each country has to give up, Annastasia has a comparative advantage in the production of R.

In A, the relative cost of producing one X is 3R. In B. the relative cost of producing one X is 2R. So, B has a comparative advantage in the production of X. Relatively speaking, B gives up less to produce X.

2. In a two-good world, it is definitionally impossible for a country to have a comparative advantage in the production of both goods. However, in a many-good world, one country will *always* have a comparative advantage in something.

3. Prices do not need to be measured in money terms—they can be measured in terms of the other good.

VI. MULTIPLE CHOICE QUESTIONS

These questions are organized by topic from the chapter outline. Choose the best answer from the options available.

A. The Principle of Comparative Advantage

1. In terms of comparative advantage, the *most correct* explanation of why bananas are imported instead of being grown commercially in the United States is that:
   a. bananas cannot be produced in the temperate zones.
   b. it would take a great deal of effort to produce bananas in the United States.
   c. bananas can be produced with less effort in other countries than they can in the United States.
   d. U.S. resources are better employed in producing other commodities, and tropical-country resources are better employed in banana production than in other things.
   e. the U.S. climate does not lend itself to banana production.

2. Before international trade begins, a country will have an equilibrium ratio of prices (determined by relative

production costs in the classical Ricardo model) between any two commodities. If trade involving these commodities begins with another country, then this price ratio will ordinarily be altered:

a. only if a change in production costs results within the country.

b. in all cases (except when the volume of international trade proves to be too small to affect it).

c. only in cases where the volume of international trade is small.

d. not at all, since it is an equilibrium relationship.

e. only in cases where the volume of international trade is exceedingly large.

Use Table 19-2 to answer questions 3 through 7. The table records the output of labor (assumed to be the only input involved) in the production of wine and cloth in two countries, A and B.

Table 19-2

Production per Hour	Country A	Country B
Yards of cloth	5	15
Liters of wine	10	20

3. Comparing the two countries and contemplating trade between them on the basis of production advantages, it would be correct to say that Country A has:

a. an absolute advantage in cloth production.

b. an absolute advantage in wine production.

c. a comparative advantage in cloth production.

d. a comparative advantage in wine production.

e. a comparative advantage in neither commodity.

4. Suppose that initially there is no trade between these two countries. In Country A, the currency unit is the "donaro;" in Country B. it is the "gelt." The prices of cloth in A and B in their pretrade situations are, respectively, 20 donaros and 60 gelts. For an equilibrium in which each country continues to produce both commodities, the corresponding wine prices would have to be:

a. 5 donaros, 20 gelts.

b. 40 donaros, 45 gelts.

c. 10 donaros, 45 gelts.

d. 10 donaros, 80 gelts.

e. 40 donaros, 80 gelts.

5. If trading opportunities were to open (international transport costs assumed to be zero or negligible), then we should expect Country B to:

a. import wine.

b. export wine.

c. import both commodities.

d. export both commodities.

e. neither export nor import, since its productive situation is such that there is no prospect of profitable trade with Country A.

6. Before the trading opportunity of question 5 emerged, each country had its own price ratio, reflecting domestic production costs. If trade develops between Countries A and B. this ratio—specifically, the ratio of the price of wine to the price of cloth—should:

a. rise in Country A, fall in Country B.

b. fall in Country A, rise in Country B.

c. rise in both.

d. fall in both.

e. not change in either country, except perhaps during a short transitional period before equilibrium is reestablished.

7. Once international trade has been established and a new equilibrium has been reached, then the ratio of cloth price to wine price (transport costs still assumed to be zero) might reasonably be:

a. 1.2 in both countries.

b. 1.6 in both countries.

c. 1.3 in A, 2.1 in B.

d. 2.1 in A, 1.3 in B.

e. 2.3 in both countries.

8. Differences in comparative production costs are usually cited as the principal basis for international trade. Another (and different) possible source of international exchange is:

a. differences in climates.

b. fixed foreign exchange rates.

c. differences in transport costs.

d. differences in labor skills.

e. economies of mass production.

9. Trade between countries of comparable size but with different standards of living will be:

a. profitable to the country with lower living standards at the expense of the one with higher standards.

b. profitable to both as long as price ratios differ in the two countries, but of no profit to either once a common price ratio has been established.

c. profitable in some degree to both, even after a common price ratio has been established.

d. unprofitable to both because one country would be at an absolute disadvantage in all products.

e. profitable to the country with higher living standards at the expense of the one with lower living standards.

B. Protectionism

10. One argument for tariffs contends that they should be imposed to help a domestic producer to compete when the level of foreign wages is significantly below the level of domestic wages. This argument:

a. is conceded by most economists to be correct, although sometimes exaggerated in order to justify some level of tariff protection.

b.   is fallacious because there are almost no instances in which there is any real difference between the levels of foreign and domestic wages.

c.   ignores the fact that differences in relative costs constitute the principal basis for international trade.

d.   may be correct with respect to money wages at home and abroad but is not correct with respect to real wages.

e.   is not correctly described by any of the preceding.

11. Country A imposes a new tariff on Country B's products. Country B is considering a retaliatory tariff on A's goods. On economic grounds, B should:

a.   reject the idea of a tariff increase.

b.   make the retaliatory tariff less than A's tariff.

c.   make the retaliatory tariff more than A's tariff.

d.   impose the retaliatory tariff only if B is in a situation of full employment.

e.   adjust the price of its currency relative to A's currency.

12. The policy of the mercantilists with respect to foreign trade held that:

a.   imports should exceed exports—i.e., the country should "get more than it gives"—in order to increase real income at home as much as possible.

b.   exports should exceed imports in order to bring in gold.

c.   since this trade represented commerce, it should be encouraged to the greatest possible degree—i.e., there should be free trade.

d.   exports should be kept in balance with imports and at the lowest possible level of both.

e.   trade in agricultural products was more important than trade in industrial goods.

13. The principal reason high-wage American labor should not require tariff protection from lower-paid foreign labor is:

a.   no American labor would be thrown out of work even if there were no tariffs.

b.   the high per-worker-hour productivity of American labor in many industries is an offset to the lower cost of foreign labor.

c.   American consumers tend to buy American-made goods in preference to foreign-made goods.

d.   a high-wage American industry can be presumed to have a comparative advantage over foreign competitors.

e.   none of the preceding reasons.

14. The argument by workers in a protected industry in the United States that free trade would worsen the income position of American labor is:

a.   not valid even for workers in that industry after allowance is made for the improvement in real income afforded by cheaper imports.

b.   not valid even for workers in that industry after allowance is made for the employment effect of increased exports.

c.   valid for workers in that industry but probably not valid for American labor as a whole.

d.   valid for workers in that industry and probably valid for American labor as a whole.

e.   probably valid for workers in that industry but unquestionably invalid for American labor as a whole.

15. From a purely economic point of view, the best level at which to set a tariff (under static assumptions) is:

a.   the prohibitive point.

b.   the amount needed to bring the level of foreign costs up to the level of domestic costs.

c.   zero.

d.   a level sufficiently low so that it is not likely to invite retaliation by other countries.

e.   the level at which revenues from the tariff will be at a maximum.

16. One argument for tariff protection contends that a tariff would improve the terms of trade in dealing with other nations. This argument:

a.   is a refinement of the mercantilist argument that a nation's exports should exceed its imports.

b.   may be valid if the tariff-imposing country is a relatively large one and the tariffs a relatively small one.

c.   is a refined version of the infant-industry argument and hence has no validity.

d.   may be valid if the tariff-imposing country is unimportant in world trade for the commodity or commodities involved.

e.   may be valid if it is applied to all the country's imports, without or almost without exception.

17. It may be argued that a tariff should be imposed on a commodity if that commodity is considered essential to material well-being and/or if it is suspected that the foreign suppliers thereof might use their supply control for purposes of political blackmail. Most economists hold that:

a.   the tariff is justified if the commodity is deemed really essential.

b.   subsidy would be preferable to a tariff if the commodity is deemed really essential.

c.   the best remedy for threats of political blackmail is to insist on all-around free trade.

d.   although the imposition of a tariff might be used as a threat, political moves should be met by political countermoves (even to the threat of war), not by economic moves.

e.   its domestic production should be nationalized if the commodity is deemed really essential.

18. If we reduce the flow of import goods by imposing heavy tariffs, our exports are likely to be affected in which of the following ways?

a.   They will likely be reduced when other countries retaliate by imposing tariffs against those exports (as is likely), but not otherwise.

b.   There is little reason to expect that they will be affected at all, since retaliatory tariffs have usually proved ineffective.

c.   They will likely be increased, since other countries will find it necessary to buy more from us to compensate for the higher cost of the goods they sell us.

d.   They will likely be increased if the tariff raises the level of employment and national product at home, but not otherwise.

e.   They are likely to be reduced in all or almost all circumstances.

19. A valid counter to the argument that a tariff results in increased money wages in the protected industry is that:

a.   workers in that industry will in all probability suffer a loss in real wages.

b.   workers in other industries will suffer a loss in real wages.

c.   the increase in money wages in the protected industry will cause unemployment.

d.   tariffs cannot increase money wages in any industry.

e.   any increase in real wages is likely to lead to inflation.

20. Arguments cited in favor of a protective tariff frequently note that tariffs (a) protect domestic industry against foreign competition and (b) bring revenue to the government. In response to these arguments, it may be said that:

a.   the tariff reduces rather than increases the sales of the domestic industry.

b.   if the industry in question enjoys an absolute advantage in production, it stands in no need of such a tariff.

c.   the emphasis on government revenue may lead to a tariff per unit much higher than the domestic industry needs for protection.

d.   an effective tariff will actually bring in no government revenue at all.

e.   none of these statements is correct.

21. A difference between a tariff on an imported good and a quota on the same good is that:

a.   a quota can never be made to yield revenue for the government, whereas a tariff can.

b.   a tariff can never be made to yield revenue for the government, whereas a quota can.

c.   a quota can be used to shut off all, or virtually all, the inflow of the imported good, whereas a tariff cannot.

d.   a tariff can be used to shut off all, or virtually all, the inflow of the imported good, whereas a quota cannot.

e.   a quantity-equivalent quota will generate the same revenue only if import rights are auctioned.

22. A prohibitive tariff:

a.   was used during the Prohibition.

b.   effectively chokes off all imports.

c.   prohibits placing a tariff on certain commodities.

d.   is less restrictive than a nonprohibitive tariff.

e.   is none of the above.

VII. PROBLEM SOLVING

The following problems are designed to help you apply the concepts that you learned in the chapter.

A. The Principle of Comparative Advantage

The questions which follow build toward an examination of the theory of comparative advantage by looking at economic conditions before trade begins. The idea is to start by identifying a country's before-trade position and standard of living and then to show how the initiation of foreign trade can increase real income.

The same simplifying assumptions employed in the text are employed here. There are only two regions: "America" and "Europe." Only two commodities are involved: food (F) and clothing (C). All the costs of producing either F or C can be measured in hours of labor. For some reason, however, the yields from an hour of labor, in the making of both F and C, differ across international boundaries.

Table 19-3

Yield of 1 Labor-Hour	Units of F	Units of C
In America	20	6
In Europe	10	8

Table 19-4

	Minutes of Labor Required to Produce:	
	1 Unit of F	1 Unit of C
In America	3	10
In Europe	6	7.5

1.   The quantities of F and of C resulting from 1 hour of labor in America and in Europe are given in Table 19-3. These data translate into the input requirements recorded in Table 19-4.

a.   Assuming that "1 hour of labor" means the same thing in both countries, the figures indicate that America is more productive in (**F / both F and C / C / neither F nor C**).

b.   Europe is, meanwhile, more productive in (**F / both F and C / C / neither F nor C**).

c.   In an 8-hour day, therefore, a worker in America can produce either 8 x 20 = 160 units of F or (**10 / 48 / 64 / 80**) units of C.

d.   In Europe a worker can produce either 64 units of C or (**10 / 48 / 64 / 80**) units of **F**.

2.   This chapter assumes that all the costs of producing either commodity in either region are labor costs and that all revenue from sale of the commodity goes to that labor.

a.   If the market price of a unit of F in America were $1, then the hourly wage earned by an American worker producing F would be (**$0.05 / $0.10 / $1.00 / $10.00 / $20.00**).

b.   If, instead, F's price in America were $0.05 (5 cents), then the corresponding hourly wage for an F worker would be (**$0.05 / $0.10 / $1.00 / $10.00 / $20.00**).

c.   Similarly, if C's price per unit in America were $2, then the hourly wage of a C worker would be (**$0.30 / $0.60 / $2.00 / $10.00 / $12.00**).

d.   If the price per unit of F were £1 (1 pound) in Europe, then the hourly wage of an F worker there would be (**£1 / £4 / £6 / £8 / £10**).

e.   If C's price in Europe were £1, on the other hand, then the corresponding hourly C wage would be (**£1 / £4 / £6 / £8 / £10**).

3.   Suppose that the prices of F and C in America are both $1.

a.   A worker, free to choose an occupation in either industry, would earn more by going to work in the production of (**F / C**). Specifically, earnings per hour would be (**$1 / $6 / $8 / $10 / $20**) in the production of F and (**$1 / $6 / $8 / $10 / $20**) in the production of C.

Given freedom of labor to enter either occupation (and with no other preference between them), the prices noted above (both $1) (**could / could not**) characterize an "equilibrium" situation in America. If these prices did prevail—say, because the government tried to enforce them by law—then (**only F / only C / both F and C**) would be produced.

b.   If the prices of both F and C were somehow £10 in Europe, then (again assuming no barrier to movement between occupations) (**all the workers would move into production of F / all the workers would move into production of C / there would be no change in the production mix of F and C**).

c.   The point is that the supply of resources (here, the entire labor force) would shift away from production of the "underpriced" commodity unless the prices of F and C stand in the proper relation to one another, i.e., unless they reflect relative marginal costs. If the price of F were $3 in America, then the price of C would have to be (**$1 / $3 / $8 / $10 / $12**), if both F and C are to be produced.

If the price of C were $2 in America, then the price of F should be (**$0.30 / $0.60 / $1.00 / $1.50 / $2.00**).

Prices of $2.40 for F and $9 for C (**would / would not**) support an equilibrium.

d.   It is relative prices that matter here. In America, the ratio between p_F and p_C must be (**1:1 / 3:10 / 5:10 / 10:3**) because only that ratio matches the underlying ratio of production costs, measured in labor time needed to produce 1 unit of each commodity.

The absolute level of prices would be governed by such factors as the quantity of money circulating within the country.

e.   If prices of F and C somehow got stuck at $2.40 and $9, respectively, workers would move away from the production of (**F / C**) and into the production of (**F / C**).

In Europe, the same requirement holds, except that the relationship must match productive conditions there.

f.   If the price of F in Europe were £4, then the price of C would have to be (**£1 / £2 / £3 / £4 / £5**) to support an equilibrium in which both commodities were produced. More generally, Europe's price ratio (F to C) must be (**3:10 / 5:10 / 4:5 / 5:4**).

The questions thus far have assumed that there is no international trade between America and Europe. Now assume that the opportunity for trade between the two regions suddenly materializes. Assume, for simplicity, that the costs of shipping goods from one region to the other are so small that they can be considered zero. The prices of F and of C in America are, respectively, 60 cents and $2.

4.   In America (and in Europe), opening trade would disrupt the pretrade domestic "equilibrium." For example, in the United States, trade supplements domestic supplies of C.

a.   The price of C should therefore (**rise / remain unchanged / fall**). This in turn means that the ratio of the price of F to the price of C (i.e., p_F/p_C) should (**rise / remain unchanged / fall**).

b.   We know that workers would leave the "underpriced" occupation if America's price ratio p_F/p_C were anything other than 3:10 (or 0.3). In this case, workers would move from the production of (**F / C**) to the production of (**F / C**) as the price ratio rose, and that would be good.

Why? Because America's new export trade means that more workers are needed in the production of American exports—commodity F.

c.   In Europe, which imports what America exports, there would (**be a / not be any**) corresponding change in domestic prices. There, the ratio p_F/p_C would (**rise / remain unchanged / fall**).

The price of F would fall as imports arrived from America. The price of C would rise, meanwhile, since there would now be a new and increased demand for European C in America.

d.   Workers would leave the production of (**C / F**), moving instead to production of Europe's export—commodity C.

5.   The points of these questions can be illustrated graphically. Take the input requirements listed in question 1 as given, and suppose that Europe and America are both endowed with 10 hours of labor (not very realistic, to be sure, but a convenient number around which to build some illustrative geometry). Suppose further that both regions start, in the absence of any trade, by dividing their labor resources equally between F and C.

a.   In panel (a) of Figure 19-1, draw the production possibility frontier for America, and identify the initial

Figure 19-1

c. Start with America, which produces ___ units of F and ___ units of C; Europe begins producing ___ units of F and ___ units of C. Total "world" production of C is ___ units; total production of F is ___ units.

6. Suppose now, for the sake of argument, that America chooses to specialize in F in trade with Europe at the European domestic price ratio.

a. In panel (a) draw a budget constraint (a consumption frontier based upon specializing in the production of F and trading to get C) indicating the possible points of consumption given this strategy. If America were to continue to consume the original 30 units of C, then it could increase its consumption of F from 100 units to ___ units by selling ___ units of F for 30 units of C. Welfare in America, assuming a smooth transition from a 50-50 labor split to 100 percent concentration in the production of F. would therefore necessarily (**fall / stay the same / rise**).

Now play the same game from the other side of the Atlantic. Assume that Europe decides to specialize completely in the production of C and buys as much F as it wants given the American price ratio.

b. Draw the appropriate budget constraint in panel (b).

c. If Europe were still interested in consuming 40 units of C, it could increase its consumption of F from 50 units to ___ units by selling 40 units of C for ___ units of F. European welfare would, in this second case, also (**climb / remain the same / fall**), again making the same assumption of continued full employment during the transition.

7. The world production frontier can now be constructed.

production mix as point A. Draw the corresponding frontier for Europe in panel (b), and identify the initial production mix as point B.

b. The slope of the American frontier, equaling ___ in magnitude, represents the relative domestic price ratio of food to clothing in America. The corresponding slope of the European frontier, equaling in ___ magnitude, is similarly the relative domestic price ratio in Europe.

a. Suppose, first of all, that both countries specialize in F; production of F would equal __ units in America and __ units in Europe, for a total of __ units; total production of C would then equal __ units.

b. Plot this combination in panel (c) and label it point D.

Now reverse the specializations of both countries.

c. Total production of F would then equal __ units, with the production of C climbing to a maximum of __ units.

d. Plot this second point in panel (c) and label it E.

Halfway between these extremes are two intermediate cases of mixed specialization.

e. If Europe specialized in C and America specialized in F, then __ units of F would be produced along with __ units of C.

f. Denote this point G and plot it in panel (c), as well.

g. If the specializations were reversed, though, __ units of F would be produced in Europe and __ units of C would be produced in America.

h. This point, plotted and labeled H in panel (c), (**would / would not**) be on the frontier because the production level(s) of (**F is / C is / neither F nor C is / both F and C are**) lower at H than at G.

The world frontier is now at hand.

i. A straight line connecting points D and G would correspond to specialization by (**America / Europe**) in the production of (**F / C**) and some intermediate combination of F and C produced in (**America / Europe**). Similarly, points along a line connecting points G and E would correspond to specialization in (**America / Europe**) in the production of (**F / C**) and some intermediate combination in (**America / Europe**).

(*Note: The frontier you just drew should look like the frontier shown in the text.*)

j. Finally, plot the pretrade initial production point in panel (c) and label it I; it (**is / is not**) on the frontier. The point chosen by free trade outlined above would be (**D / E / G / H**). It (**would / would not**) be on the frontier, and it would, for both countries, be superior to the initial, pretrade position.

B. Protectionism

8. Consult Figure 19-2. Curve SS represents a domestic supply curve for some good X; if X is a competitive industry, then SS represents the horizontal sum of the marginal cost curves of many firms. Curse DD represents domestic demand for the same good. It is implicitly assumed that consumers do not care where the good was made; they simply want to buy the indicated quantities at the indicated prices.

a. The market-clearing price in the absence of trade is $___, and ___ units of X would be demanded and supplied domestically at that price. If the world price of $5 were allowed to prevail, though, then ___ units of X

would be demanded, ___ units would be supplied domestically, and ___ units would be imported.

Figure 19-2

Now suppose that the domestic government has been convinced somehow to restrict imports by 50 percent.

b. A tariff of $__ per unit imported would do the trick, but it would raise the domestic price to $__. At that price, __ units would be demanded, __ units would be supplied domestically, and __ units would be imported. The effect of the tariff, therefore, is to (**raise / lower**) the price of X, (**raise / lower**) domestic production and employment, and (**raise / lower**) imports.

c. Given the tariff of part b, the government would collect $__ in revenue; this is revenue that would be collected above and beyond the revenue that it collected from its domestic tax base. (*Hint:* To see the tax on your diagram, construct a box underneath the supply and demand curves. The length is the 7.5 units that are imported, and the height is the $2.50 tariff.)

The higher domestic price would, however, promote (**less / more**) efficient production at home, and thereby produce an efficiency (**loss / gain**) of $__.

The marginal cost of producing X at home would, quite simply, increase to a level 50 percent higher than the marginal cost incurred by the rest of the world. The domestic economy would, in other words, be wasting resources in the production of X that would have been employed more efficiently somewhere else.

d. If the government chose to impose a quota rather than a tariff, then it would award licenses to import up to __ units of X.

e. If there were no tariff, but if it cost $2.50 per unit to transport X from the world marketplace into the domestic economy, then your answers to part b (**would / would not**) be altered. The revenue in part c identified as going to the government (**would / would not**) simply go to the transport company.

9. a.   The mercantilist approach to international trade argued that a nation should try to have (**exports / imports**) in excess of (**exports / import**)—hence the phrase "favorable balance of trade." Any surplus so obtained would be used to acquire (**merchandise / gold**).

b.   The mercantilist position was thus strongly disposed toward (**protectionism / free trade**). It was a convenient argument for many (**producer / consumer**) groups seeking protection against foreign competition.

c.   It would be (**possible / impossible**) for every nation to practice mercantilism successfully, since it is (**possible / impossible**) for every nation to have a surplus of exports. A general attempt to practice this philosophy, by trying to expand exports and restrict imports, would lead to a major (**rise / fall**) in (**exports alone / imports alone / both exports and imports**).

VIII. DISCUSSION QUESTIONS

Answer the following questions, making sure that you can explain the work you did to arrive at the answers.

1.   Look back at the very beginning of the chapter and the quote from F. Bastiat. Would David Ricardo agree or disagree with the Candle Makers?

2.   Explain, in words, how two countries mutually benefit from trade.

3.   Precisely who are the winners and who are the losers when countries place tariffs and/or quotas on imported goods?

4.   It has been argued that raising tariffs generates more revenue for the government. Do you agree?

5.   List two noneconomic arguments that have been advanced for protection. Are there any alternates to tariffs and quotas?

IX. ANSWERS TO STUDY GUIDE QUESTIONS

III.   Review of Key Concepts

5	Principle of comparative advantage
8	Absolute advantage
7	Comparative advantage
10	Terms of trade
2	Consumption-possibility curve
9	Multilateral trade
12	Tariff
13	Quota
11	Mercantilism
1	Dumping
4	Optimal tariff
6	Infant industry tariff
3	"Beggar thy neighbor" policy

VI. Multiple Choice Questions

1. D 2. B 3. D 4. C 5. A 6. A
7. B 8. E 9. C 10. C 11. A 12. B
13. B 14. C 15. C 16. B 17. B 18. E
19. B 20. C 21. E 22. B

VII.   Problem solving

1. a. F
b. C
c. 48
d. 80

2. a. $20.00 ($1.00 × 20)
b. $1.00 ($0.05 × 20)
c. $12.00 ($2.00 × 6)
d. £10
e. £8

3. a. F. $20, $6, could not, only F
b. all the workers would move into production of F
c. $10 ($3.00 × 3.33), $0.60 ($2.00/3.33), would not
d. 3:10
e. F, C
f. £5, 4:5

4. a. fall, rise
b. C, F
c. be a, fall
d. F

5. a. See dashed lines in Figure 19-1, panels (*a*) and (*b*).
b. -3.33, -1.25
c. 100, 30, 50, 40, 70, 150

6. a. See Figure 19-1, panel (*a*), 162.5, 37.5 (37.5/30 = 1.25), rise
b. See Figure 19-1 (top of next page), panel (*b*).
c. 133.33, 133.33 (40 x 3.33), climb

7. a. 200, 100, 300, 0
b. See Figure 19-1, panel (*c*).
c. 0,140
d. See Figure 19-1, panel (*c*).
e. 200, 80
f. See Figure USA, panel (*c*).
g. 100, 60
h. See Figure 19-1, panel (*c*), would not, both F and C
i. America, F. Europe, Europe, C, America
j. See Figure 19-1, panel (*c*), is not, G. would

8. a. $10, 10, 20, 5, 15
b. $2.50, $7.50, 15, 7.5, 7.5, raise, raise, lower
c. $18.75 (2.50 × 7.5), rectangle CEFG in Figure 19-2; less, loss, $3.125 (2.5 × 2.5 × 0.5), triangle ABC in Figure 19-2 (bottom on next page)
d. 7.5
e. would not, would

9. a. exports, imports, gold
b. protectionism, producer
c. impossible, impossible, fall, both exports and imports

(a)

Figure 19-1

(c)

VIII. Discussion Questions

1. David Ricardo would vehemently disagree with the Candle Makers. Ricardo's principle of comparative advantage points out that both countries can gain and be made wealthier by trade, even if one nation is much wealthier than the other.

2. When countries trade, each country specializes in the production of the commodity that it can produce relatively cheaper than the other. So in each country, resources are moved into the industry where productivity is highest. As a

result, total combined output is greater. Besides, countries would not trade if trading made them worse off.

3. The winners are the domestic industry that gets protected and the government that brings in the tariff revenue. The losers are everyone else: domestic consumers who pay more, efficient foreign firms that export less, and efficient domestic industries that now will export less if the foreign government retaliates with a tariff of its own.

4. Tariffs do indeed raise money for the government. However, there are efficiency losses and losses in consumer surplus that must be taken into consideration as well.

5. Noneconomic arguments for tariffs include national security, protection of the environment, and the preservation of culture or tradition. Some of the alternatives to tariffs and quotas are voluntary export restrictions and nontariff barriers such as licensing restrictions and bureaucratic red tape.

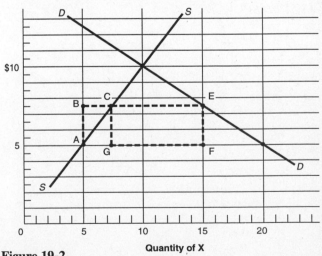

Figure 19-2

CHAPTER 20
Managing the Global Economy

I. CHAPTER OVERVIEW

This concluding chapter focuses attention on the workings of the international financial system and the global economy. Coverage begins with a discussion of the different types of exchange-rate mechanisms. In order for the nations of the world to trade, markets must exist to facilitate the exchange of currencies. Whether it is the old gold standard and its fixed-exchange-rate regime, the marketplace and its pure flexible-exchange-rate regime, or the intermediate managed-float mechanism and its goal to minimize inefficient exchange-rate variability, the rules of exchange must be clearly understood by all trading nations. The second part of the chapter provides a description of the evolution of the international financial system from the Bretton Woods agreement of 1945 to the managed-float regime of the 1990s. The international coordination of macroeconomic policies and the economic linkages that exist between economies are central to this discussion. The impact of recent wide swings in the value of the dollar on both the United States and the rest of the world is also discussed.

In the final section there is as an assessment of the main international economic issues that we face as we near the end of the millennium. At the forefront here is a discussion of the planned monetary union in Europe. If nothing else, it should be clear that no nation is an island—at least as far as the global economy is concerned.

II. LEARNING OBJECTIVES

After you have read Chapter 36 in your text and completed the exercises in this *Study Guide* chapter, you should be able to:

1. Contrast the fixed-exchange-rate system of the gold standard with the pure floating of a flexible-exchange-rate system. Describe the intermediate managed float that characterizes the contemporary international system.
2. Explain David Hume's gold-flow equilibrating mechanism.
3. Outline the worldwide effects of an overvaluation in the currency of a large economy like that of the United

States and the various means by which an overvaluation might be corrected under a fixed-rate system (gold flows), a flexible system (market forces), and a managed system (official intervention).
4. Sketch a brief chronology of the evolution of the international financial system from the Bretton Woods fixed-rate system that was created following World War II, through today's managed-float system.
5. Discuss the roles of the International Monetary Fund and the World Bank in the global economy.
6. Discuss the economic linkages that exist between nations and provide a rationale for the need for international coordination of macroeconomic policies.
7. Describe how the wide swings in the value of the U.S. dollar have been caused by, and have been the causes of, major worldwide economic events.
8. Understand the difference between *competitiveness* and *productivity* especially as these terms apply to the United States' position in the global economy.
9. Describe the crisis in the European monetary system and the resulting plans for monetary union in Europe.

III. REVIEW OF KEY CONCEPTS

Match the following terms from column A with their definitions in column B.

A	B
__ Exchange-rate system	1. In this system, a group of nations link their currencies together to stabilize exchange rates among themselves while allowing their currencies to be more flexible relative to those of the rest of the world.
__ Floating exchange rates	2. This is measured by the out put per unit of input; for example, output per person-hour.
__ Fixed exchange rates	3. Occurs when a government buys or sells its own or foreign currencies to affect exchange rates.

__ Gold standard

__ Four-pronged mechanism

__ Managed exchange rates

__ Intervention

__ Bretton Woods system

__ International Monetary Fund

__ World Bank

__ Gliding or crawling peg system

__ Currency bloc

__ Monetary union

__ Overvalued currency

__ Real net exports

__ Competitiveness

4.   Measures the difference between exports and imports where both are measured in constant or inflation-adjusted dollars.

5.   Measures the extent to which an industry is exposed to the world leader in that industry.

6.   Set of rules, arrangements, and institutions under which payments are made and received for international transactions.

7.   Refers to a situation in which the value of a nation's money is high relative to its long-run sustainable level.

8.   Refers to the extent to which a nation's goods can compete in the marketplace.

9.   Exchange rates are completely flexible and move purely under the influence of supply and demand.

10. Exchange rates are basically determined by market forces, but governments intervene to affect exchange rates.

11. The government specifies the rate at which its currency can be exchanged into other nation's currencies.

12. Established a system of exchange rates that were fixed but adjustable; also laid foundations for the International Monetary Fund, the World Bank, and the General Agreement on Tariffs and Trade.

13. Part of Hume's explanation of international payments equilibrium.

14. Administers the international monetary system and operates as a central bank for the central banks of member countries.

15. In this system smaller nations tie the value of their currency to that of a major currency or basket of currencies.

16. Fixed-exchange-rate system in which a country defines the value of its currency in terms of a fixed amount of gold.

__ Productivity

__ Globalization index

__ Optimal currency area

17. Area in which differential shocks among regions are small or labor mobility high enough to ensure rapid adjustment.

18. Industrialized nations lend money to this institution, which then makes low-interest loans to countries for projects which are economically sound but which cannot get private-sector financing.

19. The decision of the countries in Europe to adopt a common currency.

IV. SUMMARY AND CHAPTER OUTLINE

This section summarizes the key concepts from the chapter.

A. The International Monetary System

1.   In a system of pure floating exchange rates the forces of supply and demand determine the value of a nation's currency. The government neither announces a predetermined exchange rate nor takes steps to affect the exchange rate. If, for example, the price of Country X's currency is too high, it will find itself exporting fewer goods and services. Similarly, imports will be relatively cheaper for the citizens of Country X and they will import more. The increase in imports will increase X's demand for foreign currencies, while the reduction in exports will, in turn, reduce the demand for its own currency. As a result, the market will "float" to a new equilibrium exchange rate.

2.   In 1752 David Hume discussed a **four-pronged mechanism**, based on the **gold standard** and **fixed exchange** rates, which automatically restored equilibrium if there was an imbalance in international payments between nations. Suppose that Country A has a trade deficit with Country B. According to Hume, the following sequence of events occurs to restore equilibrium in the international marketplace:

a.   A must ship gold to B to pay for its trade deficit. Since A now has less gold, it must reduce its domestic money supply, and prices in A will fall. As a result, imports will become relatively more expensive and imports will decrease.

b.   Since prices in A are now lower, A's exports will increase.

c.   When B receives the gold from A its money supply will increase and prices there will go up. This increase in prices in B contributes to its decrease in exports—to A and elsewhere.

d.   In response to higher domestic prices, citizens in B will import more goods and services from abroad.

So as a result of being on the gold standard, A's initial trade deficit will turn around, as will B's initial trade surplus. International trade equilibrium is restored, but Country A will suffer a decrease in its money supply and thereby will experience deflation, if not recession; Country B will have to deal with higher prices and inflation.

3. In a system of **managed exchange rates**, market forces determine exchange rates, but governments or central banks may intervene when they want to influence the market exchange rate. **Intervention** occurs when the government buys or sells its own or foreign currencies, or changes its monetary policy with the goal of affecting exchange rates. For example, if a currency is appreciating in value, and the government has some holdings of this currency, it may sell this currency in the foreign exchange market. This action would increase the supply and, everything else held constant, tend to lower its price. Alternatively, the central bank could, via monetary policy, lower interest rates. This action would decrease the demand for the nation's currency by foreigners looking for high-interest investment opportunities.

B. International Institutions

1. At the end of World War II the nations of the world recognized the need to coordinate economic policies and seek common solutions to their problems. The discussions held at Bretton Woods, New Hampshire, led to the creation of the **International Monetary Fund (IMF)**, the **World Bank**, and the **General Agreement on Tariffs and Trade (GATT)**. According to the Bretton Woods system, exchange rates would be fixed but adjustable.

The intended goal behind the IMF's formation was to maintain, to the extent possible, stable exchange rates. No nation would have to push itself deliberately into recession or depression just to maintain a steady international value for its currency, but each participating nation did deposit a supply of its own currency (and, in some cases, gold) with the IMF. These deposits established a "lending pool" from which any nation could borrow if it found itself temporarily losing reserves in its maintenance of a fixed rate. It was of course understood that persistent losses of reserves indicated some form of "fundamental disequilibrium" which could not be sustained by continual borrowing. A nation could then devalue its currency value by up to 10 percent if it wished. Further devaluation required "consultation with the fund"— in effect, international approval.

2. The economies of the world are all interconnected. Samuelson and Nordhaus discuss several important economic linkages, as outlined below:

a. Multiplier Link: As income in Country A increases, A's imports increase. This increases the exports of other countries and consequently their incomes increase as well.

b. Monetary Link: As the interest rates in Country A decrease, there are two offsetting effects in Country B.

With lower interest rates in A, fewer foreign investors will want to invest in A. The resulting reduction in the demand for A's currency will cause A's currency to depreciate relative to that of other countries. This in turn will reduce A's imports and, thereby, B's exports and income. Alternatively, the lower interest rates in A will encourage foreign investors to keep their money at home. The increase in financial capital in B will lower interest rates in Country B. With lower interest rates, domestic investment and output in B will increase.

c. Savings and Investment Link: Changes in domestic saving and investment have a two-pronged effect on other countries. If there is a decrease in the U.S. budget deficit (i.e., an increase in public saving), domestic interest rates would fall. This will lead to a depreciation of the dollar, and increases in net exports and domestic investment. The lower U.S. interest rates would also tend to depress interest rates in Europe. This would lead to increased domestic investment in Europe. However, Europe's net foreign investment should decrease as its exports to the U.S. fall. Bottom line: the composition of saving and investment in Europe will change as a result of the savings change in the United States.

3. The experience of the United States in the 1980s supports many of these relationships. The United States began the decade with rates of inflation and unemployment that were unacceptably high. The Fed focused on the inflation problem, restricted the growth of the money supply, and pushed interest rates higher. The higher-than-normal interest rates in the United States decreased domestic investment spending and attracted financial resources from abroad. The subsequent increase in demand for the dollar contributed to its overvaluation while the drain of financial resources from foreign economies tended to increase their interest rates as well.

The overall increase in interest rates contributed to the recession felt in most of the industrialized world. The higher interest rates also exacerbated the loan-payment problems of poor and middle-income nations. Additionally, the increased value of the dollar tended to reduce U.S. exports and increase imports. The U.S. current account trade surplus quickly turned into a deficit.

4. Although the old international gold standard and Bretton Woods system are both gone, their influence persists, particularly in two important respects. First, nations still consider their gold stocks as reserves for settling international balances. (But now they tend to regard gold as an Emergency" reserve; they do not part with gold unless events force them to do so.) Second, the desire for relative stability in exchange rates persists. The gold standard is not the only possible mechanism to this end. You can hold the price of your currency steady by simply maintaining a sufficiently large inventory of foreign monies.

C. International Economic Issues at Century's End

1. While U.S. competitiveness declined during the 1980s, U.S. productivity did not. Samuelson and Nordhaus contribute the declining position of the United States in the global marketplace to the appreciation of the dollar, which increased U.S. prices relative to prices in other nations.

Domestic productivity is enhanced when foreign leaders in productivity invest abroad. For example, the U.S. automobile industry has benefited from Japanese production facilities in the United States. Open markets increase the exposure of new technology and stimulate competition.

2. In 1978 many of the large economies of Europe agreed to keep exchange rates, amongst themselves, within a rather narrow range of prices. This attempt to insulate themselves from exchange-market fluctuations could only be successful if each country was willing to sacrifice some autonomy over its domestic interest rates.

When Germany was reunited in 1990 it experienced a large increase in inflation as it converted East German marks into West German marks. The German central bank raised interest rates to reduce inflationary pressure. The higher interest rates attracted financial resources from foreign countries and increased the demand for the German mark. As a result, other members of the European Monetary System (EMS) had to raise their interest rates to keep their currencies from depreciating vis-à-vis the mark. Before long, this became too costly for the other countries to sustain, and the market reacted as speculators realized that the currencies were artificially overvalued. The EMS collapsed.

3. As a result of the EMS crisis, a plan was developed to create a common currency (the "Euro") for Europe. A common currency would eliminate all exchange rate problems between the countries, eliminate speculation and lower transaction costs. A newly-created European central bank would conduct monetary policy for the nations in this new European Union. Some economists worry that due to wage and price rigidity, and lack of labor mobility, that some areas will be left behind with chronic unemployment and low growth.

4. While no one can say precisely what lies ahead, most countries now agree that international cooperation and coordination is the best way to avoid global economic problems and increase the welfare of all. Finally, it remains for society, not the economist, to decide how to allocate scarce resources: for guns or butter, for the present or the future.

V. HELPFUL HINTS

1. Do not spend all of your time trying to *memorize* the economic linkages discussed in this chapter. Your time would be better spent by *learning and understanding* economic relationships. This is easy to say, but hard to do. Read about different economic examples and work through as many problems and questions as you can.

2. Figure 36-3 from your text is reproduced here as Figure 20-1. It illustrates the relationship between domestic savings rates (as a fraction of GDP) and investment rates.

Samuelson and Nordhaus write that normally, we should expect this scatter diagram to "be flat, with a slope of zero." A flat line means that there is no relationship between the variable measured on the horizontal axis (the domestic savings rate) and the variable on the vertical axis (the domestic investment rate). In this case we observe a positive relationship between national savings and investment.

Figure 20-1 National Savings and Investment Rates, 1960-1986
Over the long run, higher savings rates lead primarily to higher domestic investment. (Source: Adapted from Rudiger Dornbusch, "Comment," in B. Douglas Bernheim and John S. Shoven, *National Saving and Economic Performance* (University of Chicago Press, 1991).]

VI. MULTIPLE CHOICE QUESTIONS

These questions are organized by topic from the chapter outline. Choose the best answer from the options available.

A. The International Monetary System

1. For a country to be fully on the gold standard, the government of that country must:

    a. set a fixed price at which it is prepared to buy or sell gold in any quantity without restriction.

    b. be prepared to buy or sell gold at any time without restriction, but at a price which it is free to vary from day to day as it chooses, provided the same price (or almost the same price) applies to both purchases and sales.

    c. be prepared to buy gold in any quantity without restriction at a fixed price, but not necessarily to sell it.

    d. be prepared to sell gold in any quantity without restriction, but not necessarily to buy it.

    e. maintain a fixed gold content in its money unit, but not necessarily be prepared to buy or sell gold at any fixed price or without restriction.

2. Suppose that the exports of Country A to Country B have increased substantially and that both A and B operate on the gold standard. According to David Hume's gold-flow mechanism:

    a. A's domestic price level will fall, but B's domestic price level may or may not change.

    b. A's price level may or may not change, but B's will fall.

    c. A's price level will rise; B's will fall. d. A's price level will fall; B's will rise.

    e. none of the above will happen.

3. If the exchange rate between Canadian and U.S. dollars is a floating one, and if the demand for Canadian dollars increases, then:

    a. the supply of Canadian dollars has decreased or will decrease.

    b. the price of the Canadian dollar in U.S. currency will fall.

    c. the supply of U.S. dollars has decreased.

    d. the price of the U.S. dollar in Canadian currency will fall.

    e. the U.S. dollar has been devalued.

4. The primary advantage of the gold standard, or any other fixed-exchange-rate system, is its:

    a. flexibility.

    b. predictability.

    c. link to a precious metal.

    d. universal acceptance.

    e. relationship to the International Monetary Fund.

5. The main difficulty in all fixed-exchange-rate systems is that:

    a. one currency may dominate the others.

    b. gold is expensive to mine.

    c. economic adjustment may be impeded if prices fluctuate widely.

    d. there is no mechanism to counteract trade surpluses.

    e. none of the above.

6. Under a system of managed exchange rates:

    a. exchange rates are basically determined by market forces.

    b. a government may purchase its own currency in the foreign exchange market.

    c. monetary policy may be used to influence exchange rates.

    d. all the above.

    e. none of the above.

B. International Institutions

7. If GDP falls in the United States and exchange rates are floating, then:

    a. imports will tend to decrease and the price of the U.S. dollar will tend to increase.

    b. imports will tend to decrease and the price of the U.S. dollar will tend to decrease.

    c. imports will tend to increase and the price of the U.S. dollar will tend to increase.

    d. imports will tend to increase and the price of the U.S. dollar will tend to decrease.

    e. none of the preceding statements will be true.

8. One of the principal tasks of the International Monetary Fund is to:

    a. serve as a partial substitute for the gold standard in maintaining stable exchange rates.

    b. help countries with short-term balance-of-payment difficulties.

    c. make loans to private companies in any country where the funds could not otherwise be borrowed at any reasonable interest rate.

    d. facilitate the development of free-trade "regions" similar to the European Common Market.

    e. coordinate the views of the larger and more developed nations concerning exchange-rate and trade problems.

9. It could also be said that a principal task assigned to the International Monetary Fund is to:

    a. act as the world's banker in matters of both short-term and long-term credit.

    b. make direct long-term loans to less developed nations when necessary, so as to assist in their economic development.

    c. control international credit sufficiently to enable member nations to maintain their price levels at reasonably noninflationary levels.

    d. work toward the gradual reduction of tariffs and the elimination of protectionist policies among nations.

e.   none of the above.

10. Which alternative in question 9 would be correct had that question referred to the World Bank rather than the International Monetary Fund?

a.
b.
c.
d.
e.

11. A disturbance in its balance of payments may cause any nation to lose gold or foreign exchange reserves.
This danger of loss is most acute whenever that nation:

a.   increases its exports.
b.   seeks to maintain a flexible exchange rate.
c.   seeks to maintain a fixed exchange rate.
d.   increases its borrowing from other nations.
e.   experiences a drop in GDP—i.e., whenever a recession occurs.

12. A "managed float" means:

a.   an increase in the protectionist policies by some device other than a tariff increase.
b.   refusal by a nation to allow its currency to appreciate even though its reserves are large and increasing.
c.   a beggar-thy-neighbor policy.
d.   introduction of a split exchange rate—a fixed rate for some transactions, a floating rate for others.
e.   periodic intervention by a central bank to check excessive fluctuation in an otherwise floating exchange rate.

13. As part of the Bretton Woods system:

a.   the industrialized economies adopted a system of floating exchange rates.
b.   the ideas of John Maynard Keynes were widely discredited.
c.   the U.S. dollar was recognized as the preeminent currency of the world.
d.   all the above.
e.   none of the above.

14. Which of the following is typically expected to have the largest influence on the rate of investment in a country?

a.   The policies of the World Bank.
b.   The rate of saving in that country.
c.   The productivity of capital in that country.
d.   The foreign exchange rate.
e.   None of the above.

15. If a country wants to increase its own real income it should probably attempt to:

a.   overvalue its currency.
b.   depreciate its currency.
c.   export its inflation problems.
d.   coordinate its economic policies with other nations.
e.   employ a beggar-thy-neighbor policy.

C. International Economic Issues at Century's End

16. When interest rates in France increase, we should expect:

a.   domestic investment in France to decrease.
b.   foreign financial capital to flow into France.
d.   interest rates in Belgium to increase.
d.   the French franc to appreciate.
e.   all the above.

17. The U.S. dollar's sharp decline in the mid-1980s can be attributed to:

a.   the sale of dollars by some governments.
b.   the actions of speculators who sold dollars.
c.   higher relative interest rates outside the United States.
d.   all the above.
e.   none of the above.

18. A speculative attack occurs when speculators:

a.   believe a currency is about to be devalued and start purchasing it.
b.   believe a currency is about to be devalued and start selling it off.
c.   coordinate their activities in a financial cartel.
d.   move assets from stocks to bonds to currency.
e.   do any of the above.

19. One reason for the decline in U.S. competitiveness during the 1980s was:

a.   the decrease in U.S. productivity.
b.   the U.S. recession.
c.   the appreciation of the U.S. dollar.
d.   all the above.
e.   none of the above.

20. In order for the "Euro" to succeed as a common European currency:

a.   a European central bank needs to be created.
b.   wage and price rigidities in some European economies need to be reduced.
c.   labor should be freely mobile between markets.
d.   participating countries need to have inflation and interest rates that are close to those in the lowest countries.
e.   all of the above.

VII. PROBLEM SOLVING

The following problems are designed to help you apply the concepts that you learned in the chapter.

A. The International Monetary System

1.   Suppose that a widespread taste for Scotch whiskey develops in the United States.

a.   This would create an increase in the demand for (**dollars / pounds sterling**).

b.   If the United States were on the gold standard and if this demand increase were sufficiently large, then there would be a flow of gold (**away from / toward**) the United States.

c.   If this demand increase persisted without a countering effect for a long time, then the United States might be drained of its entire stock of (**gold / Scotch whiskey**).

The gold standard kept exchange rates steady by definition, but demand-and-supply forces were still at work. Why didn't some nations run out of gold while trying to maintain that standard? A nation did, indeed, have to "go off" the gold standard if it lost all or most of its gold because of a major rise in imports or a sufficient drop in exports. There were, however, some "equilibrating" forces that operated to brake any such overwhelming gold outflow. The first major attempt to describe an equilibrating mechanism was laid out by David Hume in the eighteenth century.

2.   Suppose, as in question 1, that the U.S. demand for imports increases to a point where imports exceed exports.

a.   According to Hume's analysis, the resulting gold flow (**out of / into**) the United States (**increases / decreases**) the U.S. money supply, causing the price level to (**rise / fall**).

b.   The (**same / reverse**) situation occurs in one or more foreign exporting countries. The gold which has left the United States flows into these countries, increasing their money stock and causing their prices to (**climb / fall**).

c.   Since American prices have gone down while foreign prices have gone up, (**more / fewer**) American goods will be bought by foreigners, while Americans will tend to buy (**more / fewer**) foreign goods.

d.   That is, in America, exports will (**rise / fall**), imports will (**rise / fall**), and the rise in the U.S. imports which began the process would be offset.

In rough outline, for sufficiently large movements, Hume's analysis may have some validity. There is today, however, almost no link between a nation's total gold stock and its total money supply. Moreover, Hume's analysis relies heavily on the quantity theory of money and its assumption of full employment. Both of these caveats leave the Hume analysis wanting as a description of modern-day responses to an imbalance in its current account.

3.   Assume that the nations of Germany and France have agreed to maintain fixed exchange rates between themselves. In Figure 20-2 the initial exchange rate is 3 French francs per German mark. Suppose something happens so that the demand for marks increases (dotted demand curve).

a.   What is one possible reason for the rightward shift in the demand curve?

Suppose that the German government wants to reestablish the original exchange rate.

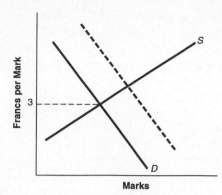

Figure 20-2

b.   What is one reason why the German government might want to do this? _____

c.   What action might the German government take to bring about this change? _____

4.   Assume that Japan and England have agreed to a system of floating exchange rates. Figure 20-3 illustrates the foreign exchange market between these two countries. Assume that the initial exchange rate is 320 Japanese yen per English pound.

a.   At the initial exchange rate, there is an excess supply of (**pounds / yen**).

b.   One possible explanation for the excess supply is that relative prices of goods and services in England may be too (**high / low**).

c.   As the exchange rate falls, Japanese citizens will want more (**Japanese / British**) goods and services.

d.   As this happens, there will be a (**movement along / shift in**) the demand and supply curves to a new equilibrium point.

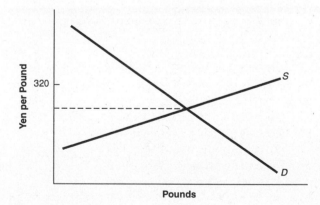

Figure 20-3

B. International Institutions

5.   The World Bank's task, in brief, is to channel money from richer nations to less developed ones.

a.   In slightly more detail, the bank's function is to (**make short-term loans / make long-term loans /**

provide foreign exchange for balance-of-payments shortages) to the world's poorer countries.

b.   It provides funds for a less developed nation (**even if that nation can / only if that nation cannot**) borrow privately at a reasonable interest rate.

6.   One of the most significant problems of international finance in the early 1980s was the overvalued U.S. dollar.

a.   The dollar was estimated by some to have been (**10 / 25 / 50**) percent overvalued from 1981 into 1984.

b.   The scenario that produced this overvaluation began with the (**tight / loose**) monetary policy and (**stimulative / contractionary**) fiscal policy of the Reagan administration that drove real interest rates in the United States (**up / down**).

c.   Foreign investment therefore flowed (**into / out of**) the United States, (**increasing / decreasing**) the demand for dollars and thus causing the dollar to (**appreciate / depreciate**) in money markets all around the world.

d.   Exports from the United States therefore became (**more / less**) expensive, while imports from abroad became (**more / less**) costly.

e.   Net exports (**expanded / contracted**) by nearly (**$50 / $140 / $250**) billion, as a result, and created an enormous (**deficit / surplus**) in the current account.

f.   This discrepancy was, though, almost canceled by a (**deficit / surplus**) in the capital account, so the overvaluation persisted and drove interest rates abroad (**up / down**).

g.   The result was a tendency for foreign economies to move into (**recession / boom**), and (**depressed / overextended**) export- and import-competing industries called for (**free trade / protection and subsidy**) in the United States.

C. International Economic Issues at Century's End

7.   In a global economy, higher interest rates in one country may have a series of effects on its neighbors.

a.   As interest rates in Germany increase, Germany will attract (**more / less**) foreign financial resources from the United States.

b.   This will lead to (**an appreciation / a depreciation**) of the dollar.

c.   As a result, both exports and GDP in the United States should (**increase / decrease**).

d.   At the same time, the higher interest rates in Germany should cause interest rates in the United States to go (**up / down**), since financial resources may be leaving (**the United States / Germany**).

e.   Consequently, investment spending and GDP in the United States would go (**down / up**).

f.   In conclusion, the effect of higher interest rates in Germany on the U.S. economy is (**ambiguous / clear cut**).

8.   Figure 20-4 illustrates the relationship between industry, productivity and globalization.

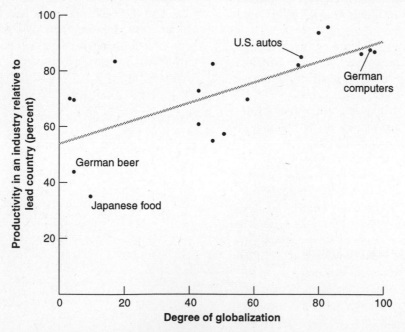

Figure 20-7 Exposure to Leading Technologies Improves Relative Productivity

The globalization index measures the extent to which an industry is exposed to the world leader in that industry either through free and unprotected trade or through transplants from the leader country. When industries are exposed, as were U.S. automakers and German computer manufacturers, they must compete vigorously to survive and they therefore close the gap with the leading country. When domestic industry is protected, as were German beer and Japanese food producers, competition is weak and relative productivity is low. [Source: McKinsey Global Institute, *Manufacturing Productivity* (Washington, D.C., 1993).]

a. List two ways in which domestic industries are exposed to the world leaders in their industry.
(1) _____
(2) _____
b. According to Figure 20-4 there is (**a positive / a negative / no**) relationship between the degree of globalization and productivity in an industry.

VIII. DISCUSSION QUESTIONS

Answer the following questions, making sure that you can explain the work you did to arrive at the answers.
1. Briefly explain the four steps in Hume's gold-flow equilibrating mechanism.
2. Briefly discuss the two main ways in which a country can intervene in the foreign exchange market to influence the exchange rate of its currency.
3. What factors contributed to the collapse of the Bretton Woods exchange-rate system?
4. Explain the relationship between the savings rate in a country and the investment rate. Differentiate between the short and long run in your answer.
5. What has happened to competitiveness and productivity in the U.S. economy in the last 10 years?
6. Discuss some of the economic considerations that must be addressed before Europe can act as a truly unified single economy.

IX. ANSWERS TO STUDY GUIDE QUESTIONS

III. Review of Key Concepts

6	Exchange rate system
9	Floating exchange rates
11	Fixed exchange rates
16	Gold Standard
13	Four-pronged mechanism
10	Managed exchange rates
3	Intervention
12	Bretton Woods system
14	International Monetary Fund
18	World Bank
15	Gliding or crawling peg system
1	Currency bloc
19	Monetary union
7	Overvalued currency
4	Real net exports
8	Competitiveness
2	Productivity
5	Globalization index
17	Optimal currency area

VI. Multiple Choice Questions

1. A 2. C 3. D 4. B 5. C 6. D
7. B 8. B 9. E 10. B 11. C 12. E
13. C 14. C 15. D 16. E 17. D 18. B
19. C 20. E

VII. Problem Solving

1. a. pounds sterling
   b. away from
   c. gold
2. a. out of, decreases, fall
   b. reverse, climb
   c. more, fewer
   d. rise, fall
3. a. There could be an increase in demand by the French for German goods and services. There could also be an increase in the flow of financial capital from France into Germany.
   b. As the mark appreciates, German exports become more expensive for the French. Also, the relative price of French goods and services will fall in Germany, so German citizens will import more products from France and purchase fewer domestic goods and services.
   c. The German government could sell marks, or it could purchase francs. Germany could also use an expansive monetary policy to lower domestic interest rates. This would encourage investors to move funds out of Germany and toward France. As a result, the demand for marks would decrease.
4. a. pounds
   b. high
   c. British
   d. movement along
5. a. make long-term loans
   b. only if that nation cannot
6. a. 50 percent
   b. tight, stimulative, up
   c. into, increasing, appreciate
   d. more, less
   e. contracted, $140, deficit
   f. surplus, up
   g. recession, depressed, protection and subsidy
7. a. more
   b. a depreciation
   c. increase
   d. up, the United States
   e. down
   f. ambiguous
8. a (1) Through free trade
      (2) Through transplants from the leader country
   b. a positive

VIII. Discussion Questions

1. a. When a country runs a trade deficit, it must pay for it with gold. The reduction in gold decreases its money supply and price level. The fall in prices makes imports relatively more expensive, so imports decrease.

   b. Exports will increase due to the fall in prices.

   c. The country receiving the gold will experience an increase in its money supply and an increase in prices. Since prices are higher, exports will decrease.

   d. The increase in prices will also encourage citizens to import more goods and services.

2. A country can purchase or sell its own currency or the currency of other nations. A country can also use monetary policy to change domestic interest rates. This will influence the flow of foreign financial capital and thereby affect the demand and exchange rate for its currency.

3. As the economies of the world recovered from the Second World War, nations (especially Germany and Japan) developed trade surpluses with the United States. Trade barriers were lowered, and technological advances quickened the pace of financial capital flows between countries. Large federal budget deficits in the United States, which kept upward pressure on interest rates, attracted financial resources from abroad. All these factors made it more and more difficult for the United States to maintain the exchange-rate parities that were established at Bretton Woods.

4. A major determinant of investment in a country is the productivity of capital in that country. As long as financial resources are globally mobile, they should flow into countries where the productivity of capital is the highest. If domestic savings are too low, relative to the rate of investment, the shortfall in savings can be compensated by an inflow of foreign financial capital. This appears to have happened, at least in the short run, in the United States. In the long run, however, Feldstein and Horioka have found a very high positive correlation between the domestic savings rate and the rate of investment.

5. Competitiveness depends upon the relative prices of goods and services in the marketplace. The competitiveness of U.S. products was diminished during the 1980s by the appreciation of the dollar. Productivity, which measures output per unit of inputs, increased during the 1980s. A study by the McKinsey Global Institute indicates that productivity in an industry is enhanced by free market competition and direct exposure to industry leaders. The productivity in domestic industries appears to be improved when foreign industry leaders produce in the domestic economy.

6. Once a common currency is agreed upon, a single central bank needs to be established to create a uniform monetary policy (no small matter). Price and wage rigidities need to be reduced so that markets can adjust to shocks and disturbances. For the same reason, labor needs to be mobile between regions and countries! Both interest rates and the inflation rate need to be similar among the nations—hopefully at a low level. In addition, participating countries need to control their federal government budget deficits and national debt. A great deal needs to be accomplished, but the payoff could be enormous!